AN INTRODUCTION TO
COMMUNICATION THEORY

AN INTRODUCTION TO COMMUNICATION THEORY

Don W. Stacks

The University of Miami
Coral Gables, Florida

Sidney R. Hill, Jr.

Mississippi State University
Starkville, Mississippi

Mark Hickson, III

The University of Alabama at Birmingham
Birmingham, Alabama

Holt, Rinehart and Winston, Inc.
Fort Worth   Chicago   San Francisco   Philadelphia
Montreal   Toronto   London   Sydney   Tokyo

Acquisitions Editor   Janet Wilhite
Developmental Editor   Barbara J. C. Rosenberg
Project Editor/Text Design   Publications Development Company
Production Manager   Kathleen Ferguson
Cover Design   Guy Jacobs

Library of Congress Cataloging-in-Publication Data

Stacks, Don W.
    An introduction to communication theory / by Don W. Stacks, Sidney R.
Hill, Jr., Mark Hickson, III.
        p.   cm.
    Includes bibliographical references and index.
    ISBN 0-03-033433-0
    1. Communication.   I. Hill, Sidney R.   II. Hickson, Mark.   III. Title.
                P90.S78   1991
                302.2—dc20   90-5044
                                                                    CIP

Credits appear on p. 312.

Address for editorial correspondence: Holt, Rinehart and Winston, Inc.,
301 Commerce Street, Suite 3700, Fort Worth, Texas 76102

Address for orders: Holt, Rinehart and Winston, Inc., 6277 Sea Harbor Drive,
Orlando, FL 32887. 1-800-782-4479, or 1-800-433-0001 (in Florida)

Printed in the United States of America

1 2 3 4   090   9 8 7 6 5 4 3 2 1

Holt, Rinehart and Winston, Inc.
The Dryden Press
Saunders College Publishing

Contents

SECTION TWO
The Materials of Communication Theory:
Nonverbal and Verbal Codes

SECTION THREE
Framing the Edifice: Rhetorical Perspectives on Communication

SECTION FOUR
Building the Edifice for the Individual: Psychological Approaches to Communication

SECTION FIVE
Building the Edifice for Society:
Sociological Approaches to Communication

SECTION SIX
Integrating and Living with the Edifice

Preface

The study of human communication is hundreds of years old, yet only recently has the concern for communication theory come to the forefront. Usually, communication theory as a course is reserved for upper-division or graduate students; at least this was true during the great expansion of the communication field in the late 1960s and early to mid-seventies. Today, however, communication scholars have correctly pointed out that the need to *understand* is as important, if not more important, than the need to *perform.* Many communication departments are redesigning their curricula to provide a central core of knowledge and understanding based on a grounding in theory for undergraduate students.

This book is designed for the *first* course in communication theory. It is concerned with the student's understanding the many and varied approaches to the study and analysis of human communication. The book's purpose is to provide the student with an understanding of (1) the background, principles, and implications of particular approaches or theories; (2) the ways these differing approaches and theories "color" the way we see and interpret behaviors around us; and (3) the ways these approaches and theories make differing predictions. Hopefully, an understanding of theory will make for an easier transition to the practice of communication skills and allow for refined predictions and better control over our communication.

A major concern of communication educators is the ability of the student to master information and increase skills. This we hope to enhance via a treatment that is deep enough to provide the major assumptions and critical knowledge needed to understand a particular theory or approach, and sufficient to provide a base from which the student can move to more advanced treatments of the material. This book, then, is aimed at establishing a foundation from which students can make critical judgments about the phenomena they study. A better understanding of the diverse nature of communication should lead to more accurate predictions of human communication. These predictions are based in large part on the knowledge integration function that is built into the study of communication theory.

This book is the result of more than 15 years of analysis of what the undergraduate student needs *before* he or she begins to practice professional communication skills. As many potential employers have noted, communication majors need to understand *why* people behave as they do and, based on this knowledge, provide communication strategies that have the best opportunity to succeed. We have found through our courses that this is best learned by demonstrating that there are many ways of perceiving, each of which produces different results. The study of communication requires the student to understand many approaches and theories that seem to contradict one another at times.

Part of the concept of communication as a continuous process involves the retention of experiences, events, and knowledge with the addition of new experiences, events, and knowledge that help us to change and adapt to differing circumstances in our lives. Communication is more critical now than ever before. The social problems involved with divorces and the consequent "divided family," street violence, family violence, and international terrorism should cause us to take notice that the communication process in our world is not as effective as it should be. Although some of these social problems have always occurred and some would occur regardless of the effectiveness of our communication, there is, nevertheless, a tendency to place part of the difficulty on the shoulders of communication.

One advantage of looking at the various perspectives that we have chosen to discuss is that having a memory bank of differing views allows us to withhold our assumptions momentarily for the purpose of communicating with the other person, as opposed to speaking words at each other.

In an introductory text, such as this one, the number of theoretical approaches and names and terms sometimes seems endless to the neophyte. Part of the purpose of this book is to assist in the synthesis and analysis of these approaches. This book does not include every possible perspective on human communication theory. Perhaps some notable ones have been omitted. However, we have attempted to write a text that includes most of the important perspectives that have brought us to where we are now in human communication theory. We have attempted to illustrate where some of the approaches still have an influence and where the influence of others has given way to some other approach.

Each chapter contains all that is necessary to understand the approach(es) surveyed. Additionally, each chapter defines important terms (also found in Appendix B, the glossary), provides a review and critique of each theory explored, and offers the student a summary table of central concepts, theorists, and limitations of each theory. Finally, a summary of all the theories and approaches to the study of human communication is provided.

One final comment is necessary. All three authors of this text believe in the integrative function of communication. All come from integrated schools that include rhetoric with the social sciences, as well as mass communication, interpersonal communication, public relations, and the performing arts. As such, this text seeks to cover a plethora of approaches that symbolize both the old and the new, the contemporary and the future. Perhaps its treatment will lead one of its readers to build a new theory. In the end, that is what theory is and what it is about.

This book is the combined efforts of the three authors, with each working primarily in his area of expertise. Writing this book has been both exhilarating and exasperating. Over the years, teachers, in conversations with us, have indicated that how one really approaches communication depends on both their training and preferences; interestingly, they typically contradicted each other as to what was "important." From all these conversations, we came to believe that communication is truly a diverse and open area of study.

We especially owe a great deal to the late Professor B. Aubrey Fisher who critiqued this text in a hard but not harsh fashion. Many of his comments and suggestions made their way into the current version, to include the analogy of communication theory as *architecture.*

We gratefully commend our colleagues Marion Couvillion, who first gave us the impetus to write this book, and Janis Williams and M.L. Sandoz for their proofreading. To Becky Smith, we owe much for the artwork in these pages. And to Marietta Tubb, whom we refer to as "V," we cannot provide enough thanks for assistance with artwork, proofing, typing, and so on.

We would also like to thank some of our former teachers who contributed to our knowledge, allowing us to write such a book. Our teachers include Larry L. Barker (Auburn University), Judee K. Burgoon (University of Arizona), Michael Burgoon (University of Arizona), Thomas J. Pace (Southern Illinois University), Don Richardson (Auburn University), John D. Stone (formerly of North Carolina State University); and Gordon Welty (Wright State University). We also want to thank all those teachers with whom we discussed both the project and our feelings about what was needed to introduce communication theory at the introductory level; they are too numerous to cite individually, but they know who they are.

This book has benefited from the careful reading and thoughtful criticism of a group of expert reviewers. The authors thank Halina Ablamowicz (State University of New York at Fredonia), John Crawford (Arizona State University), Gary Cronkhite (Indiana University), Jesse Delia (University of Illinois), H. Lloyd Goodall, Jr. (University of Utah), Colan T. Hanson (North Dakota State University), Suzanne Lindsey (University of Alabama at Birmingham), Peter Marston (California State University at Northridge), Gail Mason (Eastern Illinois University), C. David Mortenson (University of Wisconsin), Mark Wallenhorst, (State University of New York at Buffalo, and Joanne Yamauchi (The American University).

The authors thank Barbara J. Rosenberg for her editorial help. We owe much to Janet Wilhite, the speech editor for Holt, Rinehart and Winston, who assisted in producing what we all hope is the kind of textbook the field of speech communication has been seeking.

Our traditional criterion of success, initially developed in the arts and later in the political arena, asks: "Will it play in Peoria?" The basis of this contention rests with the idea that *the audience ultimately judges matters of communication value.* Peoria, Illinois, (at least at one time) was considered the typical American community. If the people in Peoria accepted an idea, the inference was that the idea would probably be accepted elsewhere.

For many years, what has been accepted as theory in the field of human communication has met with little acceptance among researchers in the discipline, although they may have known about the *Peoria criterion.* The idea that theory needs acceptance as does a play, a movie, or a political candidate is not new. However, the first problem for scholars is acceptance within their own community. A theory must be accepted by the insiders first, just as the directors or political experts must accept a candidate before the audience tests them in Peoria. In the case of this book, many people have accepted it. Only if the disciplinary audience can accept the script, however, can the show go on the road. We hope we "break a leg" in Peoria.

Finally, we would like to thank our hundreds of current and former students in the introductory theory course who have suffered through drafts of this book since 1974.

DWS
SRH
MLH

SECTION ONE

Introduction to Communication Theory: Setting the Bases

The study of human communication has evolved from a performance theory of oratory to a social–psychological theory of knowledge and action. This text introduces the student to the ways communication has been studied over the ages and the directions it may be going in the future. As such, we will establish just what communication is about and how changing theories alter how we study communication.

We begin with the notion that how we *perceive* an event "colors" the way we react to it. We then examine three basic "lenses" that have influenced how we see communication events over the past 25 years. This examination sets the parameters for the in-depth analyses of later chapters.

We view communication theory as an architect does when designing a building for a client. Obviously, the architect develops ideas of what is "right" for the client, based on perceptions of what the client desires and what is appropriate for the current society. Section One establishes the different ways we think and the footings for future design. Based on these foundations, we can classify communication theorists as we would architects, who might be viewed as "modern," "classical," or "neoclassical." Modern communication architects (theorists) usually align with either "lawlike" or a "rules," or a "systems" approach to communicative behavior.

After exploring the ways that we can view communication, we turn our attention in Section Two to the materials with which the architect works. After this section, we examine the traditional "roots" of the communication discipline: the oral message as reflected back to the ancient Greeks. Section Four focuses on the person as a communicator (intrapersonal, humanistic

1

perspective), examining communication from individual and interpersonal (two-person) perspectives. Section Five expands the focus of communication theory to society in general. Finally, Section Six integrates theory and attempts to examine the impact of both people (biological–psychological) and social forces operating in everyday communication.

We begin our study of communication design by examining what communication is. We look at how different ways of knowing create different ways to communicate our views of events occurring around us. The model we create will guide us through the various perceptions (theories) of communication.

1

Communication and Perception

*Our everyday, traditional ideas of reality are
delusions which we spend substantial parts of our
lives shoring up, even at the risk of trying to force
facts to fit our definition of reality instead of vice
versa. And the most dangerous delusion of all is that
there is only one reality. What there are, in fact, are·
many different versions of reality, some of which are
contradictory, but all of which are the results of
communication and not reflections of eternal,
objective truths.*[1]

I n this quotation, Paul Watzlawick tells us much about what we
know about communication. The notion that reality is created
through communication with others is extremely important. It
is through communication that we create our own social reality. It is through
communication that we decide *what is* and *what is not* knowledge.[2] We find
that communication, knowledge, and reality are intertwined. All three are
based on our views of a world that vary from person to person. With these
perceptions, and with our tools of communication, we attempt to convince
others to share our perceptions.

In this chapter, we introduce the most fundamental variables in day-
to-day communication. We begin with a discussion of *perception*, a phenomenon that "filters" the way we "see" the world around us. We begin our
study of communication with the ways we perceive the actions and reactions of others. As discussed later, perceptions determine our approaches
for using communication to build our own *reality*. This building, what we
call "theory," yields *knowledge*.

For humans, the concern for perceiving and sharing knowledge and
reality is significant. Most students of communication agree that humans
alone share this concern. Although monkeys, chimpanzees, and dolphins

3

have some capacity for "communication," recent scientific investigations indicate that humans may be the only "concerned" communicators, at least in our solar system.[3]

This discussion of human communication may seem egocentric, but it should be viewed as a particular burden for our species. Only humans expect reasons and feel the need to provide them. Only humans derive joy from a well-written poem. Only humans create extravagant rituals for phrases and events that they consider important. Humans, then, are thinking and feeling animals who share territoriality and aggression with other species. Humans are animals that share love, friendship, hatred, fear, confidence, shame, benevolence, pity, envy, and other feelings with their peers.[4]

We should remember, however, that sharing is no easy task. As perceivers, we are all different. We cannot be certain whether a particular color is bluish green or greenish blue. Neither can we be absolutely certain of what we said a week ago, a day ago, or even a few minutes ago. Therefore, sometimes, we say, "I meant to say," or "I thought I said," or "You didn't understand me correctly."

Many researchers have discussed the problems of communication and perception, which serve as interesting balances for one another: Communication brings us together and perceptions tend to separate us. Our contention is that the sharing (communication) aspects of humans can be improved dramatically if we learn how *others* perceive themselves, other persons, events, objects, and indeed communication itself, in ways quite different from how *we* see the same things. To provide a perceptual base, we have created a simple model of the communication process (see Fig. 1–1).

Figure 1–1 shows two communicators, A and B, each having different perceptions of "reality." Perceptions arise in two steps: First, we sense (through the use of sight, sound, smell, taste, touch) phenomena in "reality." Then, we interpret (through thinking, synthesizing, analyzing) the data that have been sensed. There are many different kinds of perceptions. In addition to different senses, there are also different *modes of analysis* (filters or different ways of interpreting data sensed from "reality"). When one communicator senses reality and interprets it, *intrapersonal* (self-to-self) communication has taken place. When one's reality has been sensed, interpreted, and communicated to the other, the message sent becomes part of reality. This is *interpersonal* communication. The sensed message is interpreted by the second communicator, and so on. A perception that is retained and becomes part of the perceptual memory bank is called *knowledge*. Knowledge, as filtered through the senses and memory itself, becomes a second filtering agent. Over time, perceptions change in part because of this internal filtering process. Through the intrapersonal and interpersonal communication processes, we interpret our sensings of "reality" and develop personal knowledge.

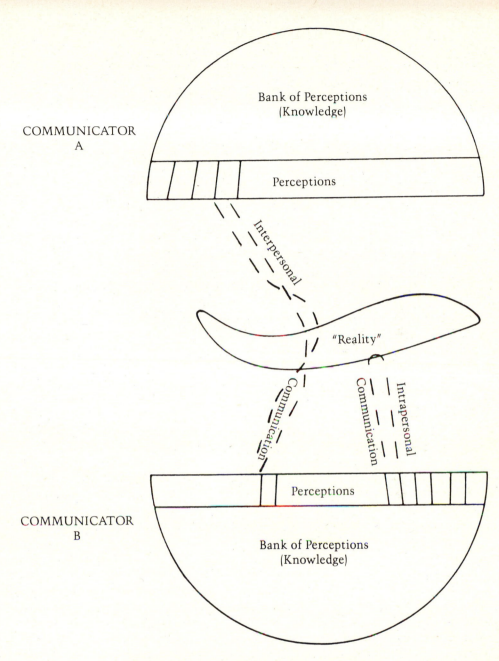

FIGURE 1–1   Perceptions and Communication.

MODES OF ANALYSIS

Data gathered from reality are just that—data. To bring data to communication requires that the information be sensed and interpreted. We sense data all the time, but we interpret or analyze selectively. In Section One, we explore some of the ways that we interpret and analyze data that we sense. As we discuss these modes of analysis, note which modes you are aware of in analyzing events around you. Modes of analysis become "lenses" through which we perceive reality's data.

Modes of the Individual: Cultural and Demographic

The first mode of analysis concerns the individual and his or her culture. Each of us belongs to a culture that establishes our views and values. For example, people from Eastern and Western *cultures* perceive events differently. Within cultures different societies exist, each capable of changing how people "see" their reality. Within our culture, for instance, we perceive that Californians and New Yorkers communicate differently, as do people from rural and urban areas. The real difference is in perception: Each culture, subculture, or society subtly refocuses perceptions of reality. Going to college is an example of how culture (high school versus college) changes our perception and communication. How different are your friends who did not go to college? Are they different, or have the cultures in which you and they belong changed?

The second lens of this mode is more personal—it is *you*. Here, we might look at *demographic* variables associated with the individual. (Remember, although you are part of a culture, you interpret that culture from within your perceptions.) Hence, demographic variables such as sex, race, age, status, education, and so forth, change how you perceive your reality. For example, a long-term relationship with the opposite sex sometimes changes your demographic identity from "single" to "going steady" or "married." With such changes also come changes in perceptions for yourself, your "spouse," and your friends.

Modes of Focus: Similarity, Time, Agreement, and Change

A second set of perceptual lenses concerns the focus of perception. The second mode of analysis has to do with simple similarities or differences. When we stereotype a person as a member of a group, we are looking at *similarities*. When someone stereotypes one of our friends, we often see the differences between the friend and his or her associates and point out those *differences* to others.

A third mode of analysis focuses on *time*. We may see an event from the present, the past, and/or the future. How we interpret the advances of a friend in a potential relationship differs if our focus is on the past and those relationships that failed or on the future and those relationships that are yet to be. We all know people who dwell in the past. We also know those who live in the *now*, forgetting the past and avoiding the future. Each perception of time affects how we analyze reality's data.

A fourth mode of analysis is based on *agreement/disagreement*. When we disagree with another, we tend to focus on those points with which we differ. When we are in the process of agreeing, our future responses tend toward agreement. Think back to a recent argument you had with someone. Was your perception of reality one of difference or agreement? How did that interaction turn out? Was it predetermined by your perception of the argument's focus on agreement or difference?

A fifth mode of analysis is *stability/change*. Some of us tend to view the importance of keeping "reality" the same as it has been; others see the need for change to take place. Are you a stable person? Do you set up your room or apartment one way and then keep it that way, or do you constantly change things? Assuming you are one or the other, your perceptions of change or stability will influence your reaction to situations requiring one or the other.

Modes of Language: Space, Voice, and Vocabulary

A major set of perceptual lenses deals with the way we describe reality. As humans, we use language, which allows us to incorporate time and space factors into our analyses. The first language lens is *spatial*. We see the world from different perspectives. Prepositions in the English language make this mode easier for us. We can see through, around, over, under, between, and so forth. Additionally, languages make use of the depth of space differently. English has three tenses (past, present, future). Other languages may have many more (French, Spanish) or even fewer (some Polynesian and American Indian languages are relegated to the immediate present). Arabs describe their world as a broad panorama, whereas Americans focus on a smaller perception of time and space.

Another language factor is the *voice* used in structuring the message via verbs. For example, an art critic (passive) may view an art object quite differently from the artist (active) who created it. Another mode is *specific knowledge* (i.e., *vocabulary*). The specificity of language helps us to see objects differently. Although many different varieties of pine trees are seen by a forester, most of us see only "pine trees." One less knowledgeable might simply see a "tree."

Modes of Logic: Logic, Strange Loops, and Vertical/Lateral Thinking

How we use language to *reflect* reality comprises the last set of perceptual lenses. These modes of analysis involve perceptions of traditional versus nontraditional thinking. The first lens deals with logical/affective analyses. A story is told of how we attempt to logically argue a case. In ancient Greece, a man named Euthalus visited with Protagorus, who was a teacher of rhetoric (persuasion). Euthalus, who wanted to attend Protagorus's school but did not have the tuition, offered to pay after he had won his first case in court. Protagorus, having confidence in his own ability to teach the lad, accepted the offer. Several months after graduating, Euthalus had yet to be involved in any court case. Thus, Protagorus decided to sue Euthalus for tuition.

Protagorus reasoned that he would win the tuition no matter what happened. Should the judge rule in favor of Protagorus, Euthalus would have to pay because that was the judgment of the court. If the judge ruled in favor of Euthalus, Euthalus would still have to pay because he would have won his first court case in agreement with the original contract. Euthalus, too, reasoned that he would win in any case. If the judge ruled in favor of Protagorus, Euthalus would still not have won his first case and the original contract would still be binding. Should the judge rule in favor of Euthalus, Euthalus would not have to pay because that was the judgment of the court. In short, it depended on how one perceived the situation.[5] Thus, even logic involves perceptions of reality. In fact emotion (affect) is somewhat involved in logic by way of seeing an argument from one's own egocentric perspective.

Another (tenth) mode of analysis is the *strange loop*.[6] According to Douglas Hofstadter, sometimes our thinking brings us to a conclusion that would otherwise seem contradictory or impossible. In a sense, the loop always returns to itself.

Affectively, when a student comes to a teacher with an excuse for an absence from a test, one teacher might analyze the absence in terms of the student's setting priorities. Another might perceive a different reason. A second example might be two teachers grading the same essay. Both will probably perceive the essay differently and assign different grades. As mentioned, there are other modes that help us to interpret the same sensed data differently.

A final mode of analysis is the result of using what Edward DeBono refers to as *vertical versus lateral lens*. The examples in Figure 1–2 are helpful in explaining these modes of analysis.

The first three glasses are filled with wine; the last three are empty. By moving *only one glass*, can you create a situation where no empty glass is next to any other empty glass and no full glass is next to any other full glass?[7] This is a riddle, a problem, and a puzzle—all these things. The point is, you must learn to take an alternative mode of thinking to correctly answer

FIGURE 1–2   Wine Glass Puzzle.

the question. This is what DeBono has called *lateral thinking*, as opposed to the ordinary *vertical thinking*.

DeBono provides a second example:

> Many years ago when a person who owed money could be thrown into jail, a merchant in London had the misfortune to owe a huge sum to a money-lender. The money-lender who was old and ugly, fancied the merchant's beautiful teenage daughter. He proposed a bargain. He said he would cancel the merchant's debt if he could have the girl instead.
>
> Both the merchant and his daughter were horrified at the proposal. So the cunning money-lender proposed that they let Providence decide the matter. He told them that he would put a black pebble and a white pebble into an empty money-bag and then the girl would have to pick out one of the pebbles. If she chose the black pebble she would become his wife and her father's debt would be cancelled. If she chose the white pebble she would stay with her father and the debt would still be cancelled. But if she refused to pick out a pebble her father would be thrown into jail and she would starve.
>
> Reluctantly the merchant agreed. They were standing on a pebble-strewn path in the merchant's garden as they talked and the money-lender stooped down to pick up the two pebbles. As he picked up the pebbles the girl, sharp-eyed with fright, noticed that he picked up two black pebbles and put them into the money bag. He then asked the girl to pick out the pebble that was to decide her fate and that of her father.

What can the girl do? The answer to the young woman's plight lies in her perception of reality. Indeed, perceptual problems do not differ from the way in which we see problems with our eyes.

Take, for example, the triangles in Figure 1–3. Look at them. Then, write down on a sheet of paper what they say.[9] Look at them again. Read each slowly and aloud. After rereading the information inside the triangles, you probably noticed that "the" was used twice in one, and "a" was used twice in the other. Using vertical thinking patterns, we often miss information that is there or that may be unnecessary. However, using lateral thinking, you probably resolved the problem of the wine glasses by picking up the second glass and pouring the wine into the fifth glass. You probably also discovered that the young lady "accidentally" dropped her selected pebble

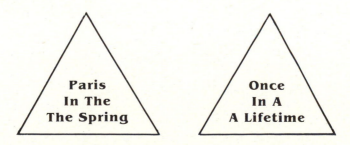

FIGURE 1–3   Verbal Perception Distortion.

onto the pebble-covered path. She then asked the money-lender to look into the moneybag and remove the remaining pebble. Since the remaining pebble was black, she must have drawn the white pebble. Vertical thinking, then, is based on the ordinary assumptions that we make about "reality." Lateral thinking questions those basic assumptions, leading to a different view of reality.

SUMMARY

As we communicate with others, we try to get the other person to feel the same as we do and employ the same modes of analysis. We also tend to try to verify our own perceptions in our communication with others. We must remember, however, that because perceptions differ, our attempts to persuade others and ourselves are based upon our perceptions of reality. Our own views limit our potential for perceiving.

DEFINITION OF COMMUNICATION

In this text, we look at perceptions of the particular phenomenon we refer to as *communication.* We provide a *working* definition of communication that incorporates the commonalities across modes of analysis and across theoretical perspectives discussed in the remainder of this book: *Communication is a symbolic process in which human beings act to exchange perceptions and ultimately to build the knowledge bank for themselves, one another, and society as a whole, for the purpose of taking future actions.* We will find, however, that those who have theorized about communication look at the process quite differently. They use one or more of the different modes of analysis that we have discussed: (1) culture/demographics, (2) similarities/differences, (3) time, (4) agreement/disagreement, (5) stability/change, (6) space, (7) active/passive voice, (8) specific knowledge, (9) logic/affect, (10) strange loops, and (11) vertical/lateral thinking.

Through a discussion of theory, we hope that you will learn to view communication from several different perspectives. As you progress through the text, you will "see" communication as a complex phenomenon that is not a reflection of any eternal, objective truth. These perceptual views (*theories of knowledge*) influence how we try to persuade others (*theories of action*), as well as how we behave (*theories of performance*).

REVIEW

Like Euthalus and Protagorus, we all are trying to find a way of v̶i̶e̶w̶i̶n̶g "reality" similar to our own interests and goals. In this book, our ̶ ̶ ̶ ̶ ̶ ̶ to illustrate that there have been a number of different views of ̶ ̶ ̶ ̶ ̶ication reality." There are many analogies we could use to show this; ̶ ̶ ̶ ̶ we have chosen architecture. Architects build edifices for different purposes; some are aesthetic, whereas others are functional. Some are large and encompass a large area; others are small but "work" in a number of locales.

Communication theorists have developed some good ideas, some good plans, and some good edifices. In this text, we look at a few of them. In Chapter 2, we explain three *blueprints* of a communication theory. The three blueprints we discuss are laws, systems, and rules. In Chapters 3 and 4, we discuss the two primary *materials* of communication: nonverbal and verbal communication. In Chapters 5 and 6, we discuss the *framing* of communication theory through a discussion of classical and contemporary rhetorical theories. Chapters 7 and 8 are concerned with *building the edifice for the individual* through a discussion of the psychological aspects of communication theory. Chapters 9 through 12 are concerned with *building the edifice for society.* These are sociologically based theories. Chapter 13, the biosocial approach, is concerned with how many of the theories may become an *integrated edifice.* Finally, in Chapter 14, we discuss *living with the communication edifice,* or how these theories may be used in your study of the human communication process.

At the end of each chapter is a *summary table.* Each one lists the major theories, the primary theorists, basic principles, constructs, criteria, and approach discussed in the chapter. Additionally, limitations to the theories are presented. Two appendices are included: Appendix A explains how theories are generated. Appendix B is a glossary of terms found throughout the text.

CRITIQUE

In this chapter, we have discussed communication as a process used to create and share perceptions as well as a phenomenon used to store perceptions (generate knowledge). We have provided a model of how we view the integration of reality, knowledge, and communication, including eleven different modes of analysis for perceiving. Finally, we have provided the outline for the remainder of the text.

What have we learned about building communication? The architect must understand intuitively how a building will look, how functional it will be, and how much aesthetic appreciation it will receive. The communication architect must impose certain restrictions on him- or herself prior to developing a blueprint. The communication architect must understand how to approach communication in general, what parts are important, and how results can be tested. Using this approach, we (1) perceive a situation or person, (2) test that perception via some result, and (3) learn from anticipated results how the theory functions. This day-to-day theorizing someday will yield a formal theory of how to communicate, with what effect, and with what limitations. Fortunately, there are many theories already stated and tested that allow us to understand, predict, and ultimately control communication. With a knowledge of general theory building, like the architect, we have the basic knowledge needed to evaluate and choose a blueprint format (a "metatheory").

Chapter 2 expands our discussion of communication theory to the three dominant blueprints of the late 1970s and early eighties. As you read and study this material, remember that a general blueprint will depend upon the amount of adaptability or flexibility that is needed. Chapter 2 provides the blueprints from which we can design our communication. That design, however, must be built upon a solid foundation, one cemented in effective theory.

NOTES AND REFERENCES

[1] P. Watzlawick, *How Real is Real? Confusion, Disinformation, Communication* (New York: Vintage, 1976), xi.

[2] P. L. Berger and T. Luckmann, *The Social Construction of Reality: A Treatise in the Sociology of Knowledge* (New York: Anchor, 1966); R. A. Cherwitz and J. W. Hikins, *Communication and Knowledge: An Investigation in Rhetorical Epistemology* (Columbia: University of South Carolina Press, 1986); D. R. Hofstadter, *Godel, Esher, Bach: An Eternal Golden Triad* (New York: Vintage, 1980). See also R. M. Pirsig, *Zen and the Art of Motorcycle Maintenance* (New York: Morrow, 1974); D. R. Hofstadter and D. C. Dennett, *The Mind's I: Fantasies and Reflections on Self and Soul* (New York: Bantam, 1981); D. R. Hofstadter, *Metamagical Themas: Questing for the Essence of Mind and Pattern* (New York: Basic, 1985).

[3] Watzlawick, pp. 147–239.

[4] L. Cooper, trans., *The Rhetoric of Aristotle* (Englewood Cliffs, NJ: Prentice–Hall, 1932), pp. 90–143; N. K. Denzin, *On Understanding Emotion* (San Francisco: Jossey–Bass, 1984).

[5] B. Russell, *A History of Western Philosophy* (New York: Simon and Schuster, 1945), p. 76.

[6] Hofstadter, *Godel, Esher, Bach*, pp. 8–16.

[7] K. R. Krupar, *Communication Games: Participant's Manual* (New York: Free Press, 1973), p. 103.

[8] E. DeBono, *New Think* (New York: Avon, 1968), pp. 21–22.

[9] B. D. Ruben and R. W. Budd, *Human Communication Handbook: Simulations and Games* (Rochelle Park, NJ: Hayden, 1975), pp. 30–31.

2

The Blueprints of Communication Theory: Systems, Rules, and Laws

A structure is only as good as the plans from which it is drawn. Each of us sees the uses for our structures differently. Some people prefer to live in houses with formal living rooms, whereas others prefer family rooms. This preference is reflected in the architect's blueprints. If an architect's perception of a space is multifunctional, that space is designed to be used in many ways. Adaptability, or flexibility, may be important in living areas; however, in bathrooms, where the functions are more limited, the architect's purpose is to design for the specific uses.

This chapter outlines three traditional types of blueprints available to the communication architect. Our discussion of use and flexibility is tied to the concepts of *generality* and *necessity*, which help the communication architect determine how specialized a plan should be, how permanent the edifice may be, and how different variables (materials) are used in planning the structure.

In this chapter, we focus on three ways to organize or plan theoretical approaches: systems, rules, and laws. These approaches differ primarily in the degree of generality and necessity.[1] Donald P. Cushman and W. Barnett Pearce have indicated that each approach generates "different questions for inquiry, employs alternative principles of explanation, prediction and control, and advocates diverse criteria of truth" (p. 174). However, all three require a consideration of generality and necessity.

GENERALITY AND NECESSITY

Generality refers to a theory's degree of potential application. Theory generality is tested two ways, using tests of (1) *syntactical* generality and

13

(2) *domain* generality. Syntactical generality is identified as the degree to which the words "all" or "none" are used in the principles of the theory. When qualifications ("some," "most") are used, the theory is less than absolutely general. Domain generality can be tested by determining how many conditions or specifications must be met for a given principle or statement to hold true.

For example, consider the hypothesis that tall women are expected to talk more than short women, under the conditions that (1) they were talking to a male stranger and (2) they were in the first four minutes of conversation. If we add other conditions (e.g., at business conventions), we *decrease* the domain generality by adding another restriction to our principle. The syntactical generality would be affected by whether we are talking about *all* women who are five feet nine inches and taller, or *most* or *some.* To the extent that we can use the word "all," we increase the level of generality.

In addition, three types of necessity indicate how theoretical statements are related to one another: (1) *nomic* necessity, (2) *logical* necessity, and (3) *practical* necessity. Nomic necessity concerns the idea that the principle *must* hold true. For example, if our intent is that "All women five feet nine inches or taller talk more to a male stranger in the first four minutes than do shorter women," then the nomic necessity is based on whether we can say "All women five feet nine inches *must talk* more . . ." That is, one condition predicts the next. Logical necessity, based on definitional forces, is determined by whether a logical formula or *calculus* can be derived from theoretical propositions (see the next section, "Systems Approach"). Practical necessity depends on the extent to which a person feels obligated to perform in a certain way (or the extent to which he or she operates according to social norms). We discuss this in more detail later, under "Rules Approach." All theoretical relationships are indicated by the necessity and generality—or adaptability—of each of the three blueprints, which are sometimes called *metatheoretical* approaches:

Quality	High Generality	Midrange Generality	Low Generality
	SYSTEMS	RULES	LAWS
Necessity	Logical	Practical	Nomic
Form	A affects B,C,D, . . . *n*	A wants to do C.	All A's are B's.
	B affects A,C,D, . . . *n*	Before A can do C,	All A's are B's
	C affects A,B,D, . . . *n*	A must do B; therefore,	under condi-
	and so on.	A does B as a means	tions 1, 2,
		of achieving C.	3, . . . *n*.

Each approach includes a level of generality and a type of necessity. In this chapter, we define each approach and provide examples. Any particular theory could be geared to any of the three approaches, depending on how its principles are written. We begin with the systems approach, which in many ways is more general or adaptive than the other two.

SYSTEMS APPROACH

A system has been defined as "any continuing entity capable of two or more states. A *communication* system is one in which the states are connections or nonconnections among objects."[2] A system is something that seeks to *describe* the interrelationships between states.

This section examines first what constitutes a system. We then examine how systems "theory" can be used in communication research. Finally, we review some objections raised by people advocating more "substantive" theoretical positions.[3] We turn now to an understanding of what a system is and how it operates.

Communication Systems

Structural Theory.   Ithiel de Sola Pool defines a communication system in terms of the "connections or nonconnections" among objects (p. 3). In so doing he presents a *structural* view of what a system is and indicates what a system does: It transmits information in some network of interconnected objects or people. Specifically, he argues (pp. 3–4) that communication systems differ in six ways (see Fig. 2–1):

1. The number of "objects" or people connected to each other
2. The message capacity of the connections or networks between people
3. The capacity of each channel, network, or connection; the volume of information (messages) that flows between people
4. The network structure, including direction of message flow, number of connections ("links"), and probability of channel use
5. The form of messages carried (verbal, nonverbal, written)
6. The "triggering mechanism" that activates change from state to state or dimension to dimension

The structural view, then, examines who says what to whom through what channel with what effect. It serves to describe the flow of information, or energy, within the system. For instance, a researcher interested in the flow of messages within a group discussion may wish to *map* messages as part of the structure of a discussion. The researcher's goal is to describe how messages *flow* in the group which becomes the system under study. Similarly, an organizational researcher may be interested in the upward, downward, and horizontal flow of messages in a complex organization. He or she may examine how those messages *flow* between people, what types of messages flow, and how messages *change* as they move through the system.

General Systems Theory.   An alternative view examines systems in a more general manner, as more than interconnections between people or

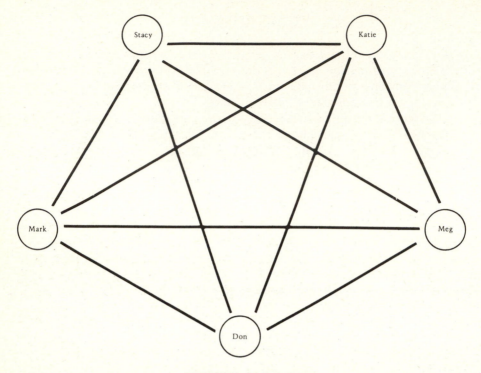

FIGURE 2–1   Systems.

objects. This view, general systems theory (GST), operates as an interactive system "fed" on information.[4] According to Brent Ruben, GST implies three propositions. The first states that communication is multidimensional and multidirectional. Any number of inputs (people, information, objects) may affect communication (multiple causation), or a "single" message may have multiple effects. Also implied is that these effects can go in *any* direction and result in different outcomes (this is termed *equifinality*).

For example, if a boss has a meeting with workers and states that this year's salary increase will be limited to 5 percent, worker interpretations will differ. Perceptions will vary depending on whether an individual just bought a new car, on what 5 percent is in real dollars, and on what percentage of salary increase had been expected. Thus, even a simple message to a few people is multidirectional and multidimensional.

Second, effective communication has at its core the *control* or manipulation of the receiver of that communication. That is, an effective message maximizes the system's potential resources. This implies, however, an understanding of the system and the ways it operates. Third, both sender *and* receiver determine the system. That is, "What we see in, and say about, other people (and things) says far more about us than about them" (p. 121). A system, then, is transactional. To deal with a communication system, we need to understand its "holistic" nature, that is, communication is more than the simple addition of a source and a receiver; it is that *plus* the perceptions of *each* communicator.

Components

Whether one identifies more with structure (de Sola Pool) or with effect (Ruben), all systems contain properties that tie them together as a "theory." A system in its simplest form is a way of "mapping" or "describing" some communication relationship. Communication systems consist of several elements, each relating to the others. When we think of a system, we must first place it in some location, or *environment*.

Different environments change the way the system operates, as you have found in your transition between high school and college, or simply dating and going steady. How a system relates to the environment is a function of its *openness* to the environment and to other systems. With openness comes new ideas or energy which takes the system to different states. Your reading of this book should provide new ideas, assuming of course you are open to what we are saying. Openness, then, creates more energy or ideas than you originally had—your system is said to be *holistic*.

Finally, all systems comprise other systems which are related in some form of *hierarchy*. Your system may be composed of college classification: freshmen, sophomore, junior, and senior. You begin in the system as a freshman, receive information, and move to the next higher subsystem—sophomore—and so on. As your system grows, it experiences *feedback*, which provides information to the system as to where it is going. For instance, passing the first test in a difficult class provides stabilizing feedback. If you do not pass a crucial class in your major, however, that information may encourage you to shift majors: The feedback provides information for change.

Communication systems can be found at many levels: intrapersonal, interpersonal, organizational, or societal. Furthermore, analysis of the system can take on several forms. We begin with a general overview of systems terminology and relationships and then move on to two different interpretations of how communication systems theory operates.

Environment.   All systems operate in some *environment*. Ruben suggests that one way to look at systems is to examine the basic relationships of all systems (see Fig. 2–2). A system is simply a set of interacting objects, units, or elements. The system in which you are interested is probably one of several that might be said to compose the *suprasystem*. Within the suprasystem are numerous *systems*, each having a number of *subsystems*. Figure 2–2 also suggests that there are areas that separate the various systems and subsystems. These are *boundaries*, which may be physical, spatial, temporal, or even symbolic in nature. The boundary is a buffer area that separates the system from its environment. It allows for the exchange of information between the various systems, subsystems, and the environment, or it inhibits that same flow.

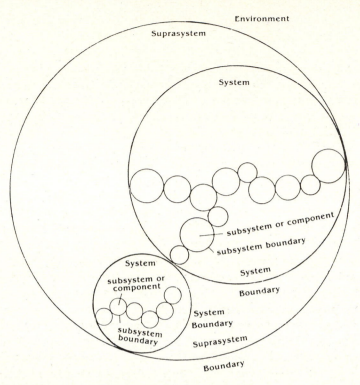

FIGURE 2-2   Suprasystems, Systems, and Subsystems.
Source: B. D. Ruben, "General System Theory: An Approach to Human Communication," in *Approaches to Human Communication,* eds., R. W. Budd and B. D. Ruben (New York: Spartan Books, 1972), p. 127.

Environments include elements of both time and place. Returning to our earlier example, a 5 percent raise may be perceived in terms of the cost of living. If that cost increase is 8 percent, 5 percent may not look good. If it is 2 percent, 5 percent may be attractive. In terms of time, if there were no cost of living increases over the last two years, this year's 5 percent increase may not be perceived as attractive.

Openness.   In general, there are two types of systems.[5] *Open* systems are composed of prescribed, semipermeable boundaries that are interdependent on other systems or subsystems. The open system is characterized by a *metabolism* in which inputs (energy, information) are shared between system, subsystem, and environment.[6] At the other extreme are *closed* systems, systems contained and isolated from the environment. Such systems move toward a state of *entropy* (deterioration). All systems move toward entropy, but open systems can control this movement through *negentropy*, actions or forces that reduce or redirect the entropic course. Again, new energy may be created by the 5 percent raise, if benefits were also increased.

It would be nice if all systems were either open or closed. Actually, human systems closely *approximate* open systems. B. Aubrey Fisher notes that since "communication presupposes a social system, a communication system is always open to some degree and more nearly open than closed."[7] Because human systems tend toward openness, they are more complex. An anomaly of human communication theory is that as complexity of theory increases, so too does understanding. One problem associated with systems theory is that it is too "simple," too all encompassing, and does not put concepts and behavior into neat pigeon holes. At the same time, however, it does tend to describe our communication.

Holism.   The concept underlying holism is that a system is greater than the sum of its parts.[8] Because a system is composed of related elements connected to each other, metabolism can be added by each interconnection. It also can be reduced by the same. If we were interested only in the elements of the system, we would be stuck with a taxonomy—or listing—of which part is which. Instead, systems people advocate studying the *process* by which the system operates. The functioning of the system is the preferred level of analysis, an analysis presupposing knowledge of the various elements comprising the system.

For instance, suppose each wheel of your car holds each tire on with five nuts. As you are changing a tire, your nephew throws the four nuts into an adjacent ditch. Instead of throwing your nephew into the ditch, you simply remove one nut from each of the remaining three wheels. You place these nuts on the wheel where you were replacing the tire, enabling you to get the car far enough to purchase more nuts. The system still works, with fewer parts, simply by placing them in a different relationship with one another.

Hierarchy.   If systems reflect natural order as found in life, then those same systems tend to range from very simple to very complex. Within any suprasystem are a number of systems, each differing in terms of complexity and hierarchy. Human communication systems are part of the larger social (supra)system. Each system, however, can be identified as being related to others above, below, or at the same level of hierarchy. Arthur Koestler describes this as the "holon" or "system of relations which is represented on the next higher level as a unit."[9] For example, the small group is a holon of the larger group. The individual is a holon of the small group. The self-concept is a holon of the individual (as its own system).

Feedback.   All systems that lean to openness possess the ability to control themselves. This ability, referred to earlier as "negentropy," is based in the principle of *feedback* and *feedback systems.* In one sense, the feedback system operates to maintain the system, to achieve *homeostasis* (stability). In this model, feedback operates much like a thermostat looking for deviations or errors in the system (temperature) and then returning the system to the original state. This is called *negative* feedback.[10] Feedback that amplifies the deviations and moves the system to another state is called *positive* feedback. Typically, open systems use both negative feedback, to stabilize the system (especially when that system is experiencing entropy), and positive feedback, to move it to the next higher state.

A Humanistic Perspective—The Person as a System

Theorists advocating a humanistic approach to communication view the person as a human being. They dislike the often-applied person–machine analogy to the systematic study of behavior and communication.[11] They argue that the relationship a person has with himself or herself is as complex as relationships with others. Underlying this sense of relationship is a feeling that one of the major goals of science, *predictability*, in some way has been relegated to the machine–person analogy; that is, we are more concerned with understanding a group of people based on some characteristic (e.g., sex or race) than with what makes one person act. The personality is complex and varies from situation to situation.[12] The person is his or her *own* system.

Understanding that a person is a changing whole opens the study of human communication to systems analysis. Humanistic tradition maintains that the person is a system constantly monitoring information (subsystem and environment inputs and outputs) and making decisions based on information gained from both.

The humanistic approach sees each of us as part of the larger system that yields a mutual dependency on each other. We are active users (subsystems) of information stored within ourselves. With this information, which comes from others and ourselves, we evaluate our environments and communicate according to our perceptions of others and self. This is what we earlier defined as an "open system." Information is metabolized as both positive and negative feedback, and either changes or maintains the person at any given time.

One major drawback to the systems perspective is found in the concepts of entropy and homeostasis. Living human systems almost never reach a state of complete entropy and they never reach homeostasis. Ludwig von Bertalanffy noted this and argued that within the human system the tendency is for order and ordering.[13] He suggested that the person can and does act in ways that are "highly statistically improbable." This human system quirk is identified as the process of *human adaptation*; that is, people behave in ways that may cause "disequilibrium" within the system.[14] The person is acting on information derived from *within* his or her system instead of stimuli from the outside.

The tendency of the human system to seek order over time and to alter the energy/information it receives suggests a system moving through psychological space. That is, the person may be different due to several factors at any given time (environment, information, internal states, personality). Hence, the person is highly susceptible to the principle of *equifinality* and *holism*. Multiple effects or causes of behavior within the system make us more than we know at any moment in time. However, an understanding of the person as a whole provides predictability. Prediction is accomplished by examining *life cycles* or the "sequences of a person's inner experiences and production."[15] To really know someone, we must closely observe that person under a variety of situations and understand how that person interprets his or her own experiences. Systems analysis views each person as a suprasystem, with systems dealing with such things as personality, fears, intelligence, sex drives, and so forth.

Systems theory allows the humanistic approach to understand the person as a whole. Such understanding comes not from an analysis of the parts of the system alone, but from the parts *and* the interconnectedness of the parts with each other. As Paul Watzlawick, Janet Beavin, and Don Jackson have noted, a person "does not originate communication; he participates in it."[16]

A Pragmatic Perspective

Not all agree with the humanistic perspective. A second model of systems (the pragmatic view) has been offered by Fisher, whose concern is with the interrelatedness of people in a social unit. The *social system* as a whole is the central concern in Fisher's perspective. He believes that "any understanding of communication focuses on the pragmatic and highly observable connectedness between human actions belonging to the social system *as a whole.*"[17] Actions are messages that can be observed and are found in the nature of people's relationships.

Fisher's concern is the *behavior* exhibited by a person and its influences on relationships among people within the system. He believes that all behavior *is* communication, and, since we cannot help but behave, we cannot *not* communicate. The system is founded on actions defined in terms of behaviors that link the person with the social system of relevance. This behavioral perspective does not rule out internal feelings, attitudes, or beliefs, but it centers on the behavioral manifestations of those thoughts or feelings.

Since behavior is that which "counts," the behavioral patterns of people in the system are measured. Fisher measures the sequences of people's behavior over time, observing how the system moves from one psychological state to another. Behavioral sequences are reduced to "sequential interaction patterns" of behavior which, through redundancy, become interpretable. The basic unit of analysis in such an interpretation is the "interact"—the linkage of two behaviors. *Interacts* yield sequences of behaviors that yield meaning over a period of time.

A major problem in this form of systems analysis is the randomness found in human behavior ("disequilibrium"). This, however, can be accounted for by the sequential nature of the pattern. As noted earlier, our social system tends toward order and ordering. Fisher has labeled this ordering process as *stochastic probability* (p. 213). He notes that systems are patterned by the nature of the interconnectedness of its parts, and that the relationship between behaviors yields patterns rather than randomness. We can interpret the system through people's interaction. Increased behavioral redundancy leads to patterning from which interpretations are inferred.

For instance, if you are part of a group that has met over a period of time, as time passes you predict how other members will act. Sometimes a member reacts to a *new* stimulus (e.g., a new member) in a random manner at first. (The behavior is not patterned and is idiosyncratic.) Over time, it will become a pattern if this person acts in a similar manner each time a new group member is added.

The pragmatic view of systems is more concerned with *change* than with structure. As such, it looks for systems use of information over time. Structure, however, is not totally excluded, but is viewed as a *part* of the process through which communication is studied. A change in structure (interacts) may explain a change in behavior.

The Structural–Functional Perspective

A third systems perspective stresses the *uses* of information within communication networks. Peter Monge has presented a systems model that has an

---

TABLE 2–1   Logical Conditions To Be Met

General Systems Theory

Open Systems
1. Identification of the components of the system.
2. Specification of relations in the system.
3. Determination of system behavior:
    a. Exchange of inputs and outputs between system and environment (through system boundaries)
    b. Attainment of steady state (some distance remaining from true equilibrium)
    c. Attainment of steady state independent of initial conditions (concept of *equifinality*)
    d. Decrease of entropy
4. Stipulation of the environment.
5. Determination of system evolution.

Closed System
1. Identification of system components.
2. Specification of set states (behavior) in the system.
3. Change due to transformation because of:
    a. Isolation from environment
    b. True equilibrium attained
    c. Increase in entropy

Cybernetic Theory
1. Setting of parameters for the system (signals).
2. Control over the system defined as exerted by some "center."
3. Feedback systems or subsystems provided to the control center.
4. Location of error signals from tests of system or subsystem parameters.
5. Corrective action may be taken by control center to maintain or move system.

Source: P.R. Monge, "The Systems Perspective as a Theoretical Basis for the Study of Human Communication," *Communication Quarterly,* 25 (1977), 22.

interest in the structure of the networks *and* the message flow between the various parts of that system.[18] Monge's model incorporates the open and closed systems associated with GST to a *cybernetic system*, which focuses on feedback mechanisms and self-regulation. This model is called *structural–functional* (see Table 2–1).

Although GST was examined earlier in this chapter, a quick review helps to understand Monge's perspective. GST generally describes the system and its operations, and is concerned with identification of the relevant systems parts, units, or subsystems. GST examines the interactions between those parts within the particular environment, which may be either open or closed. The type of system, then, defines the way in which the system will operate. Predictions of how the system evolves are made based on structural knowledge.

In contrast to GST, cybernetic systems (CS) are concerned with determining system control and regulation.[19] They examine the feedback systems (positive or negative) or subsystems that *control* the system through processes described earlier. As Monge has noted, feedback systems tend to be composed of three types of feedback "loops" (see Fig. 2–3).[20] These may be *self-loops*, which specify that a particular unit influences itself at a later point in time; *mutually causal loops*, each directly influencing the other either simultaneously or almost instantaneously; or *indirect loops*, each unit influencing another in some sequential process. Obviously, different forms of control are obtained, depending on the type of feedback loop used in a particular feedback system. All three types of systems (GST-open, GST-closed, CS) are used in the structural–functional system (SFS).[21]

Monge argues that GST provides the identification of key structural considerations. We look first at the system to identify the subsystems and environment(s) in which the system operates, then at the feedback loops used to regulate the system. Of critical concern are those subsystems most essential to the system's survival. These are then described, each contributing subsystem identified, and its role in system maintenance determined. It should be noted that what is emphasized in SFS is the structure in which information or behavior is communicated. This view of systems is concerned more with the description and analysis networking than with the change that occurs; it assumes that change occurs (it takes an *open* systems approach). Furthermore, change can be analyzed by identifying essential subsystems and their controlling devices (type of feedback system and loop).

Analysis from the SFS approach is found in many organizational settings (where the organization serves as the suprasystem). For instance, within a large state university system, various systems operate within the suprasystem environment. Those systems are, of course, the various state universities, but those that are private are not part of the system, although they may still affect the system. The analysis focuses on how the university system operates; on which subsystems are essential; and on funding, recruitment of students, and the win–loss record of the various athletic teams at each system (which, of course are subsystems within the system [university] at the same level as the various colleges and schools within the particular

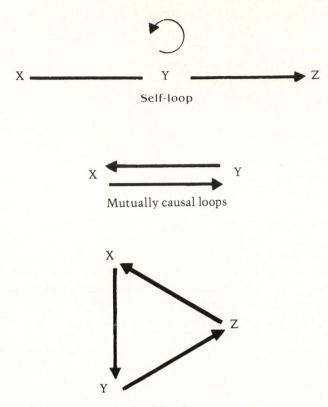

FIGURE 2–3   **Forms of Feedback Loops.**
Source: P. R. Monge, "Systems Theory and Research in the Study of Organizational Communication: The Correspondence Problem," *Human Communication Research, 8* (1982), 250.

system [university]). After all this has been identified, the researcher describes how the system as a whole maintains itself or, if it is in danger of entropy, what must be done to balance the system.

_____ REVIEW _____

Systems theory places emphasis on reflecting or describing the "real" world. In systems theory, we examine the logical relationships between elements taken as a whole.[22] Systems theory is a *metatheory*. It should be obvious by now that a number of different theories fall under the umbrella of "systems," from very general to very specific. Additionally, as we note in the next sections, both law and rule theories may fall under systems theory. Systems theory allows for a logical analysis of the total communication over time. It accounts for those variables of interest *to the researcher* at the researcher's level of interest. As was demonstrated, systems can be analyzed at the intrapersonal, interpersonal, small group, or complex organization level. Finally, systems theory takes into account the total communication process. Although the pragmatic and the structural views differ in what they consider to be the central concern—change or network flow—systems theory provides a method to analyze complex human behavior in its "natural" form.

CRITIQUE

As might be expected, a number of criticisms have been aimed at the various systems theories. Perhaps the most significant criticism is that systems theory lacks substance.[23] This criticism may be a little unfair and is aimed more at structural than pragmatic theories. Systems theory has also been attacked for being overly complex and the systems theorist, by advocating complexity, for making too much of very little.[24] Some argue that systems theory has not produced empirical support relative to its advocates.[25] It may be that only now methods are becoming available to adequately test theories (we point the reader to Monge's 1982 treatment of this criticism).[26] That systems theory is logical, as pointed out in both Fisher's and Monge's works, has been supported in the literature. It is heuristic. It has produced new theory. How reliable systems theory is, however, is dependent on two things: (1) the ability of the researcher to identify the relevant components, and (2) the ability of the researcher to measure the interactions/networks/patterns that result from the interconnectedness of the whole.

RULES APPROACH

Although systems theory provides an explanation of how communication is structured and functions, some theorists find that its stress on description reduces its impact. These theorists' concerns with the pragmatic aspects of day-to-day communication naturally point them to studying how we coordinate our communications. The goal is to understand *why* people communicate as they do. Theorists advocating this approach identify with a rules orientation to communication.

In studying the rules approach we examine two different theories. The first, more formal treatment, consists of a formal logic, complete with relationships, variables, and prediction. The second is a "looser" rules approach to day-to-day communication. We begin by looking at rules in general, then an example of a rules theory (coordinated management of meaning) and, finally, a second example, dramaturgical analysis.

Donald P. Cushman has outlined several ways that the term *rules* can be applied in the social sciences. In this context, we are concerned with a "class of human activity where significance is largely dependent on the existence of consensually-shared rules [norms that we usually subconsciously agree to]" (p. 38). Communication, in this approach, is "the transfer of symbolic information"

(p. 39). Communication functions to regulate this consensus for the coordination of behavior. Structure is determined by code (language) and network rules. Here, for instance, the goal of interpersonal communication is to develop, present, and validate the self-concept (p. 39). When we meet a friend, for instance, we normally do not begin conversation at the same place or level we previously ended. Instead, we agree to begin at a particular place, say, probing to see what has happened previously, then moving into more intimate or important topics. As relationships intensify over time, however, that general rule changes and we informally agree with the friend how to initiate a new conversation; that is, we agree to communicate in a particular way with each other.

According to Cushman and Pearce, "A theory of human communication, according to this perspective, takes the form of a practical syllogism. An individual, or group A intends to bring about C; A considers that to bring about C, he must do B; and therefore A sets himself to do B."[27] Furthermore, there are two categories of rules: (1) *movements*, which are stimulus–response behaviors governed by nomic necessity, and (2) *actions*, which are choice-governed responses derived from practical necessity (p. 177). In communication, actions are the basis for prediction. Cushman and Pearce suggest a rule-governed theory of action.

Coordinated Management of Meaning

One theory employing the rules approach is represented in the work of Pearce and his colleagues.[28] It is important to remember that this theory assumes a pluralistic society, in which many different value systems are held by its members. In this society, we can explain our actions in many ways. In particular, we may use two types of rules. First, *influenced behavior* varies as a result of the actor's "meanings and volition."[29] These types of behavior are like taking turns using a number at an ice cream store or bowing to another, as in Japanese society. Second, *creative behavior* involves "following rules in a novel way or acting independently of the rules" (p. 19). Thus, for example, when we continually bend a rule or behave in ways inappropriate to the general rule (*norm*), we are engaged in creative behavior. Suppose that the rule is to stop at all stop signs. Will you stop at a stop sign in the middle of nowhere? When your view of traffic is unrestricted? At midnight? With no other traffic? Or will you create a "new" rule: when nobody is present, slow down and roll through the stop sign? Because creative behaviors will be somewhat idiosyncratic, most of the rules we are concerned with are for influenced behavior.

Pearce's theory is referred to as the *coordinated management of meaning* (CMM). It is important to note the meaning of each word in the name of the theory because it is composed of constructs (terms in a theory). *Meaning*, according to Pearce, is episodic, organized over various conversations. Meaning is organized into units and may be organized in one of two ways.

Meaning is determined *synchronically*, by locating a meaning in the context of related meanings (when something was said), or *diachronically*, "by providing an interpretation of past messages and the prediction of future ones" (pp. 20–21) (e.g., "Let me say all that I wish to say; then you can talk").

An episode is determined or *coordinated* by the actors (communicators) in a situation. The communication has some imposed internal structure, but that structure is dependent on the actors involved. Overall, an episode answers the question, "What do you think he is doing?" (p. 21). According to Pearce, there are three types of episodes: "Episodes 1" include factors outside of the actors, significant symbols according to the symbolic interactionists (see Chapter 9). They include rituals, social rites, and so forth. "Episodes 2" are in individual minds, definitions of situations, according to the symbolic interactionists (see Chapter 9). "Episodes 3" are "communicators' interpretations of the actual sequence of messages that they jointly produced" (pp. 21–22).

Management involves the methods we use to analyze our episodes. According to Pearce, there are four types: "(1) predicted agreement confirmed (PAC); (2) predicted agreement disconfirmed (PAD); (3) predicted disagreement confirmed (PDC); and (4) predicted disagreement disconfirmed (PDD)" (p. 23). Thus, the *mode of analysis* (agreement/disagreement) is an important variable in Pearce's theory.

In such an analysis, the following predictions might be made: In a PAC situation, if Bob expects Nancy will go out with him, he asks her for a date. She agrees to go. Predicted agreement is confirmed (PAC). If Bob asks her and she does not go, she has done the unexpected. The predicted agreement is disconfirmed (PAD). Now Bob must try to figure out what the problem is.

If Bob goes into his boss' office predicting that he will not get the raise he is asking for and the boss does not give him the raise, the predicted disagreement is confirmed (PDC). If Bob is given the raise, however, Bob is delighted (PDD), yet he feels obligated to try to figure out why he got an unexpected raise.

Pearce indicates that we contract with each other concerning a particular episode (create a consensually shared rule). Early in conversations we negotiate with one another about the contract. We may indicate that it is or is not all right to bring up a particular topic, for example. This indication may be verbal, nonverbal, or both. Each of us expects the other to accept his or her Episode 2 (definition of the situation). Over time, many Episode 2s are negotiated through three negotiation strategies: casting, mirroring, and negotiation.

Casting is used to train others for a part. For example, over time office workers learn they may interrupt the boss if the door is open. If the door is closed, the workers know not to interrupt. Casting is similar to casting in a play; it is teaching others to play a particular role.

Mirroring is the opposite of casting. Mirroring is *taking on* whatever role is needed in the particular episode by the other. Anyone can take on casting or mirroring roles, although success is dependent on relationship and role. It is easy to see, for example, that parents provide roles and attempt to cast their children in them; however, as children mature they often mirror adult roles, such as playing "marriage" or "doctor."

Negotiation involves compromising. Individuals may talk about the episode (and previous episodes) in what we call "metacommunicating." They may create shared experiences to forge a common ground for future interactions. (In initial interactions, people may ask, "Where are you from?" "What are you majoring in?" etc.) They may ingratiate (bargain) by operating in an episode, hopeful that the other will reciprocate. Or, they may use invocation, "inviting the other to take a complementary role" (p. 25) (i.e., to "see this from my point of view"). Thus, we work together to establish episodic rules. These episodes are combined into *conversations*, a series of which becomes a relationship. Eventually relationships are formed, changed, and terminated as a combination of conversations.

Dramaturgical Analysis

Sociologist Erving Goffman has also researched the rules involved in conversations. He has analyzed the general rules of human interaction using drama as the basis or metaphor for his theory.

Goffman's general approach to the study of social interaction was to observe behavior without any contrived constructs, variables, hypotheses, or specific research questions. His general question was how a performer (social actor or communicator) goes about staging and acting out his or her social role in a variety of contexts. He refers to these presentations as *self-presentations*.[30] In the preface of one of his first books, Goffman wrote, "The perspective employed in this report is that of the theatrical performance; the principles derived are dramaturgical ones" (p. xi). Thus, he contended that we are constantly "on stage" when around others. The performance, then, is "the total range of behaviors displayed by an individual in the presence of a specific group of observers and upon whom the behaviors are designed to achieve some impact."[31] Each performance takes place at a particular location or *stage.* Goffman, then, developed a rule-governed theory of communication as *performance.*

The *front* of the stage in real-life performance is similar to the theatrical stage front. Here are located the "props" or objects needed to carry out the performance. The *manner* of the performer indicates to the audience what kind of performance is about to take place. Performances, then, are essentially *social games* that take place with groups of interactants, some of whom take on other roles, one of which may be simply the audience.

A social game may occur at any time. Change the audience, the actor, or the stage, however, and you change the interpretation. For instance, a social game may be a "fun" argument or fight with a friend before class. The classroom is the stage, and your books are the props used in the argument. Other class members are the audience. As you "fight," you pick up a book and toss it at your friend, who ducks and laughs. However, at that point, the teacher enters the room and observes what happens. From his or her perspective, the behavior is inappropriate for the stage. The key is that certain roles (friend, student, teacher) are taken, each with its own expectations of how to behave on the stage. Similar role problems are found with tutors who fall in love with their students. If the student also falls in love, the two must take care to ensure that the stage for their "loving" behavior differs from the stage for their "tutoring" behavior.

In his book, *Encounters: Two Studies in the Sociology of Interaction*, Goffman discusses two important aspects of playing games and providing performances: games and role distance.[32] Goffman discusses focused interactions that occur "when people effectively agree to sustain for a time a single focus of cognitive and visual attention, as in a conversation, a board game, or joint task sustained by a close face-to-face circle of contributors" (p. 7). The factors involved in such interactions include "embarrassment, maintenance of poise, capacity for nondistractive verbal communication, adherence to a code regarding giving up and taking over the speaker role, and allocation of spatial position . . . the participants' maintenance of continuous engrossment in the official focus of activity" (p. 11). Tension in these encounters occurs when the focus of attention is threatened by various distractions.

In *Relations in Public: Microstudies of the Public Order*, Goffman outlines some of the behaviors that we should follow according to social rules.[33] He describes humans as *vehicular units*. With these units (whether walking down the street or driving one's car) there are definite paths that people should take, based on social rules that are similar in function and scope to traffic regulations. One particularly important factor is *intention display*, where we indicate or signal to others where we intend to go and what we intend to do (p. 11). In interaction studies the individual can be different things. Besides being a vehicular unit, for example, we can be a participation unit. As a vehicular unit we are "a shell of some kind controlled (usually from within) by a human pilot or navigator" (p. 6). The individual can be considered the pilot "encased in a soft and exposing shell, namely his clothes and skin" (p. 7). We also appear in public as either a "single" or in a "with." A single is a party of one. A "with" is a party of more than one whose members are perceived to be "together." "Social settings and social occasions are not organized in terms of individuals but in terms of participation units" (p. 21).

"At the center of social organization is the concept of claims" (p. 28). Claims include personal space, the space surrounding the individual and "the stall," the territory immediately around the individual which he or she can use temporarily. In addition, the individual may claim a "turn," personal effects, information about oneself and "conversational preserves." "The claim to a preserve is made visible by a sign of some kind, which, following ethological practice, may be called a *marker*" (p. 41).

The central offense in conversation is an encroachment or other violation of the above claims and preserves. These violations may result from the placement of the body, a stare, disruptive noise, words, or other actions that fail to follow societal rules.

Under the heading of "supportive interchanges," Goffman discusses interpersonal rituals:

> Interpersonal rituals have a dislogistic character, and this definitely impinges on positive and negative rites. When . . . one individual provides a sign of involvement in and a connectedness to another, it behooves the recipient to show that the message has been received, that its import has been appreciated, that the affirmed relationship actually exists as the performer implies, that the performer himself has worth as a person, and finally, that the recipient has an appreciative, grateful nature (p. 63).

Supportive rituals involve such things as greetings, farewells, acts of courtesy, reassurance displays, and avoidance of openly denying the worth of others.

In addition to supportive interchanges, there are also "remedial interchanges":

> When persons are present together, many contingencies arise that could reflect discreditably on them. The individual finds that he has acted (or is about to act) so as to give the appearance of encroaching on another's various territories and preserves; or finds himself about to give a bad impression of himself; or both. In these circumstances he is likely to engage in remedial activity to reinforce a definition of himself that is satisfactory to him. (p. 183).

Goffman claims that actors have developed a specific process for handling these remedial interchanges. This process, called a *full remedial cycle*, involves four steps: remedy, relief, appreciation, and minimization. An example of this process can be noted with an individual's attempting to break in line at the grocery market:

Violator: "Excuse me. I'm late for Sunday School. Do you mind if I get in front of you?" (remedy)

Victim: "No. Go ahead." (relief)

Violator: "Thank you." (appreciation)

Victim: "You're welcome." (minimization)

According to Goffman, the remedial cycle requires that all four steps be taken in order. In this way, the violator provides an *account* to the victim, transforming what could otherwise be unacceptable behavior into acceptable behavior.[34] Thus, there are rules for breaking rules.

In this dramaturgical analysis, Goffman also discusses *backstage* behavior. The kinds of behavior that occur backstage are those one engages in preparing to be on stage. Judee K. Burgoon and Thomas J. Saine analyzed Goffman's works and developed five principles for the successful staging of behavior (think back to the classroom example earlier as you read through these):

1. A performer must separate audiences.
2. A performer should be aware of and adhere to requirements of decorum that accompany dramatic action.
3. A performer must coordinate verbal and nonverbal codes to create an impression.
4. For a performance to be accepted by an audience, the actor must be judged sincere.
5. An actor must appear satisfied with the role.[35]

Goffman's performances are similar to Pearce's episodes. When analyzing a performance, however, Goffman refers to the *frame*[36] (similar to Pearce's coordination of episodes). The central concept in frame analysis is the *key* (pp. 40–82). Keys are used primarily to establish how serious a particular interaction is at a particular time. It is important to know, for example, when one is "only playing." For Goffman, then, humans interact by playing out roles as within a play except that the actors are simultaneously the writers of dialogue, the producers, and the directors. The better we can coordinate these roles and the easier we can adapt to rules, the more successful we will be in achieving a position resulting from our communication.

REVIEW

The rules perspective provides a good heuristic base for communication theory. It has the capacity for dealing with either verbal or nonverbal communication, or both. It has the capacity for information exchange and rhetorical intercourse (persuasion). Through the use of both influenced behavior and creative behavior, it can be useful with an exchange (reciprocity) model or a conflict model. However, it is extremely important for rules theorists to discover the rules for *why* one chooses to follow influenced behavior or creative behavior.

CRITIQUE

Rules are governed by practical necessity, but the rules approach has been criticized for its ambiguity (What constitutes a rule?) and for not answering the why question (Why did the rule develop?). For the most part, a communication rules approach accounts for influenced behavior but not for creative behavior. Although the underlying practical syllogism can be tested, relatively few studies have done so. The theory is logical for everyday interactions, but rarely accounts for exceptions to social conversation. It is supportable, but to some extent it cannot be refuted. If a particular behavior falls outside influenced behavior, the theorist can argue that it was a creative behavior. This problem is critical for the rules theorist, unless, like Goffman, he or she formulates rules for violations. The reliability of the theory is questionable without accounts for rule violations. Rules theory, as Stephen Littlejohn notes, has been very heuristic and will continue to be, partly because of its ambiguity.[37]

COVERING LAWS PERSPECTIVE

A *covering laws* perspective involves a set of universal propositions and their stipulated initial conditions. For example, in the natural sciences we say that water boils at 100°C (212°F). This universal proposition, however, holds true *only* under the initial condition, *at sea level* (i.e., at 760 millimeters of mercury of pressure). A law will not hold true *unless* the condition(s) is (are) specified. Although those taking a laws view have dwindled significantly in the social sciences over the past twenty years, many communication theorists and researchers still strive for the parsimony (theoretical simplicity) of this approach.

According to Cushman and Pearce, systems, laws, and rules operate under different philosophical expectations, but all three must apply the expectations of generality and necessity. The level of generality is associated with the number of conditions placed on the universal proposition. Laws approaches use nomic necessity because they are what they are by name and definition, they necessarily *are* the case. According to Charles R. Berger, the functions of laws are to predict and explain. He argues that explanation is more important of the two, quoting Dray:

> What the theory maintains is that explanation is achieved, and only achieved *by subsuming what is to be explained under a general law.* Such an account of the basic structure of explanation is sometimes referred to as "the regularity analysis" but because it makes use of the notion of bringing a case under a law, i.e., "covering" it with a law I shall speak of it hereafter as "the covering law model."[38]

Laws are either deductive or inductive. A deductive–nomological statement is equivalent to "All X is Y." By substitution we might say, "All bachelors are unmarried men." These statements are not restricted by time or space. They are deductive because we can conclude, if Bill is a bachelor, he is an unmarried man. They are nomological because the universal is true because the variables are labeled or named "unmarried men" and "bachelors." A deductive–statistical statement might be "the probability that an event X is also true of Y is r" (p. 10). An example might be the law of genetics. If both parents have brown eyes, we can predict with certain accuracy the probability as to how many of their ten children will have brown eyes. It is deductive because we can provide probabilities for a specific case, and it is statistical because the probabilities are based on generalized statistics. Finally, there are inductive–statistical explanations. If our theory holds that people with similar attitudes will like one another, and if we know that both the members of Gamma Rho and a rushee have similar attitudes, we can ascertain the probabilities that they will like one another (pp. 10–11).

To help you further understand the covering laws approach, we examine two representative theories. The first, uncertainty reduction, applies to initial interactions among strangers. The second, violations of spatial expectations, applies to communication where the function is to influence others.

Uncertainty Reduction Theory

One example of a communication theory from the covering laws view is Charles R. Berger and Richard J. Calabrese's uncertainty reduction theory. They suggest that communication functions to reduce interpersonal uncertainty in initial interactions with strangers. Berger and Calabrese argue that the initial interaction is predictable by taking into account the relationships of twenty-one theorems (theoretical statements), yielding seven axioms. The axioms reflect the deductive nature of the theory:[39]

> Axiom 1: Given the high level of uncertainty present at the onset of the entry phase, as the amount of verbal communication between strangers increases, the level of uncertainty for each interactant in the relationship decreases. As uncertainty is further reduced, the amount of verbal communication increases.
>
> Axiom 2: As nonverbal affiliative expressiveness increases, uncertainty levels decrease in an initial interaction situation. In addition, decreases in uncertainty level cause increases in nonverbal affiliative expressiveness.
>
> Axiom 3: High levels of uncertainty cause increases in information-seeking behavior. As uncertainty levels decline, information-seeking behavior decreases.
>
> Axiom 4: High levels of uncertainty in a relationship cause decreases in the intimacy level of communication content. Low levels of uncertainty produce high levels of intimacy.
>
> Axiom 5: High levels of uncertainty produce high rates of reciprocity. Low levels of uncertainty produce low reciprocity rates.
>
> Axiom 6: Similarities between persons reduce uncertainty, whereas dissimilarities produce increases in uncertainty.
>
> Axiom 7: Increases in uncertainty level produce decreases in liking, whereas decreases in uncertainty level produce increases in liking.

In the context of the above axioms, nonverbal affiliative expressiveness refers to touching, making eye contact, showing positive facial expressions, and so forth. Information-seeking behavior means trying to get the other person to disclose information. The intimacy level of content concerns the degree to which the content of the conversation is personal. Hence, increases or decreases in one set (or subset) of behaviors produce explainable and predictable changes in another set of behaviors.

The key here is that the cause–effect relationship operates as if it were lawful, or *lawlike*. We use the term lawlike to imply that, unlike the natural sciences, the social sciences theorize an active and reactive subject—people— who react to one change in slightly different ways. The boiling water example may produce a lawlike analogy where the differing degrees of atmospheric pressure are equivalent to attitudes or temperament in individuals; they may differ slightly from each other from one "atmosphere" to another.

The resultant predictions are then tested much like those in the natural sciences. Berger and Calabrese, for instance, predict that both verbal and nonverbal "affiliative expressiveness" are related in a positive manner; as one increases, so does the other—unless, of course, another variable can be deduced to change that one-to-one-increase.

Violations of Spatial Expectations

In a similar manner, Burgoon theorized the communicative outcomes that are achieved by violating interpersonal distancing expectations.[40] In deriving her theory, Burgoon sets forth thirteen propositions about the relationships between the distances people adopt when interacting. These propositions are the function of three principles: (1) the reward value of the initiator of the deviation (e.g., the initiator's physical attractiveness, race, credibility), (2) the direction of the deviation (closer or further than the established distancing norm), and (3) the amount of that deviation.

According to this model, we can predict how persuasive a source will be based on knowledge of the key variables of reward, deviation, and deviation direction. Figure 2–4 indicates the predicted outcomes for a rewarding and nonrewarding source.[41] To use the theory, we would need to know two initial conditions: (1) our reward value and (2) the normative distance appropriate for any interaction with another person. If we know that others generally perceive us as physically attractive, we might see ourselves as possessing a high reward value. Based on Figure 2–4, we would predict that our best results would come if we deviated somewhat from whatever distance norm was established. Suppose, for example, that we were selling clothes. As attractive—rewarding—salespeople, we would allow the customer to approach us. After noting what distance norm was established, we would then deviate closer or further from the "norm." Actual strategy would have to take into account the age of the customer. For sake of argument, however, we might note that with customers closer to our own age, the closer deviation would produce more persuasion ("sales") than the further-than-norm deviation. For older customers, greater distance might provide more sales.

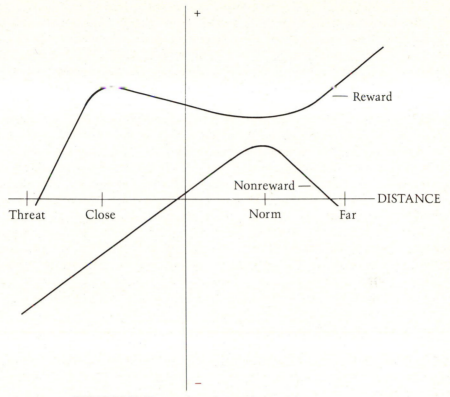

FIGURE 2–4   Predicted Outcomes for Violating Spatial Expectations.
Source: M. Hickson and D. W. Stacks, *NVC: Nonverbal Communication Studies and Applications,* 2nd ed. (Dubuque, IA: Brown, 1989), p. 65.

REVIEW

The covering laws model has met with little agreement in communication theory, perhaps due in part to its relative inflexibility in accounting for human communication. Positivists, or "variable testers" have had better results for specific cases, given specific subject pools. For a laws perspective to hold up, however, more general statements are needed from larger subject pools.

CRITIQUE

To an extent, theories that employ a laws approach (uncertainty reduction or spatial violations) are testable; however, because generality is necessary, "real world" testing is difficult. Law theory is best employed in the confines of the social scientist's laboratory. Law theory is troubled, for example, by variables that cannot be controlled, such as culture. It has trouble with such questions as, "To what extent are axioms culture bound, if they are culture bound." On the surface, the theory is logical. It is supportable or refutable, but *any* unexplained exception throws a wrench into a covering laws theory that does not indicate a probability level; hence, the term lawlike is often used instead of "law." Berger and Calabrese's theory, like most lawlike theories, is highly parsimonious, using uncertainty reduction as the primary construct. It appears to be reliable if given cultural constraints and so on. This theory has been quoted often in the literature but has not proven particularly heuristic as yet. The same may be said of Burgoon's spatial violations theory; that is, there is not a voluminous quantity of literature arguing for or against the case. Thus, the laws or lawlike approach has gained little favor among communication researchers. Lawlike approaches, nevertheless, are valuable tools for the communication theorist to help assess the limiting factors in a theory, as well as to ascertain at what point rules-based theories begin to approach lawlike consistency.

_____ SUMMARY _____

The approaches discussed in this chapter are summarized in Table 2–2. Each of the three theory approaches discussed is based on a different kind of necessity: The systems approach uses logical necessity, the rules approach uses practical necessity, and the laws approach employs nomic necessity. A laws approach, therefore, gains its force through the use of principles worded in such a way that they *must* hold true. The rules approach is based on the extent to which individuals in a society obey the *norms* of that society.[42] The systems approach is more concerned with the *logical relationships* among the elements of the system, as well as the relationship between the system and its environment. (See Table 2–2.)

This chapter has provided the basic blueprints to develop a more specific theory. Almost any theoretical approach examined in the next few chapters can be undertaken from a systems, rules, or laws blueprint. The manner in which each theory is written allows us to determine which approach the theorist has taken.

When the communication theorist desires to include a large number of constructs, all of which may interrelate to produce differing outcomes, he or she most likely will adopt a systems perspective. When the approach is concerned with pragmatic assessments, the theorist will tend to take a rules approach. Rules that occur consistently over a period of time may approach a lawlike accuracy, and a laws approach may be most appropriate.

In each case, however, the communication architect must gather the appropriate materials with which to begin construction. The materials for the communication theorist are found in the nonverbal and verbal codes. The verbal code deals with semantics—the meanings of symbols—as well as their structure; the nonverbal code may be perceived as the affective (emotional) cement that adds intensity to a meaning. In Section Two, we present several nonverbal (Chapter 3) and verbal (Chapter 4) approaches to

TABLE 2-2 Summary Table

Name of Theory	Primary Theorists	Basic Principle	Constructs	Criteria	Analytic Approach	Limitations
Systems approach	L. von Bertalanffy B. A. Fisher P. Monge	To maintain its existence, a system must be open (adapt to its environment) and adapt internally.	• System • Suprasystem • Subsystem • Open system • Closed system • Entropy • Negentropy	Constant adaptation	None	As a metatheory, this approach is useful for classifying other approaches.
Rules approach Coordinated management of meaning	B. Pearce	Communication is structured in accordance with a practical syllogism.	• Influenced behavior • Creative behavior • Episode • Casting • Mirroring	Effectiveness of practical syllogism	Practical syllogism	Does not explain how rules are created in the first place. Does not explain how to determine the existence of a rule. Does not account for rule violations.
Dramaturgical approach	E. Goffman	There are social rules for both violating and obeying rules. The rules are based on creating impressions for others.	• Stage • Front • Manner • Social games • Intention display • Backstage • Vehicular unit	Adapting to norms	A play	Accounts for rules violations by establishing rules.
Laws approach Uncertainty reduction	C. Berger R. Calabrese	In the initial stages of a relationship, individuals reduce uncertainty.	• Nonverbal affiliative expressiveness • Intimacy level • Information-seeking behavior	Increasing communication should reduce uncertainty.	—	Does not provide a causal model for the interaction between other communication events and uncertainty reduction.
Proxemic violations	J. K. Burgoon	People react to distancing deviations according to the direction and degree of deviation and reward value of the deviator.	• Distance • Norm violations • Reward	Norms are set according to personal spacing expectations and the reward value of the other	—	—

communication. Use of these materials, then, begins the formal construction of communication.

──────── Notes and References ────────

[1] D. P. Cushman and W. B. Pearce, "Generality and Necessity in Three Types of Human Communication Theory—Special Attention to Rules Theory," in *Communication Yearbook I*, ed. B. D. Ruben (New Brunswick, NJ: Transaction Books, 1977), pp. 173–182.

[2] I. de Sola Pool, "Communication Systems," in *Handbook of Communication*, ed. I. de Sola Pool et al. (Chicago: Rand McNally, 1973), pp. 3–26.

[3] J. G. Delia, "Alternative Perspectives for the Study of Human Communication: Critique and Response," *Communication Quarterly*, 25 (1977), 46–62.

[4] For excellent reviews see P. R. Monge, "The Systems Perspective as a Theoretical Basis for the Study of Human Communication," *Communication Quarterly*, 25 (1977), 19–29; B. D. Ruben, "General Systems Theory: An Approach to Human Communication," in *Approaches to Human Communication*, eds. R. W. Budd and B. D. Ruben (New York: Spartan Books, 1972), pp. 120–144; B. A. Fisher, *Perspectives on Human Communication* (New York: Macmillan, 1978).

[5] S. W. Littlejohn, *Theories of Human Communication*, 3rd ed. (Belmont, CA: Wadsworth, 1989), p. 35.

[6] A. Rapoport, "Forward," in *Modern Systems Research for the Behavioral Scientist*, ed. W. Buckley (Chicago: Aldine, 1968).

[7] B. A. Fisher, "The Pragmatic Perspective of Human Communication," in *Human Communication Theory*, ed. F. E. X. Dance (New York: Harper and Row, 1982), p. 199; Fisher, *Perspective*.

[8] See, for example, A. D. Hall and R. E. Fagen, "Definition of a System," *General Systems*, 1 (1956), 18–28; Rapoport; L. von Bertalanffy, *General Systems Theory: Foundations, Development, Applications* (New York: Braziller, 1968); E. Laszlo, *The Systems View of the World* (New York: Braziller, 1972).

[9] A. Koestler, "Beyond Atomism and Holism—The Concept of the Holon," in *Beyond Reductionism*, eds. A. Koestler and J. R. Smythies (London: Hutchison, 1969).

[10] Ruben; W. Buckley, "Society as a Complex Adaptive System," in *Modern Systems Research for the Behavioral Scientist*, ed. W. Buckley (Chicago: Aldine, 1968), pp. 490–513.

[11] M. Polani, *Personal Knowledge: Towards a Post-Critical Philosophy* (Chicago: University of Chicago Press, 1958).

[12] W. Mischel, *Personality & Assessment* (New York: Wiley, 1968).

[13] L. von Bertalanffy, "Problems of General Systems Theory," *Human Biology*, 23 (1951), 302–312; L. von Bertalanffy, "General Systems Theory and Psychiatry," in *American Handbook of Psychiatry*, *III*, ed. S. Arieti (New York: Basic Books, 1966).

[14] C. Buhler and M. Allen, *Introduction to Humanistic Psychology* (Monterey, CA: Brooks/Cole, 1972), p. 34.

[15] Buhler and Allen, p. 37.

[16]P. Watzlawick, J. H. Beavin, and D. D. Jackson, *Pragmatics of Human Communication* (New York: Norton, 1967), p. 70.

[17]Fisher, *Perspectives*, p. 202.

[18]Monge.

[19]See N. Wiener, *Cybernetics or Control and Communication in the Animal and the Machine* (New York: MIT Press, 1961).

[20]P. R. Monge, "Systems Theory and Research in the Study of Organizational Communication: The Correspondence Problem," *Human Communication Research, 8* (1982), 250.

[21]R. V. Farace, P. R. Monge, and H. M. Russell, *Communicating and Organizing* (Reading, MA: Addison–Wesley, 1977), pp. 50–69.

[22]Littlejohn, p. 17.

[23]For a detailed discussion see Delia, pp. 50–54.

[24]Littlejohn, p. 48.

[25]D. P. Cushman, "The Rules Perspective as a Theoretical Basis for the Study of Human Communication," *Communication Quarterly, 25* (1977), 30–45.

[26]Monge, "Systems Theory and Research."

[27]Cushman and Pearce, p. 177. See also D. P. Cushman and G. C. Whiting, "An Approach to Communication Theory: Toward Consensus on Rules," *Journal of Communication, 22* (1972), 219–220.

[28]W. B. Pearce and V. E. Cronen, *Communication, Action, and Meaning: The Creation of Social Realities* (New York: Praeger, 1980); W. B. Pearce, "The Coordinated Management of Meaning: A Rules-Based Theory of Interpersonal Communication," in *Explorations in Interpersonal Communication*, ed. G. R. Miller (Beverly Hills, CA: Sage, 1976), pp. 17–35; V. E. Cronen, W. B. Pearce, and L. M. Harris, "The Coordinated Management of Meaning: A Theory of Communication," in *Human Communication Theory: Comparative Essays*, ed. F. E. X. Dance (New York: Harper and Row, 1982), pp. 61–89.

[29]Pearce, p. 19.

[30]E. Goffman, *The Presentation of Self in Everyday Life* (Garden City, NY: Anchor, 1959).

[31]J. K. Burgoon and T. J. Saine, *The Unspoken Dialogue: An Introduction to Nonverbal Communication* (Boston: Houghton Mifflin, 1978), p. 247.

[32]E. Goffman, *Encounters: Two Studies in the Sociology of Interaction* (Indianapolis: Bobbs–Merril, 1961).

[33]E. Goffman, *Relations in Public: Microstudies of the Public Order* (New York: Harper and Row, 1971).

[34]P. W. Blumstein et al., "The Honoring of Accounts," *American Sociological Review, 39* (1974), 551–556; Goffman, *Encounters*, pp. 29–34.

[35]Burgoon and Saine, pp. 249–250.

[36]E. Goffman, *Frame Analysis: An Essay on the Organization of Experience* (New York: Harper and Row, 1974), pp. 21–39.

[37]Littlejohn, p. 129.

[38]C. R. Berger, "The Covering Law Perspective as a Theoretical Basis for the Study of Human Communication," *Communication Quarterly, 25* (1977), 8, taken from W. Dray, *Law and Explanation in History* (Oxford: Oxford University Press, 1957), p. 1.

[39]C. R. Berger and R. J. Calabrese, "Some Explanations in Initial Interaction and Beyond: Toward a Developmental Theory of Interpersonal Communication," *Human Communication Research, 1* (1975), 99–112.

[40]See J. K. Burgoon and S. B. Jones, "Toward a Theory of Personal Space Expectations and Their Violations," *Human Communication Research, 2* (1976), 131–146. See also J. K. Burgoon, "A Communication Model of Personal Space Violations: Explication and an Initial Test," *Human Communication Research, 4* (1978), 129–142.

[41]See J. K. Burgoon, D. W. Stacks, and W. G. Woodall, "A Communicative Model of Violations of Distance Expectations: Further Tests and a Critique," *Western Journal of Speech Communication, 43* (1979), 153–167; D. W. Stacks and J. K. Burgoon, "The Role of Nonverbal Behaviors as Distractors in Resistance to Persuasion in Interpersonal Contexts," *Central States Speech Journal, 32* (1981), 61–73.

[42]For more information on the rules approach, see S. B. Shimanoff, *Communication Rules: Theory and Research* (Beverly Hills, CA: Sage, 1980).

SECTION TWO

The Materials of Communication Theory: Nonverbal and Verbal Codes

Good builders understand the materials with which they must work. This section introduces the two major types of materials communication architects use: nonverbal and verbal communication codes. (A code is a type of material used in communication to establish meaning or some type of communicative expectation or norm.) Verbal and nonverbal materials establish how we perceive communication to work, at which levels we build, and how we distinguish subcodes within each code. This process is similar to what structural architects do when they specify materials to be used in constructing a building. The architect establishes which materials meet the specifications of the project. Communication architects begin to create their edifices by choosing with care the codes necessary to complete messages.

In examining codes, however, the communication architect needs to understand that there are various ways to analyze these materials. We may analyze the nonverbal codes (Chapter 3) through an ethological approach, a linguistic (structural) approach, or a functional approach. With the verbal code (Chapter 4), we briefly examine the influence of two different theories of language use: semantics (the use of words) and syntactics (the use of grammar and structure). Our concern throughout this section is on *meaning in communication*. We believe that meaning is the material that makes communication so human an experience.

We begin our study of the materials of communication theory by discussing how the materials are used for *coding*, that is, how to put our ideas into some form so that others can understand them. We discuss several

41

complementary and contradictory approaches to verbal and nonverbal coding. We begin our study of codes with the nonverbal code that employs the following "dimensions": spatial, physical appearance, overt body and vocal expressiveness, and covert body–temporal expressiveness. Use of space is referred to as *proxemics*, one nonverbal area in which theoretical approaches have been developed. The same is true of overt body expressiveness (or *kinesics*), the study of facial expression, eye movement, and body movement. The other dimensions, or subcodes—physical appearance, vocal expression, and covert body–temporal expressiveness—are still in developmental theoretical stages.

3

Nonverbal Communication

The study of communication has centered traditionally on the spoken or verbal form of discourse. Attention has been aimed at the symbolic components of communication associated with "language." However, two component "codes" are involved in human communication. The language code is predominantly "verbal" and is associated with spoken and written language. The second code, the *nonverbal code*, communicated via forms other than words, is less well understood.

The importance of nonverbal communication is best understood when considering how we apply meaning to any communication. Consider, for instance, the following phrase: I love you. This phrase has any number of *actual* meanings. How we interpret this statement of relationship is dependent upon accompanying nonverbal *cues*. Albert Mehrabian has suggested that the meaning of communication may be as much as 93 percent nonverbal. In his research, Mehrabian found that the *emotional* meaning ascribed a communication (in this case an actor uttering *only* the word "maybe") broke down as follows: 38 percent was found in the voice, 55 percent in facial expression, and 7 percent in the verbal statement.[1]

In looking at Mehrabian's findings, it is obvious that nonverbal communication is very important in day-to-day interaction; however, this research does not reflect the reality of communication. We seldom communicate in one-word sentences when trying to establish a relationship, discuss something, or transmit important information. A more reasonable guess is that 60 to 70 percent of the emotional meaning is nonverbal, and that the verbal statement accounts for only 30 to 40 percent of the emotional meaning.[2]

If nonverbal communication is so important, why do we study it so little? One reason lies with the nature of nonverbal communication. It does not easily lend itself to study. Also, nonverbal communication is more "naturalistic" than its verbal counterpart. Another reason is found in ourselves: We simply overlook the nonverbal, except when failure to understand expected nonverbal behavior causes inappropriate communication. As Paul Ekman and Wallace Friesen note:

> Most people do not know what they are doing with their bodies when they are talking, and no one tells them. People learn to disregard the internal cues which are informative about their stream of body movements and facial expressions. Most interactive behavior seems to be enacted with little conscious choice or registration, efforts to inhibit what is shown fail because the information about what is occurring is not customarily within awareness.[3]

Hickson and Stacks suggest that one reason for this lack of understanding is found in the *normative nature* of nonverbal communication.[4] We communicate nonverbally based on cultural and societal expectations or norms, which are not always expressed, but are learned through socialization and observation. As such, nonverbal communication changes or modifies the verbal message as situations change.

If nonverbal communication is "unconscious" or "normative," how do we study it? What are the many "parts" of nonverbal communication? People differ in their understandings of *how* to—and *what* to—interpret when studying nonverbal communication. This chapter is concerned with these and other concerns. After a cursory examination of what nonverbal communication is, we examine three theoretical approaches that help us interpret and understand nonverbal communication. We begin by studying how nonverbal communication differs from verbal communication.

DIFFERENCES BETWEEN VERBAL AND NONVERBAL COMMUNICATION

Nonverbal communication differs from verbal communication in a number of ways; however, *both operate together* to establish "meaning." Although this chapter seeks to understand nonverbal "theory," keep in mind that one code cannot effectively exist without the other. In many instances, our verbal communication simply reflects what we observe nonverbally.

Definition

Although it is important to define what we study, the definition of nonverbal communication is as elusive as that of verbal communication. Frank E. X. Dance and Carl E. Larson, for instance, offer over one hundred definitions of verbal communication, but offer only one definition of nonverbal communication. To them, nonverbal communication is "a stimulus not dependent on symbolic content for meaning."[5] Dance and Larson's definition offers us little more than Edward Sapir's 1949 observation that nonverbal communication is "an elaborate code that is written nowhere, known to none, and understood by all."[6] Judee K. Burgoon and Thomas J. Saine offer a working definition: "*nonverbal communication* [is] *those attributes or actions of humans, other than the use of words themselves, which have socially shared meaning, are intentionally sent or interpreted as intentional, are consciously sent or consciously received, and have the potential for feedback from the receiver.*"[7] Hickson and Stacks widen this definition by including the senders of a nonverbal communication as their own receivers. They also suggest that some communicative stimuli may not be *consciously* shared in terms of meaning, due to the *normative* or *expected* nature of nonverbal behaviors in human interaction.[8]

With all this in mind, how do verbal and nonverbal communication differ? Nonverbal communication differs from verbal communication in four major ways: the *intentionality of the message*, the *degree of symbolism* in the act or message, the encoding and decoding *processing mechanisms* of communication, and the *difference between behavior and communication*.

Intentionality. One major difference between verbal and nonverbal communication is found in the perception of *intent*. In general, intent is more important when considering the verbal code. Michael Burgoon and Michael Ruffner assert that a verbal message is communication when it is (1) intentionally sent by the source and (2) intentionally received by the receiver.[9] This interpretation of intent dramatically reduces what is considered to be verbal communication.

Nonverbal communication is much less restricted by intent. The simple *perception* of intent by a receiver is sufficient to be considered nonverbal communication, because nonverbal communication tends to be less conscious and less refined than verbal communication. Also, because nonverbal communication deals with norms, intent is not as clearly defined. Behaviors we intend may be due to the norms associated with the behavior, or they may be due to someone else's perception that the communication was caused by these norms. Consider, for instance, the norms for physical appearance. We all wear clothes, but how often do we consciously dress for a specific effect? How many times has a friend commented on your appearance, yet you have done nothing consciously different in dressing? The receiver's perception of intent is enough to satisfy the definitional qualifications of nonverbal communication.

Symbolic Differences. Sometimes intent is perceived because of some *symbolic impact* of our communication. Wearing a particular color or style, or choosing not to wear the same, may be perceived as a "message" by others (e.g., dressing in black may be an option—style—or a conscious message, such as "mourning"). Verbal communication by its nature is a *mediated* form of communication. That is, we *infer* what meaning has been applied to a particular word choice. The words we use are abstractions with agreed upon meanings. Verbal communication is intentional and must be "shared" between people. Nonverbal communication, however, is more natural and, while shared by people, may not be consciously understood.

Nonverbal communication operates best as norms and behavioral expectations based on such norms.[10]

Mehrabian suggests that verbal communication is more *explicit* than nonverbal communication, which he sees as being *implicit:* "Verbal cues are definable by an explicit dictionary and by rules of syntax, but there are only vague and informal explanations of the significance of various nonverbal behaviors."[11] This dichotomy reflects the difference between mediated versus normative communication. While we may verbally comment on some behavior, that behavior reflects one or more nonverbal norms (e.g., appearance, touch, speech rate, smell).

Finally, a distinction must be made between sign and symbol. A *sign* is a natural representation of an event or act. It is what we see or feel. A *symbol,* however, is something that takes the place of something else. The symbol represents the sign through abstraction. For example, the sign of a desk is the actual desk; how we describe that desk is through abstraction. We know what is physically attractive to us (sign) and create arbitrary differences (symbols) to indicate degrees of attraction. Verbal communication has the advantage of being more specific (in terms of being able to distinguish between similar things in an arbitrary way), whereas nonverbal communication is better at conveying feeling or emotions (natural reactions). In many cases, however, a nonverbal sign may yield a symbol (it becomes an *emblem* as the sign becomes an abstraction) which reflects abstract thoughts. "Peace," "bedtime," "give me a ride," or "happiness" are emblems, or gestures that have direct verbal equivalents.

Processing Mechanisms.   A third difference between verbal and nonverbal communication concerns how we process information. All information, including communication, is processed by the brain. The brain interprets this information via the mind, which in turn controls both physiological (reflex) and sociological (learned/social) behaviors associated with it. The way that the brain processes that information, however, differentiates the two codes.

A major processing difference is found in the type of information each brain hemisphere processes. Typically, the left hemisphere processes more discontinuous and arbitrary types of information, and the right processes more continuous and natural types of information. (For more information on this, see Chapter 13.) Paul Watzlawick, Janet Beavin, and Don Jackson define such differences as being digital (discontinuous, arbitrary) or analogical (continuous, natural).[12] Digital information reflects the symbolic nature of language and is found predominantly in the left hemisphere. The right hemisphere is predisposed toward analogical processing. It is concerned with the natural units representing emotion or sensory information associated with nonverbal communication.

Based on such differences, verbal and nonverbal messages differ in terms of the final structure of the message. Nonverbal communication is much less structured. The rules by which we communicate nonverbally are much simpler than the complex grammar and syntax of verbal communication. Nonverbal communication is typically expressed in the present. Unlike the verbal message, nonverbal communication is limited for expressing past or future. Nonverbal communication also requires an understanding of the *context* in which the interaction occurs. Verbal communication can *create* that context.

    Behavioral Considerations.   Finally, nonverbal communication allows for more *behavior* to be "counted" as communication. Burgoon and Saine state that information, behavior, and communication are related, much as demonstrated in Figure 3–1.[13] Here we see that all around us is information, some of which may be behavior. Some of this behavior may be communication. Hickson and Stacks further refine this model to include verbal communication as a subset of nonverbal communication (see Fig. 3–2).[14] This model suggests that we can distinguish among information, behavior, and communication. It also suggests that verbal communication is a refinement of nonverbal communication, a suggestion based in part on neurological processing and evolutionary evidence.[15] Information is both conscious and unconscious. You are conscious of the page color of this book, but not the subtle smell it may have. Information is used to guide behavior; that is, we take information from our physical (immediate, natural) and mental (perceived, influenced by a sense of past and future) environments and use it to guide our behavior or actions and reactions.

    Some behavior constitutes communication in a general sense. Some behavior becomes expected or normative and nonverbal in nature. This may yield at least one *perceiver* in the environment who views the behavior as either intentionally originating from another or from within him- or herself (unconscious). If the behavior becomes symbolically linked to another and

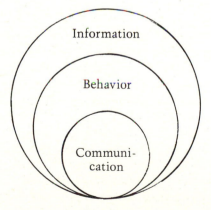

FIGURE 3–1   Relationship Between Information–Behavior–Communication.
Source: J. K. Burgoon and T. J. Saine, *The Unspoken Dialogue: An Introduction to Nonverbal Communication* (Boston: Houghton–Mifflin, 1978), p 6.

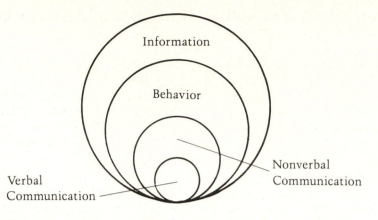

FIGURE 3-2   Information–Behavior–Communication Relationships II.

that person has intentionally produced the behavior as a message with symbolic meaning, it is considered verbal communication.

NONVERBAL/VERBAL FUNCTIONS

Although nonverbal and verbal communication differ, both are needed for effective communication. The nonverbal code functions with the verbal code to produce communicative meaning. Through a combination of sensory inputs (multiple channels), the nonverbal message modifies the verbal message (sends multiple messages). Historically, the nonverbal code, as a multichannel/multimessage phenomenon, was thought to modify the verbal message through six related functions: repetition, contradiction, substitution, regulation, accentuation, and complementation.

In 1965, Paul Ekman suggested that the nonverbal message may *repeat* or reinforce the verbal message (i.e., holding up one finger to indicate the number of orders you are placing while verbally stating "one").[16] Nonverbal messages also may function to *contradict* or negate the verbal message, as in sarcasm. Sometimes, nonverbal communication *substitutes* for the verbal message. A sign becomes associated with and replaces some symbol (e.g., "peace" or "time out"). Another function of nonverbal communication is the *regulation* of the verbal message. Nonverbal messages serve to control an interaction in a synchronous or smooth manner (e.g., head nodding or proper turn sequencing during conversation). At other times, the nonverbal message serves to *accentuate* the emphasis of the verbal message (e.g., raising your voice or shaking your fist). Finally, the nonverbal message functions to *complement* the verbal message by modifying the verbal message (e.g., smiling to show pleasure).

More recently, a different functional perspective has been suggested.[17] This view sees nonverbal communication functioning as holistic messages rather than as a simple information processing function. Holistic functions include identification, impression formation and management, deception, emotion, and conversational structure. Nonverbal communication, then, serves primarily a controlling function, where we attempt to get another person to do our bidding. Hickson and Stacks suggest that these holistic functions can be broken into eight "practical" functions: control of the conversation, control of another's behavior, affinity or likableness, rejection or dislikableness, display of cognitive information, display of affective information, self-deception, and deception of others. Judee K. Burgoon, David Buller, and Gill Woodall take a parallel perspective, noting six "social" functions: identification, impression formation, and impression management; mixed messages and deception; relational communication; emotional expression; structuring interaction and conversational management; and social influence and facilitation. Both sets of functions reflect the growing concern over the total communicative message, or, as Burgoon et al. note, "the verbal and nonverbal codes are closely coordinated to produce messages [e.g., processing functions], and they are well integrated for achieving most other communicative functions [e.g., practical or social]" (p. 181).

Nonverbal communication serves to ensure that the proper meaning of the verbal message is understood (or not understood in some instances). Nonverbal messages may serve rather simple modification functions, such as suggested by Ekman, or more complex purposeful functions, such as advocated by Burgoon et al. and Hickson and Stacks. However, neither verbal nor nonverbal communication can operate alone. Each needs the other to be effective.

NONVERBAL SUBCODES

Nonverbal communication is divided into many different "parts," called *subcodes*, that comprise the different areas of nonverbal study or emphasis. Different people, however, have different organizational patterns for what they believe constitutes nonverbal communication. One of the earliest codification attempts was devised by Jurgen Ruesch and Weldon Kees, who created a three-part code.[18] *Sign language* includes all forms of codification in which words, numbers, and punctuation signs are supplanted by gesture; *action language* includes all movements that are not used exclusively as signals; and *object language* includes all intentional or unintentional displays of material things, such as implements, machines, art objects, architectural structures, the human body, and clothing. Other coding systems range from these three areas to the eighteen identified by Larry Barker and Nancy Collins (see Table 3–1).[19] Most students of nonverbal communication, however, recognize seven or eight subcodes: *environment* (objects or artifacts), *proxemics* (personal space and territory), *haptics* (touch or zero-proxemics), *physical appearance* (body and clothing), *kinesics* (body, hand, and leg

TABLE 3–1 Subcodes of Nonverbal Communication

Reusch & Kees	Barker & Collins	Knapp	Burgoon & Saine	Hickson & Stacks	Harrison
Sign language	Animal/insect	Environment	Artifacts	Spatial	Artifactual
Object language	Culture	Proxemics:	Proxemics:	Environment	Spatiotemporal
Action language	Environment	Territory	Territory	Territory	Performance
	Kinesics	Personal space	Personal space	Personal space	Mediatory
	Human behavior	Touching	Time	Touch	
	Interaction patterns	Artifacts	Touch	Social	
	Learning	Physical appearance	Physical appearance	Physical	
	Machine	Paralanguage	Vocalics	Appearance	
	Media	Kinesics	Kinesics	Overt bodily	
	Mental processes			Kinesics	
	Music			Paralanguage	
	Physical appearance			Covert bodily	
	Physiology			Time	
	Pictures			Olfaction	
	Space			Telepathic systems	
	Touch				
	Time				

gestures and facial expressions), *paralanguage* (use of voice, sometimes called "vocalics"), *chronemics* (time), and *olfaction* (smell).[20]

Subcode division reflects the large degree of diversification involved in the study of nonverbal communication. Historically, however, the study of nonverbal communication has been less diversified, reflecting a less refined and unencumbered view of communication.

HISTORICAL OVERVIEW

The first treatment of nonverbal communication is found in the time of Aristotle, about 400 to 600 years B.C.[21] Most modern students of communication trace the scientific study of nonverbal communication to Charles Darwin and include Sir Charles Bell's earlier (1844) work. However, the study of nonverbal communication is first mentioned in the ancient Greek and Roman treatment of rhetoric.[22]

Cicero's work on *pronuntiatio,* or delivery, was probably the first systematic treatment of nonverbal communication. His work, however, was limited to the use of the voice and bodily movements in public speaking contexts. From this beginning, others examined the nonverbal code for its influence on communication, albeit almost entirely in public speaking situations. In 1775, Joshua Steele focused on the voice as an instrument, or on the concept of *prosody.*[23] Steele's concept was that language in drama or poetry could be "read" much like a musical score (see Fig. 3–3). Later, in 1806, Gilbert Austin concentrated on the bodily movements associated with language.[24] This approach, modeled after the natural gestures associated with communication, provides an *elocutionary system* where "appropriate" gestures are learned and used in dramatic presentation (see Fig. 3–4). A more complex view of nonverbal communication was developed by Francois Delsarte.[25] Delsarte incorporated both voice and bodily movement and was interested in expressing attitude and persuading an audience that the nonverbal messages were "agents of the heart."

Early attempts at systematizing nonverbal communication theory, given their emphasis and level of sophistication, are considered lacking today. Up to the middle of the nineteenth century, nonverbal theory was aimed at providing taxonomies (systems) of nonverbal messages appropriate in performance contexts. In view of what we explained in Chapter 1, these approaches are theories of performance.

What impact do these early approaches have on our interpretation of communication? Consider the ways that people adapt their gestures and voice for effect in day-to-day interactions. Although few "systems" are truly found across our culture, subcultures do adopt certain elocutionary systems, thereby increasing the complexity of communication. Most students exposed to an acting class are influenced by this early approach: certain "methods"—gestures and vocalizations—are identified with specific emotions or outcomes. Many public speakers adopt an elocutionary system as

First manner. *Bombaſtic, by an exceſs in the extenſion of acute and grave, and of the piano and forte, and the tones not ſoſtenuto or equally ſupported.*

* *Ordinary walking meaſure.*

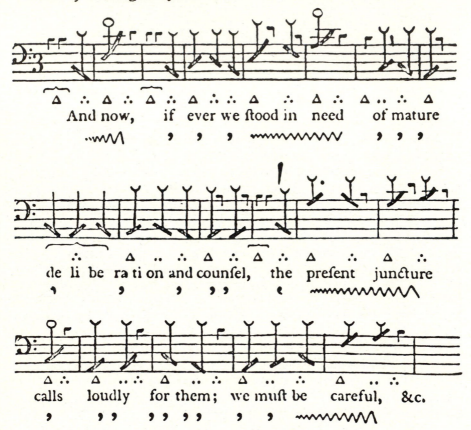

* *Walking meaſure* means, that the duration of the whole quantity of ſyllables and pauſes contained in *one cadence* (that is, as much as are marked between two bars), ſhould be equal to the time of making one ſtep of walking; which admits the varieties of *ſlow, ordinary,* and *quick walking;* the next degree above which, in velocity, is *running meaſure.*

FIGURE 3–3   Steele's Musical Prosody.
Source: J. Steele, *Prosodia Rationalis* (London: 1779), 51.

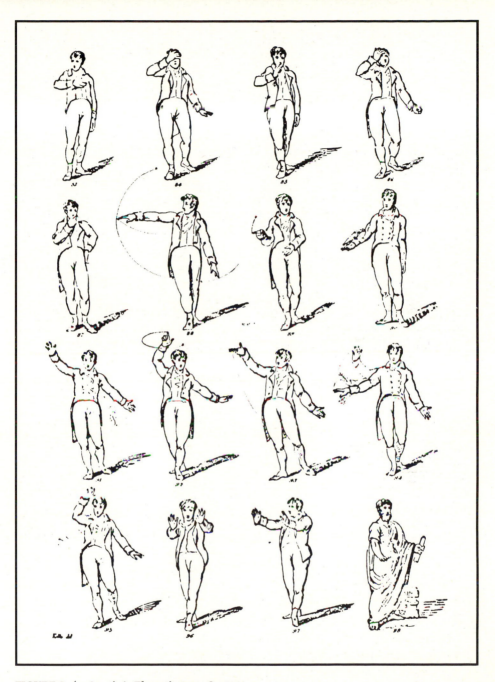

FIGURE 3-4   Austin's Elocutionary System.
Source: G. Austin, *Chironomia or a Treatise on Rhetorical Delivery*.

they master the art of public address. In politics and religion, for example, certain physical and vocal gestures have been systematized in ways similar to Delsarte's and Steele's treatments of delivery.

CONTEMPORARY NONVERBAL APPROACHES

The beginning of the *modern* study of nonverbal communication is most closely identified with the seminal work of Darwin, *The Expression of Emotions in Man and Animals.*[26] Darwin's concern with nonverbal communication was as a theory of performance, a *mode of delivery* that indicated mood, attitude, or feeling. As it was developed, it became a theory of knowledge, as discussed below. Darwin's influence on the study of communication in general and his influence on a number of theoretical verbal and nonverbal approaches to communication cannot be stressed enough. Darwin's influence is seen in many disciplines and in the work of many nonverbal theorists, as apparent in Figure 3–5.

This disciplinary analysis suggests the lines of influence that form modern nonverbal theory. The focus most similar to Darwin's, for instance, is the *zoological.* This nonverbal approach sees a direct relationship between us and other animals in the origin and use of nonverbal communication. It suggests that nonverbal communication is a product of evolution and is explained in terms of survival value. Researchers including Robert Ardrey and Desmond Morris represent the zoological approach.[27] From this perspective developed the *ethological* approach (the study of similarities between the behavior of other animals and the behavior of humans). Ekman and Friesen are representative of this approach.

Closely related is the *anthropological* approach, as represented in the works of Ray L. Birdwhistell and Edward T. Hall. This view incorporates culture and society in the study of nonverbal communication.[28] Anthropological researchers argue that nonverbal communication is more than simply an evolutionary model of behavior, that the society/culture in which we live modifies our nonverbal repertoire. All three approaches, however, are theories of knowledge.

A fourth approach developed from Darwin is *psychological* in nature. The psychological approach examines the impact of nonverbal communication as an attitudinal or behavioral modifier. It incorporates cultural and individual differences that alter perceptions of communication. Representative of this approach are Albert Mehrabian and Miles R. Patterson.[29] Psychological approaches tend to represent theories of action.

From the original work of Darwin, the focus on nonverbal communication has grown *across* academic disciplines. Based on his work, three theoretical perspectives evolved: the ethological approach, the anthropological approach, and the functional approach. People in particular disciplines have tended to use an approach because of the research methods they employ; however, some have incorporated several approaches. Ekman and Friesen, for

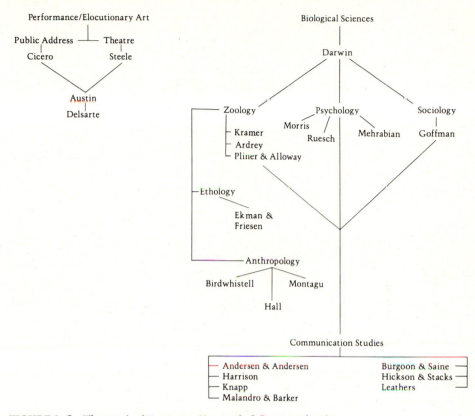

FIGURE 3-5 Theoretical Focus on Nonverbal Communication.
Adapted and extended from M. Hickson and D. W. Stacks, *NVC: Nonverbal Communication Studies and Applications* (Dubuque, IA: William C. Brown, 1985), p. 13.

example, have used the ethological approach even though they work in the field of psychology. Some nonverbal researchers in the field of speech communication have employed the ethological approach (e.g., Ross Buck) and the functional approach (J. K. Burgoon).

ETHOLOGICAL APPROACH

According to Darwin, human's emotions, like those of other animals, are displayed in the face. For genetic reasons, Darwin assumed that the nonverbal communication of different species is similar. For this reason, the ethological view is supportive of the *nature* argument in what is often referred to as the "nature–nurture controversy." Individuals who support Darwin's view (Buck; Morris; Ekman and Friesen) believe that nonverbal expressions are basically similar across cultures. Nonverbal communication is not learned— it is a natural part of being human. Two often cited ethological examples are the smile and the eyebrow flash, facial expressions found across cultures.

Cumulative Structure Theory

Ekman and Friesen's approach to nonverbal communication centers on the *meanings associated with* kinesic or bodily behavior.[30] Their perspective has been called "cumulative structure" or "meaning centered" in its approach because it centers more on the meanings associated with gesture and facial expression than on the structure of the behavior. Ekman and Friesen assume that all nonverbal communication behavior reflects two concerns: whether the act is intentional and whether the behavior *must* accompany the verbal message.

Consider, for instance, a conversation with a male friend. As he talks, some gestures may have a clear meaning to you. Other gestures may not and must be verbally referred to. Suppose that the conversation is about shooting pool. As your friend describes a particularly difficult pool shot, he gestures as if lining it up and then "shoots" the cue ball. As the imaginary balls move about the imaginary table, his face explodes in happiness as the ball goes in the pocket. Here, we have an example of both concerns. The act of lining up the shot makes no sense without a verbal explanation (think of what others might think if that behavior was observed in isolation, with no other person present). The action is intentional and has some meaning. Unfortunately, we do not know what the meaning is without being privy to the conversation. The facial expression of happiness is different. That gesture (facial expression) stands alone and is interpretable regardless of the verbal message. Both gestures add to the meaning associated with the interaction as *expressive behavior*.

Ekman and Friesen have identified five categories of expressive behavior: emblems, illustrators, regulators, adaptors, and affect displays. Each category provides insight into the meaning associated with the communication event. In some cases, the behavior adds to the message as a purposeful act; in others, it performs an information function, clarifying or adding to the meaning associated with the verbal messages.

The *emblem* is a gesture or facial expression that has a direct verbal equivalent. It is clearly intentional (the behavior represents a symbolically linked thought) and may stand alone (it has its own symbolism). Representative emblems within *our* culture include the "O.K.," "peace," or "I want a ride" gestures. In other cultures, however, the same gestures may have different or no meanings. Emblems, then, serve both informational and purposeful functions.

Illustrators are gestures and facial expressions that support and complement the verbal message. Illustrators are intentional behaviors, but, because they accompany the message, they cannot be used with any precision alone. Ekman and Friesen further identify eight classes of illustrators that serve to add to the verbal message, such as batons, pictographs, or rhythmic movements.[31] Illustrators serve primarily an informative function.

Ekman and Friesen's third general category concerns the regulation of conversation. *Regulators* are intentional acts that indicate a desire to interact but, as they are linked to the source, cannot stand alone. These gestures or facial expressions allow people to regulate when to talk and when to listen. For example, Americans tend to regulate their interactions through a synchronous, "I speak, you speak, I speak, you speak, I speak . . . ," regulatory sequence.[32] Typical regulators include smiles and head nods (*backchanneling behavior*), pointing gestures, raised eyebrows, opening of the mouth, gaze direction, and facing behaviors—all gestures that regulate the flow of information in a conversation.

The fourth category is *adaptors*. Adaptors are intentional acts that may or may not stand alone. Ekman and Friesen suggest that adaptive behaviors are used to adjust the body and satisfy some bodily or emotional need. Adaptors are usually classified in one of two subcategories: *self* (touching the self, straightening clothing) or *object* (biting a pen during a test, playing with keys). They are usually seen as reflecting nervous or negative behavior. Such behaviors usually serve an information function.

Ekman and Friesen's fifth category deals with emotional display. *Affect displays* are intentional or unintentional displays of emotion that may or may not accompany a verbal message. They suggest that there are seven affect displays that are universally expressed: anger, contempt, disgust, fear, happiness, sadness, and surprise. Ekman and Friesen also note that different affect displays can be expressed at the same time. This they call an *affect blend* which includes an eighth emotion (or lack of emotion), the neutral expression. Affect displays serve both informative and purposeful functions.

Consider again the discussion about pool between you and your friend. As he talks, much of the meaning associated with the interaction is reflected in his nonverbal communication. Aside from facial expression (an emblem or affect display), there may be other cues that tell you how your friend feels, how important the topic was, and when to talk. Looking back, such cues might have included scratching his head while thinking about the "shot," drawing the pool cue several times through the fingers, nodding when you comment on the setup of the shot, and so forth. From a cumulative meaning approach, the nonverbal behaviors provide a better understanding of the interaction, and perhaps even a prediction of how the interaction will go.

Action Theory

Morris also proposes a view of kinesics based on expression, or, more specifically, on actions.[33] He is interested in understanding how we acquire particular nonverbal behaviors. Morris bases his study on the assumption that behavior is not "free-flowing," but is divided into a long series of separate events. He suggests five categories of actions: inborn, discovered, absorbed, trained, and mixed. *Inborn actions* are instinctive and occur at birth, such as suckling behaviors. *Discovered actions* are barely conscious and are limited to the genetic structure of the body, such as crossing one's legs. *Absorbed actions* are unconsciously acquired from friends, such as mirroring a friend's facial expression or gesture. *Trained actions* must be learned, such as typing, walking, or snapping fingers. *Mixed actions* are acquired in a number of ways, to include the four previously mentioned. As such, action theory sees nonverbal behavior serving both an informative and purposeful function.

How would action theory differ from cumulative structure in the interpretation of the pool shot conversation? First, the behaviors exhibited by you and your friend would be classified according to the behavioral category they best fit. Second, the interaction would be examined through each behavior alone, unless, of course, it were a mixed behavior. What actions would Morris find? The way that the breath is held prior to the shot (this might be similar to a golfer addressing the ball before beginning to swing) may be inborn. Discovered actions might include how the pool cue is held at first, then changed as the shot is mentally played out. Absorbed actions might include your face mirroring the concentration of your friend's, or a particular stance may indicate a stance borrowed from a respected other. Trained actions might include drawing the cue or positioning of the head for the shot. Mixed actions could be any of the above in tandem.

Adaptation Theory

Ross Buck incorporates some nonverbal communication functions into what is essentially an ethological view. Buck indicates that the two primary aspects of motivation and emotion are *adaptation* and the *maintenance of homeostasis;* that is, we use nonverbal communication to adapt to various situations and to maintain ourselves. These behaviors are functions that we tend to have in common with other animals. In addition, Buck states that we must externally express our emotions. Finally, he indicates that we must have a "direct subjective experience of motivational/emotional states which may be useful for self-regulation in species with significant cognitive capabilities."[34]

In your imaginary pool conversation, we noticed that your friend's facial expression during the pool shot was fearful. We might predict the outcome differently if the expression was neutral—cool. However, it might be that the expression—or lack of expression—was more indicative as a maintaining of a perception of "cool" than was felt. We would have interpretation problems without knowing your friend's past behavior in similar situations.

SUMMARY

Ekman and Friesen, Morris, and Buck support Darwin's basic assumption that human nonverbal communication is similar across cultures. In the pool shot interaction, similar behaviors can be found in any culture where a similar game is found. Nonverbal communication, then, is a natural function. In addition, the expression of emotions through nonverbal communication is similar between humans and other animals.

ANTHROPOLOGICAL APPROACH

The anthropological approach, which examines nonverbal communication as influenced by culture or society, is quite different from the ethological approach. As noted earlier, the anthropological approach is represented by the work of Birdwhistell and Hall.

Linguistic Analogy

Birdwhistell's contributions to the study of nonverbal communication are in the area of kinesics. In one of his more important publications, *Kinesics and Context: Essays on Body Motion Communication*, Birdwhistell outlined six principles for the study of kinesic behavior.[35] Based on these six principles, he then outlined his "linguistic analogy of nonverbal communication." As discussed later in Chapter 4, language is *structured* on sounds and combinations of sounds, which form what we call words. Combinations of words form sentences when placed in the proper context. Sentences then form paragraphs. Birdwhistell's approach to nonverbal communication is quite similar; that is, there are nonverbal "sounds," which he refers to as *allokines* (body movements often small enough to be undetectable). Allokines combine to form *kines* in a fashion similar to that of language, which is why this approach is often referred to as a *linguistic analogy.* Birdwhistell's six principles are as follows:

1. There is a high degree of interdependence among the five body senses (visual, aural, gustatory, olfactory, and tactile) which, together with the verbal, form the *infracommunicational system.*
2. Kinesic communication varies according to culture and even among microcultures.
3. There is no universal body language symbol.
4. The principle of redundancy, as stated in information theory, is not applicable to kinesic behavior.
5. Kinesic behavior is more primitive and less controllable than verbal communication.
6. We must compare and contrast nonverbal codes time and time again before we can make accurate interpretations.

These principles establish the foundation for the linguistic analogy of nonverbal communication. They state (1) that the five senses work together or interact to create perception and (2) that at times one or more of the senses may dominate the others. According to Birdwhistell's model, kinesic behaviors are unique to each culture or subculture. Individual differences in nonverbal communication are a function of the culture or subculture under study and must be accounted for. Birdwhistell, in his third principle, notes that nonverbal behaviors are learned rather than passed genetically from generation to generation. He also perceives nonverbal communication to be complementary to rather than redundant with verbal communication; that is, nonverbal works with the verbal to create meaning and cannot replace the verbal in establishing meaning (compare Ekman and Friesen's theory, especially their view of the emblem). Finally, because our nonverbal communication is not always conscious and is more primitive, we tend to forget about what we are "saying" nonverbally. Because of this and the many differences in kinesic behaviors between people and cultures, we must be careful when studying nonverbal behavior even within a particular culture.

In his linguistic analogy, Birdwhistell felt that *parakinesic phenomena*, a combination of the movements associated with verbal language, could be studied through the structure of gesture. This structure, he felt, was roughly equivalent to the linguistic view of verbal language and comprised three factors: (1) the intensity of muscular tension shown, (2) the duration of the movement shown, and (3) the range of the movement. Based on these factors, Birdwhistell suggests that we can analyze the following classes of movement behavior: *allokine, kine, kineme, and kinemorpheme*. The allokine and kine are the smallest behaviors, with at least 20,000 different allokines in the facial area alone. These minute behaviors are usually beyond any meaningful interpretation and must be combined with other allokines and kines for analysis. At the first meaningful level of analysis is the kineme (a grouping of kines), which is equivalent to the word. Combinations of kinemes create kinemorphemes, equivalent to sentences. Thus, we may analyze nonverbal communication as we would verbal communication, but the units of analysis move from sounds and words to movements and gestures.

Figure 3–6 provides an example of how Birdwhistell analyzes an interaction. Note that the linguistic analogy serves basically an information function. The focus of interpretation is on the *structure of the movement*, rather than the purpose behind it. In interpreting our earlier pool example, we would break movements within the interaction to smaller units and then recombine them to create "meaning." We would use a series of symbols (see Fig. 3–6) as a shorthand method to the analysis, then compare the gestures to the verbal communication. In some ways, this is a systems approach: the theorist decides what level constitutes the suprasystem and system and makes interpretations accordingly.

Birdwhistell's approach tries to place the kines and kinemes into a socially significant motion. Such motions, when considered in their cultural setting, complement the verbal to form the total message. Consider, for instance, if this approach could identify those movements that were persuasive. Once identified as persuasive in a particular culture, their use might increase a source's effectiveness. Conversely, if we knew which movements indicated agreement or persuasability, we might be reluctant to accept the message.

KINESIC CODING

1. This situation was observed on a bus at about 2:30
   P.M., April 14, 1952. The little boy was seated next to
   the window. He seemed tired of looking out of the
   window, and, after surveying all of the car ads and the
   passengers, he leaned toward his mother and pulled at
   her sleeve, pouted and vigorously kicked his legs.

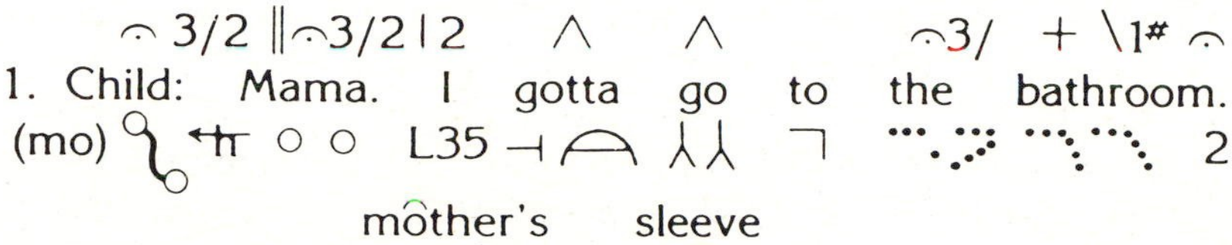

      ⌒ 3/2 ‖⌒3/2 ｜2   ∧   ∧   ⌒3/ + \1# ⌒

1. Child: Mama. I gotta go to the bathroom.

(mo) ⌒ ⇆ ○ ○ L35 ⊣ ⌒ ⋀⋀ ⌐ ⋯⋰⋯ ⋯⋱⋯ 2

           mother's   sleeve

NOTE: The upper codes (ones above the descriptor) are
          paralinguistic cues. The kinegraphs are below the
          descriptor. See if you can match Birdwhistell's
          coding system to his description.

FIGURE 3-6 Birdwhistell's Kinesic Coding.
Source: R. L. Birdwhistell, *Kinesics and Context: Essays on Body Motion Communication*
(New York: Ballantine, 1980), p. 358.

Cultural Analogy

Hall's work encompasses at least two major areas of nonverbal communication: proxemics and chronemics. Hall's proxemic theory refers to the
"interrelated observations and theories of man's use of space as a specialized
elaboration of culture."[36] Hall includes what has been further defined as
environmental (or artifactual), territorial, and personal spacing behaviors.
He suggests three types of space, each with differing norms and expectations:
informal space, the space immediately surrounding us (personal space);
fixed-feature space, the relatively fixed or hard to move features of the environment, such as buildings, walls, and the like; and *semifixed-feature space*,
which is more mobile and consists of furnishings and objects found within
the fixed-feature space.

    One of Hall's major contributions comes from his analysis of personal
spacing preferences. Our spacing preferences are influenced, Hall notes, by
eight interrelated factors found in each culture: (1) the sex of the interactants
and whether they are standing, sitting, or lying (*sexual–postural* factor);
(2) the angle formed by the shoulders and chests/backs of the interactants

(*sociofugal–sociopetal axis* factor); (3) the positioning of the body within the interaction, to include opening the possibility of touching (*kinesthetic* factor); (4) touching and type of touch (*zero-proxemic* or touch factor); (5) the amount and manner of eye contact (*visual* code factor); (6) the perception of personal bodily heat from the interaction (*thermal* code factor); (7) the odors and smells involved in the interaction (*olfactory* code factor); and (8) the loudness or volume of the voice in the interaction (*voice loudness* factor).

These factors result in cultural and subcultural norms of expected behavior. For instance, in our culture we expect to greet people, strangers or friends, at a distance of about 24 to 36 inches. We expect that any touch will be, at least initially, nonintimate and relegated to the hand or forearm area. This greeting is ritualized within the culture. If you were in the Middle East, however, the greeting distance would be closer, close enough to smell the other's breath, and you would place your hand on the other's shoulder. Again, if you were in parts of Europe, the greeting might entail close physical contact, a hug and perhaps a kiss on the other's facial cheek.

Hall has also contributed in the area of *chronemics,* the study of time. In *The Silent Language* and *The Dance of Life: The Other Dimension of Time,* Hall notes that time norms are found across cultures in many forms.[37] Time, for instance, is perceived in terms of how it is taught (*formal time*), how it is reacted to (*informal time*), and how it is used for precise measurement (*technical time*). When we learn our culture's formal time, we learn that time has six functions. Time is ordered and cyclic, has value, has duration and depth, and is tangible. These six features of the formal system may be taught differently from culture to culture. Informal time, however, is more loosely defined within a culture and operates on a more psychological or sociological level; it is expressed through individual or group idiosyncrasies. Use of such time labels as "in a while," "later," or "now" take on specific but unstated meanings. Finally, technical time represents the most precise use of time. Miles per hour, the solar year, feet per second, and $e = mc^2$ are representative samples of technical time.

Hall's views express cultural or social differences in how we perceive and use nonverbal communication. Although his perceptions incorporate concepts that are similar across cultures or societies, one's subculture may alter them. Hall's approaches reflect an anthropological focus and have influenced other approaches to nonverbal communication.

SUMMARY

Birdwhistell's *linguistic analogy* theory and Hall's *cultural analogy* theory view culture as important to the study of nonverbal communication. Although Birdwhistell and Hall study different nonverbal subcodes, they appear to agree that nonverbal communication is learned through social rules that vary from culture to culture, subculture to subculture. Other nonverbal communication theorists are more concerned about specific nonverbal *functions* than about how the codes developed in the first place. In a sense, then, we can say that the ethologists support the nature argument in the nature–nurture controversy, whereas the linguistic analogy theorists support the nurture argument in the controversy. The functionalists, however, are relatively unconcerned about either.

FUNCTIONAL APPROACH

Functionalists see nonverbal communication as purposive and limited by a particular time frame. They see discrete beginnings and endings to the nonverbal behavior under study. This differs from the ethological approach, in which nonverbal communication is seen as a continuing evolutionary process from the lower species to the human. It also differs from the anthropological approach in that the particular function under study may occur in any culture. Cultural norms are a "given" in functional theory and are accounted for in the time frame as "cultural variation." The problem with the functional approach is that researchers have proposed and found a number of different functions, some of which appear to be similar, others which are not. In this section, we look at several important functional nonverbal theories.

Mehrabian's Metaphorical Approach

Mehrabian's approach places nonverbal behaviors into *functional* groupings.[38] He sees nonverbal communication as falling on three continuums: dominance–submissiveness, pleasure–displeasure, and arousal–nonarousal. Nonverbal behavior can be placed on each continuum and analyzed via three *metaphors* dealing with power and status, liking, and responsiveness. The power–status metaphor reflects the degree to which the nonverbal behavior communicates dominance or submissiveness. The liking metaphor is based on the pleasure–displeasure continuum, with nonverbal behaviors falling on the pleasurable end communicating increased liking. The responsiveness metaphor is based on the arousal–nonarousal continuum, where high levels of arousal are seen as responsive (see Fig. 3–7). Almost any nonverbal message can be analyzed by each function and interpreted from one or a combination of functions. For example, a smile might indicate pleasure, arousal, and liking. A grimace, on the other hand, might indicate displeasure, arousal, and disliking.

Mehrabian's approach accounts for most nonverbal communication, but is most applicable to the kinesic, paralanguage, touch, and distancing subcodes. Mehrabian also is interested in the interrelatedness of the three dimensions and their relation to the total communicative interaction. His approach has been used to examine such communication-related effects as relationship development.[39] Suppose, for instance, we are interested in the

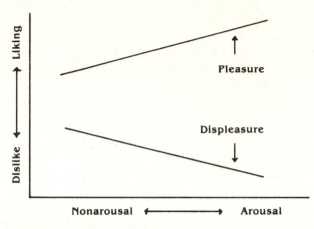

FIGURE 3–7   Mehrabian's Functional Coding.
Source: A. Mehrabian, *Silent Messages: Implicit Communication of Emotions and Attitudes* (Belmont, CA: Wadsworth, 1981), p 12.

relational messages of attraction during Bob and Jane's first meeting. We might establish the degree of attraction by the pleasure, arousal, and dominance–submissiveness represented in their nonverbal behaviors. If Bob and Jane were responsive to each other, their gestures and facial expressions would indicate interest, and they would adopt a close distance from each other. Our interpretation of these behaviors would be pleasure–liking, arousal–responsiveness, and equal power–status (i.e., neither dominant nor submissive).

Equilibrium Theory

Michael Argyle and Janet Dean propose a view of nonverbal communication based on an *intimacy–equilibrium* metaphor.[40] They suggest that all interaction is bound in conflict between *approach and avoidance forces.* Forces that pull people toward and away from each other tend to equalize a relationship. Such forces are found in the nonverbal behaviors associated with approach (closer distances, more eye contact, increased touch, increased gestures) and avoidance (larger distances, less eye contact, decreased touch, reduced gestures). Argyle and Dean note that as we interact, we examine *all* the available channels of communication.

In our initial interaction example, if Jane is approaching and Bob is avoiding, we would find two sets of behavior: intimacy seeking on the one hand (attempts at decreased distance, increased gesturing, positive facial expression, more eye contact) and intimacy avoiding on the other (increased distance, decreased gesturing, negative or neutral facial expression, less eye contact). A change in one nonverbal channel or subcode results in compensatory change in other channels.

Patterson's Functional Approach

Patterson suggests that nonverbal communication has five functions: (1) providing information, (2) expressing intimacy, (3) regulating interaction, (4) exercising social control, and (5) facilitating service or task goals.[41] Providing information involves letting someone know about your feelings or expressing your feelings about how the other person feels. Expression of intimacy can easily be accomplished nonverbally through the use of touch. Regulation of conversation is the same as expressed in Ekman and Friesen's system. Exercising social control is used when trying to express your particular viewpoint. Service–task functions are relatively impersonal, for example, the touch behavior that takes place when a barber or beautician cuts your hair.

In our initial interaction example, Bob and Jane's nonverbal communication provides information as to the degree of the relationship. As in Mehrabian's and Argyle and Dean's approaches, there is information regarding the relational dimension of the interaction—the two people may be approaching a degree of intimacy not initially present. In arriving at intimacy, however, the regulative function of nonverbal communication may actually make Bob and Jane's early communication less refined and more awkward as they seek to find a common norm for their behaviors. As they begin to exchange nonverbal cues of intimacy and to feel more comfortable in the interaction, one may exercise control over the interaction and some structure to the conversation may evolve. As Bob and Jane share information, they establish their relationship. As the relationship progresses, control will be agreed upon and their conversations smoothed out.

A Taxonomy of Metafunctions

J. K. Burgoon and Saine have grouped differing theories by the assumptions each makes about the way nonverbal communication should be studied.[42] They suggest that six major theoretical approaches may be found in the nonverbal literature: body language, ethological, psychoanalytic, linguistic, physiological, and functional. Their approach might be considered *metafunctional;* that is, within the frame of nonverbal communication, certain approaches are examined for their impact on a functional nonverbal theory of communication.

Representative of the *body language approach*, which interprets nonverbal communication as latent, sexually related behavior, is the work of Julius Fast and that of Gerald Nierenberg and Henry Calero, all of whom rely on an anecdotal treatment of communication whereby incidents and observations are made into factual, predictive statements of cause and effect.[43]

The *ethological approach* closely approximates the zoological focus and relies heavily on an evolutionary perspective. Representative theoreticians include W. John Smith and J. A. R. A. M. van Hoof.[44] The *psychoanalytic approach* examines internal motivation as the cause of nonverbal communication. This approach, associated closely with the works of Sigmund Freud, is tied to the idea that the "individual is constantly attempting to outgrow the psychological and physical inadequacies of childhood. Our behavior attempts to compensate for past failures."[45] A large number of researchers have resorted to the psychoanalytic view in trying to explain nonverbal behavior.

Burgoon and Saine divide the *linguistic approach* into two views similar to Littlejohn's analysis.[46] This division yields a *structure-centered* model and a *meaning-centered* model. Birdwhistell's kinesic theory is representative of the structure-centered approach, as is Albert Scheflen's theory of social order.[47] Ekman and Friesen are representative of the meaning-centered approach.[48] Both approaches examine the bodily forms of communication (voice, gesture, gross bodily movements, facial expression, etc.).

The *physiological approach* advocated by Burgoon and Saine is also divided into two models. The *sensory model* examines how nonverbal data are perceived by the senses as communicative conduits and what physiological constraints limit sensory communication. The *neurophysiological* model focuses on nonverbal information processing by the brain. The work of Peter Andersen, John Garrison, and Janis Andersen, of Stacks, and of others is representative of the neurophysiological model, whereas Gorden Hewes and Hower J. Hsia are representative of the sensory model.[49]

The metafunctional view, according to Burgoon and Saine, represents a more *communicative* approach to nonverbal communication.[50] This approach is interested in predicting communicative outcomes based on knowledge gained from (1) an understanding of what the communication process is and (2) what specific characteristics surround it. They view this approach as more objective, relying on what is revealed, given an understanding of what was expected. The approach also suggests a coordinated use of differing nonverbal subcodes and is capable of incorporating the other approaches.

A Communicative Functional Approach

Based on her earlier work, J. K. Burgoon has advocated a functional theory of communication. This approach focuses on the "purposes, motives, or outcomes of communication."[51] It focuses on the role nonverbal communication has on communication outcomes, such as persuasion and deception. It moves the focus from an understanding of how nonverbal communication operates to what nonverbal communication *does.* Burgoon suggests at least nine functions, from emotional communication to information processing and comprehension. As noted earlier, other functional theorists have developed similar functional analyses.[52] Such approaches would view an initial interaction as multifunctional and as an important part of the communication *process.* The focus is not simply on the nonverbal behaviors being exhibited, but also on the relationship between that behavior and the purposes behind it.

—————— REVIEW ——————————————————————

This chapter has examined how we study nonverbal communication, which serves many important functions *with* verbal communication.

TABLE 3–2 Summary Table

Name of Theory	Primary Theorists	Basic Principle	Constructs	Criteria	Analytic Approach	Limitations
Nature (ethological)	Charles Darwin Paul Ekman Wallace Friesen Ross Buck Desmond Morris	Most nonverbal behaviors are genetically transmitted.	• Emblems • Illustrators • Regulators • Adaptors • Affect displays	Relate universal behaviors among humans. Test human behavior against animal behavior.	Intercultural similarity	A lawlike approach that does not account for rules-based or singular culture behavior.
Nurture (linguistic analogy)	Ray Birdwhistell Edward T. Hall	Most human nonverbal behavior is learned, varies from person to person and culture to culture.	• Allokines • Kines • Kinemorphemes • Kinemes • Fixed space • Informal space • Semifixed space	Systematize nonverbal behavior in a way similar to systematizing language.	Notational system	Does not account for some coding as "natural," animalistic behavior.
Functional	Albert Mehrabian Miles Patterson Judee K. Burgoon	Most nonverbal behavior is functional (i.e., it has a purpose).	• Pleasure • Arousal • Dominance	Study nonverbal behavior through purpose.	Varies	Does not deal with the nature–nurture issue.

Although different people have different ideas of how the nonverbal code should be broken down, there are three major theoretical approaches, as summarized in Table 3–2. Following the historical analysis, we discussed how people related differing nonverbal approaches to the study of communication.

_____ CRITIQUE _____

Each theoretical approach (ethological, anthropological, and functional) provides differing points of reference for the study of nonverbal communication. Some approaches are more "efficient" and some are more "elegant," but all try to further our understanding of nonverbal communication. No one approach is better than any other, but each is representative of current thought in the study of nonverbal communication. It is up to the individual student of communication to decide the usefulness of each.

In examining nonverbal theory, several things should be evident. Nonverbal communication theory in general—as well as most individual theories—is not parsimonious. This criticism is not an indictment, but rather a problem found in any area that tries to be as all-inclusive, as do many of the nonverbal theories (i.e., ethological- and anthropological-based theories). There are problems with testability and reliability, especially when research tries to compare findings of different approaches to similar behaviors. Many nonverbal theories predict logical relationships between constructs and concepts, although the underlying assumptions often differ. Additionally, most have received *some* support. Finally, each theory examined has served a heuristic function. Each theory has generated a great deal of research, yielding a better understanding of the functional relationships between verbal and nonverbal forms of communication.

We now turn to the second major communication code: verbal communication. Chapter 4 examines the impact of the symbolic nature of communication and strives to introduce an understanding of what we mean is not always what we say.

_____ NOTES AND REFERENCES _____

[1]A. Mehrabian, *Silent Messages: Implicit Communication of Emotions and Attitudes* 2d ed. (Belmont, CA: Wadsworth, 1981), p. 77.

[2]R. Birdwhistell, *Kinesics and Context: Essays on Body Motion Communication* (Philadelphia: University of Pennsylvania Press, 1970).

[3]P. Ekman and W. Friesen, "Nonverbal Behavior in Psychotherapy Research," *Psychotherapy*, 3 (1968), 181.

[4]M. Hickson and D. W. Stacks, *NVC: Nonverbal Communication Studies and Applications*, 2nd ed. (Dubuque, IA: William C. Brown, 1989), p. 4.

[5]F. E. X. Dance and C. E. Larson, *The Functions of Human Communication: A Theoretical Approach* (New York: Holt, Rinehart and Winston, 1976), p. 194.

[6]E. Sapir, "The Unconscious Patterning of Behavior in Society," in *Selected Writings of Edward Sapir in Language, Culture, and Personality*, ed. D. Mandelbaum (Berkeley, CA: University of California Press, 1949), p. 556.

[7]J. K. Burgoon and T. J. Saine, *The Unspoken Dialogue: An Introduction to Nonverbal Communication* (Boston: Houghton Mifflin, 1978), pp. 9–10.

[0]Hickson and Stacks, p. 8.

[9]M. Burgoon and M. Ruffner, *Human Communication* (New York: Holt, Rinehart and Winston, 1978), pp. 15–18.

[10]Hickson and Stacks, pp. 8–10.

[11]Mehrabian, p. 31.

[12]P. Watzlawick, J. Beavin, and D. Jackson, *Pragmatics of Human Communication: A Study of Interactional Patterns, Pathologies, and Paradoxes* (New York: Norton, 1967).

[13]Burgoon and Saine, pp. 5–6.

[14]Hickson and Stacks, pp. 9–11.

[15]H. J. Jerrison, "Evolution of the Brain," in *The Human Brain*, ed. M. C. Wittrock (Englewood Cliffs, NJ: Prentice–Hall, 1977), pp. 39–62.

[16]See, for example, P. Ekman, "Communication Through Nonverbal Behavior: A Source of Information About an Interpersonal Relationship," in *Affect, Cognition, and Personality*, eds. S. S. Tompkins and C. E. Izard (New York: Springer, 1965).

[17]See J. K. Burgoon, D. B. Buller, and W. G. Woodall, *Nonverbal Communication: The Unspoken Dialogue* (New York: Harper and Row, 1989), pp. 179–180; M. Hickson and D. W. Stacks, pp. 132–137.

[18]J. Ruesch and W. Kees, *Nonverbal Communication: Notes on the Visual Perception of Human Relations* (Berkeley, CA: University of California Press, 1970), p. 189.

[19]L. L. Barker and N. B. Collins, "Nonverbal and Kinesic Research," in *Methods of Research in Communication*, eds. P. Emmert and W. D. Brooks (Boston: Houghton Mifflin, 1970).

[20]See Burgoon and Saine; Hickson and Stacks; M. L. Knapp, *Nonverbal Communication in Human Interaction*, 2nd ed. (New York: Holt, Rinehart and Winston, 1978); D. G. Leathers, *Nonverbal Communication Systems* (Boston: Allyn and Bacon, 1976); D. G. Leathers, *Successful Nonverbal Communication* (New York: Macmillan, 1976); L. A. Malandro and L. L. Barker, *Nonverbal Communication* (Reading, MA: Allyn and Bacon, 1983).

[21]R. P. Harrison and M. L. Knapp, "Toward an Understanding of Nonverbal Communication Systems," *Journal of Communication*, 22 (1972), 339–352.

[22]Harrison and Knapp; C. Darwin, *The Expression of Emotion in Man and Animals* (London: John Murray, 1872), republished, 1965 by University of Chicago Press; C. Bell, *The Anatomy and Philosophy of Expression: As Connected with the Fine Arts*, 3rd ed., 1844, cited in Harrison and Knapp; Cicero, *On Oratory and Orators*, trans. J. S. Watson (New York: Harper and Brothers, 1860).

[23]J. Steele, *Prosodia Rationalis* (London: 1779), 51, as reprinted in M. M. Robb, *Oral Interpretation of Literature in American Colleges and Universities* (New York: H. W. Wilson, 1941), 62.

[24]G. Austin, *Chironomia or a Treatise on Rhetorical Delivery*, eds. M. M. Robb and L. Thonssen (Carbondale, IL: Southern Illinois University Press, 1966).

[25]J. W. Zorn, ed., *The Essential Delsarte* (Metuchen, NJ: Scarecrow Press, 1968).

[26]C. Darwin, *The Expression of Emotions in Man and Animals* (New York: Greenwood, 1955).

[27]R. Ardrey, *The Territorial Imperative* (New York: Atheneum, 1966); D. Morris, *The Naked Ape* (London: Jonathan Cape, 1967).

[28]Birdwhistell, *Kinesics and Context: Essays on Body Motion Communication*; R. T. Hall, *The Silent Language* (Garden City, NY: Doubleday, 1959); R. T. Hall, *The Hidden Dimension* (Garden City, NY: Doubleday, 1966).

[29]A. Mehrabian; M. L. Patterson, *Nonverbal Behavior: A Functional Perspective* (New York: Verlag–Springer, 1983).

[30]P. Ekman and W. V. Friesen, *Unmasking the Face: A Guide to Recognizing Emotions from Facial Expressions* (Englewood Cliffs, NJ: Prentice–Hall, 1975).

[31]*Batons* serve to emphasize what is being said (e.g., shaking of the fist or pointing as a means of emphasis). *Ideographs* represent thought processes and are used when speakers cannot get their thoughts out (snapping of fingers or rolling of the hands as if trying to get the point out). *Pictographs* are used to create the shape of what is being talked out, such as talking about money and "drawing" a dollar symbol ($) in the air. *Kinetographs* represent forms of bodily action, such as kicking a leg or making an expansive gesture. *Emblematic illustrators* are, as the name suggests, gestures that take on emblematic meaning (substitute for some word or phrase) during the interaction, but after the interaction have no particular meaning. Finally, Ekman and Friesen suggest three categories of specific movements: *deictic movements* are indications of locations in space ("over there" by pointing to the left), *rhythmic movements* indicate the timing of an event or occurrence, and *spatial movements* represent spatial relationships and differences.

[32]See S. Duncan, "Some Signals and Rules for Taking Turns in Conversations," *Journal of Personality and Social Psychology*, 23 (1972), 282–292; S. Duncan, "Interaction Units During Speaking Turns in Face-to-Face Conversations," in *Organization of Behaviors in Face-to-Face Interaction*, eds. A. Kendon, R. Harns, and M. Key (The Hague: Mouton, 1975); S. Duncan, "Speaking Turns: Studies of Structure and Individual Differences," in *Nonverbal Interaction*, eds. J. M. Weimann and R. P. Harrison (Beverly Hills, CA: Sage, 1983).

[33]D. Morris, *Manwatching: A Field Guide to Human Behavior* (New York: Henry N. Abrams, 1977).

[34]R. Buck, *The Communication of Emotion* (New York: Guilford, 1984), p. 29.

[35]Birdwhistell.

[36]Hall, *The Hidden Dimension*; Hall, *The Silent Language*; E. T. Hall, "A System for the Notation of Proxemic Behavior," *American Anthropologist*, 65 (1963), 1003–1026.

[37]Hall, *The Silent Language*; E. T. Hall, *The Dance of Life: The Other Dimension of Time* (New York: Doubleday, 1984).

[38]A. Mehrabian, *Nonverbal Communication* (Chicago: Aldine–Atherton, 1972).

[39]N. J. Henley, *Body Politics: Power, Sex, and Nonverbal Communication* (Englewood Cliffs, NJ: Prentice–Hall, 1977).

[40]M. Argyle and J. Dean, "Eye Contact, Distance, and Affiliation," *Sociometry, 28* (1965), 289–304.

[41]Patterson, pp. 7–9.

[42]J. K. Burgoon and T. J. Saine, *The Unspoken Dialogue: An Introduction to Nonverbal Communication* (Boston: Houghton Mifflin, 1978).

[43]J. Fast, *Body Language* (New York: Pocket Books, 1971); G. I. Nierenberg and H. Calero, *How to Read a Person Like a Book* (New York: Pocket Books, 1971).

[44]W. J. Smith, "Displays and Messages in Intraspecific Communication," in *Nonverbal Communication*, ed. S. Weitz (Oxford: Oxford University Press, 1974), pp. 332–336; J. A. R. A. M. van Hoof, "A Comparative Approach to the Phylogeny of Laughter and Smiling," in *Non-Verbal Communication*, ed. R. A. Hinde (Cambridge: Cambridge University Press, 1975).

[45]Burgoon and Saine, pp. 47–48.

[46]S. W. Littlejohn, *Theories of Human Communication*, 2nd ed. (Belmont, CA: Wadsworth, 1983), p. 87.

[47]Birdwhistell; A. E. Scheflen, *How Behavior Means* (Garden City, NY: Anchor, 1974).

[48]Ekman and Friesen, *Unmasking the Face.*

[49]P. Andersen, J. Garrison, and J. Andersen; D. W. Stacks, "Toward a Preverbal Stage of Communication"; D. W. Stacks, "Hemispheric and Evolutionary Use: A Re-Examination of Verbal and Nonverbal Communication and the Brain," paper presented at the annual meeting of the Eastern Communication Association, Hartford, CT, May 1982; D. W. Stacks and L. A. Dorsey, "Toward a Psychoanalytic–Neurophysiological Interpretation of Nonverbal Communication, *Journal of Communication Therapy* (in press); D. W. Stacks and D. E. Sellers, "Toward a Holistic Approach to Communication: The Effect of 'Pure' Hemispheric Reception of Messages," *Communication Quarterly, 34* (1986), 266–285; G. Hewes, "The Anthropology of Posture," *Scientific American*, 1957, 123–132; H. J. Hsia, "The Information Processing Capacity and Modality of Channel Performance," *Audio/Visual Communication Review, 19* (1971), 51–75.

[50]Burgoon and Saine, pp. 47–48.

[51]Burgoon, Bullard, and Woodall, p. 22.

[52]Hickson and Stacks.

4

Language: Verbal Communication

To build an edifice, an architect must specify the materials that are essential to completing the building. In Chapter 3, we focused on the mortar, the material that binds the bricks together in forming the building. This chapter focuses on the bricks themselves. Just as architects must consider different kinds of bricks for aesthetic and supportable qualities, communication theorists work with the bricks of language: semantics (color and shape of brick) and syntax (density).

The question of how we acquire and use language—verbal communication—to communicate has been a theoretical concern for centuries. Our ability to symbolize and talk separates us from lower species animals. This chapter seeks to understand how and with what effect language is used. Much like nonverbal communication, however, there are many perspectives on language and its influences. We begin with a view of language that suggests that language is genetically preset (a nature approach). We simply learn the particular combination of words that reflects the way we encode and decode the message(s). A second approach examines the impact of language in creating reality, that is, the way we label our world and how those labels yield "reality" (a nurture approach). We then turn to a "functional" view of language, which seeks to answer the question, "Why do we react to language as if words were the things they represent?" Finally, we discuss a "message-centered" approach to language, which examines the thinking process associated with language prior to the message's actual transmission.

The psychology and sociology of language takes us to several competing views of human communication. These theories differ in the way they presume language began and in the function they see language having in day-to-day communication. Not all theories of language, however, have been "grand." Consider, for example, the following "theories" of language and language acquisition:

Language is inherently necessary by nature to interact with others ["Nature" theory; Plato]; Language arose when the mouth and vocal organs tried to

72

pantomime gestures made by the body ["Pantomime" theory; Darwin]; Language arose out of the imitation of sounds in nature [called the "Bow-Wow" or "Onomatopoeic" theory; Herder]; Language is derived by interjections of fear, astonishment, pain, etc. [from the nonverbal communication of affect; Condillac]; Language arose from the grunts of physical action ["Yo-He-Ho" theory; Noire]; and a theory which posited that in primitive times every object in nature had its own sound, primitive man could hear and distinguish these sounds, while through evolution, we lost the ability to hear them ["Ding-Dong" theory; Muller].[1]

As strange as these theories may sound, only fifty years ago, some theorists suggested that language was developed by imitating the speech of elders.

In looking at the various theories of language, keep in mind that we use *symbols* to discuss *symbols*; that is, the very nature of language is mediated. This makes its study ever more difficult.

NATURE VIEWS OF LANGUAGE

The focus on language acquisition has been central to a linguistic approach to communication. One theorist concerned with language acquisition is Noam Chomsky, who approaches the learning of language as a biological function, similar to the way Darwin approached nonverbal communication.[2] Chomsky's theory, *deep structure*, suggests that an innate grammar—or structure—underlies all languages. This theory encompasses a general, universal (laws) approach. Based on a large body of research, Chomsky enumerated three structures that exist in all languages.

First, there is the "*subject–predicate relation* by which what is named in the subject is shown, in terms of logic to be 'a function of' what is said of the predicate."[3] No matter what the subject is, the predicate indicates what kind of action the subject takes. No matter what the predicate, the subject indicates who or what is taking that action. For example, "the man eats," "the elephant eats," "the turkey eats," all indicate that the subject is taking the action of *eating*. From the predicate's view, "the man eats," "the man plays," "the man runs," all indicate that *the man* is taking the action, whatever it may be. Second, the *verb–object relation* expresses the "logical relationship between cause and effect" (p. 200). This relationship indicates *to whom or to what* the action is taken. "The man wears the hat," "the man wears the suit," "the man wears the shirt," all indicate that the object (whatever it is) is being worn by the man. Third, *modification* "represents what logicians call 'the intersect of classes'" (p. 200). "The man wears the blue hat," "the man wears the red hat," "the man wears the white hat," all indicate the intersection of hat and some color.

Thus, Chomsky suggests that all humans are born with a natural ability for language. We are able to formulate certain kinds of combinations of words that, even in their least sophisticated versions, make sense. "Man eat big fish," while not a perfect English sentence, encompasses all of Chomsky's grammatical, structural notions: the subject–predicate relation (man–eat), the verb–object relation (eat–fish), and the modifier (big–fish).[4]

That language can be broken into grammatical structure, however, does not explain how that language takes on meaning. Dan I. Slobin argues that, rather than being born with a programmed sense of grammar, the child has a processing mechanism or system for organizing the linguistic information that is picked up from his or her environment.[5] Slobin suggests that cognitive development precedes linguistic development. He offers evidence from a variety of languages. Children of varying languages, he notes, learn language in relation to each language's degree of difficulty. Complex languages take longer to acquire, Slobin argues, because the child must make *exceptions* to the innate operating principles associated with all language. Slobin suggests that four principles operate in all languages (pp. 39–66):

1. *Pay attention to the order of words.* Correct word order seems to be easy for children to learn in any language. Children usually use the correct word order from the time they first begin forming sentences.

2. *Avoid exceptions.* In all languages, children tend to overgeneralize and overregulate when they learn a rule. For example, after learning the *-ed* ending, children tend to apply it to all verbs: "He goed away."

3. *Avoid interruption or rearrangement of linguistic units* (as in the use of negatives). In English, a child first formulates a negative sentence by placing the word "no" at the beginning of each negative sentence, "No I do this," progressing to "I no do this," to finally "I cannot do this." The same progression has been found for children acquiring Russian and Japanese languages.

4. *Pay attention to the ends of words.* Children who learn languages with postpositions learn the language faster than those with prepositions. For example, the Turkish child learns to say "The book is table-on" much faster than the American child learns "The book is on the table."

Which theory is correct? Which is better? What do these theories tell us? First, both theories are theories of knowledge, as discussed in Chapter 1. Second, both nature views of language tell us how a language is used, but do not tell us what meanings are associated with the *use* of that language. Third, although Chomsky's notions revolutionized the study of language, critics such as Slobin have added much to its perspective. Nevertheless, knowing the grammar (deep structure) and its relationship to words (surface structure) in either perspective does not tell us the meanings we associate with the words or grammar. For this we must turn to another perspective: the nurture views of language.

NURTURE VIEWS OF LANGUAGE

Edward Sapir and Benjamin Whorf oppose the nature perspective.[6] Focusing primarily on *semantics* (the meaning of words; vocabulary), Sapir and Whorf developed a *cultural* theory of language. In Whorf's words,

> The background linguistic system (in other words, the grammar) of each language is not merely a reproducing instrument for voicing ideas but rather itself a shaper of ideas, the shaper and guide for the individual's mental activity, for his analysis of impressions, for his synthesis of his mental stock in trade. Formulation of ideas is not an independent process, strictly rational in the old sense, but is of a particular grammar and differs, from slightly to greatly, between different grammars.[7]

Thus, language is cultural (similar to Birdwhistell's notion of nonverbal communication; see Chapter 3). Even the rules of language vary from culture to culture. Because of this variation, individuals from different cultures vary in the ways they perceive their worlds. Some languages have many words for what we call "snow." Others have no words for such a concept, especially if they have never seen snow. According to Sapir and Whorf, the culture's language is directly associated with how we think in that culture. This thesis gives credence to the anthropological notion of *cultural relativity*, which suggests that, because different cultures have different languages and different views of the world, they also hold different values. Thus, we view "hostage taking" very differently than do Middle Eastern cultures. Also, past, present, and/or future are viewed in different ways, depending on how cultures translate words into feelings. For instance, Hickson and Stacks argue that because of the differing views of Arab and Israeli culture, the Camp David Peace Accords may have been doomed even before they were signed.[8]

These contrasting theories of language illustrate that, to some extent, Chomsky's view of language is similar to Darwin's, and Ekman's and Friesen's approach to nonverbal communication (the nature view). The Sapir–Whorf approach to language is similar to Birdwhistell's approach to nonverbal communication (the nurture view). As such, both fall into the theories of knowledge category of communication theory.

A FUNCTIONAL VIEW OF LANGUAGE—GENERAL SEMANTICS

Few language theories are similar to the nonverbal functional approach discussed in Chapter 3. One of the closest is pertinent to the English language in particular. Focusing only on the meaning of words (and how those meanings influence behavior), the *general semanticists* feel that language needs to be more reflective of the world in which we live. Although this theory has been criticized for its prescriptiveness and its simplicity, it contains some important ideas for the beginning communication student. General semantics, nevertheless, reflects a view prominent in the communication discipline from the 1940s through the middle 1960s.

The underlying assumption of general semantics is that "The word is not the thing." Words are considered abstractions of reality. For this reason, the general semanticists consider it important that words come as close as possible to representing reality. This is a challenge. They realize that, while words appear as static concepts over long periods of time, "reality" is in a constant state of change. To understand what concerns the general semanticist, we must examine the nature of symbols and how we use them. In the following sections, we assign meaning to the symbols and structures comprising *our* language.

Symbol Use

As Leslie A. White has written, "All human behavior originates in the use of symbols."[9] No one believed this statement more than Alfred Korzybski, the founder of general semantics. Stuart Chase has described Korzybski:

> He had the general aspect of an amiable Buddha, bald as a newel post, with kindly, intelligent eyes behind vast, rounded spectacles, and with a rich Polish accent. He wore as a kind of uniform a khaki shirt, open at the throat, which sometimes kept him out of hotel dining rooms. He was rude, formidable, over-verbalized, and strangely appealing—for all I know, an authentic genius.[10]

As a physicist, Korzybski was concerned about the lack of precision in our everyday use of language. His basic contention was that humans "live" in two different environments, a physical environment and a symbolic environment. To compare these two environments, we will use as an analogy, "The map is not the territory." For example, if you were driving from New Orleans to Chicago, and you were at the Arkansas–Missouri border, you might ask your passenger to estimate how far it is to Chicago. Your passenger might answer, "According to the map, we have about two and one-half inches to go." This information (as such) would be valuable to you only if you knew the map's scale; however, most scales are not 1:1. If they were, maps would be the same size as the territories they represent. Instead, maps operate as a kind of shorthand. A similar idea serves to illustrate our use of words. Words are a kind of shorthand. A well-known example of the principle, *"The word is not the thing,"* is the joke concerning a hitchhiker and an automobile driver. At a stop sign the driver asks his rider if there is anything coming? The hitchhiker replies, "Only a dog, man." Only after they had run into a Greyhound *bus* was the semantics of the word "dog" understood by both.

Why is the word *not* the thing? Words (in fact, any symbols) are not the same as the phenomena they represent. *Symbols are representations of ideas, and ideas are representations of "things."* This point is illustrated by C. K.

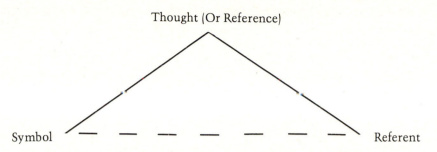

FIGURE 4–1   Ogden and Richard's Relationship of Language to Thought and Referent.
Source: C. K. Ogden and I. A. Richards, *The Meaning of Meaning: A Study of the Influence of Language Upon Thought and of the Science of Symbolism* (New York: Harcourt, Brace, and World, 1923), p. 11.

Ogden and I. A. Richards (see Fig. 4–1).[11] As you can see, a word symbolizes a thought, a thought refers to a "thing" (the referent), and a word stands for the "thing." All three, however, are different phenomena.

A *referent* may be any object, event, phenomenon, and so on, found in our physical environment. For example, our referent might be a snake. Because of our thinking capacity, we also have thoughts, references, or ideas of referents (mental "pictures" of snakes). Thus, we can think about a snake even when one is not physically present. The snake may take the form of a mental picture, an emotion, a past event, and so forth. We also have *symbols* for referents; we have the word "snake." We all know that the word "snake" is not really a snake. Finally, we have an idea of symbols. These ideas are most significant when higher level abstractions are used. We all have ideas of "love," "hate," "God," and perhaps even "infinity"—abstract ideas based upon symbols.

An interesting phenomenon occurs, however, when we *act* as if words are the things they represent. We know that people who fear snakes are afraid when they see one; however, some people are so frightened that their pulse rates and blood pressures increase when they hear the word "snake." In communication, simply thinking about giving a "speech" produces similar behavior in many people. This interaction among words, their meanings, and human behavior is what Korzybski was considering when he proposed the theory of general semantics.

To investigate this theory further we discuss a number of constructs: (1) silent assumptions, (2) reactions and responses, (3) the use of identity, (4) time-binding and space-binding, (5) multiordinality, (6) intensional and extensional orientations, and (7) levels of abstraction.

Silent Assumptions

Dan P. Millar and Frank E. Millar demonstrate that the meaning of a word is not limited to what is found in a dictionary. The consequences of semantic misunderstanding in most instances are minimal compared with the following example:

> The Johnsons live at 1204 Westminster Street in northwestern Washington, D.C. The Pells are their next door neighbors. Over a period of years the two families begin to predict one another's behavior. Mr. Johnson mows the lawn each Saturday morning from April through October. Mrs. Pell goes grocery shopping on Tuesday and Friday mornings.
>
> During the past year numerous prowlers and robbers have invaded the neighborhood. Last month the Johnsons were robbed while out of the house.
>
> Two weeks later, it was dark at 6:30 P.M. Mrs. Johnson thought she heard someone inside the Pell home. Noting that the lights were not on in the Pell house, Mrs. Johnson called the police.
>
> About 20 minutes later, there was a noise outside the Pell home. Mr. Pell, who had been resting from a hard day's work, got up from bed. Suddenly the front door was forced open, and Mr. Pell fired three shots into the intruder's stomach.
>
> The intruder was a man in blue from the Washington police force. This is a rather dramatic, but true, story of what can happen when individuals assume too much about the behavior of others. (The names and addresses have been changed.)[12]

Because we use silent assumptions too often, general semanticists ask us to learn to be silent, to keep still. This time of relief allows us to *respond* to words as human beings rather than to *react* as our compatriot animals do.

The general semanticists note that we have a tendency for dealing with "things" at an abstract level. For example, we do not deal with phenomena at the atomic level (protons, electrons, neutrons), although the phenomena are changing at that level. Korzybski has stated that the "objective level" is not words and cannot be reached by words alone:

> We must point our finger and be silent or we shall never reach this [objective] level. . . . Stress that we must handle, look, and listen, never speak, but remain silent outwardly as well as inwardly, in order to find ourselves on the objective level. This silence on the objective level involves checking upon neutral grounds of a great many 'emotions,' 'perceived ideas,' (etc.).[13]

The silent assumption of which we are probably most guilty is anticipating what another may say. While keeping silent, we should ask ourselves three questions about what the other person is saying (as well as what *we* are saying).[14]

1. *What does he or she mean?* What he or she means is different from what he or she is saying. Quite often people do not say what they mean. We must listen with all of our senses to pick up the answer to this question. Determining what a person is saying is very difficult,

especially in *metacommunication* (see Fig. 4–2) where levels 2 and 3 are indicative of the idea that two parties often have different interpretations of level 1.

2. *How does he or she know?* So often, with rumor for example, we repeat information without recalling the source. We need to have an idea about the source of the message. Without being too undiplomatic, we can discover the answer to this question.

3. *Why is he or she telling me this?* The concern with this question is whether you are the appropriate listener. We need to understand why we are the targets of the words we hear. A few years ago, one of this book's authors had a student come into the office and complain that the graduate assistant had not been coming to class to teach her Spanish lab. It was suggested that she talk to the head of the foreign language department, which was a suitable response because she actually had a problem she wanted to solve. At other times, a person may want only a listener. Many times, on a bad day, the wife may come home and complain to the husband about a problem at work. She is not so much seeking an answer to the problem as she is seeking a target for her frustrations. (This is called *catharsis.*)

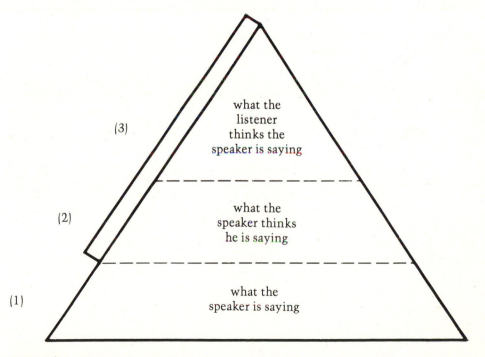

(3) what the
     listener
     thinks the
     speaker is saying

(2) what the
     speaker thinks
     he is saying

(1) what the
     speaker is saying

FIGURE 4–2   Metacommunication.

Source: G. I. Nierenburg and H. H. Calero, *Meta-Talk: A guide to Hidden Meanings in Conversations* (New York: Cornerstone, 1973), p. 12.

Reaction/Response

One difference between humans and other animals is the degree to which we have learned to use our language's symbol-using capacity. We often fall into semantic traps, regarding humans as simply another animal with an ability to use symbols. One way to know how humans function is to study other animals and then apply the findings to ourselves.

Korzybski disagrees with this idea and sees great danger in viewing the problem *additively* instead of *nonadditively*. Pavlov, for instance, experimented with dogs by ringing a bell and simultaneously introducing food. The sound of the bell was associated with food. The bell's ring was the neutral stimulus from which the process of abstraction took place. The dog was conditioned or trained to make the additive association between sound and food. Korzybski speaks of *inborn* and *acquired* responses. Similarly, when food is placed into the mouth of an organism, salivation takes place with no learning or acquisition of this response. It is inborn. The use of a neutral stimulus elicits an acquired response that comes through experience with the stimulus.

Humans often react as other animals do in terms of conditioned responses. There is great similarity between the reaction of Pavlov's dogs to bells and food and the response of Hitler's followers to swastikas and other signals. *People can be easily induced to react to slogans, names, desires, and so forth, in much the same way as animals are conditioned.* Examples of such conditioning include reacting to such symbols as "AIDS" or "herpes," with which most of us would not want to be associated.

Korzybski stresses that we must *not* copy other animals. Our most significant responses must be conditional, not conditioned; that is, the response should be delayed and modified, not automatic. Humans can be trained to behave like animals, to make undelayed reflexlike actions, instead of delayed, evaluative symbol reactions (responses). Because we can be trained, it is essential that we be conscious of the basic principles and methods through which our behavior can be perverted. In this regard, the English language is seen as two-valued; it does not facilitate the multiplicity of ideas. We must avoid learning an invariable reaction (stereotype) to a class of people, and recognize differences among the individual members of a class and vary our responses accordingly. Although other animals function exclusively in a physical environment of the body, we operate in both physical (body) and symbolic (mind) environments (see Table 4–1). Later in this chapter, we describe some "coping mechanisms" for dealing with this mind–body dualism. It is important to understand that, by simply reacting, our only coping mechanism is physical restraint.

Identity

A primary reason we tend to react instead of respond is that we see an absolute sameness or identity in the world. There are at least three reasons

TABLE 4–1   Human Environments

Aspect	Environment	Action Mechanism	Coping Mechanism
Body	Physical	Reaction	Physical restraint
Mind	Symbolic	Response	Etc.
			Quotes
			Dating
			Indexing

for this tendency: (1) The *name* is an important characteristic of the "thing"; (2) the uniqueness of the thing is in the name; and (3) if a thing has no name, it is either nonexistent or inconceivable. Thus, we have people who believe all divorces are alike, all teachers are out "to get" their students, and so on; however, even extremely similar situations, people, and so forth, differ. For example, John Dewey has pointed out that in each case the response is a new response to a new stimulus.[15] This adds to Korzybski's principle that life is an ongoing process with various electrons continually in motion (at least the elements are always in motion). Dewey suggests that the reason for unique responses was that, in each case, a new situation evolves.

For example, if we were subjected to a stimulus–response test 344 times, on the 345th time we would be subjected one more time, but to a new stimulus, different from that presented the 344th time, 343rd time, and so forth. This is similar to Korzybski's *dating system*, for time itself is always in motion. Because no time is the same as any other time, even the most similar situations, stimuli, and responses differ.

Dewey also implied that a stimulus–response relationship does not occur as a reflex action, but in fact these responses are "delayed responses." Neither Korzybski nor Dewey has suggested a definite time period break prior to response. Responses, then, are made after some delay, although there is no specific time period of the delay.

The concept of identity causes two additional problems based on our sometimes inappropriate uses of time through the verb "to be": First, "is" can lead to the identification of different levels of abstraction, implying in the utterance that one "thing" can exist as another. For example, in saying that "Ann is a Phi Mu," the implication is that Ann is *only* a Phi Mu and without Phi Mu Ann would be nothing. Second, "is" can lead to the predication of "qualities." For example, in saying that "Tommy is a good boy," the implication is that "good" and "Tommy" always go together. The construct of identification is closely associated with two other constructs in general semantics theory: nonallness and nonadditivity.

The concept of *nonallness* refers to the idea that we cannot say everything about anything. We cannot sense all of anything; thus, we cannot say everything about it. When we see the similarities in things (as we do through identity), we tend to disregard the differences. General semanticists, therefore, recommend that we use "etc." to illustrate that there are other "unknowns" that we are describing when we speak.

A related factor of identification is that of *nonadditivity*. When we add things and say they are something else, we have used this concept. One example is "4 apples plus 4 apples equals 8 apples." A typical example in everyday situations may be, "Can you take just one more student in the class?" Because no two things are exactly alike, taking a student who simply sits in class is different from taking a student who participates a lot. Therefore, adding together does not simply give us more of the same any more than being conditioned to a word or sound yields *communicative* behavior.

Time-Binding and Space-Binding

As we pointed out in Chapter 1, because two people have 20/20 vision does not mean that each perceives things in the same way. General semanticists suggest that things in the physical environment are constantly evolving. We are not the same as we were 10 years ago. But would you agree that you are not the same person you were 10 *seconds* ago? Obviously, you are not, for cells are growing, cells are dying, and so forth. The same is true even of nonliving phenomena because molecules are shifting. This phenomenon we call time-binding. Space-binding also occurs. Because people are in different places, they perceive things differently. The various accounts of what happened in an automobile accident support this point. Also, the number of "calls" of a referee that were judged "wrong" by someone watching the game on television may differ from the number judged wrong by someone attending the game. (Does the television [the medium] affect perceptions?) Considering that you probably will never be in the same space twice in a lifetime (because of the earth's rotation and revolution), there can be little argument that these changes occur.

Time-Binding.   Time-binding is treated as something through which all events, actions, perceptions, and so forth, must pass. Time is not considered an active agent, but rather a necessary passive catalyst. The effect of time is determined by a number of factors. For instance, there is the state of the "thing" at a given point in time (1_1). An infant, a teenager, and a senior citizen are different at time 1_1. Indeed, this is one reason that the terms for various ages have developed, each signifying the object's place in time. Simultaneously, things offer different physical appearances and often undergo different biological phases. While an infant and a teenager are growing, a senior citizen is deteriorating. An infant or a teenager can deteriorate through malnutrition or disease, but not by the aging (time) process itself.

Time changes must be viewed subjectively. For us, there appear to be at least three levels to view time. First, as previously discussed, there is the *physical* level in which objects' external appearances differ from one time to the next. Second, we undergo changes with time that must be considered at the *psychological* level. This is illustrated in the form of anxiety. When considered in this way, anxiety is simply the desire of the object at time 1_1 to pass through time at a faster rate to reach time 1_2. What makes communication difficult is that we undergo the process of change independently, yet we simultaneously pass through time together.[16] The third level of time is *cultural*; various cultures perceive time differently. The cultural level of time is also noted in the pace of human motion in New York City, on the one hand and in rural Mississippi, on the other. Technology is also a primary factor on the cultural level. Whereas going 250 miles for a weekend trip is considered usual today, certainly it was unusual 100 years ago. Taking a "long time" is related to cultural and personal experience.

Time itself becomes a changing concept even as abstract, arbitrary, and objective as time may be. Within time, then, one should include the physical level, the psychological level, the cultural level, and the phenomenal level— where time itself changes as *it* "passes"—as aspects of the communicative context.

Space-Binding.   As a corollary to the time dimension, semanticists have discussed the spatial dimension, more commonly called "space-binding."[17] Two aspects of this dimension are proximity and relative position. As with time, space is a passive, catalytic phenomenon. "Things" must exist within a space, they must be close to or far away from other things, and, even at the same distance apart, they must occupy different positions. The spatial dimension includes the physical level (perception and proximity), the psychological level (mood, state, etc.), and the cultural level (norms, values).

The *physical* level is understood easily. If we are standing face-to-face with a friend six feet away, our perception of that person is different than if only three feet separates us. Likewise, if we are interacting (at a distance of, say, four feet) face-to-face, perception is different than if we were interacting back-to-back at the same distance.

Psychologically, one who is drunk perceives space differently from his or her sober counterpart. This is detectable in driving behavior. Additionally, a person often "looks good" if the perceiver "feels good," and vice versa.

Space also differs with culture, as noted by Julius Fast in *Body Language:*

> Culture is still a guiding factor in all body language, and this is particularly true of body zones. Dr. [Edward] Hall goes into the cross-cultural implication of his proxemics. In Japan, for example, crowding together is a sign of warm and pleasant intimacy. In certain situations, Hall believes the Japanese prefer crowding.
>
> Donald Keene, who wrote *Living Japan*, notes the fact that in the Japanese language there is no word for privacy. To the Japanese, privacy exists in terms of his house. He regards this area as his own and resents intrusion into it. The fact that he crowds together with other people does not negate his need for living space.
>
> Dr. Hall sees this as a reflection of the Japanese concept of space. Westerners, he believes, see space as the distance between objects. To us, space is empty.

The Japanese see the shape and arrangement of space as having a tangible meaning. This is apparent not only in their flower arrangements and art, but in their gardens as well where units of space blend harmoniously to form an integrated whole.[18]

Fast explains that Arabs have almost "too much" space because their houses have large unused areas. Space-binding and time-binding, then, are necessary frameworks from which one should analyze any communicative context.

Three frames of reference (usually all different) operate simultaneously in defining time–space relationships to people in the communicative process. One framework exists for each person's perception, and a third exists for their "together" perception. Each framework contains different perceptions of time and space caused by varying physical conditions, psychological states, and cultural experiences. The object of communication, then, becomes focusing each frame of reference upon the other two frames, enabling the two individuals to "understand" one another. Never will all three frames appear exactly the same, but the process must be continued until there is enough similarity to make the exchange understandable.

We should be aware of the dimensions and the levels within those dimensions in which the communication context is molded. Then we can begin to understand the difficulty in communicating, and perhaps be more patient in our attempts. Too often scholars have emphasized the transmittal aspects of communication without giving proper attention to these receptive–perceptive aspects. Understanding perceptual phenomena is prerequisite to structuring the transmittal of messages, and only through this understanding can one effectively communicate.

Multiordinality

The construct of multiordinality has been adequately described by Wendell Johnson:

> When we speak, for example, of a statement about a statement, we use the word "statement" in two different ways. . . . let us say, hypothetically, that we make a statement on one level and then on the "next higher level" we make a statement about that statement. For example, we may say, "Blue pigeons fly faster than white pigeons." Now we may go to the "next higher" level of abstraction and make one of a number of statements about this statement, such as, "It is true" or "It is false" or "It is interesting if true" or "To the extent that this statement is true, it implies a relationship between pigmentation and muscle structure." These statements are on a higher level of abstraction than the first statement because they are statements about the first statement. But we can say of the first one and of each of the others, also that it is a statement. Thus the word statement is seen to be *multiordinal* in that it can be used on different levels, or orders, of abstraction, and its particular meaning varies from level to level. Consequently, to the question "What is a statement?" no general, absolute answer may be given.[19]

Thus, we can use the same words at different levels of abstraction, as exemplified by Harry L. Weinberg:

> Take the word "love." I can love a steak, a building, a woman, a painting, a theory, a horse, a bloody fight. All these loves are on the same level of abstraction. But love can also move to other levels. Thus I can love my love of a woman, a horse, a theory, etc. This is a second-order love and differs from a first-order love in an extremely important way, namely, that because it is on another level of abstraction, it involves, apparently, different and/or additional psycho-neurological processes.[20]

Multiordinality is further explained, depending on one's orientation.

Intensional and Extensional Orientation

According to Irving J. Lee, quoting Korzybski, "Intensional orientations are based on verbal definitions, associations, etc., largely disregarding observations as if they would involve a 'principle' of 'talk first and never mind the life facts.' Extensional orientations are based on ordering observations, investigations, etc., *first*, and the verbalization next in importance."[21] The differences between the two orientations are found in Table 4–2.

General semanticists support the extensional orientation, meaning that one should "Check the facts first." Additional terms characterizing this approach include "observation," "curiosity," "discovery," "inquiry," and "verification."

Let us characterize the perhaps more typical *intensional* orientation:

1. *People pay more attention to the names of things and what are said about things than they do to the "life facts."* For example, the name "Skinny Shake" was developed by a fast-food store to increase sales of milkshakes to people on diets. The result was that people on diets bought the drinks because they liked milkshakes, regardless of the fact that the ingredients in a Skinny Shake were the same as in a regular milkshake.

TABLE 4–2   Intensional/Extensional Characteristics

Intensional	Extensional
• Opposed to survival order and nervous structure	• Survival order and nervous structure
• Looks at generalities, similarities, classes	• Recognizes uniqueness
• Logical analysis	• Empirical, experimental
• A priori assumptions	• Enumeration of particulars
• Philosophy, aesthetics, theology	• Mathematics

Adapted from A. Korzybski, *Science and Sanity: An Introduction to Non-Aristotelian Systems and General Semantics* (Lakeville, CT: The Institute of General Semantics, 1958).

2. *People respond to words as if they were the objects themselves.* If a person were to say the word "vomit," it may cause another to respond to the word as if it were the thing.

3. *People do not abide by the life facts they are exposed to.* Examples of this are smoking cigarettes, not wearing seat belts, and driving while intoxicated.

4. *People use verbal proofs instead of the life facts.* For example, they assume that if Purdue beat Texas and Texas beat Ohio State, then Purdue will beat Ohio State.

We may look at some statements to determine the extent of intensional or extensional meaning (see Table 4–3). The differences among statements are affected by our *inside-the-skin* views (our affective states and disturbances and how we express them). We should, then, be aware of using an intensional approach (when we use it). We might make a statement such as, "I can't really tell you how I feel, but . . ."

In summary, we should not assume that A *is* A, or that something *has to be* A or non-A. We should look at details first. We should begin with observations and use extensional devices.

Extensional Devices

General semanticists suggest that several linguistic devices can help to handle the problems we have with language. These include the use of dating, indexing, the use of "etc.," and the use of quotations. *Dating* involves the use of some notation indicating that things change through time. Thus, we may talk about $Jeff_{1973}$ and $Jeff_{1988}$ as two different people. In fifteen years people go through a number of changes. The general semanticists suggest that we indicate this development by dating. *Indexing* involves the use of a subscript to show that each individual of a group is not the same. In a sense, a social security number operates in this way: There may be hundreds of George Johnsons, but each one has a separate and distinct social security number. The use of the term *"etc."* simply shows that we cannot say everything about a given phenomenon at any point in time. The use of *quotation marks* around

TABLE 4–3   Degree of Intensional/Extensional Meaning

No Intensional Meaning*	Can Have Extensional Meaning	No Extensional Meaning
Hablar en voz alba.	This room is 15 feet long	Angels watch over my bed at night.

*For one who does not know Spanish

Adapted from: S. I. Hayakawa, *Language in Thought and Action,* 4th ed. (New York: Harcourt, Brace and World, 1978), pp. 52–54.

ABSTRACTION LADDER

Start reading from the bottom *UP*

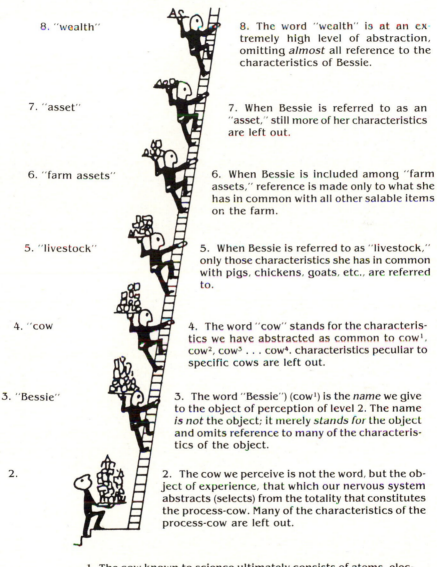

8. "wealth"

8. The word "wealth" is at an extremely high level of abstraction, omitting *almost* all reference to the characteristics of Bessie.

7. "asset"

7. When Bessie is referred to as an "asset," still more of her characteristics are left out.

6. "farm assets"

6. When Bessie is included among "farm assets," reference is made only to what she has in common with all other salable items on the farm.

5. "livestock"

5. When Bessie is referred to as "livestock," only those characteristics she has in common with pigs, chickens, goats, etc., are referred to.

4. "cow

4. The word "cow" stands for the characteristics we have abstracted as common to cow^1, cow^2, cow^3 . . . cow^4. characteristics peculiar to specific cows are left out.

3. "Bessie"

3. The word "Bessie") (cow^1) is the *name* we give to the object of perception of level 2. The name *is not* the object; it merely *stands for* the object and omits reference to many of the characteristics of the object.

2.

2. The cow we perceive is not the word, but the object of experience, that which our nervous system abstracts (selects) from the totality that constitutes the process-cow. Many of the characteristics of the process-cow are left out.

1. The cow known to science ultimately consists of atoms, electrons, etc., according to present-day scientific inference. Characteristics (represented by circles) are infinite at this level and ever-changing. This is the *process level*.

FIGURE 4–3   Abstraction Ladder.
Source: S. I. Hayakawa, *Language in Thought and Action* (Orlando, FL: Harcourt Brace Jovanovich, Inc., 1978).

a word indicates that although the two of us may use the word differently, there is enough similarity in meaning to use it.

Levels of Abstraction

As seen in Figure 4–3, we often talk at various levels of abstraction. We need to recognize this and, when possible, we need to operate at the lower (most concrete) level.

Recommendations

Although the general semanticist recommends that we use the principle of the "word is not the thing" as a basic way of thinking, many people do not operate on this principle. John C. Condon, Jr., believes we should further distinguish among four types of statements: (1) description, (2) inference, (3) judgment, and (4) tautology.[22] The differences are shown in the following statements:

1. The dog is barking. [description]
2. The dog is healthy. [inference]
3. The dog is man's best friend. [judgment]
4. The "dog" is a four-legged animal that barks. [tautology]

We should learn to look for similarities and differences as well as the differences within the similarities and the similarities within the differences.

General semantics, as a theory of language, is clearly a theory of knowledge. As a theory, it points out the problems inherent with symbols, especially for symbol-using animals such as the human. (We note in Chapter 7 that we are also symbol-*mis*using animals.) Although "dated," the ideas are important in building an understanding of communication. This is true when we consider that "meaning" is "found" in the words/symbols we use to communicate. Thus, perhaps those who suggest that the general semantics approach to language is obsolete or passé are reacting to their own language needs.

A MESSAGE-CENTERED PERSPECTIVE OF LANGUAGE: CONSTRUCTIVISM

Since the rise and subsequent "fall" of general semantics in the late 1960s, one of the most dominant language development theories has been developed by Jesse G. Delia and Ruth Anne Clark and their colleagues at the University of Illinois.[23] Their theory is often referred to as "constructivism" and is more concerned with the thinking process that occurs before the message is transmitted than the actual transmission. They refer to this thinking process as *social cognition.* Delia and Clark have been especially concerned with how children learn to adapt their messages before they speak. In essence, they are concerned with how one establishes and changes an *impression* of the other person. They also observe how the impression is used to establish a *message strategy* and how people rationalize such strategies. Several principles can be derived from this approach:

1. *Episodic and dispositional construals of persons are organized by interpersonal schemata.* These interpersonal schemata are cognitions (thoughts) about how we think the other person will behave. They are organized around some system (schema). The patterns in these organizations include interpretations and inferences, but they also include "constructed" patterns on which we elaborate to explain the behavior of another.

2. *The organization of interpersonal impressions provides context–action–relevant understandings and anticipations of others.* According to Barbara J. O'Keefe and Delia, "the perceiver acts . . . as a social psychologist attempting to elaborate a pattern of concepts for explaining, understanding, and predicting the other's behavior within a range of contexts."[24]

3. *Systematic variations in interpersonal constructs and schemata that develop as a function of social experience provide differential capacities to form stable, organized impressions across time and contexts.* Basically, research has found that individuals who have more choices available to them in assessing others, and those who are more abstract in their notions of interpersonal constructs, appear better able to formulate organized views of other people.

Consider, for example, an interaction with Bruno, someone you truly dislike. How you think about him is "colored" around your general feelings of people you dislike in general. You may see Bruno as simply "bad" for one or two reasons (cognitions), or you may have a well-developed dislike for him based on a variety of cognitions. Each cognition helps to forge an impression of this disliked other. Over time, and without competing cognitions, the impression becomes stable. You tend to understand and predict his behaviors based on that impression. In a given situation, then, you can construct how he will act and react. The more complex your cognitive interpersonal schemata and the greater the number of cognitions, the more precise will be your predictions about Bruno's messages. Thus, over a period of time you find many reasons to dislike or hate Bruno. As such, you can construct how he will respond to communication.

Thus, Delia, Clark and others have stated that language is used to assess how the other person will feel about a message before the message is fully formulated. Individuals with better language skills, therefore, formulate clearer and more precise messages that are oriented toward a particular receiver within a particular situation.[25] As such, constructivism falls into our general category of theories of knowledge.

_____ REVIEW _____

In this chapter, we have viewed three major perspectives of language in human communication, as well as a contemporary theory on the premessage importance of language. A summary is provided in Table 4–4. The nature view has been represented by the work of Chomsky; the nurture view has been represented by Sapir and Whorf. A functional view, presented in the works of Korzybski and his followers, has shown how language can be better used to make language more correspondent with "reality." The constructivist approach by Delia, Clark, and others illustrates the importance of language prior to sending a message. Some other views, with the argument centering around the relationship between thought and language, are found in the theories of Jean Piaget and others.[26] Almost all of these theorists would agree, however, that language and thought work together. Language is a coding system used for transmitting and receiving informational messages, whereas the nonverbal code is better suited for expressing feelings and the intensity of the message.[27]

What do we know about the communication materials with which we work? With the nonverbal code, we can change the emphasis of a message or we can contradict the verbal message. The approach we take to nonverbal communication, be it ethological, linguistic, or functional, will define how we use and interpret the possible effects of nonverbal codes. The way we approach the meaning of the verbal code also has a significant effect. Together, the nonverbal and verbal materials provide the basic meaning in the messages we send. Language, however, is an abstraction, and some words are more abstract than others.

The process of communication, then, requires that the communication architect understand how both nonverbal and verbal messages influence meaning, as well as how they influence the meanings inherent in one another. The most effective messages are those in which the verbal and the nonverbal materials are used together. Verbally, we can "create" nonverbal messages, describing, narrating, and scripting the movements and objects around us; however, we cannot "create" verbal messages through the nonverbal code, except in limited circumstances.

In the next section, we discuss one of the primary uses of communication materials. Traditional and contemporary rhetorical theory relies heavily on the verbal code, although nonverbal materials may be used to a lesser extent. Rhetorical theorists add the dimension of *framing* to the communication process. These theorists have developed the communication materials into a system to be used to persuade others to take actions.

_____ CRITIQUE _____

The nature–nurture problem is practically without resolution. Studies in the past, concerning identical twins who have been brought up in different contexts, have provided mixed results. It would appear, however,

TABLE 4–4 Summary Table

Name of Theory	Primary Theorists	Basic Principle	Constructs	Criteria	Analytic Approach	Limitations
Nature	Noam Chomsky Dan Slobin	Language has an apparent structure.	• Subject–predicate • Verb–object • Modification	Study language through its structure	Analyze the structure of language	Does not account for diverse differences among cultures.
Nurture	Edward Sapir Benjamin Whorf	Language varies from culture to culture.	• Cultural relativism	Cultural comparison	—	Does not account for the capacity to learn language in all cultures.
General semantics	Alfred Korzybski S.I. Hayakawa Irving J. Lee	Language must be a reflection of "reality."	• Silent assumptions • Reaction/response • Identity • Nonallness • Nonadditivity • Time- and Space-binding • Multiordinality • Intensional and extensional orientations • Levels of abstraction	Change the nature of language to Letter reflect its referents	—	Unrealistic therapeutic device.
Constructivism	Jesse Delia Ruth Anne Clark	Language is prestructured through social cognition.	• Social cognition • Message strategy	—	—	Difficult to get "inside one's head."

that any one exception disproves the nature theory. Korzybski's system may be beneficial as a therapeutic device, but it has had little heuristic value of late. Delia and Clark have written extensively about the constructivist approach, and at this time constructivism may be the most heuristic.

For us, it is important to remember that verbal and nonverbal codes form the bases for the study of human communication. These two coding systems are used to transfer information, with a purpose and with some intensity. Combined with psychological and social strategies, these coding systems give humans a means of perceiving their worlds, exchanging their worlds with others, and making decisions about which perceptions should be retained and which should be discarded. The strategies used to exchange these worlds with others will be the topic of the next chapter on rhetorical theories.

NOTES AND REFERENCES

[1] G. W. Gray and J. M. Wise, *The Bases of Speech*, 3rd ed. (New York: Harper and Row, 1959), pp. 455–472.

[2] See N. Chomsky, *Syntactic Structures* (The Hague: Mouton, 1957); *Aspects of the Theory of Syntax* (Cambridge, MA: MIT Press, 1965); *Cartesian Linguistics: A Chapter in the History of Rationalist Thought* (New York: Harper and Row, 1966); *Topics in the Theory of Generative Grammar* (The Hague: Mouton, 1966); *Language and Mind* (New York: Harcourt Brace Jovanovich, 1968); *The Sound Pattern of English* (New York: Harper and Row, 1968); *Current Issues in Linguistic Theory* (The Hague: Mouton, 1970); *Problems of Knowledge and Freedom* (New York: Pantheon, 1971); *Reflections on Language* (New York: Pantheon, 1975); *The Logical Structure of Linguistic Theory* (New York: Plenum, 1975); *Essays on Form and Interpretation* (New York: North Holland, 1977); *Rules and Representations* (New York: Columbia University Press, 1980).

[3] J. Britton, *Language and Learning* (Baltimore: Penguin, 1970), p. 200.

[4] J. S. Bruner, R. R. Oliver, P. M. Greenfield, et al., *Studies in Cognitive Growth* (New York: Wiley, 1966), p. 43.

[5] D. I. Slobin, *Psycholinguistics* (Glenview, IL: Scott Foresman, 1974).

[6] E. Sapir, *Language: An Introduction to the Study of Speech* (New York: Harcourt, Brace, and World, 1949), p. 207.

[7] B. L. Whorf, *Language, Thought, and Reality: Selected Writings of Benjamin Whorf*, ed. J. B. Carroll (New York: Wiley, 1956).

[8] M. Hickson and D. W. Stacks, *NVC: Nonverbal Communication Studies and Application*, 2nd ed. (Dubuque, IA: William C. Brown, 1989).

[9] L. A. White, *The Science of Culture: A Study of Man and Civilization* (New York: Farrar, Straus, and Cudahy, 1949), p. 22. See also P. Watzlawick, *The Language of Change: Elements of Therapeutic Communication* (New York: Basic, 1978); C. K. West, *The Social and Psychological Distortion of Information* (Chicago: Nelson–Hall, 1981).

[10] S. Chase, *Power of Words* (New York: Harcourt, Brace, and World, 1954), p. 125.

[11]C. K. Ogden and I. A. Richards, *The Meaning of Meaning: A Study of the Influence of Language Upon Thought and of the Science of Symbolism* (New York: Harcourt, Brace, and World, 1923), p. 11.

[12]D. P. Millar and F. E. Millar, *Messages and Myths: Understanding Interpersonal Communication* (New York: Alfred, 1976), pp. 29–30.

[13]A. Korzybski, *Science and Sanity: An Introduction to Non-Aristotelian Systems and General Semantics* (Lakeville, CT: The Institute of General Semantics, 1958), p. 399.

[14]Adapted from W. Johnson and D. Moeller, *Living With Change: The Semantics of Coping* (New York: Harper and Row, 1972). Johnson developed two of these questions; the third was developed by M. Hickson.

[15]M. Hickson, III, "Dewey's Reflex Arc and Reflective Thought: A Comparison with Korzybski," *ETC: A Review of General Semantics, 30* (1973), 127.

[16]M. Hickson, III, "A Receiver's View of the Communicative Context: A General Semantics Model," *ETC: A Review of General Semantics, 31* (1974), 377.

[17]W. Johnson, *People in Quandaries* (New York: Harper and Row, 1946), p. 164.

[18]J. Fast, *Body Language* (New York: M. Evans, 1970), pp. 37–39.

[19]Johnson, p. 155. Italics added.

[20]H. L. Weinberg, *Levels of Knowing and Existence: Studies in General Semantics* (New York: Harper and Row, 1959), pp. 98–99.

[21]I. J. Lee, *Language Habits in Human Affairs: An Introduction to General Semantics* (New York: Harper and Row, 1941), p. 123.

[22]J. C. Condon, Jr., *Semantics and Communication,* 3rd ed. (New York: Macmillan, 1985), pp. 122–129.

[23]J. G. Delia, R. A. Clark, and D. E. Switzer, "Cognitive Complexity and Impression Formation in Informal Social Interaction," *Speech Monographs, 41* (1974), 299–308; J. G. Delia and R. A. Clark, "Cognitive Complexity, Social Perception, and the Development of Listener-Adapted Communication in Six-, Eight-, Ten-, and Twelve-Year Old Boys," *Communication Monographs, 44* (1977), 326–345; J. G. Delia, "Change of Meaning Processes in Impression Formation," *Communication Monographs, 43* (1976), 142–157; J. G. Delia and B. J. O'Keefe, "Constructivism: The Development of Communication in Children," in *Children Communicating,* ed. E. Wartella (Beverly Hills, CA: Sage, 1979); J. G. Delia, B. J. O'Keefe, and D. J. O'Keefe, "The Constructivist Approach to Communication," in *Human Communication Theory: Comparative Essays* (New York: Harper and Row, 1982); R. A. Clark and J. G. Delia, "Cognitive Complexity, Social Perspective-Taking, and Functional Persuasive Skills in Second- to Ninth-Grade Children," *Human Communication Research, 3* (1977), 128–134; J. L. Applegate and J. G. Delia, "Person-Centered Speech: Psychological Development, and the Contexts of Language Usage," in *The Social and Psychological Contexts of Language,* eds. R. St. Clair and H. Giles (Hillsdale, NJ: Erlbaum, 1980); B. J. O'Keefe and H. E. Sypher, "Cognitive Complexity Measure and the Relationship of Cognitive Complexity to Communication: A Critical Review," *Human Communication Research, 8* (1981), 72–92.

[24]B. J. O'Keefe and J. G. Delia, "Impression Formation and Message Production," in *Social Cognition and Communication,* eds. M. E. Roloff and C. R. Berger (Beverly Hills, CA: Sage, 1982), p. 43.

[25]O'Keefe and Delia, pp. 33–72; see also J. A. Daly, R. A. Bell, P. J. Glenn, and S. Lawrence, "Conceptualizing Conversational Complexity," *Human Communication Research, 12* (1985), 30–53.

[26]See, for example, J. Piaget, *Structuralism*, trans. and ed. C. Maschler (New York: Harper Colophon, 1970); J. Piaget, *Main Trends in Inter-Disciplinary Research* (New York: Harper Torch Books, 1973); L. S. Vygotsky, *Thought and Language*, trans. W. Hanfmann and G. Vakar (Cambridge, MA: MIT Press, 1962), pp. 9–24; Bruner et al. See also J. R. Searle, *Speech Acts: An Essay in the Philosophy of Language* (Cambridge: Cambridge University Press, 1969); P. Saugsad, *A Theory of Communication and the Use of Language: Foundations for the Study of Psychology* (Oslo: Universitetsforlaget, 1977).

[27]R. L. Lanigan, "The Speech Act Theory of Interpersonal Communication: Stimulus for Research," *Journal of Applied Communications Research, 2* (1974), 98–101.

SECTION THREE

Framing the Edifice: Rhetorical Perspectives on Communication

The study of human communication is over two thousand years old. This history gives the communication student an understanding of his or her past, providing a *frame of reference.* From this frame, we apply psychological (individual), sociological (social), and biological blueprints into a recognizable edifice. The enduring study of human communication provides the communication theorist a rich sense of tradition from which to explain human behavior. These traditions are present today in a variety of communication theories, which generally *describe* communication events. Much of what we study today was laid down by the classical Greek theorists. We are proving (and improving) their "theory." Also, to truly understand a person, an organization, a society, or a discipline, we must examine its past to better predict its future.

Chapter 5 begins this examination with the classical rhetoric of the early Greek and Roman "theorists." This focus is on the impact of *oratory*—the creation and delivery of messages—within a *monolithic* society. The contributions of the Sophists and the rhetoric of Aristotle provide a firm base for the study of oratory. The restructuring of this foundation by the Romans is then examined through the works of Cicero and Quintilian. Finally, the classical impact on education in the early Middle Ages is explored.

Chapter 6 extends this analysis to the study of contemporary rhetorical thought and the use of argument in a *pluralistic* society. The rhetoric of communication versus the rhetoric of confrontation is explored through such "new" rhetoricians as Kenneth Burke and Chaim Perelman.

95

Section Three uses the materials of communication discussed in Chapters 3 and 4 to build a frame for the study of communication. This frame transcends the centuries and, it might be argued, consciously or unconsciously influences the communication architect's design of his or her edifice for later use.

5

Classical Rhetorical Theory: Protagorus, Aristotle, Cicero, and Quintilian

As students of communication, we are influenced by those who taught us, their teachers, their teachers' teachers, and so on. To design and use effective communication—to theorize and test those theories—requires an understanding of our communication roots. Examining early Greek society and its contributions to the study of communication is the first step in the long journey culminating in contemporary communication theory.

Cultural historians have suggested that civilization may be defined as the deliberate pursuit of an ideal.[1] Accepting this definition, we may accurately say that Western civilization began in Greece. Modern Western man is indebted to Greek civilization. Greek thinkers provided the origins for much of our philosophy, the beginnings of our medicine, and the first systematic study of the natural sciences. In fact, the influence of the early Greeks pervades Western civilization. For this reason, the study of *rhetorical* communication theory begins with ancient Greece.

Many students consider *communication* to be a twentieth century field of study. In fact, however, communication is one of the most ancient of academic studies. Many of the theories we use were first developed over two thousand years ago. Understanding how these theories evolved helps us use them in personal and professional situations.

THE NATURE OF GREEK SOCIETY

You should understand that *rhetoric* (the study and delivery of messages; oratory) was a principal interest of the Greeks, reflecting the essentially oral

97

nature of Greek society.[2] The Greek judicial system was oral in its mechanics: Any verbal complaint was pleaded by a citizen before a magistrate. The magistrate held public hearings where the litigants argued their own causes to a jury of citizens. The presentation of documentary evidence was extremely rare. Politics and the political system were similarly dependent upon oral communication. Citizens shaped policy directly through speech among themselves and to their chosen leaders. Political agitation was a process of public communication. Documents were used to maintain records rather than to influence minds.

Greece had no newspapers, magazines, or public billboards. Information was spread among its citizens orally. Even entertainment was oral: the human voice—in song, drama, or public discourse—was the most common form of diversion. Literature was written to be heard, and even when reading to oneself, the Greek read aloud.

The Nature of Greek Thought

Greek concern with universals led to, or in some respects was a consequence of, their tendency to view the world as an ordered whole. The Greeks' attempt to explore and explain the universe and the human role in it led to the development of philosophy. Inevitably, the role of oral communication within their society created a special place for rhetoric in Greek philosophical systems.[3] The value systems of ancient Greece emphasized idealism. (Today, this concept continues in such phrases as "maximizing our potential.") The Greeks had little respect for anyone who allowed his or her body or mind to deteriorate through lack of training or use. The growth of education resulted from the Greeks' concern with the individual development of each citizen to the fullest potential. The nature of Greek society placed the creation and delivery of oral messages in a position central to the functioning of the state. Thus, training in rhetoric became equally central to the education of the citizen.

The Emergence of the Sophists

The ancient Greeks took a practical view of education. Because it benefited the recipient, it was the citizen's responsibility to acquire whatever education desired. The Greeks sought education not from a school, but from a teacher. In the period 550–500 B.C., a set of teachers emerged whom we know as *Sophists*.[4] The Sophists accepted students for a set fee and taught them rhetoric. The best remembered of these early teachers was Protagorus.

Protagorus was totally practical in his teaching. He wished to equip his students to function within the activities of the state. Although most of his teachings are lost, evidence remains of works on ethics, law, and grammar, in addition to rhetoric. Protagorus's teaching method was based on the imitation of model speeches. In his teachings on delivery, Protagorus exemplified a plain, direct style of speaking. This became known as the "Attic" style (from Attica, the southeastern portion of Greece around Athens).

Two major rhetorical principles—doctrines—are generally attributed to Protagorus. The *doctrine of subjectivity* taught that we are the measure of all things. Truth exists in a relativistic sense only. All matter, said Protagorus, must be seen as in a state of constant change, of flux. For this reason, we must be the judge of what is true. The *doctrine of opposites* held that, irrespective of the subject, we can always find at least two contradictory positions that can be rationally defended. As a logical extension of these doctrines, Protagorus taught that the function of rhetoric is to air all opinions, and thus to allow the best (i.e., the most truthful) to prevail. In this position we find the forerunner of the eighteenth century basis for the concept of freedom of speech. However, you should realize that, logically, freedom to advocate *all* points of view can be defended as a special policy *only* if we deny our ability to determine *absolute* truth. The example of Euthalus and Protagorus in Chapter 1 illustrates the doctrine of opposites.

Whether these ideas were original to Protagorus is unknown, although he was the first recorded teacher of them. Protagorus was highly respected in Athens during the fifth century B.C. Even Plato, who despised the Sophists, described Protagorus as a man of high character. Protagorus's philosophical relativism may best be expressed in the statement that "absolute truth is unknowable, and perhaps non-existent."[5] Unfortunately for Protagorus, he carried his philosophy to its logical extension. In an essay entitled "On the Gods," he declared that he did not know whether the gods existed. Greek society, like many monolithic societies, was not especially tolerant. Protagorus was banished and his writings were ordered to be destroyed by the Athenian assembly. However, other sophistic schools also had a significant influence.

The Flowering of the Sophists

Sophists generally fall into four fairly distinct groupings. The *literary-cultural* sophists were primarily interested in the study of language and grammar. Prominent among this group was Prodacus. Perhaps the most prominent of the *rhetorical* sophists was Gorgias, whose efforts exemplify the teachers of rhetoric and oratory. Another group of teachers, represented by Isocrates, focused primarily on *statesmanship*. Hyppius is typical of the group of *eristic* sophists whose primary study was formal logic.

The earlier relativism of Protagorus reached full flower in the works of Gorgias.[6] Our first record of Gorgias comes from 427 B.C., when he arrived in Athens from the city–state of Leontini to enlist the aid of Athens in defeating the invasion of Leontini by Syracuse. He was so effective that he persuaded Athens to send her entire army and navy into the war. Unfortunately, they were soundly defeated. As a result of the war, Athens was occupied and the defensive walls of the city were destroyed.

Gorgias remained for a while in Athens as an orator and teacher. He had developed a flowery style of speaking that became the rage of Athens.[7] Gorgias believed in the relativity of language. He taught that (1) words and things are different, (2) objects themselves do not contain the words used to label them, and (3) words are a human tool inherently different from the things they describe. His philosophy of human affairs is summarized in the statement, "Nothing exists outside of human senses; if it did, we could not know it; and if we could, we could not prove it to anyone."[8]

The comments of later writers, including Aristotle, seem to make it clear that Gorgias's works did not include any systematic discussion of rhetoric. He focused on the teaching of oratory, whose purpose he saw as *persuasion.* The persuasive method used was the theory of probabilities which Plato so violently attacked, but Gorgias defended its use as the essence of logic.[9] All of the Sophists suffered, of course, from the attacks of Plato and his disciples. Nothing seemed to goad Plato more than the sophistic concept of relativistic truth.[10] Disagreement over the basic nature of knowledge is bound to lead to conflict, and the clash between Platonists and Sophists has lasted some twenty-five hundred years.[11]

In addition to logical argument, Gorgias recognized the persuasive force of emotion. The rhyming style of Greek oratory was conducive to emotional appeals based on the sound of the language. Gorgias and his students were major figures in the development of many stylistic devices.[12] Because they were widely imitated, such devices were later condemned as trite and artificial. In evaluating Gorgias, however, we must remember that he was the first to study these devices as an essential characteristic of style.

Gorgias also influenced the theory of style with the application of the sophistic theory that two antithetical statements can be made on each subject. If this is true, it creates a dilemma for the orator: How do we know which position to take? How is truth to be determined? To Gorgias, this problem demanded the consideration of three factors in arriving at the correct action: *time, place,* and *circumstance.* For example (as it might be applied to contemporary situations), both of the following statements may logically be defended:

1. To interfere in the activities of other people which do not affect us is wrong.

2. To fail to act in order to prevent the abuse of innocent victims is wrong.

In resolving this dilemma, Gorgias applied the principle of *kairos:* he would consider the kinds of actions involved, the likelihood that intervention would be successful, the seriousness of the abuse, and other factors in the context of the situation. Gorgias thought that *appropriateness* rather than correctness should be the standard for behavior. Communication practices are neither "right" nor "wrong" in and of themselves; they are right only because they are appropriate to the context in which they occur. Of course, since what is appropriate will vary according to our perception of the context, there is no way to say *absolutely* what ought to be done.[13]

In rhetorical theory, *kairos* is the orator's standard used to decide such matters as choice of organization, the means of proof, and particularly the style to be employed. Marion Untersteiner has defined it as "the adaptation of the speech to the manifold variety of life, to the psychology of speaker and hearer."[14]

Gorgias never claimed to be a teacher of virtue. He acknowledged that speaking about virtue and justice might make the speaker a better man simply due to an association with the material. His teaching method was imitation and drill. Like others, he used a collection of *commonplaces* (stock arguments) in teaching, but Gorgias did not establish a rigid system of rules for their use. Gorgias's major contributions to classical rhetorical theory were (1) the production of one of the earliest textbooks on the proper development of logical argument and (2) his recognition of the function of emotion and the importance of language in persuasion. Gorgias taught a theory of rhetoric that may be summarized in the statement, "Since knowledge cannot be gained with certainty, rhetoric must aim at opinion. Since there will always be conflicting opinions, it all ultimately becomes a matter of persuasion."[15] Although Gorgias was slighted by many scholars, twentieth century studies have begun to recognize the importance of what he had to say. The contemporary approaches to language studied in Chapter 4 and to human decision-making to be studied in later chapters make Gorgias seem very modern. In our modern view of theory, the artistic Sophist's rhetoric would fall within our theories of knowledge.

Prescriptive Rhetorical Theories

If we view the artistic approaches of Sophists such as Protagorus and Gorgias as one branch of Greek rhetorical theory, the other and the oldest branch, the prescriptive approach to rhetoric, began with Corax of Sicily. Traditional scholarship has identified Corax as the author of the first work on rhetoric.[16]

Artistic rhetorics, as discussed earlier, are those in which the theorist establishes general standards against which the finished work is to be measured. *Prescriptive* rhetorics, on the other hand, provide the practitioner with a set of very specific rules to be followed in the construction of oratory. The prescription serves as a sort of recipe by which the speech may be made. In our breakdown of communication theory, such rhetorical practices fall into theories of performance. Both schools of rhetoric typically provided multitudes of examples to be imitated by students. The prescriptive approaches, however, were known for the development of *handbooks*, manuals of rules that could be used by the student to develop speeches on any subject.

Our records of this period are at best imprecise. We must piece together what we can from the shreds of facts now available, recognizing that this is only an approximation. At any rate, around 467 B.C. there was a major political upheaval on the island of Sicily. The reigning tyrants were overthrown. In the aftermath, lawsuits were instigated to recover lands and properties seized by the tyrants and/or their court favorites. Since these seizures took place over many years, most crucial witnesses had died or disappeared. Moreover, the political disruption led indirectly to the destruction of many written records. In such a situation, absolute proof of ownership generally is impossible to achieve. In response to these circumstances, Corax is said to have developed the practice of arguing by probabilities.[17]

Much of Corax's theory was "after-the-fact," a study of the most successful speakers and what they did in the courts. He defined rhetoric as *the art of persuasion*, and laid out a system for the arrangement of speeches which called for a five-part division: introduction, narration, argument, digression, and epilogue.

As previously mentioned, Plato objected to the views of the Sophists on knowledge, rhetoric, and society. To Plato, the truth was absolute, knowable—at least by some—and capable of being communicated. Plato felt that the rule of society should be reserved for those capable of knowing the truth. Rhetoric, which adapted to the views of the audience, was judged by Plato as only a sham, as a way of spreading false truths.[18] Instead, Plato recommended *dialectic*, a question-and-answer search to absolute truth, over the "unethical" format of rhetoric. This debate over the nature of truth that began between Plato and the Sophists shows up repeatedly in the history of communication. In many respects, Aristotle's life work was devoted to the search for some middle ground in this debate.

THE RHETORIC OF ARISTOTLE

Of the books and fragments of books on rhetoric and oratory surviving from classical Greece, the most important is Aristotle's *Rhetoric.* Sufficient manuscript evidence exists to provide a clear picture of the methodology and philosophical position from which Aristotle operated.

Sometimes attacked, but seldom ignored by any scholar of rhetorical theory, Aristotle, in opposition to Plato, his mentor, is perhaps the most highly esteemed figure in ancient rhetoric. His *Poetics* and *Rhetoric* comprise an analytically thorough treatment of the phases of writing and speaking dealing with the art of imaginative appeal and public address. The *Rhetoric* is generally considered the most important work in the literature of speechcraft.[19]

In many respects, the *Rhetoric* accepts, elaborates, and systematizes doctrines set forth by Plato. Aristotle adopted three typically Platonic principles: (1) Contemporary writers treated rhetoric in an unscientific manner, (2) rhetoric was closely related to dialectic, and (3) orators should be familiar with the laws of human nature because they influenced the responses of the audience.

The *Rhetoric* reveals philosophical and temperamental divergences from Plato's ideas. Aristotle seemed to be more interested in reorganizing theory about life than in reform; for this reason, the *Rhetoric* is largely detached from morality. It is neither a manual of rules nor a collection of injunctions. It is an amoral and scientific analysis of the means of persuasion.[20] As such, Aristotle's theory of rhetoric best represents a theory of knowledge.

The *Rhetoric* is divided into three books, or sections. Book I generally deals with the necessities and opportunities of the speaker, Book II with the audience, and Book III with the speech itself.

Book I

Aristotle opened Book I with the statement, "Rhetoric is the counterpart of Dialectic."[21] He argued that these subjects are of concern to all and belong to no definite science, since all of us "attempt to discuss statements and to maintain them, to defend themselves and to attack others" (Book I, 11, 135a). Rhetoric is defined "as the faculty of observing in any given case the available means of persuasion" (Book I, 1, 1355b). In other words, it enables us to find suitable material for achieving persuasion in any field of inquiry. Unlike other disciplines, the subject matter of rhetoric is technique or method. As with logic, rhetoric is a means of bringing out truth, or making us see what is true and fitting.

The tool best adapted to achieving persuasion is the *enthymeme*, or approximate syllogism. A certain amount of academic disputation has centered around Aristotle's definition of an enthymeme.[22] Traditional scholarship said that an Aristotelian enthymeme was merely a syllogism with one of its premises omitted. Some contemporary scholars argue that this is not true.[23] A syllogism, by contrast, was a statement that could be objectively proven.

Consider, for example, the classical syllogism: All men are mortal; Aristotle is a man; therefore, Aristotle is mortal. The proof is *deductive*. We begin by noting that all men are mortal and that Aristotle belongs to the class "men." Based on this knowledge of class mortality, the logical conclusion may be drawn. The enthymeme, however, omits reference to one of the parts: Aristotle is a man; therefore he is mortal.

Aristotle argued that the practice of rhetoric had four basic values (Book I, 1, 1355a): (1) Truth and justice may be guarded against falsehood and wrong. (2) The ignorant may be persuaded. (3) The opposition may be refuted. (4) People may defend themselves against attack. This last argument was probably the most important to Aristotle himself, for he stated that "it is absurd to hold that a man ought to be ashamed of being unable to defend himself with his limbs, but not of being unable to defend himself with speech and reason, when the use of rational speech is more distinctive of a human being than the use of his limbs" (Book I, 1, 1355a).

Aristotle's basic method was to subdivide. Persuasion is achieved in three ways. "The first kind depends on the personal character of the speaker [*ethos*]; the second on putting the audience into a certain frame of mind [*pathos*]; the third on the proof, or apparent proof, provided by the words of the speech itself [*logos*]" (Book I, 1, 1356a). The types of oratory are defined, as well as the purpose of each type, and detailed suggestions are presented on the various topics that are appropriate in each instance.

Aristotle recognized the crucial role of the audience in the total speech situation. His model of speech consisted of three parts: the speaker, the subject of the speech, and the people who hear the speech. He categorized audiences, suggesting that the object of a speech should be determined by the audience.

The emphasis on ethos, or proof created by the personal character of the speaker, remains one of Aristotle's great legacies. The workings of ethos were explained by Aristotle with the observation, "We believe good men more fully and more readily than others; this is true generally whatever the question is, and absolutely true where exact certainty is impossible and opinions are divided" (Book I, 1, 1356a). Some of the most sophisticated twentieth century research in communication theory has confirmed the contention of Aristotle that "his character may almost be called the most effective means of persuasion a speaker possesses" (Book I, 1, 1356a).

About half of Book I is devoted to a detailed analysis of the various common subjects, such as virtue, happiness, love, honor, and so forth, that provide the basis for motivation and serve as avenues for achieving proof in *deliberative* (the subjects are argued for the good or advantageous), *forensic* (judicial argument that the subject is criminal [just or unjust]), and *epideictic* (argument that the subject is praiseworthy and noble) oratory.

Book II

Aristotle turned in Book II to an analysis of human emotions, a study of the characteristics of people, and a survey of the traits usually observed in people of wealth and power. The overriding importance of ethos is again stressed, but Aristotle also observed that, "When people are feeling friendly and placable, they think one sort of thing; when they are feeling angry or hostile, they think something totally different" (Book II, 1, 1378a). It is important for the orator to possess the ability to influence the emotions of this audience.

Aristotle treated emotions in pairs of opposites: anger and calm, friendship and enmity, shame and shamelessness, and so forth. In each instance, the emotion is defined: "Anger may be defined as an impulse, accompanied by a pain, to a conspicuous revenge for a conspicuous slight directed without justification towards what concerns oneself or towards what concerns one's friends" (Book II, 1, 1378a). Calmness is the opposite of anger. Having provided a precise definition, Aristotle discussed what types of acts produce each emotion and the rhetorical devices used to create it in the audience's mind. Some suggest that Aristotle was too prescriptive in his analysis of human motives, but the degree to which they have retained their relevance—in spite of more than two thousand years of social evolution—is amazing.

In the concluding sections of Book II, Aristotle continued his analysis of the common topics begun in Book I. He examined two forms of extrinsic proof common to all types of speeches: the example and the enthymeme. Careful attention was paid to the concept of probabilities as a method for establishing proof of either past or future facts.[24]

The detailed lists of subjects for enthymemes provided in Book II served as the basis for Aristotle's logical system and his analysis of the position of logic in persuasion. Aristotle made probability the essential substructure of his rhetorical system. In so doing, he expressed his awareness of the variance operating in human affairs.

Book III

In Book III, Aristotle dealt with delivery, linking it in a general way with style. Interestingly, Aristotle was somewhat apologetic in this treatment. He considered the importance of delivery to be the result of "defects in our political institutions" (Book III, 1, 1403b). Aristotle made quite clear that he would prefer audiences to be swayed solely by the proof introduced in support of the speaker's arguments. He recognized, however, that this is not what happens: "just as in drama the actors now count for more than the poets, so it is in the contests of public life" (Book III, 1, 1403b). The art of delivery, according to Aristotle, consists of three parts: (1) understanding the proper use of volume, (2) the proper use of accents and pitch, and (3) the use of rhythm. Style is analyzed, and presented as four elements: clarity, propriety, uniqueness, and naturalness. Each is examined in detail and advice on how to achieve style is provided.

REVIEW

Aristotle's *Rhetoric* provides an orderly, systematic attempt to set down the principles of the art of public speaking. This alone is sufficient to justify its study as a milestone in rhetorical theory. Aristotle's work has also served as the foundation for much of the work of the theorists who followed him.

General agreement is that Aristotle's *Rhetoric* successfully established four major postulates concerning the practice of oratory: (1) that rhetoric was a useful art and a valuable social tool, (2) that rhetoric could be taught, (3) that good rhetoric avoided extremes, and (4) that logic was the essential prerequisite for proof. By establishing these premises, Aristotle essentially rehabilitated rhetoric in Greek culture and thought.

THE LATIN INFLUENCE

It is indicative of the basic nature of the society that when we go to Greece our eyes are drawn to the remains of the beautiful. Going to Rome, we find our attention focused on the utilitarian. Ancient Rome was an eminently practical civilization, and the monuments she left through the ages are those of a practical nature.

So it is with Roman contributions to rhetorical theory. The Greeks invented the science of rhetoric, but the Romans perfected it. Roman training in rhetoric began at the elementary age with a teacher called a *grammaticus.* He taught his pupils grammar, spelling, and phrasing, and gave them a foundation in correct use of the language. Advanced rhetorical education centered around a practice known as *declamation:* set-piece speeches or debates on hypothetical issues drawn from similar events in real life. The ultimate goal of Roman education was to produce the philosopher–orator–statesman.

Cicero

Rome's greatest orator was Cicero.[25] Cicero, or Tully as he was known in the medieval period, was one of the few great practicing orators who also wrote on the theory of oratory.[26] His books and monographs comprise a complete system of rhetoric, comparable in coverage to the work of Aristotle. Although Cicero created little original theory, he systematized the works of earlier thinkers in such a way as to merit our attention.[27]

The most comprehensive of Cicero's works is *De Oratore*, completed around 55 B.C. Consisting of three books, *De Oratore* is the setting in which Cicero presents his *five canons of rhetoric*. Because they dominated rhetorical thinking for more than fifty generations, the *canons* deserve discussion in detail.[28]

The first canon was invention (*inventio*). Public speaking students today would call this research: going to the library or interviewing some expert on a topic. To Cicero, it was the discovering of all available materials that the orator could use in preparation of his discourse through painstaking research and investigation of facts. To master invention, the orator must consider the nature of proof.

The second canon was disposition (*dispositio*), or what we would call organization. It concerned the arrangement of material in the most compelling manner. Cicero relied heavily on Aristotle's schema. A speech, said Cicero, has six parts: *exordium* (introduction), the passage that prepares the mind of the listener to receive the rest of the speech; *narratio* (narrative), the exposition of events that have occurred or are supposed to have occurred; *divisio* (partition), a statement of the topics to be discussed in the speech; *confirmatio* (confirmation), that part of the oration that, by marshaling arguments, lends credit, authority, and support to the case; *confutatio* (refutation), the part of the speech that anticipates the objections or arguments of the opposition and disposes of them in advance; *conclusio* (peroration), the end of the speech, providing a summary of what has been said along with emotional appeals to win the sympathy of the audience.

The third canon was that of style (*elocutio*): word choice, composition, and various stylistic devices or *figures of speech*. Cicero classified and described the three kinds of style: plain, moderate, and grand. He identified the characteristics of a good style as correctness, clearness, appropriateness, and ornament.[29]

The fourth canon is that of memory (*memoria*), the study of the materials so that they may be presented in a fluent fashion. Stress was placed on structure because order serves as an aid to memory.[30] Because rhetorical theorists of the past two centuries have so frequently ignored it, memory is often known as "the lost canon."

The final canon was that of delivery (*pronuntiatio*), or the manner in which the speech is delivered. Cicero felt that delivery was of the highest importance. He noted that without effective delivery, "a speaker of the highest capacity can be held in no esteem, while one of moderate abilities, with this qualification, may surpass even those of the highest talent."

Cicero's greatest strength may be found in his functional approach to rhetoric. An orator himself, he was most concerned with explaining what worked effectively in communicating to his audience. Cicero also stressed the importance of philosophical study and general education, in addition to training in the practice of oratory. His concern with the character of the orator set the foundation for a moralistic rhetoric closely aligned to Plato that has continued to "contaminate" rhetorical theory into the twentieth century.[31]

Cicero provided no new departure in theory. He asked no generative questions. He was, in the best tradition of Rome, an eclectic. He took the best of what had gone before and synthesized it into a coherent package. We would probably best categorize his theory as both a theory of knowledge and a theory of performance. He set a stage for medieval rhetorical theory that endured for over a thousand years.

Quintilian

The second significant Roman contributor to classical rhetorical theory was Quintilian. The major work for which Quintilian is known is his *De Institutione Oratoria* (*On the Education of the Orator*), a careful and systematic description of the method by which a young orator should be trained. It was primarily a compendium of ancient theories on rhetoric.[32] Quintilian examined the methods of instruction practiced in the schools and the objectives of classical education, and made numerous comments and suggestions for improvement.[33] He strongly expressed his displeasure with stylistic abuses and advocated a return to simpler styles.

Quintilian condemned artificiality in language. He taught that the effective orator avoided styles that were inconsistent with ordinary speech. He did not claim that using metaphors or figures of speech was wrong, but that clarity and understanding were the first priority.[34] Finally, Quintilian followed Cicero with his insistence that *the good orator must be a good man.* The moral development of the young orator thus became a major concern of the process of rhetorical education.[35] Hence, Quintilian is best aligned with the theories of performance theorists.

ad Herennium

A treatist entitled *Rhetorica ad Herennium* also emerged from the Roman era.[36] Its author is unknown, although for many centuries it was thought to be the work of Cicero. Written somewhere around 86 B.C., *ad Herennium* was a treatise in four books. As did the classical Greeks, it viewed oratory as being of three kinds: deliberative, demonstrative, and judicial. Approximately half of *ad Herennium* is devoted to style, and it came to be looked upon as the definitive treatment of stylistic ornamentation. The work emphasizes the use of practice and the imitation of model speeches as a means of improving an orator's ability.

LATIN INFLUENCE ON RHETORIC IN THE MIDDLE AGES

Saying that Cicero and Quintilian were the only well-known Latin theorists in the medieval period is no exaggeration. Cicero's influence is apparent in the number of medieval allusions to his work, the library holdings of his books, the wide uses of his rhetorical doctrines, the translations of his works, and the commentaries made upon them. Quintilian, on the other hand, had supplied the medieval world with a broad plan of instruction for the Roman schools. His influence can be seen in the teachings carried on in the schools of the Middle Ages.[37] These two theorists were widely known by medieval scholars, and their ideas were a vital force in motivating their scholarship.

Rhetorical theory evolved little between the decline of the Roman republic and the rebirth of learning in the West around 1100 A.D. This can be attributed primarily to the society of that era.

Where rhetoric had practical application, it flourished. In Greece and republican Rome, the ability to speak effectively was essential to the political life of the citizenry. But the emergence of totalitarian regimes marked the end of citizen input into the political process, and thus the loss of any need for effective speaking skills. Throughout the first millennium, this condition prevailed. Political structure was essentially totalitarian. There was no opportunity to sway masses of people through rhetoric. Thus, there was no reason for theorists to be concerned with rhetoric. Intellectual life was dominated by the Church, with her already established virtues and complete control of religious activities. In such an environment, even preaching fell into disuse and provided no stimulus to rhetorical growth.

The *form* of rhetoric remained, but it was a sterile art. Imitation was the practice until a new society emerged. It is difficult, however, to discover a major medieval writer who did not mention Cicero when there was occasion to treat public speaking. Alcuin called upon Ciceronian rhetoric in writing his doctrine of kingly behavior directed toward Charlemagne.[38] Cassiodorus, Isidore, and Capella, early encylopedists, assumed Cicero the greatest example and followed his teaching dutifully. In each case, Cicero was praised for both his eloquence and his philosophy.

St. Augustine: Christian Rhetoric

The first truly medieval treatise dealing with the communicative arts, St. Augustine's *De Doctrina Christiana*, was based on Augustine's experience as a teacher of Ciceronian rhetoric. This work is especially interesting because it tried to justify the rhetorical training of priests. A hint of Aristotle is apparent when Augustine argues that for the clergy to be effective defenders of the truth, they should possess rhetorical skills. An Aristotelian practicality is seen when Augustine condemns people who are overly concerned with grammatical precision and the niceties of language. After all, he writes, "there is no reason for speaking if what is said is not understood by those [to whom] we speak."[39]

As a bishop, Augustine was deeply interested in increasing the effectiveness of Christian preaching. He dismissed as excessive pride the idea that the preacher could rely on divine inspiration for his sermons and homilies.[40] Since by this time, the Christian Church was the established religion, Augustine dealt extensively with how rhetoric could be used to move and to inspire audiences. His treatment of style is based primarily on Cicero (pp. 156–157). The importance of *De Doctrina Christiana* to later writers was enormous. It became *the* authoritative statement of Christian rhetoric (p. 159).

Rhetoric and Education

That Cicero was so pervasively regarded as the great example in rhetoric implies that his work must have enjoyed enormous circulation and use.[41] Although he wrote seven books on rhetoric, the most frequently used prior to the fifteenth century were his early works. Only the *De Inventione*,[42] the *Rhetorica ad Herennium* (thought at the time to be Ciceronian), and the *Topica* (known chiefly through versions of Boethius) are widely known.[43] The remaining works were neglected during the Middle Ages.

The seat of learning in the Middle Ages was the university. Although rhetoric was not taught as such in the northern universities, Sorbonne in Paris held twenty-four of Cicero's works in its library by 1342. Cicero was also represented in the library at Oxford. Cicero and the study of rhetoric were of vital interest in the universities of the south. In Italy, the Ciceronian tradition was significant throughout the Middle Ages. The Italians adapted oratory to their legal studies. Examples of this adaptation can be found in Isidore's *Etymologia*, Alcuin's *Dialogus*, and an anonymous work entitled *Rhetorica Ecclesiastica*. Through such use, the rhetorical principles of Cicero remained alive through the Middle Ages.[44]

Another key to the popularity of Cicero's rhetoric was its availability. Only Cicero's rhetoric was translated from Latin during the Middle Ages. By the thirteenth century, *De Inventione* was available in French and Italian. About 1266, Guidotto da Bologna was working on a paraphrased version of *Ad Herennium* in Italian under the title *Rettorica nuovo di Tullio*. An important French translation of *De Inventione* and *Ad Herennium* was produced by Jean d'Antioche de Harens in 1282 under the title *Rettorique de Marc Tulles Cyceron*. No such translations were attempted in northern Europe until Thomas Wilson's English translation of 1530, called simply the *Arte of Rhetorique*. Since the scholars of this period could easily read the works of Cicero in Latin, such wide translation can be taken as evidence of its popularity and use.

In addition to the translations, another indication of the high regard for Cicero is found in the commentaries on *De Inventione* and *Rhetorica ad*

Herennium. The existence of such commentaries in a medieval society could only refer to the use of a book in the schools. Thierry of Chartres composed in the twelfth century what is believed to be the first medieval commentary on *De Inventione* (p. xiv). Thierry's *Super Cicero de Inventione* also refers the reader to Quintilian's *Institutio Oratoria* for a different approach. Victorinus and Boethius wrote on Cicero's work, and more than one hundred commentaries of unknown origins exist, at least in part.

An interesting tangent in the development of rhetorical theory is the period from approximately 1100–1300 A.D., when Cicero's scheme was applied to the art of letter writing. This study of model letters is still found today (usually in business administration courses, often titled "Business Letter Writing," "Business Communication," etc.), but in the early medieval period, it provided an invaluable tool to a largely illiterate age. Teachers of the art, which was known as *ars dictamen,* were highly prized members of university faculties. Dictamen manuals, containing sample letters for a variety of situations, were widely circulated.[45] Almost all consisted of examples that applied the Ciceronian canon of *inventio* to the process of writing a letter.[46]

The effect of Quintilian upon medieval society was overshadowed by that of Cicero, yet Quintilian as a teacher is not to be forgotten. Although the study of grammar lost the larger meaning that Quintilian had given it, the basic principles remained. It was reduced from a springboard to the study of rhetoric to a limited and technical study aimed at "introducing men to the language and literature of the church." John of Salisbury, a great scholar of the Middle Ages, relied upon Quintilian's theories when he compounded his *Metalogicus,* the most extensive medieval survey of language study.[47] This alone would have ensured Quintilian's place in the Middle Ages, but as in the case of Cicero, his theories on education and rhetoric were known and used throughout the scholastic world.

Cicero and Quintilian had profound influences upon medieval thinking. As the only two well-known Latin theorists, their writings served to preserve the best classical thought on rhetoric. Cicero once defined the ideal orator as a "complete man." His orator must have been well versed in philosophy, supplemented with logic and moral science, and knowledgeable in public affairs, taking an active part in society. By these standards, both Cicero and Quintilian were "complete men."

REVIEW

After Plato, the early Greeks saw rhetoric as a device for persuading others of differing viewpoints. Protagorus and Aristotle provided the philosophical background in proof (*inventio*). Gorgias provided a background style (*elocutio*). The Romans, Cicero and Quintilian, systematized the work of the Greeks focusing upon the five canons of rhetoric and the nature of credibility (*ethos*). Table 5–1 summarizes traditional rhetorical theory.

TABLE 5-1 Summary Table

Name of Theory	Primary Theorists	Basic Principle	Constructs	Criteria	Analytic Approach	Limitations
Traditional Rhetorical Theory	Protagorous Aristotle Gorgias Cicero Quintilian	The speaker must adapt his speech to the needs of his audience to accomplish his persuasive end.	• Five canons of rhetoric: —*Inventio* (proof) —*Dispositio* (organization) —*Elocutio* (style) —*Memoria* (memory) —*Pronuntiatio* (delivery) • Rhetoric • Three means of proof: —*Ethos* —*Pathos* —*Logos*			

Today's modern theorist owes much to the classical architects. The frame they created focused on the structure of messages, although delivery techniques were also examined. For the most part, the classical rhetorician, and their Latin and Middle Ages counterparts, focused on the practical, building a solid form that withstood the ages. If today's architect is concerned with prediction and control, the ancient architect was concerned with prescription and description. The focus on divining the truth, persuasion, and creating rhetorical rules set the stage for—trained—the modern communication architect, whether that architect follows in the rhetorical tradition or moves to other interpretations of what constitutes communication.

CRITIQUE

Because of its focus on persuasive discourse, the work of the classical theorists is easily testable. In fact, a great deal of contemporary experimental research has been devoted to testing various hypotheses drawn from the classical theories. Perhaps more importantly, these tenets are testable for each of us in our own daily communication. One essential premise, the lack of a provable absolute truth, must be accepted as a foundation. Granted that premise, the classical theorists constructed highly logical systems. In Aristotle's concept of ethos, we find one of the most important theoretical developments in the field of communication.

NOTES AND REFERENCES

[1]W. Jaeger, *Paideia: The Ideals of Greek Culture,* trans. G. Highet (New York: Oxford University Press, 1943).

[2]The central role of oral communication in Greek society is widely acknowledged. See, among others, R. L. Enos, "The Persuasive and Social Force of Logography in Ancient Greece," *Central States Speech Journal,* 25 (1974), 4–10; G. A. Kennedy, *The Art of Persuasion in Greece* (Princeton, NJ: Princeton University Press, 1963), pp. 26–29.

[3]J. Benjamin, "The Greek Concept of Dialectic," *Southern Speech Communication Journal,* 48 (1983), 357–358.

[4]A comprehensive treatment of the Sophists, their rhetoric, and their influence on classical culture is beyond our purpose here. We aim only at a general understanding of the major sophistic theses. Those who want to explore this important chapter in the history of rhetoric might begin with Jaeger, vol. 1; F. Copleston, *A History of Philosophy* (New York: Image Books, 1962); W. K. C. Guthrie, *The Sophists* (London: Cambridge University Press, 1971); or any of the various works of G. A. Kennedy cited herein.

[5]Kennedy, p. 13.

[6]For a more detailed discussion of Gorgias and his approach to rhetoric, see Kennedy, pp. 61–68.

[7]G. A. Kennedy, *Classical Rhetoric and Its Christian and Secular Tradition From Ancient to Modern Times* (Chapel Hill: University of North Carolina Press, 1980), pp. 29–31.

[8]For an interpretation of Gorgias's meaning, see B. E. Gronbeck, "Gorgias on Rhetoric and Poetic: A Rehabilitation," *Southern Speech Communication Journal*, 38 (1972), 29–31.

[9]Plato, of course, caricatured Gorgias in his dialogue by that name. Given Plato's notion of a knowable, absolute truth, this is perhaps understandable. However, those who know Gorgias's rhetoric only from the Platonic perspective will have a distorted view. This is well documented by Gronbeck and in the essay by R. L. Enos, "The Epistemology of Gorgias' Rhetoric: A Re-examination," *Southern Speech Communication Journal*, 42 (1976), 35–51.

[10]For a discussion of Plato's own rather totalitarian view of the proper application of rhetoric, see C. Kauffman, "The Axiological Foundations of Plato's Theory of Rhetoric," *Central States Speech Journal*, 33 (1982), 353–366.

[11]A representative sample of this clash is illustrated in T. M. Perkins, "Isocrates and Plato: Relativism vs. Idealism," *Southern Speech Communication Journal*, 50 (1984), 49–66.

[12]Kennedy, *Classical Rhetoric*, p. 30. Such stylistic devices included *antithesis* —the use of opposites of terminology or meaning in contrasting clauses; *isocolon* —the repetitive use of two or more clauses with the same number of syllables; *parison* —the use of parallel structures; *homoeoteleuton* —the use of a series of two or more clauses ending with the same or rhyming words.

[13]Gorgias's use of *kairos* is examined in R. A. Engnell, "Implications for Communication of the Rhetorical Epistemology of Gorgias of Leontini," *Western Speech*, 37 (1973), 177–178.

[14]M. Untersteiner, *The Sophists*, translated by K. Freeman (London: Oxford University Press, 1954), as quoted in Kennedy, *Persuasion in Greece*, p. 67.

[15]Enos, "Epistemology of Gorgias," pp. 45–46.

[16]D. L. Clark, *Rhetoric in Greco–Roman Education* (New York: Columbia University Press, 1957), p. 25.

[17]Kennedy, *Persuasion in Greece*, pp. 58–61. See also D. C. Bryant, "Rhetoric: Its Function and Its Scope," *Quarterly Journal of Speech*, 39 (1953), 401–424; and B. Smith, "Corax and Probability," *Quarterly Journal of Speech*, 7 (1921), 13–42.

[18]Although this evaluation of Plato is by far the most widely accepted, there are scholars who take a different point of view. See E. Black, "Plato's View of Rhetoric," *Quarterly Journal of Speech*, 44 (1958), 361–374; R. W. Quimby, "The Growth of Plato's Perception of Rhetoric," *Philosophy and Rhetoric*, 7 (1964), 71–79; and D. S. Kaufner, "The Influence of Plato's Developing Psychology on His Views of Rhetoric," *Quarterly Journal of Speech*, 64 (1978), 63–78.

[19]An interesting survey of other Aristotelian works is provided by K. V. Erickson, "The Lost Rhetorics of Aristotle," *Communication Monographs*, 43 (1976), 229–237.

[20]The extent to which Aristotle's work was based on systematic observation is examined in D. J. Stanton and G. F. Berquist, "Aristotle's Rhetoric: Empiricism or Conjecture?" *Southern Speech Communication Journal*, 41 (1975), 69–81.

[21]Book I, Chapter 1, 11, 135a. Unless otherwise noted, citations are from the translation by W. R. Roberts (New York: Modern Library, 1954).

[22]T. M. Conley, "The Enthymeme in Perspective," *Quarterly Journal of Speech, 70* (1984), 168–187; E. W. Wiley, "The Enthymeme: Idioms of Persuasion," *Quarterly Journal of Speech, 42* (1956), 19–24; R. L. Lanigan, "Enthymeme: The Rhetorical Species of Aristotle's Syllogism," *Southern Speech Communication Journal 39* (1974), 207–222.

[23]Kennedy, *Classical Rhetoric,* pp. 70–71.

[24]C. S. Baldwin, *Ancient Rhetoric and Poetic* (Gloucester, MA: Peter Smith, 1959), pp. 19–20.

[25]A detailed biographical sketch is provided in G. A. Kennedy, *The Art of Rhetoric in the Roman World* (Princeton, NJ: Princeton University Press, 1972), pp. 103–108.

[26]For a discussion of Cicero's career in the Roman courts, see R. L. Enos, "Cicero's Forensic Oratory: The Manifestation of Power in the Roman Republic," *Southern Speech Communication Journal, 40* (1975), 377–394.

[27]Baldwin, *Ancient Rhetoric,* pp. 38–39.

[28]Kennedy accords *De Oratore* equal status with Aristotle's *Rhetoric.* See: *Rhetoric in the Roman World,* p. 205.

[29]Clark, *Greco–Roman Education,* pp. 83–84.

[30]Baldwin, *Ancient Rhetoric,* p. 53. See also W. E. Hoogestraat, "Memory: The Lost Canon?" *Quarterly Journal of Speech, 46* (1960), 141–147.

[31]Cicero's concern with the character of the orator is not controversial. The implications of that concern are. For a review, see S. M. Halloran, "Tradition and Theory in Rhetoric," *Quarterly Journal of Speech, 62* (1976), 234–241.

[32]Baldwin, *Ancient Rhetoric,* p. 62.

[33]G. A. Kennedy, *Quintilian* (New York: Twayne Publishers, 1969), pp. 47–50.

[34]W. Taylor, *Tudor Figures of Rhetoric* (Whitewater, WI: Language Press, 1972), p. 4.

[35]Clark, *Greco–Roman Education,* pp. 264–265.

[36]Kennedy, *Classical Rhetoric,* pp. 96–99. See also R. Nadeau, "*Rhetoric Ad Herennium:* Commentary and Translation of Book I," *Speech Monographs, 16* (1949), 57–68.

[37]Kennedy, *Quintilian,* pp. 139–141.

[38]R. K. Eich, "When Rhetoric Flourished in the Carolingian Empire," *Journal of the Western Speech Communication Association, 40* (1976), 57–61; Kennedy, *Classical Rhetoric,* pp. 182–184.

[39]Augustine, *On Christian Doctrine,* trans. D. W. Robertson, Jr., *The Library of Liberal Arts* (Indianapolis: Bobbs–Merrill, 1958), p. 134.

[40]Kennedy, *Classical Rhetoric,* p. 153.

[41]J. Bliese, "The Study of Rhetoric in the Twelfth Century," *Quarterly Journal of Speech, 63* (1977), pp. 365–366, 377–378.

[42]Kennedy, *Classical Rhetoric,* pp. 90–91.

[43]J. O. Ward, "Glosses and Commentaries on Cicero's *Rhetorica,*" in ed. J. J. Murphy, *Medieval Eloquence* (Berkeley: University of California Press, 1978), pp. 53–56.

[44]J. J. Murphy, ed., *Three Medieval Rhetorical Arts* (Berkeley: University of California Press, 1971), pp. ix–x.

[45]A detailed treatment of dictamen can be found in S. R. Hill, Jr., "Dictamen: That Bastard of Literature and the Law," *Central States Speech Journal*, 24 (1973), 117–124; P. E. Kane, "Dictamen: The Medieval Rhetoric of Letter Writing," *Central States Speech Journal*, 21 (1971), 224–230. See also Kennedy, *Classical Rhetoric*, pp. 185–187; C. B. Faulhaber, "The *Summa Dictaminis* of Guido Faba," in ed. Murphy, *Medieval Eloquence*, pp. 85–111.

[46]Murphy, *Three Medieval Arts*, pp. xv–xvi, 3–4.

[47]C. S. Baldwin, *Medieval Rhetoric and Poetic to 1400* (Gloucester, MA: Peter Smith,

6

Contemporary Rhetorical Theory:
Burke, Perelman, and Their
Counterparts

Building on the foundation provided by Greek and Roman theorists, contemporary rhetoricians frame communication as it influences decision making in modern society. The labels used by society vary with time. We may talk about rhetoric, or oratory, or discussion, or interpersonal relationships, but what we study remains the same: the process of social influence. Modern theorists, like their Greek forebears, want to know how the people in a society use communication as a tool to achieve their personal goals.[1]

We have seen that communication is essentially a social act that takes place within a context. As society changes, the context of communication changes. Thus, modern theorists cannot rely solely on the classical works. Aristotle's analysis of the motives of ancient Athenians is simply not an accurate description of modern Americans. We must reach an understanding of the nature of *our* society to understand how we communicate within it.

THE ORGANIZATION OF MODERN SOCIETY

Obviously, there are basic differences in the organization of society from classical to modern times. Modern technology, economics, government, religion, and science are all dramatically different from those of Plato and Aristotle. Among the most important differences is our willingness to tolerate competing value systems, or, as it is most commonly labeled, a *pluralistic* society.[2]

Classical societies tended toward monolithic ethical and philosophical structures. They were marked by a tendency for competing systems to struggle for institutional supremacy. Whenever one ethical or philosophical system

116

emerged as dominant, it ruthlessly eradicated the system that it had supplanted. It claimed all "truth" for itself. As a consequence, decision making in classical societies was unique. In the Middle Ages, that decision-making process became known as *scholasticism.* In essence, scholasticism was *a priori* reasoning: all the "truths" were already known and referenced to the established values (great masters, scripture, etc.). When a question arose, people got the answer by referring to the "truths."[3] If the answer was not directly available, then they engaged in interpretation. The method of interpretation has generally been labeled *dialectic,* or the search for truth among truths.

Contemporary Western society has gradually realized that differing value systems can coexist. This pluralistic society created the need for decision-making theory in communication. *Decision-making theory* in a pluralistic society demands the understanding of three assumptions:

1. *There is no such thing as a universally accepted absolute truth.* Put simply, there is *nothing* that *everybody* believes.

2. *Humans are the measure of all things.* Decisions are made by people, and the decision maker must recognize that it is the interaction between idea and individual that leads to action. We can bewail the blindness of our society if we will, but if we want to communicate effectively, we must perceive and accept it as reality.[4]

3. *The influence of emotions on decision making is an inescapable consequence of our humanness.* We are not purely logical beasts. It is an error to assume absolute rationality on the part of decision makers. Furthermore, it makes little sense to talk about adapting to the emotional situation of participants as "bad." There is nothing debasing or wrong about studying human transactions from a psychological analysis of the people who are doing the transacting.

Communication or Confrontation?

Acceptance of a new understanding of communication has not come easily. Problems have arisen because of two premises about human communication which began to gain adherents only within the last two hundred years. One premise is that *in situations of human conflict, symbolic interaction (or communication) is to be preferred to physical encounter.* Civilized humans settle more differences through discussion than through force. The other premise is that *maximum communication is always to be preferred to the restricting or preventing of social influence.* Americans have zealously guarded freedom of speech and freedom of the press. We have assumed that our society must keep open the channels of exchange. The revered "marketplace" philosophy has taught that the truth wins in any open exchange. Important as these two beliefs seem, they are *not* part of the long tradition of Western society.

In the second half of the twentieth century, both premises have come under siege. For some, the first premise, the doctrine of communication, has been discarded in favor of the *doctrine of confrontation*. Some people have declared that communication is capitulation and that physical encounter *should* become the preferred mode for bringing about social change. (The symbolic drama of the peaceful demonstration has given way to direct force, seizure, and even violence.) Urban terrorism has become a fact of life for much of the Western world.[5] The second premise has been discarded on two grounds: (1) maximizing communication in conflict situations intensifies the problem without solving it, and (2) worthy ends can justify obstructing or interfering with freedom of speech by members of a *corrupt* establishment. (Heckling and clamor often have been used deliberately to prevent speaking by those who oppose the new social revolt.) Many people seem to be aiming at a return to the days of scholasticism and monolithic values, where only the strongest survived through brute force, not logic.

Our society is only beginning to sort out the claims made for the doctrine of confrontation in its challenge to the doctrine of communication. Rhetorical theorists have always been intensely practical, and our concern today is the search for what will work, for what is genuine and functional rather than self-defeating. We can assume neither that the past is universally good nor that new claims have been proved merely because they have been shouted with great enthusiasm.[6]

THE NEW RHETORICIANS

Two theorists, Kenneth Burke and Chaim Perelman, stand out as offering significant contributions to our understanding of modern rhetoric. The first was Burke.[7] Widely hailed as the foremost rhetorical theorist of the early twentieth century, Burke advanced a comprehensive theory of human interaction. He argued that, in the process of understanding the world around us, we perceive of people as either "friendly" or "unfriendly." Friendly people were defined as those individuals sufficiently sensitive that they perceive our problems without explanation, and sufficiently concerned for our best interests that they take action to alleviate problems without our pleading. All other people, in Burke's eyes, were part of the large group of "unfriendlies" in the world. Having reached such an evaluation, we select strategies for dealing with the situation. For us, that strategy is rhetoric. Unfriendlies are the ones to whom rhetoric is addressed.

It is important to understand several terms.[8] *Rhetoric*, to Burke, is the use and study of persuasive resources. In Burke's words, the basic function of rhetoric is "the use of words by human agents to form attitudes or to induce actions in other human beings."[9] *Identification* and *consubstantiality* are terms introduced by Burke in his analysis of the means by which the function of rhetoric is achieved. They are used to denote the process through which the speaker establishes psychological unity with the audience. Another way of looking at these terms is to say that "friendlies" are people with whom you are consubstantial. Identification is the process by which you go about changing unfriendlies into friendlies. *Division*, in Burke's lexicon, is the complement to identification. It is the state of human affairs which gives rise to rhetoric. Because we perceive the world differently, we stand apart from each other. Yet standing apart, we still must cooperate in society. The creation of a motive for cooperation is the role of rhetoric.

Burke's Rhetorical Theory

Burke constructed a rhetorical theory from the classic Aristotelian definition of rhetoric as the art of persuasion. Humans, to Burke, are symbol-using animals. Through the manipulation of symbols, we establish the motive for cooperation among people. Burke saw manipulation as inherent in the nature of language. Thus, all literature falls within the province of rhetoric because it is intended to have an effect on the reader. Art is a means of communication because the artist intends to secure some sort of response from the observer.

Although he is consistent with classical theorists, in at least two ways Burke went beyond them in drawing the bounds of rhetoric. First, he included among rhetorical acts those things that are done *unconsciously* as well as those that are deliberate. To Burke, intent was not necessary for a specific symbolic act to function persuasively. Second, Burke incorporated *nonverbal elements* into his theory of communication. He observed that equipment in a doctor's office should be seen not only for its diagnostic usefulness (apparatus), but also as a function of the rhetoric of medicine (imagery).

Burke's additions to the classical understanding of the nature of rhetoric have provided a theoretical footing for many scholars as they examine the rhetoric of clothing, of mass or mob actions, of witchcraft, or of hysteria. Burke believed that communication is *the* central process of society. We use symbols to relate to each other and to achieve cooperation. Without symbols, there would be no communication, thus no social structure.

Burke also observed that society depends on order. No government can survive very long solely through the use of force. Communication provides the means of creating images that legitimize authority. As children, we are taught that certain symbols (the flag, the president, etc.) uphold the established social order. Social movements arise from the failure of communication between groups in the society. The result is a rejection of the symbols of authority and of the established hierarchy. Burke argued that four basic motives arise in human communication: *hierarchy*, which reflects the human desire for order; *guilt*, which comes from the rejection of an established hierarchy; *victimage*, the sacrifice of a scapegoat to epitomize the evils of society; and *redemption*, the restoration of order through the establishment of a new hierarchy.[10]

For example, political order is important to Americans. When Richard Nixon was first implicated in Watergate, many people simply could not believe the president could be involved in an illegality (even though our history is filled with such involvement). Our desire for order, on which Nixon played in his successful presidential elections, Burke would argue is a motive for hierarchy. Once people realized that Nixon was guilty, they felt guilty, too. Psychologically, many people were still longing for a return to the hierarchy. To restore order, to reach redemption, scapegoats were needed (John Dean, H. R. Halderman) on whom we could heap our scorn. Replacing Nixon with Ronald Reagan and substituting Oliver North as the scapegoat provides a similar example.

In deriving his definition of rhetoric, Burke examined meanings already associated with the term. His studies led him to accept the view of rhetoric as persuasion, where rhetoric was "addressed" to a specific audience and aimed toward a particular purpose. Burke then asked, "How is persuasion accomplished? How is the audience manipulated by the rhetor so that his purpose may be achieved?" He supplied the answer in his concept of "identification." You can, said Burke, persuade a person only to the degree that you "talk his language." By "language," Burke referred not to English or Russian, for example, but to images, ideas, attitudes, and values. Persuasion is accomplished by presentation of the message in such gestures, order, tones, and content that the audience identifies with the speaker. It is the sense of being identified, the feeling of being united with the speaker, that makes a particular message persuasive. When Person A identifies with Person B, then Person A is made consubstantial with Person B. The greater the degree of identification, the more signs of consubstantiality will emerge, and the more effective the persuasive effort will be.

You may be interested to notice the impact of Burke's concept on a *sociological* approach to human interaction. Identification provides the source or motive for cooperation in social endeavor. The greater the identification or evidence of consubstantiality, the greater the cooperation among members of a social order. This is verified in primitive societies, which tend to have a high homogeneity (i.e., members of the society are more alike in their wants, attitudes, values). Such societies tend toward greater cooperation among individuals than is the norm in modern, industrialized societies. The same differences in cooperation may frequently be observed in small towns versus large cities, and may be attributed to the more heterogeneous nature inherent in a city.

Implied in the notion of identification is the concept of *division*, which Burke defined as the sense of having different values or attitudes toward the world. If division did not exist, if we were not set apart psychologically, there would be no need to be concerned with the establishment of identification. If pure identification existed, there would be no disagreement and no strife because there would be no motive for strife.

In the same sense, strife would be impossible in a state of absolute separation. Unaware of each other, we would not quarrel. We would have no sense of a necessity for cooperation, and thus no possibility for disagreement over action. In Burke's terms, strife must first come through the symbolic ground of communication, the first necessary condition for verbal combat.

The nature of society, however, is that identification and division exist simultaneously. The degree to which one or the other dominates a particular situation is ambiguous. This, to Burke, is what constitutes the "invitation to rhetoric."

Alistair Cooke, in discussing the role of critic in society, wrote, "The existence of critics, good, bad, or indifferent, is a firm clause in the social contract between the governors and the governed in any nation that is not a dictatorship."[11] In *A Grammar of Motives*, Burke advocated a "dramatistic" approach to the analysis of our actions and motivations.[12] This critical structure is appropriate to rhetoric because of Burke's position that language and thought serve as modes for inducing action. By focusing on the goal of rhetoric as persuasion, Burke clearly falls within the framework of classical rhetorical theory. Burke himself was quite comfortable in harness with the classicists. He saw his statements as supplemental to, not as a substitute for, traditional definitions of rhetoric.

Burke observed that sometimes the aim of rhetoric is an immediate response or action. In those cases, clearly, rhetoric is best understood as the process of persuasion. At times, however, the goal of rhetoric aims not at our actions but at our thoughts. Although the association is indirect, Burke insisted on pointing to the function of thoughts or attitudes as precursors to action. Thus, by viewing attitudes as incipient action, attitudinal appeals remain tied to the persuasive process and thus to our objects of rhetoric.

The *pentad* is Burke's label for the organizational pattern or structure that he designed to study rhetorical motivations. Its terminology is drawn from the analysis of drama, which led to the use of the term "dramatistic" in describing his critical method.[13] The elements of the pentad are identified briefly as follows:

1. *Act* —The communicative message. In terms consistent with Burke's theory, the act is the block of symbols chosen to achieve persuasion. In everyday terms, it is the speech of the politician or the sermon of the minister. In contemporary life, it may include a commercial message you listened to on your car radio or an advertisement on a billboard. Burke is perfectly willing to extend the definition of act to encompass symbolic behavior, so that act may be the march of civil rights demonstrators, or the brick heaved through an administration building window by an irate alumnus, or the self-immolation of a Buddhist monk.

2. *Scene* —Now generally called "situation" by political commentators. It is the broad background against which the act is performed. It is an America torn by the Great Depression listening to the voice of a new president declaring, "All we have to fear is fear itself." Analysis of scene in Burke's method extends to a consideration of all the economic, political, social, and rhetorical factors present in the mind of the audience when the act occurs.

3. *Agent*—The source of the communicative message. The agent may be Martin Luther King, Jr., standing on the steps of the Lincoln Memorial affirming his dream, or John F. Kennedy announcing the passing of power to a new generation of Americans, or the anonymous television figure in a white lab jacket assuring us that a new drug product is more effective than its competitors, or Karl Mauldin selling the safety of travelers' checks. The Agent is the speaker, the actor, the politician, the writer. The agent is the one who acts.

4. *Agency*—The means or instruments used in the communicative act. Agency refers to how the agent went about carrying out the act. In a physical sense, agency might include the brick thrown through the window. In the symbolic sense, agency is most often the style and phrasing that the agent uses to frame his or her act.

5. *Purpose*—The aim or goal of the act. Since Burke defined the function of rhetoric as persuasion, he saw purpose as the response from the audience that the agent sought. The purpose includes thought as well as action and both long-range and short-range objectives.

For the student who plans a career as a practitioner of rhetoric, Burke's pentad is most useful as a sort of "checklist" in planning persuasive messages. It serves as a reminder that effective communication must go far beyond the mere composition of the words of a message.

The Rhetoric of Perelman

Among the most acclaimed efforts at sorting out the conflict between communication and confrontation is the work of Chaim Perelman of the University of Paris. Perelman's major work, *The New Rhetoric: A Treatise on Argumentation*, examines the process of argument and the ways argument functions within the larger framework of the communication process.[14] Although Perelman's ideas are consistent with the classical rhetorical theories of Aristotle, Cicero, and Quintilian, they go much further in their treatment of *the process of argument.*

Perelman began his work by breaking away from the intellectual evolution of reason and reasoning that dominated Western thought for over three hundred years.[15] Descartes, in his systemization of traditional theory, viewed the world as consisting of "rights" and "wrongs." This position is best summarized by the statement, "Whenever two men come to opposite decisions about the same matter, one of them at least must certainly be in the wrong." The philosophical orientation comes from the Aristotelian notion of division and categories: *A* must either be *B* or not-*B*; it cannot be both. Growing out of such notions are the ideas of the "necessity" of proof and the "self-evident" nature of truth.[16] Perelman did not deny that there may be self-evident truths.[17] He questioned if necessary, self-evident truths have any application whatsoever to the realm of rhetoric. He observed that the very nature of argumentation is opposed to necessity or self-evidence, since we do not rationally deliberate when the solution is obvious or self-evident. Some of our acts are necessary in the sense that they must occur. Such acts, however, are *not* the subject of deliberation. If you are in a building when a fire breaks out and are aware that there is only one exit from the building, it makes no sense to deliberate over what action to take. Argument is restricted to the arena of the credible, the plausible, the probable, at least to the degree that this latter eludes the certainty of numerical calculations.[18]

The concept of *dialectic*, then, is properly defined as a subject that is concerned *not* with facts or truths or reality (whatever these terms might mean), but with opinions. Opinions, Perelman insisted, are nothing more than theses adhered to with varying degrees of intensity. Recognition of variance in the intensity of belief led Perelman to see that argument must be developed in terms of the specific audience that will be the target of the argument.[19] We must understand that a change in audience demands a change in the argumentation.[20] If the purpose of argument is to act on the mind of the audience, then in evaluating that argument, we must not lose sight of the *quality* of minds that the argument has successfully convinced.[21] Perelman suggested that the intellectual value of a belief can be measured by the intellectual qualities of its adherents.

Prerequisites for an Argument.   An examination of the process of argument requires an understanding of the essential prerequisites for the existence of an argument. Perelman suggested three such prerequisites. First, for argumentation to exist, there must be an effective community of minds realized at a given moment. There must be agreement, at least in principle, on the formation of the intellectual community. After that, the parties must agree on debating a specific question together. Perelman did not argue that these conditions must be stable or prolonged in any way; they must simply exist at the time that argumentation is to take place. A fairly complex set of conditions is needed for the formation of community of minds. Among the most important are some evidence of *a common language* and some *reason why discussion should begin.* When Perelman referred to a common language, he used the phrase in the same way as Burke: Participants in a dialogue must share sufficient semantic space to decode language in reasonably similar ways. One reason why academicians and manual laborers seldom engage in argument is that in most cases they do not share a common language.

A second necessary prerequisite for argument emerges when we consider that the speaker's audience may vary considerably from situation to situation. It never includes *all* human beings. There are some people with whom contact may be superfluous or even undesirable, others with whom we cannot be bothered to talk, and others to whom we give orders. Therefore, to engage in argument, we must attach some importance to gaining the consent of the other, to securing his or her mental cooperation. Note, as an adjunct to this condition, that it is a compliment to be engaged in argument. One's engaging in argument with another affirms the worth and importance of that person. It also affirms an equality of status between parties, since, in the case of wildly superior status, the most likely avenue is to issue orders rather than to engage in argument.

Perelman's third essential requirement for the existence of argument is that there must be a willingness to listen. Argument, by definition, is a two-way interaction. H. L. Mencken, in his "Rules for an Argument," wrote,

> What I admire most in any man is a serene spirit, a steady freedom from moral indignation . . . When he fights, he fights in the manner of a gentleman fighting a duel, not in that of a longshoreman clearing out a waterfront saloon. That is to say, he assumes that his opponent is as decent a man as he is, and just as honest—and perhaps, after all, right.[22]

Argument presumes that both parties will have the opportunity to express conflicting views. In many situations, the argumentative format is deliberately designed to ensure that opposing sides have an equal opportunity to express their views. Listening, to Perelman and other contemporary theorists, goes beyond simple hearing. Listening implicitly admits the possibility of accepting the other's point of view. Perhaps some of the difficulties arising in communication (between parents and children, teachers and students, workers and managers, etc.) can be traced to the perception of one party that their view will never be accepted. Such a perception must inevitably produce frustration and a sense that we have been cheated. Surely, we can say that to engage in pseudo-argument, to hear without listening, to give another the chance to "have their say" when the decision is already rendered, is an intellectually fraudulent act.

The Speaker and Audience.

There is an illusion, or at least a frequently used phrase, common to the scientific community that facts "speak for themselves." Facts make such an irresistible and indelible imprint on our minds that we are forced to adhere to them regardless of our inclinations. The scientist is frequently guilty of assuming that facts exist in such a way that they are perceived identically by everyone. In terms of the way in which the human mind works, of course, this is a naive assessment of information-processing systems. Therefore, attention must be paid by the arguer to draw the attention of an indifferent public to the premises under debate.

If the purpose of argument is to secure adherence to a premise, it is easy to understand that "truth" is always relative to *the audience whom the arguer wishes to influence.* This is not the same as saying the audience to whom the argument is physically presented. A trusting person might believe, after perusing the *Congressional Record*, that the daily business of the Senate and the House of Representatives is to sit alertly as members present hour after hour of speeches on various topics. In fact, this is not what happens. Most speeches in Congress are delivered before practically empty chambers. Many were never "given" at all. They were inserted into the *Record* to create the appearance of presentation. The officials whose words are thus recorded are not so much concerned with influencing their fellow legislators as they are with "speaking" to their constituents back home.

The speaker needs to know who his or her actual audience is. The great orator is one who possesses the art of taking into consideration, in argument, the composite nature of the audience. In assessing argumentation, the important thing is not knowing what the speaker regards as true or important, but knowing the view of those being addressed. Gracian long ago summarized the matter by observing that a public speech "is like a feast, where the dishes are made to please the guests, and not the cooks." Arguments that are appropriate to one set of circumstances may appear ridiculous in others. The speaker must always adapt.

Occasions for Rhetoric.   In ordinary dialogue, we try to persuade our audience to bring about some immediate or future action. Most of our daily arguments develop at this practical level. It is, indeed, in daily conversation that the opportunity to engage in argumentation most commonly presents itself. With this view of argumentation, it is easy to understand why modern rhetorical theorists view argument as *central* to the communication process. Even if most of us will never engage in courtroom fight, or battle over a crucial bit of legislation, we cannot avoid the "give and take" of social interaction. By effectively using rhetorical skills, we improve our own power to influence others and achieve goals that are important to each of us.

Rhetoric and the Process of Education.   Perelman posed a series of interesting questions in his examination of the rhetoric of education. He began by looking at the ancient puzzle of the difference between the concepts of "education" and "propaganda." Common usage finds no problem in making a distinction: Education is good and propaganda is bad. This distinction, however, is based solely on the point of view of the person who attaches the labels. Americans commonly define as "education" the attempts by schoolteachers to inculcate values such as self-reliance, cooperation, nonviolence, and patriotism. However, the attempts by Soviet or Chinese educational systems to promote analogous values in their students are dismissed as "propaganda."

Perelman managed to make a more defensible distinction between propaganda and education. He noted that the propagandist must, prior to the effective transmission of his or her message, gain the goodwill of his or her audience. The educator, on the other hand, has been commissioned by the community to be the spokesperson for the commonly accepted values of society. As such, the educator enjoys a credibility attached to this "office" and begins without the burden of the propagandist. As the economist Gordon Tullock notes,

> The theory that we must "educate our governors" is frequently advanced to support public education in Switzerland, Sweden, etc. Further, most dictatorships favor widespread public education. In their case it is also, of course, an ideal

opportunity to indoctrinate the children in whatever happens to be the dominant ideology. Indeed, such indoctrination is presumably the basic reason that churches always and everywhere have been much interested in education.[23]

Whatever the level of subject matter, it is always assumed by society that the educational speaker's discourse will defend values that are a matter of consensus in the group that commissioned him or her. Even if, on occasion, the speaker does not express truth, it is assumed that the educator is not attempting to destroy the existing system. Instances where this assumption is shaken always lead to bitter reactions by the commissioning community. Thus, many people expressed hostility toward anti-Vietnam War college professors during the mid-1960s. At that time, the majority of American society supported the war, and felt a sense of betrayal at the discovery that many college teachers were advising students to resist the draft, to refuse military service, even to flee to Canada. The basis of the hostility was a sense that the professors, employed as educators, had violated the purpose of education. They were actively working against the values of the community paying their salaries.

His examination of education led Perelman to redefine the type of speaking known in classical rhetoric as "epideictic." In Perelman's conception, epideictic speaking serves to increase the intensity of adherence of commonly held values in both audience and speaker. In contrast, argumentation always has as its purpose the modification of existing values. Thus, argumentation and epideictic speaking are antithetical forms of communication. Remember the necessary prerequisites for argumentation. They confirm that the roles played by participants in argumentation are essentially contradictory to those of the participants in an educational (or epideictic) communication setting.

The nature of societies, as well as individuals, is to value the ideals and principles they have chosen. We prize the status quo. Because they desire to promote existing value systems, societies naturally move in the direction of encouraging epideictic speaking. We may note some prevalent attitudes toward society per se on the part of individual members. Remember that we are not considering evaluation of a particular society, but rather attitudes toward the concept of society itself. This is an important distinction. You may dislike a particular play yet remain a supporter of plays as an art form. We may equally disapprove of certain values within society while supporting the concept of a society. Most people value society. By introducing order into human relationships, society allows predictability. It is the structure of the game that gives the tokens (attitudes) meaning. It is, therefore, safer and more comfortable to exist within a society, and most choose to do so. Beyond this, societial structures are stable. They have to be stable to allow the maximum planning in the drive to secure tokens. This drive toward stability is so pronounced that we may state it almost as a law.

For society to achieve stability, it must secure the support, voluntarily given, of the people who comprise the social group. Returning to the basic premise of motivation, we know that people will support the social structure if and only if they perceive it as a means of increasing their supply of things they value.

Perelman observed that one measure of the security of any society is the degree that it allows argumentation as opposed to epideictic discourse. No established structure ever really welcomes dissent (which, with its concern for change in the status quo, is the essence of argumentation). A mature society is secure in its values and confident of its worth and is more likely to tolerate argumentation than one that is basically insecure. As observers of society, we can learn to evaluate the strength of our own nation by its attitudes toward those who challenge commonly accepted values.

Participants in Argumentation.   Argumentation demands a high degree of commitment on the part of the participants. It is impossible to regard argument as merely an intellectual exercise divorced from all concerns with the outcome of the issue. The stress of the argumentative situation is too great to expect that we will subject ourselves to it without a deep and sincere concern with the positions being advocated. Objectivity, as it applies to argumentation, does not allow the separation of an assertion from the person who makes it. Being a disinterested spectator does not give us the right to participate in and influence the outcome of the argument. Unlike scientific dispute, where the solution of some problem comes from a knowledge of the techniques that enable a solution to be reached, interference in controversy (i.e., argument) is made when we are involved in the controversy. Only to the degree that it represents impartiality is neutrality a qualification to judge. Objectivity is not a desirable quality. Thoughts that lead to action are different from scientifically stated relationships.

A *fanatic* clings to a disputed idea for which no unquestioned proof can be furnished, but nevertheless refuses to consider the possibility of submitting it for free discussion. Since rhetorical proof is never completely "necessary" proof, the thinking person adheres to conclusions only for the time and circumstances of the original argument. Argumentation aims at a choice among possible ideas. This role of argumentation in decision making is denied by both the skeptic and the fanatic. In the absence of compelling reason, they are inclined to give violence a free hand, rejecting personal commitment and a responsibility for making a decision among *possible* answers.[24]

OTHER PHILOSOPHICAL VIEWS
OF THE TWENTIETH CENTURY

Burke and Perelman are among the more important rhetorical theorists of the twentieth century. Other theorists, however, owing their allegiance primarily to the discipline of philosophy, have had an impact on the rise of rhetoric. At least three deserve mention here: I.A. Richards, Richard M. Weaver, and

Stephen Toulmin. It is important to note that the twentieth century has brought about several philosophical traditions which influence rhetoric.

In the United States, the most dominant position is that taken by the *pragmatists*. Especially notable among these philosophers are Charles Sanders Peirce, William James (discussed in Chapter 7), John Dewey, and George Herbert Mead (discussed in Chapter 9). The position of the pragmatists is that communication provides the means to an end. The primary consideration and evaluative tool, then, is effectiveness—but effectiveness over the long haul. Although these views came from philosophers, they have developed into psychological and social psychological issues and are covered in other chapters. In a way, Burke may be placed among the pragmatists.

In continental Europe, more subjective views sprang forth. Most notable among these philosophies are those based in *existentialism* and *phenomenology*. In some cases, the concepts were versed in *Marxism* as well. Psychologists such as Carl Rogers are discussed in the next chapter; others, such as Jurgen Habermas, are discussed in Chapter 12.

In England, the philosophical concept of *positivism* had a major influence. To some extent, this notion has been examined in the work of Korzybski. As noted in Chapter 4, this view sees certain problems with language and attempts to resolve some of those problems by ascertaining measurable qualities. Much of contemporary cybernetic views—especially computer programming—take this approach since coding is such an important element in the computer field.

Richards, Weaver, and Toulmin added to what we know about rhetoric in different ways. We discuss each in terms of their major contributions since none has produced such a complete view of the rhetorical act as have Burke and Perelman.

I. A. Richards

British-born Richards was a proponent of the *positivistic* view. He was greatly influenced by G. E. Moore, and he was concerned about the question, "What do we mean?" Richards and C. K. Ogden published a book entitled, *The Meaning of Meaning.*[25] They attempted to tap the laws of language. As critics of traditional views on rhetoric, Ogden and Richards felt they needed to question our underlying assumptions about the nature of rhetoric. They attempted to determine the smallest units of language (similar to Birdwhistell's allokines in nonverbal communication; see Chapter 3). Finally, they suggested that rhetoric owns a central place among the disciplines. As we discussed in Chapter 1, Richards felt that perception is very important, that every stimulus we receive leaves an imprint (an *engram*) on us, which can be revived later.[26] As discussed in the earlier section on general semantics, Richards and Ogden generated the triangle that indicates that symbols simply "stand for" referents. Like other positivists, Richards suggested that we cannot use "objective" language in the same ways that we use "subjective" language. Korzybski discussed the use of quotation marks, whereas Richards developed a series of *specialized* quotation marks (pp. 17–43). General semantics is seldom referred to these days, but students of rhetoric may still encounter the name of I. A. Richards.

Richard M. Weaver

Whereas Richards attempted to construct language to make it a better indicator of "reality," American-born Richard M. Weaver was more concerned with *knowledge* and *truth*.[27] Weaver developed a three-part division of knowledge: ideas, beliefs, and metaphysical dreams. At the first level are specific *ideas* "about things—those everyday physical entities we encounter." At the second level, we find *beliefs:* "convictions, theories, laws, generalizations, or concepts that order the world of facts."[28] Weaver discussed how we generalize about "things" we encounter in specific situations. The *metaphysical dream* is "an intuitive feeling about the immanent nature of reality." (p. 51). He compared and contrasted rhetoric and dialectic, viewing both as means of gaining knowledge. Whereas others viewed dialectic as inquiry, Weaver thought that rhetoric *used* dialectic, asked us to believe it, and motivated us to act on it. He was much more a critic of rhetoric than a rhetorical theorist. Among those items he felt were causing a deterioration in rhetoric were

> scientism, nominalism; semantic positivism; uncritical homage to the theory of evolution; radical egalitarianism; pragmatism; cultural relativism; materialism; emphasis on techniques at the expense of goals; idolization of youth; progressive education; disparagement of historical consciousness; deleterious effects of the mass media; and degenerate literature, music, and art (p. 67).

In other words, Weaver was critical of most of the ideas of the positivistic school, as well as the pragmatic school.

Stephen Toulmin

British-born Stephen Toulmin's concern was with the Aristotelian method of logic. Unlike the general semanticists, however, he attacked that logic on the basis of its structure instead of on the basis of language.[29] Like Perelman, he was concerned with *argumentation.* Toulmin attempted to formulate a practical system of logic. Like Perelman, he objected to absolutism. In so doing, he said there are two kinds of arguments: *analytic* and *substantial*.[30] The analytic argument goes no further than the premises stated in the argument; however, the substantial argument involves an inference from some data to other data. Like the general semanticists, he argued that formal logic (dependent on mathematics as the standard of logic) assumes no concept of change. He also opposed the relativistic standards, indicating that there are *no* standards at all. Toulmin's work also includes a critique of how generalized knowledge comes about. He suggested that much of what becomes "knowledge" is based on papers presented at academic conventions. To improve our knowledge,

Toulmin suggested, we must develop more sophisticated and more innovative means for critiquing data provided to us. Hence, we must constantly reevaluate our methods of evaluation.

REVIEW

Only the existence of an argumentation that is neither compelling nor arbitrary can give meaning to freedom. Freedom is a state in which a reasonable choice can be exercised. If freedom were no more than necessary adherence to a previously given natural order, it would exclude all possibility of choice. If the exercise of freedom were not based on reasons, every choice would be irrational and would be reduced to an arbitrary decision operating in an intellectual void. Because of the possibility of argumentation that provides reasons, but not compelling reasons, it is possible to escape the dilemma between adherence to a universally valid truth or recourse to violence to secure acceptance for our opinions and decisions.

The theory of argumentation helps to provide what a logic of value judgments has tried in vain to provide, namely, the justification for the possibility of a human community in the sphere of action when this justification *cannot* be based on reality or objective truth.

Table 6–1 summarizes the material discussed in this chapter.

CRITIQUE

The works of Burke and Perelman are extensions of traditional rhetorical theory. The theories are basically untestable; they deal with society as a whole. The logic of Burke is particularly difficult to test since the theory is based on an abstraction: *consubstantiality.* Because of the societal approach, contemporary theory is hardly supportable or refutable. Burke is efficient, but his definitions of scene and agency are somewhat ambiguous. Reliability is questionable because of the difficulty in describing an ongoing pluralistic society; however, his is one of the few theories that deals with society at large. Burke has been used extensively in contemporary rhetorical studies, probably because of the ease with which researchers can use the pentad. Contemporary rhetorical theory is important because it allows us to understand the difficulties involved in creating a communicative message in a complex society.

Like Plato, contemporary theorists have been concerned with the truth. While Burke was concerned with the critical analysis of performance, he, too, was concerned with truth. Perelman, Richards, Weaver, and Toulmin, however, all may be considered theorists of knowledge. Their similarity with Plato can be noted in that all appear to be idealists in what may be considered a never-ending search for the truth. Their divergence from Plato, however, appears to be that contemporary queries of truth (epistemology) believe that not only does the truth itself change (the planet Earth is flat) but also our methods for discovering truth change. In a sense, then, all are critical of

TABLE 6-1 Summary Table

Name of Theory	Primary Theorists	Basic Principle	Constructs	Criteria	Analytic Approach	Limitations
Contemporary rhetorical theory	Kenneth Burke Chaim Perelman	There is no such thing as a universally accepted truth.	• Monolithic society • Pluralistic society	Pentad (Act, Scene, Agency, Agent, Purpose) Argument versus epideictic speech Communication versus confrontation	Pentad	Uses a societal approach which is difficult to test. Analytic tool (pentad) provides too much ambiguity to be useful as a testing device.

Aristotle's traditional logic. In the case of Richards, the logic was attacked in a manner similar to that of the general semanticists. According to Weaver, the traditional methods of logic (as well as its followers) are overly positivistic and overly pragmatic. Weaver believed that we have not been innovative in our search for the truth. The base that we need to focus on, then, is in evaluating our assumptions. According to Toulmin, we need to devise methods of logic that are more consistent with the "reality" around us.

The philosophical views, from Plato to Toulmin, find us in the same predicament that we discussed in Chapter 1. In essence, Platonists advocate that there is a "reality" in the world. Thus, we need to spend a great deal of time searching for the correct method of finding that reality, and thus in finding truth and knowledge. Other philosophers indicate that the only "reality" is in our perceptions. Since we cannot physically share our perceptions, we must search for communication tools to *approximate* our perceptions to share them with others. There are many views in between, including pragmatism. Pragmatism suggests that if one person asks another to "switch off the lights," it is relatively unimportant whether the perceptions of the interactants match. All that is important is whether the other person switched the lights off.

These philosophical perspectives, and their rhetorical theories, help to frame the verbal and nonverbal codes. The matching of perspectives provides a frame through which communication can occur. When perspectives do not seem to match, then we may determine that our frames are different (a southerner and a northerner might view the American Civil War differently) or our coding processes are different (a prochoice advocate and a prolife advocate may simply define "life" differently). Finally, there may be both a coding problem and a framing problem. In the next section we will see how these codes and frames provide a building perspective for individual communicators.

─────── ## NOTES AND REFERENCES ───────────

[1] Among others who argue for this perspective, see D. Ehninger, "On Systems of Rhetoric," *Philosophy and Rhetoric*, 1 (1968), 137–139.

[2] Many authors point up the impact of pluralism on contemporary rhetoric. Among others, see D. P. Cushman and P. K. Tompkins, "A Theory of Rhetoric for Contemporary Society," *Philosophy and Rhetoric*, 13 (1980), 43–67.

[3] Chaim Perelman describes this system in his essay "Rhetoric and Philosophy," *Philosophy and Rhetoric*, 1 (1968), 15–24.

[4] A thorough discussion of the "human" orientation of rhetoric is provided by R. B. Douglas, "An Aristotelian Orientation to Rhetorical Communication," *Philosophy and Rhetoric*, 7 (1974), 80–88.

[5] For a treatment of the increasing role of terrorism and its impact on communication, see A. P. Schmid and J. de Graaf, *Violence and Communication* (Beverly Hills, CA: Sage Publications, 1982).

[6]See F. E. Jandt, *Conflict Resolution Through Communication* (New York: Harper and Row, 1973). Additionally, a number of critical analyses have been created during this period that we do not include here as theories. Most are syntheses of the works of others. A few examples include R. Murphy, "The Speech as Literary Genre," *Quarterly Journal of Speech*, 44 (1958), 117–127; G. M. A. Grube, "Rhetoric and Literary Criticism," *Quarterly Journal of Speech*, 42 (1956), 339–344; B. Baskerville, "The Place of Oratory in American Literature," *Quarterly Journal of Speech*, 39 (1953), 459–464; O. M. Walter, "On Views of Rhetoric, Whether Conservative or Progressive," *Quarterly Journal of Speech*, 49 (1963), 367–382; I. J. Lee, "Four Ways of Looking at a Speech," *Quarterly Journal of Speech*, 28 (1942), 148–155; A. J. Croft, "The Functions of Rhetorical Criticism," *Quarterly Journal of Speech*, 42 (1956), 283–291; W. Sachsteder, "The Masterpiece and Its Historical Context," *Western Speech*, 21 (1957), 164–168; H. H. Perritt, "Cybernetics and Rhetoric," *Southern Speech Journal*, 20 (1954), 7–15; L. D. Reid, "The Perils of Rhetorical Criticism," *Quarterly Journal of Speech*, 30 (1944), 416–422; E. J. Wrage, "The Ideal Critic," *Central States Speech Journal*, 8 (1957), 20–23; G. Borchers, "An Approach to the Problem of Oral Style," *Quarterly Journal of Speech*, 22 (1936), 114–117; G. E. Bigelow, "Distinguishing Rhetoric From Poetic Discourse," *Southern Speech Journal*, 19 (1953), 83–97; W. R. Brockriede, "Dimensions of the Concept of Rhetoric," *Quarterly Journal of Speech*, 55 (1968), 1–12. An excellent summary of rhetorical criticism is found in E. Black, *Rhetorical Criticism* (New York: Macmillan, 1965); a summary from a literary viewpoint is found in W. C. Booth, *The Rhetoric of Fiction* (Chicago: University of Chicago Press, 1961).

[7]A complete bibliography of Burke's rhetorical works is beyond our scope here. Perhaps the best single volume to consult is *Language as Symbolic Action* (Berkeley, CA: University of California Press, 1966).

[8]The critical importance of understanding Burke's terminology is highlighted in the excellent essay by J. Blankenship et al., "Pivotal Terms in the Early Works of K. Burke," *Philosophy and Rhetoric*, 7 (1974), 1–24. A more narrow examination of some instances of Burke's use of language is found in L. Crowell, "Three Cheers for Kenneth Burke," *Quarterly Journal of Speech*, 63 (1977), 152–167.

[9]Burke's attitude toward Aristotelian concepts is made clear in his essay, "The Party Line," *Quarterly Journal of Speech*, 62 (1976), 63.

[10]These are developed by Burke in *A Rhetoric of Motives* (New York: Prentice–Hall, 1950).

[11]A. Cooke, *Six Men* (New York: Alfred A. Knopf, 1977), p. 4.

[12]K. Burke, *A Grammar of Motives* (Englewood Cliffs, NJ: Prentice–Hall, 1965).

[13]For a detailed treatment of Burke's critical method, see M. H. Nichols, "Kenneth Burke's Dramatistic Approach in Speech Criticism," in ed. W. Rueckert, *Critical Responses to Kenneth Burke* (Minneapolis: University of Minnesota Press, 1969).

[14]C. Perelman and L. Olbrechts-Tyteca, *The New Rhetoric: A Treatise on Argumentation* (Notre Dame, IN: University of Notre Dame Press, 1971).

[15]The anti-Cartesian position of the new rhetoric is discussed in N. Rotenstreich, "Argumentation and Philosophical Clarification," *Philosophy and Rhetoric*, 5 (1972), 12–23.

[16]Florescu accurately summarizes the antirhetorical emphasis of the Cartesian tradition in his essay, "Rhetoric and Its Rehabilitation in Contemporary Philosophy," *Philosophy and Rhetoric*, 3 (1970), 195–198.

[17]Perelman's idea of the nonconclusive nature of argument is examined in D. Abbott, "The Jurisprudential Analogy: Argumentation and the New Rhetoric," *Central States Speech Journal*, 25 (1974), 50–55.

[18]Perelman and Olbrechts-Tyteca, *The New Rhetoric*, p. 1.

[19]Perelman, "Rhetoric and Philosophy," pp. 18–19.

[20]For a discussion of Perelman's concept of the relationship between audience and argument, see J. R. Anderson, "The Audience as a Concept in the Philosophic Rhetoric of Perelman, Johnstone, and Natanson," *Southern Speech Communication Journal*, 38 (1972), 39–50.

[21]An interesting development of Perelman's statement of the relationship between "truth" and the audience addressed may be found in A. Scult, "Perelman's Universal Audience: One Perspective," *Central States Speech Journal*, 27 (1976), 176–180.

[22]Excerpted from "The Public and Private Face of H. L. Mencken," as cited by Cooke, *Six Men*, p. 94.

[23]G. Tullock, *Economics of Income Redistribution* (Boston: Kluwer–Nijhoff, 1983), p. 180.

[24]Of course not all critics are comfortable with Perelman's view of the role of argumentation. For generally negative reactions, the reader might wish to examine J. W. Ray, "Perelman's Universal Audience," *Quarterly Journal of Speech*, 64 (1978), 361–375; L. S. Ede, "Rhetoric versus Philosophy: The Role of the Universal Audience in Perelman's New Rhetoric," *Central States Speech Journal*, 32 (1981), 118–125.

[25]C. K. Ogden and I. A. Richards, *The Meaning of Meaning: A Study of the Influence of Language Upon Thought and of the Science of Symbolism* (New York: Harcourt, Brace, 1930); S. K. Foss, K. A. Foss, and R. Trapp, *Contemporary Perspectives on Rhetoric* (Prospect Heights, IL: Waveland, 1985).

[26]Foss, Foss, and Trapp, p. 23.

[27]R. M. Weaver, *Ideas Have Consequences* (Chicago: University of Chicago Press, 1948); Foss, Foss, and Trapp, pp. 51–52.

[28]Foss, Foss, and Trapp, p. 51.

[29]S. Toulmin, "Logic and the Criticism of Arguments," in J. L. Golden et al., *The Rhetoric of Western Thought*, 3rd ed. (Dubuque, IA: Kendall–Hunt, 1983).

[30]Foss, Foss, and Trapp, p. 81.

SECTION FOUR

Building the Edifice for the Individual: Psychological Approaches to Communication

All communication resides in the people engaged in that communication. All communication is personal. In designing our communication edifice, we begin with an analysis of the user's needs. Just as there are various schools of architecture, there are various approaches to communication theory. In this section, we examine the most basic type of communication: that which resides in the person. Our focus in Section Four, then, is the *individual as seen by the individual.* Reflecting on our metaphor, psychological approaches portray the personal idiosyncrasies of the individual communicator, the tugging between personal wants and society's needs.

In Chapter 7, we view what are commonly referred to as *humanistic approaches*, which are concerned with the interaction of personality with the orientation to the outside world. The central concern of this approach is the *self.* As such, the humanistic approach focuses on individual differences in communicators, trying to understand better the person as a person. We examine personal reasons behind communication, and the responsibility of language and day-to-day communication.

Chapter 8 concerns the study of behavior and the attitudes that underlie that behavior. The central focus is on *understanding human attitudes.* We examine how attitudes are formed and reformed, as well as how they are used in forming and reforming the attitudes of others. A variety of behavioral and attitudinal theories are examined for their impact on how people respond to persuasive messages. Chapter 8 extends the study of communication from an introspective view of the individual communicator presented in Chapter 7 to a study of the interaction between two or more people, one of whom desires a change in the relationship.

The focus of Section Four, then, is on *us*, and how and why we communicate. We begin with an understanding of the self as its own entity. We then move to an examination of the process of one person influencing another: persuasion. At times communication architects must grasp who their clients are, attempting to define why they think as they do, and choosing particular verbal and nonverbal messages. Once they have an understanding of the self, then they attempt to introduce change in environment, change in others' messages (attitudes), and ultimately change in others' behavior.

7

Humanistic Approaches to Communication

This chapter's focus is on the issues of *personal* intent, growth, and self-knowledge. Like the architect just beginning to design his or her building, individual communicators must look inside themselves to grasp what they really want to build. The process of introspection provides the basis for future communication and helps us to (1) understand better our motives for communication and (2) accept responsibility for that communication. In our architecture metaphor, architects must grow and adapt when creating their designs. They must understand why they create their buildings, be happy with the result, and take responsibility for the edifice. In this chapter, we examine communication approaches that focus on *why* people communicate; the focus, therefore, is on the *individual.*

This chapter examines theories centering on the concept of *self* as the foundation for communication. We study how *individual differences* influence the study of communication.

Communication begins when we experience *intrapersonal* communication. Intrapersonal communication theory has been greatly influenced by the allied field of psychology. This influence, however, comes not from traditional perspectives such as behavioral or psychoanalytic theory, but from a perspective only formally stated in the middle 1960s: *humanistic psychology.* This intrapersonal perspective sets the foundations for the study of communication as both responsive and responsible. Responsibility and responsiveness are the cornerstones of a humanistic orientation toward communication, based on knowledge of self (intrapersonal) and how that self relates to others (interpersonal).

The humanistic approach to communication encompasses diverse views of how we communicate. Humanistic perceptions of self stress commitment, satisfaction, adaptation, self-expression, and organization to an organism

137

that at times seems out of control. Most humanistic approaches suggest that the human system experiences states of *disequilibrium* or internal conflict (see Chapter 3), caused by conflicting values, goals, and beliefs. One way to redress this conflict is to change our view of "self." As Gordon Allport noted, we have many selves. Integrating or adapting these sometimes conflicting views of self is often a difficult task.[1] As we move from one "self" to another, we begin to self-fulfill, and ultimately self-actualize. Doing so, however, requires a change in intrapersonal and interpersonal communication. Humanistic approaches, as a family of communication theories, fall into our general category of theories of knowledge.

THE SELF

As John Waite Bowers and James J. Bradac note, "Communication is the relationship among behaviors of interacting individuals. Hence the concept *coorientation* has become an important one to rhetorical and communication theory. Central to coorientation are concepts of *self* and *other*."[2] There are, however, many different ways to view the self. Each view offers a different interpretation of the role played by coorientation in human relationships.

Coorientation may take two basic forms: (1) the way we perceive ourself regarding ourself (I–Me), and (2) the way our selves interact with other selves (You–Me). For the first form, consider how you feel about yourself before taking an important examination. If you have a "good" I–Me relationship, you might enter the testing situation talking as if you are *really* ready for the test. Your internal dialogue will be positive. If your view of self is less than positive, however, your internal dialogue may be expressed in conflict (e.g., "I need to do well [I]" but "I just cannot take multiple choice tests [Me]"). We will examine several concepts of self and how each relates to communication.

Historically, the concept of self has been plagued with a definitional problem. The interchanging of terms such as "ego," "ideal self," "proprium," and "identity" has confused discussions of the self.[3] Two terms, for instance, have been used constantly to refer to two distinct but overlapping phenomena. Morris Rosenberg notes that "self" and "ego" have been used to refer

> to the "inner nature" or "essential nature" of man . . . the experience and content of self-awareness . . . to the center of the psychophysical field . . . to inner or subjective being, or psychological faculties or dispositions, taken concretely . . . to the individual known to the individual . . . to a constellation of "mine" experiences . . . to individual identity and continuity of personal character . . . to a set of mental processes operating in the interest of satisfying inner drives . . . and, most simply, to the person.[4]

Kenneth Gergen states that self can be defined first as a process and then as a structure. He offers the following *process* definition: "that process by which the person conceptualizes (or categorizes) his behavior—both his external conduct and his internal states."[5] He defines self on the *structural* level as a "concern with the system of concepts available to the person in attempting to define himself" (pp. 22–23). Gardner Murphy suggests that a better definition might be "the individual as known to the individual."[6] This definition anticipates a view of the self both as object and as a developing phenomenon.

The self, then, is something in constant flux. As we have positive and negative experiences, those experiences influence the way we see ourselves. Sometimes this vision corresponds to how we truly feel; at other times we try to deceive ourselves and others. The self, as a cornerstone to perception, influences how people communicate with others, if they choose to do so at all.

PERSPECTIVES ON THE SELF

Several approaches have been advanced concerning how the self (or personality) takes part in the communication process. We focus briefly on five: role theory, the developmental approach, Schutz's personality types, Gibb's "climates," and Rogers's self theory. The first of these, role theory, has been a concern of several different theorists. Perhaps the most notable are the pragmatic philosophers of the early twentieth century and the more recent works of the transactional analysts. Both are concerned with what constitutes the self in regard to the various *roles* people learn to play.

Role Theory: The Pragmatic View

Before William James's formulation of a "self" as a three-part concept of self-experience, the self was perceived as experiences of the body with an emphasis on awareness of internal organs and muscle structure.[7] James, however, argued that two interrelated constructs are found in any person: a *Me* and an *I*. The *Me* represents the empirical self, a self that can be evaluated. The *I*, on the other hand, represents a form of *consciousness* in which the person becomes his or her own self-knower; a sort of ego-relationship. Both concepts, however, are *not* different entities, but operate together to form the *self-concept*.

James visualized the empirical self, or *Me*, as everything that we can call our own. The empirical self comprises three elements, each affecting the other. The *material self* is considered the body and physical extensions thereof, including possessions and the home. The *social self* is comprised of "recognition" from "others." James noted that there are many social selves, each different according to the "others" surrounding us. The social self may be closely associated with a set of roles, such as parent, spouse, lover, employee, and deacon (see Fig. 7–1). For James, the *spiritual self* is the inner, subjective being—psychic faculties, dispositions, the "self of selves." This self is composed of several states of consciousness, one that may transcend the others.

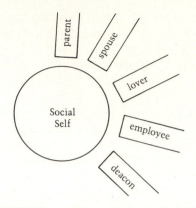

FIGURE 7–1   Roles and the Social Self.

James also considered the *I* important; it allows us to balance the *Me* by judging past and future along with the present. The *I* helps to create a healthy self, or to self-preserve. We visualize ourselves through the concept of *self-esteem*. Self-esteem, James felt, was a ratio between our successes and our expectations. Obviously, the roles we play influence our self-esteem. As long as we maintain a stable relationship between expectations and potential, we have a healthy self-esteem. When imbalance occurs, however, we "mutate" to abnormal behavior representing inner conflicts within the self.

James provided a model to study the inner psyche of man. He suggested that we consist of many "selves," some in conflict with each other. He suggested that we are self-conscious. James also suggested that we differ in the degree of self-esteem we have, which may be explained in problems associated with role expectations. In our test-taking example, a good self-esteem for the role "student" should produce a healthy concept of that role; however, pressure to be better in a subject in which we lack confidence may yield a low self-esteem (*I* less than *Me*). In other situations, the same may hold true, such as a dating situation: The greater the failure to get a date, the less one may keep up physical appearance (an indicator of personal self-esteem), and the more one may take on a "loner" role and even deprecate dating potential ("I can't even get a date, never have, never will").

Role Theory: The Transactional View

Thomas Harris suggests different roles for the self. In *I'm OK—You're OK*, he suggests that people assume one of three roles: the adult, the child, or the parent.[8] *Transactional analysis* (TA), as this approach is called, examines communication based on role expectations in which the key element is the *transaction* between the people. Harris notes that we engage in a "I do something to you and you do something back" exchange in any transaction. (This is similar to Homans's view; see Chapter 10.) This exchange creates a perception of self based on *role knowledge*.

The first role we assume is that of the *parent* (see Fig. 7–2). In this role, we learn through the imposed, unquestioned, externalized recordings of events around us. During this stage (birth through age five), children subconsciously learn to socialize from their parents and others' parents. They learn *as if* they were the parent, acting toward themselves as if they were the parent (e.g., the infant slapping his or her own hand and saying "no, no!" [the bad-me], then smiling and saying "me good" [the good-me]). The socialization process teaches us "how to" behave and gives us generalization-like imperatives such as "never" and "always." Harris notes that the parent role is found any time we feel so dependent that we are not free to question data that are stored in the parent.

The second role is the *child*. This role is full of negatives dealing with the self and others. Most data received at this stage is "sour" and externalized with messages such as "It's my fault. Again. Always is. Ever will be. World without end" (p. 25). In this role, we feel compelled to obey or lash out; if the outcome is to lash out, the child will most likely be punished. Hence, we develop an "I'm not OK" attitude. Feelings are developed in this role, feelings that reflect inward and often with hurt.

The third role is the *adult*, adopted after about 10 months of age and related to the ability to gain mobility and exercise motor coordination. The emerging adult is created by combining information from both the taught (parent) and the felt (child) through exploration and testing. The adult gets its data from more than simply the parent or child; it also gets "archaic" data from earlier adult role stages. These stages are constantly updated and contrasted with past data. Harris argues that the adult cannot "erase the recording, but can . . . choose to turn it off"; that is, we take the "I'm not OK"

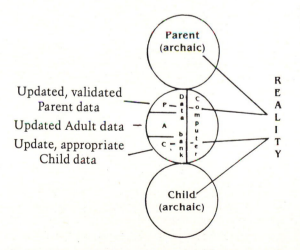

FIGURE 7–2   Transactional Analysis (Updating Function of the Adult through Reality Testing).

Source: T. A. Harris, *I'm OK–You're OK* (New York: Harper and Row, 1969), p. 32.

feelings of the child and validate the negative feelings by comparing them with the newer, better understood data.

We play each of these three roles throughout life as we interact with self and others. The development from parent to child to adult creates a self expressed in the sense of "okayness." When we think of childhood, we think "I'm not OK; you're OK." When we feel that neither the world nor we are functioning properly, we think, "I'm not OK; you're not OK." Finally, when we feel paranoid and parent, we think, "I'm OK; you're not OK." When the adult takes over, we think, "I'm OK; you're OK." According to Harris, people should strive toward the adult, a role in which we work with others to solve problems.

Our communication reflects the degree of "okayness" we feel. These feelings are communicated in our choice of language (good–bad) and related nonverbal behaviors (positive–negative). *The self is reflected in language as described by the particular role we occupy.*

In our earlier examples, the degree of okayness can be easily interpreted. In the breakup of a long-term relationship, childlike communication may include messages such as, "It wasn't right for" him or her or "I didn't work hard enough." Perhaps the other partner took on a parent role, expressing the breakup as the other's fault—that he or she "didn't put enough into the relationship; I worked harder at it." Or, perhaps both partners felt "I'm not OK; you're OK," but were unable to move to a mutual adult stage for agreement.

Developmental Approaches

The self is a product of a developing personality. As the personality develops, so does the concept of self. Table 7–1 presents the eight stages of development Harry Stack Sullivan hypothesizes we go through. Sullivan's model suggests that we begin with no knowledge of past or present in the infant stage and that maturation is a learning phenomenon guided by a "mothering one."[9] The mothering role at birth is taken by the mother and father, each serving a nurturing and a learning role. This process is continual as we move

TABLE 7–1 Sullivan's Stages of Self-Development

Stage	Period
1. Infancy	From birth to appearance of speech
2. Childhood	From appearance of speech to a need for playmates
3. Juvenile era	From need for playmates to need for close friend of same sex
4. Preadolescence	Ends with puberty
5. Early Adolescence	Begins with puberty and increased interest in the opposite sex
6. Late adolescence	Begins with the findings of ways to gratify genital drives
7. Adulthood	Begins with the establishment of a love relationship with a significant other of the opposite sex

from role to role. In learning to be a boss, for instance, we begin at the infant stage and, through the help of a mothering one—a mentor—develop into the role of boss. The same development holds true for spouse, parent, and other roles.

As we progress in each role from Stage 1 to Stage 8, three different personalities develop: the *good-me*, the *bad-me*, and the *not-me*. These personalities, which derive from our self-system, are related to states of tension brought about through personal needs and anxiety. Sullivan felt that growth was not only personal, but also socialized, a process through which we must deal with confrontations with other significant others or mothering ones. These confrontations cause anxiety and perceptions of good-me, bad-me, and not-me. In some cases, the mentoring or mothering one will make us feel good, bad, or neither.

Gordon Allport has also viewed the development of self as a chronological progression,[10] but more in line with James's concept of the *Me*. In it we perceive our self as definable in *self-awareness*. In achieving what Allport felt was the final (eighth) stage, or *the knower*, we go through the seven earlier stages that deal with identity and image (see Table 7–2). The first three stages follow from birth through infancy and establish bodily and psychological self-identities. The next two stages follow through the juvenile era to early adolescence; we extend our identity to a social awareness of our actual self-image, as opposed to our *idealized* self-image. The sixth and seventh stages take us through late adolescence and begin to mark a realization of self as opposed to others, reflecting a rational view of self. At the seventh stage, future aspirations and goals motivate behavior. Thus, Allport would view the development of the boss role as both from the aid of a mentor *and* from our ability to reflect our abilities within the role to others at similar stages of role acquisition.

Both Sullivan and Allport view the developing self as the assertion of a personality. The personality is one of the guiding forces (antecedents) of behavior, but not the necessary force for behavior; that is, the self may not be the *direct* cause of behavior, but may be one of many causes. From a communication perspective, the influence of environment and role (especially role models) suggests a fertile grounding toward an understanding of the individual communicator.

TABLE 7–2   Allport's Stages of Self-Development

Stage	Awareness	Period
1	Sense of Bodily Self	
2	Sense of Continuing Self-Identity	First three years of life
3	Self-Esteem, Pride	
4	Extension of Self	
5	Self-Image	Ages 4–6
6	Rational Self	
7	Self ("The Knower")	Ages 6–12

A problem with the developmental approaches lies in the internalized form of communication. What we know of self-perception comes from our ability to communicate at a level appropriate to our current stage. Since language is based largely on perception, we must *infer* through that language whether we are "developing." The same is true from the perspective of the person trying to develop the personality or self: actions and reactions are *perceived* by the communicator.

Schutz's Personality Types

The idea that we may not be "OK" suggests that self-perceptions may hinder our personal growth. William Schutz developed a model of interpersonal behavior predicated on the *type* of person with whom we deal.[11] Schutz felt that people fall into four general behavioral types: deficient, excessive, ideal, and pathological. Each behavior can be found in three general classifications of *intrapersonal expectations of a relationship:* a *need* for inclusion, affection, and control. All relate to the way we view ourselves. A healthy self, or personality, reflects a balancing of our needs for inclusion, affection, and control. As seen in Figure 7–3, a healthy personality is found somewhere midway between the extremes.

According to Schutz, people in the category of *inclusion* tend to be classified as undersocial, oversocial, or social. *Undersocial* people are introverted or withdrawn. They are deficient in the need for including others in

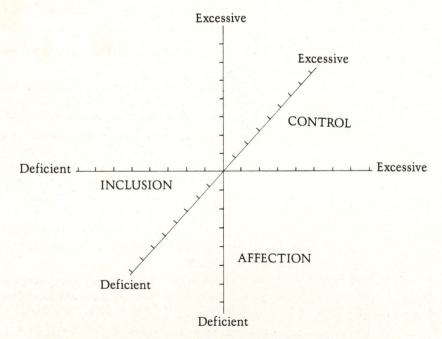

FIGURE 7–3   Schultz's Personalities (Affection, Control, Inclusion).

their life or in a feeling of being needed. They avoid association with others and reject invitations to join with others. Undersocials do not get involved, exhibit little commitment, and view themselves as worthless. At the other end are the *oversocials* or excessive people. These people fear being ignored and constantly seek the comfort of others. Between the oversocials and undersocials are the *socials*. To them, social interaction poses no problem. They feel worthwhile, that life is worth living, and they strive toward actualizing their social potential. Socials have a healthy self-concept, are creative, and are motivated by a concern for others. The pathologically extreme, however, are so concerned with inclusion that life becomes one major anxiety. They often become alienated and exist in a fantasy world.

In his second category, *affection*, Schutz defines the deficient person as *underpersonal*. These people's interactions with others are superficial. They maintain an emotional distance between self and others. The underpersonal is characterized as one who does not get involved and generally distrusts other people. At the other extreme is the *overpersonal*. They are extremely intimate, personal, and confiding. The ideal type is the *personal*, who is comfortable in relationships and who realizes that some people may not like them, but for whom this perception does not create a crisis. Personals can provide and receive genuine affection. The pathologically extreme, on the other hand, develop neuroses and psychoses regarding affection.

Schutz's third category is *control*. Deficient people are submissive, are *abdicrats*. They bow to authority at every opportunity and follow rather than lead. They refuse to take responsibility and generally exhibit hostility. Opposite the abdicrat is the *autocrat*, a bossy, dogmatic competitor. Autocrats possess a need to dominate and distrust the motives and creative potential of others. The ideal is found in the *democrat*, one who can give or receive orders, can follow or not follow, and can relinquish control. Democrats have healthy self-concepts. The pathologically extreme, on the other hand, are obsessed with power and have an extreme need for control.

Schutz's portrayal of the healthy self takes the best of humanistic psychology as his "golden mean" personality. Healthy people are responsible for their actions, are creative in relationships with others, and, while seeking order, understand that excessive control does not allow others to actualize. They are open to others and their environment. The extremes—deficient, excessive, or pathological—are people with major imbalances within their self-systems; they represent closed systems.

Gibb's Communication Climates

According to humanistic theory, healthy people are *open systems*. A major form of *entropy* in our intrapersonal systems comes from our defensive tendencies. The healthy person, although exhibiting some defensiveness or *disequilibrium*, works with others, to include different roles or selves, to establish supportive intrapersonal and interpersonal relationships. Jack R. Gibb provides an analysis of what he labels *defensive communication* as "that behavior which occurs when an individual perceives threat or antici- pates threat in the group."[12] Although his concern is with group behavior, Gibb's ideas can be extended to a humanistic model of behavior. Gibb con- tends that six factors establish a *defensive climate:* evaluation, control, strat- egy, neutrality, superiority, and certainty. All six factors are internally oriented and self-protective. Contrast these with the six factors in Gibb's *supportive climates:* description, problem orientation, spontaneity, empa- thy, equality, and understanding. We have two lists of *opposites.*

Gibb's defensive communication is based on a relationship similar to a tennis match in which one player is inherently superior to the other. The superior player "teases" the opponent until a "slam" is set up. The superior player *always* wins, creating defensiveness on the part of the other player, who anticipates losing each time. At times, the superior player is also defensive, a result of thinking that, even at the remote possibility, he or she might lose.

Supportive climates are built around equal players who both attempt to continue the "rally." A slam is viewed as "illegal." Neither wishes to chase stray tennis balls; neither plays to win or lose. Both view communication as an ongoing process; hence, they rally, complementing their abilities and help- ing each other to overcome deficiencies.

A PHENOMENOLOGY OF THE SELF

The use of phenomenology (a descriptive account of day-to-day interaction as seen by the individual) as an approach to the study of communication is relatively recent. However, the phenomenological approach is at least ninety years old, following the publication of Edmund Husserl's *Logische Unter- suchugen* in 1900.[13] For us, phenomenology may be defined four ways: (1) as a *descriptive account* of everyday life experience;[14] (2) as a *method* for studying everyday human experience;[15] (3) as a *philosophical movement* that began in Europe in the nineteenth century;[16] and (4) as a *communica- tion approach* wherein "conscious [intrapersonal] experience is composed of two absolutely correlated 'movements': [a] a psychological impending act (*noesis,* the consciousness of): and [b] object (*noema,* that which the con- sciousness is of)."[17]

Human Communication in Action

Definitions are important in understanding human communication in differ- ing ways. The *descriptive account* of everyday events and communication has been pointed out in the sociological–communication work of Julian B. Roebuck and Hickson in their study of southern rednecks, including the verbal and nonverbal communication of this social type.[18] As a *method,* the phenomenological view and the related view of ethnomethodology has been discussed in the communication contexts by Hickson and others.[19] The *philosophical movement* serves as a backdrop for many of the studies now being undertaken by members of the philosophical division of the International Communication Association. The *communication approach* has been used in the area of language and technology as well as psychology.[20] Our focus here is on the communication approach.

According to Stanley A. Deetz, the concepts of noesis and noema work together as subject–object because we cannot have a consciousness without an object, and an object cannot exist outside our consciousness. In studying language from this phenomenological view, Deetz and Georg Gusdorf arrived at five basic *communication* principles. First, a word is "an index of value."[21] Second, "thought and speaking are identical" (p. xxii). Third, "all knowledge is conscious." Fourth, "raw experience comes to us with a pre-reflective character." Fifth, "all experience inherently occurs through language."[22]

For Deetz and Gusdorf, the world is comprised of experience, which is "known" through thought and expressed only through language. *The word is the thing*, for only through words do we describe our reality. From our discussion of language, we know that symbols are *not* the objects they represent. But here we are concerned with an individual, *personal reality* where symbols have immense impact. We live, protect, and sometimes die for symbols such as "the flag," "country," or "honor." Consider the outcry at the 1989 and 1990 U.S. Supreme Court decisions allowing the desecration of the American flag. In other instances, we find labels becoming a permanent part of our personality: becoming "bad," "ugly," and so on. For us, this phenomenological approach is also important in the work of Carl Rogers, who established a phenomenologically based, self-centered psychology.[23]

Rogers's Self Theory Approach

Rogers advances the humanistic argument that we strive for self-actualization, which is defined in the attainment of goals, through the concepts of self-responsibility and self-knowledge, and through the process of socialization.[24] Rogers views the "search for self" as an outgrowth of three propositions: (1) We are in a continually changing world with ourselves as the center; (2) We can view ourselves as both subjects and objects; and (3) Our overt behavior is an indication of our self-concept.

Rogers sees people as subjective and interpretative. This phenomenological view led him to believe that we should be more concerned with the *interpretations of actions* than with the actual actions themselves. Whatever we do is reflected in the self-concept and is rooted in the subjective, not the objective, reality of the behavior. The inner self, the subject (agent) or ego, is closely related to James's concept of *I*. We have a second self, one that is more objective and empirical, more *Me*-related. This self is composed of content (images, perceptions, pictures), direction (positive to negative), intensity (high to low), salience, consistency, clarity, stability, and verifiability. As such, the objective self can be stepped away from and, with the help of a therapist (or friend), observe or bring experience to the conscious.

Rogers's propositions, as indicated in Table 7–3, are more complex than presented here. In the final analysis, however, self qualities can be determined in three different ways, each by answering simple questions:

1. Who do *you* think *you* are?
2. Who do *others* think *you* are?
3. Who do *you* think *others* think *you* are?

When answering these three questions, Rogers suggests we keep in mind the following questions *from the point of view of the other:*

1. Can I be perceived by others as trustworthy, dependable, or consistent in some deep sense?
2. Can I be expressive enough that I can communicate unambiguously?

TABLE 7–3   Propositions Concerning Personality and Self

1. Each of us is the center of our own world, a world available to our self.
2. How each of us responds to what we see in our world is guided by a desire to enhance and maintain the self we accept and to permit that self to express itself to the fullest capacity.
3. To understand ourselves, we must understand our own way of looking at the world.
4. The self-concept is derived by judging the satisfaction we get from interacting with others and the environment, realizing that some perceptions of self are more satisfactory than others.
5. We develop values from experiences that have satisfied or failed to satisfy our needs, as well as from the experiences of others in our environment.
6. All experiences do not have the same impact on us because of differing need states and values. Some experiences are consistent with our self-view, some are inconsistent, and others must be rationalized to fit that self-view.
7. Our behavior provides clues as to our self-concept.
8. We perceive most experiences not fitting our self-concepts as dangerous and build self-defenses against them for the self as we know it.
9. We revise the self-concept to fit reality as we see it; that is, we remove or change conditions leading up to experiences that are dangerous to our self-concept so that the self-concept does not change dramatically.
10. As we open up and become more aware of our sensory and physical experiences, we become more responsive, more understanding, and more accepting of others.
11. Acceptance of reality and actual experiences and reactions into the self-concept changes held value systems; thus we become more open to change. We find happiness in discovering that our self-concepts are continually changing.

Adapted from C. Rogers, *Client-Centered Therapy* (Boston: Houghton-Mifflin, 1951).

3. Can I let myself experience positive attitudes toward others—attitudes of warmth, caring, liking, interest, respect?
4. Can I be strong enough to be separate from the other?
5. Am I secure enough within myself to permit this separateness?
6. Can I let myself enter fully into the world of others' feelings of personal meanings and see these as they do?
7. Can I receive others as they are?
8. Can I act with sufficient sensitivity in the relationship so that my behavior will not be perceived as a threat?
9. Can I free others from the threat of external evaluation?
10. Can I meet others as people in the process of becoming, or will I be bound by their past and by my past?

Rogers's view of self is consistent with the humanistic perspective that we are constantly trying to achieve a degree of self-actualization. The way we do so, or our motivation toward actualization, is found in a knowledge of self and relationships with others. Rogers firmly believed that not only were other people (society) important in determining the self-concept, but the psychological environment also contributed to developing the self. The perceived relationship between self with self as well as self with others is important. Consider, for instance, what happens when we feel that we are not liked or are unwanted. We usually have two courses of action: We try harder to get others to like us, or we avoid people. Obviously, either reaction can result in a continuous cycle of events. We avoid people, so people avoid us, and we think they avoid us because they do not like us, so we avoid people . . .

COMMUNICATION VARIABLES

The humanistic theorist's central construct is the concern for self. This concern is tempered, however, with a sense of responsibility. Each theorist perceives the self as central to an understanding of ourselves and others. We understand ourselves through symbol manipulation—language. We are what we disclose. Such disclosures become variables of interest to communication researchers and theorists. Our view must include a vision of ourselves as individuals responsible for our use of sophisticated verbal and nonverbal forms of communication.

The study of communication has been strongly influenced by humanistic thought. In the area of intrapersonal communication alone, new insight into *how* we communicate is beginning to alter the way we view communication and communication outcomes (see Chapter 9). Specifically, *communication apprehension*—the communicator's internal fears about saying something to another—has probably been influenced most by the study of the individual.[25] The most common fear is in a public speaking situation, but people may also fear asking a question in a public forum, calling someone for a date, or asking for a raise. Another area influenced by the study of self is *communicator style,* the particular way that a person relates to another.[26] People differ in the ways they approach others, creating a particular communication strategy based on their perceptions of self and others. The study of *persuasion and attitude change* also has been influenced by the study of self, especially as researchers attempt to explain interpersonal influence attempts (see Chapter 8).[27] This interest has focused on the self, self-concept, self-esteem, self-monitoring, self-disclosure, and individual locus of control. Humanistic influence is also found in research on information processing.[28]

Within the study of communication, the tenets of humanistic psychology offer us a chance to study *us as us.* We *are* greater than the sum of the stimuli around us. We can create and act on a reality as if it *were* real. The humanist is concerned with people getting along with other people and of becoming, in Carl Rogers's terms, fully functioning individuals. To become fully functioning, we must understand others, be open to their self-disclosure as a way to understand better their past, and work at establishing supportive rather than defensive climates. Getting along with other people—treating others as thinking and reacting people—is one of the most important and equalizing concepts found in human communication.

REVIEW

This chapter has centered on the most important feature of any communication: the communicator. An examination of the "third force" in psychology provides the information necessary for the study of the communicator as a whole person. This person has a life history that must be taken into account to understand fully and predict his or her behavior. In this chapter, we have laid out the central tenets of humanistic psychology. In so doing, we provide the groundwork for treating communication as a central concern for personal growth and as a potential problem encountered in growth. As summarized in Table 7–4, a number of theories were examined; although each position was similar, each had its own views on what constituted the self. Based on these understandings, we get a better picture of what constitutes the human "spirit," "ego," or "self."

CRITIQUE

Humanistic theory, although having had a significant impact on communication, is not the concise, predictive theory we would like it to be. Some critics see little in this theoretical approach. The focus on the individual nature of the communication process makes humanistic theory hard to test, because each of us is unique. Tests of theory must be on a case-by-case basis, which is not amenable to mass audiences or the establishment of norms from which to work; hence, the theory's support may be questioned. Humanistic theory arose from problems with behavioral and psychoanalytic

TABLE 7-4 Summary Table

Name of Theory	Primary Theorists	Basic Principle	Constructs	Criteria	Analytic Approach	Limitations
Humanistic psychological approach	William James	The self is important	• Material self • Social self • Spiritual self	Successes versus pretensions	None	Humanistic psychological approaches assume that the individual makes choices between the stimulus and the response. This is very difficult to measure.
	Thomas Harris		• Parent • Adult • Child	Elimination of cross-interactions		The self, the central construct in this approach, is difficult to define. As we see, many researchers define self differently.
	William Schutz		• Inclusion • Affection • Control	An individual should not be "under" or "over" in any of these constructs		
	Carl Rogers			Phenomenal world		

151

approaches to understanding human behavior.[29] This concern with self has created a theoretical atmosphere conducive to new ideas and formulations. In this regard, humanistic theory has been heuristic.

The main problems associated with humanistic theory center around its reliability and logical base. Roderick P. Hart and Don M. Burks argue that humanistic theory does not add to our knowledge of communication in either a reliable or a logical way.[30] Hart and Burks see humanistic theory as simplistic and unable to explain most communicative behavior. Others, however, argue that humanistic theory provides explanations for both expression and quality of interaction as a form of openness in communication. Openness, they argue, yields a form of social control.[31]

One final criticism that may be leveled at humanistic theory is its lack of clarity and multiple use of concepts. In this regard, the theory is clearly lacking in parsimony. This, however, is not a problem for the humanistic theorist, who argues that our personal view of the world is unique and different and must accommodate some vagueness in constructs and concepts. To the humanistic researcher, then, *to really know communication is to know us individually.*

We turn next to the impact of attempting to influence others. In Chapter 8, our focus is on the interactive nature of *mutual influence.* The humanistic approaches, however, have established a starting point for the study of communication in larger contexts: interpersonal, small group, large group (organizational), societal, and mass.

NOTES AND REFERENCES

[1]G. W. Allport, *Pattern and Growth in Personality,* 2nd ed. (New York: Holt, Rinehart and Winston, 1961).

[2]J. W. Bowers and J. J. Bradac, "Contemporary Problems in Human Communication Theory," in eds. C. C. Arnold and J. W. Bowers *Handbook of Rhetorical and Communication Theory* (Boston: Allyn and Bacon, 1984), pp. 871–894.

[3]See M. Sherif and H. Cantrill, *The Psychology of Ego-Involvement* (New York: John Wiley and Sons, 1947); L. R. Judd and C. B. Smith, "A Study of Variables Influencing Self-Concept and Idea Self-Concept in the Basic Speech Course," *Speech Teacher,* 23 (1974), 215–221; G. W. Allport, *Becoming* (New Haven, CT; Yale University Press, 1955).

[4]M. Rosenberg, "Psychological Selectivity of Self-Esteem Formation," in eds. C. W. Sherif and M. Sherif *Attitude, Ego-Involvement and Change* (New York: John Wiley and Sons, 1967).

[5]K. J. Gergen, *The Concept of Self* (New York: Holt, Rinehart and Winston, 1971), pp. 22–23.

[6]G. Murphy, *Personality: A Biosocial Approach to Origins and Structure* (New York: Harper and Brothers, 1947).

[7]W. James, *Principles of Psychology* (New York: Holt, 1892); W. James, *Psychology: A Briefer Course* (New York: Holt, 1910).

[8]T. A. Harris, *I'm OK—You're OK* (New York: Harper and Row, 1969). See also E. Berne, *Games People Play: The Psychology of Human Relationships* (New York: Grove, 1964).

[9]H. S. Sullivan, *The Interpersonal Theory of Psychiatry* (New York: W. W. Norton, 1953).

[10]G. W. Allport, *Pattern and Growth in Personality* (New York: Holt, Rinehart and Winston, 1961).

[11]W. C. Schutz, *The Interpersonal Underworld* (Palo Alto, CA: Science and Behavior Books, 1966).

[12]J. R. Gibb, "Defensive Communication," *Journal of Communication, 11* (1961), 141–148.

[13]One excellent book on this topic for background and intellectual history is H. Spiegelberg, *Doing Phenomenology: Essays on and in Phenomenology* (The Hague: Martinus Nijhoff, 1975). See also M. Heidegger, *On the Way to Language* (New York: Harper and Row, 1971); M. Heidegger, *An Introduction to Metaphysics* (Garden City, NY: Doubleday, 1961).

[14]This is most notable in the works of Hans-Georg Gadamer (see chapter 12), Umberto Eco (semiotics), Maurice Merleau-Ponty (relationship between subject and object), Harold Garfinkel (ethnomethodology), and Alfred Schutz (applications in sociology.). The research in the field of communication has been focused on relationships and dialogue in interpersonal communication. See, for example, R. C. Arnett, "Toward a Phenomenological Dialogue," *Western Journal of Speech Communication, 45* (1981), 201–212; R. Anderson, "Phenomenological Dialogue, Humanistic Psychology, and Pseudo-Walls: A Response and Extension," *Western Journal of Speech Communication, 46* (1982), 344–357; D. D. Cahn and J. T. Hanford, "Perspectives on Human Communication Research: Behaviorism, Phenomenology, and an Integrated View," *Western Journal of Speech Communication, 48* (1984), 277–292.

[15]J. D. Douglas and J. M. Johnson, *Existential Sociology* (Cambridge: Cambridge University Press, 1977); S. T. Bruyn, *The Human Perspective in Sociology* (Englewood Cliffs, NJ: Prentice–Hall, 1966); M. Q. Patton, *Qualitative Research Methods* (Beverly Hills, CA: Sage, 1980); M. Natanson, *Philosophy of the Social Sciences: A Reader* (New York: Random House, 1963). In communication, see especially, S. A. Deetz, "Critical Interpretive Research in Organizational Communication," *Western Journal of Speech Communication, 46* (1982), 131–149; M. Hickson, "Ethnomethodology: The Promise of Applied Communication Research?" *Southern Speech Communication Journal, 48* (1983), 182–195.

[16]Proponents of the philosophical movement include Husserl, Heidegger, Jean-Paul Sartre, and Merleau-Ponty.

[17]See Deetz.

[18]J. B. Roebuck and M. Hickson, III, *The Southern Redneck: A Phenomenological Class Study* (New York: Praeger, 1982).

[19]M. Hickson, III, "Communication in Natural Settings: Research Tool for Undergraduates," *Communication Quarterly, 25* (1977), 23–28.

[20]R. L. Lanigan, "Semiotic Phenomenology: A Theory of Human Communication Praxis," *Journal of Applied Communications Research, 10* (1982), 62–73; R. L. Lanigan,

Semiotic Phenomenology of Rhetoric: Eidetic Practice in Henry Grattan's Discourse on Tolerance (Washington, DC: University Press of American, 1984); M. J. Hyde, ed., *Communication Philosophy and the Technological Age* (University, AL: University of Alabama Press, 1982).

[21]G. Gusdorf, *Speaking (La Parole)*, trans. P. T. Brockelman (Evanston, IL: Northwestern University Press, 1965), p. 9.

[22]S. A. Deetz, "Words Without Things: Toward a Social Phenomenology of Language," *Quarterly Journal of Speech*, 59 (1973), 40–54.

[23]C. Rogers, *Client-Centered Therapy* (Boston: Houghton Mifflin, 1951).

[24]"Chronological Bibliography of the Works of Carl R. Rogers, 1930–1985 Inclusive," *Person-Centered Review*, 1 (1986), 83–99.

[25]See S. R. Glasser, "Oral Communication Apprehension and Avoidance: The Current State of the Art," *Communication Education*, 30 (1981), 321–341; D. W. Stacks and J. D. Stone, "An Examination of the Effect of Basic Speech Courses, Self-Concept, and Self-Disclosure on Communication Apprehension," *Communication Education*, 33 (1984), 317–331; D. E. Sellers and D. W. Stacks, "Toward a Hemispheric Processing Theory of Communication Competence and Avoidance," paper presented at the World Communication Association Atlantic Area Convention, San Juan, PR, December 1984.

[26]C. R. Berger and N. J. Metzger, "The Functions of Human Communication in Developing, Maintaining, and Altering Self-Image," in eds. C. C. Arnold and J. W. Bowers, *Handbook of Rhetorical and Communication Theory* (Boston: Allyn and Bacon, 1984), pp. 273–337; R. W. Norton, "Foundation of a Communicator Style Construct," *Human Communication Research*, 4 (1978), 99–112; D. W. Stacks, "Understanding Communication Processing as a Function of Brain Hemispheric Style," paper presented at the SCA Regional Research Seminar: "Meeting the Methodological Challenges of a Process Notion of Communication," University of South Florida, Tampa, April 1983.

[27]See G. R. Miller, M. Burgoon, and J. K. Burgoon, "The Functions of Human Communication in Changing Attitudes and Gaining Compliance," in eds. C. C. Arnold and J. W. Bowers, *Handbook of Rhetorical and Communication Theory* (Boston: Allyn and Bacon, 1984), pp. 400–474.

[28]See D. W. Stacks, "Toward a Preverbal Stage of Communication," *Journal of Communication Therapy*, 2 (1983), 39–60; D. E. Sellers and D. W. Stacks, "Brain Processing and Therapy: A Conceptual and Research Frontier," *Journal of Communication Therapy*, 3 (1985), 30–50.

[29]C. Buhler and M. Allen, *Introduction to Humanistic Psychology* (Monterey, CA: Brooks/Cole, 1972), pp. 1–2.

[30]R. P. Hart and D. M. Burks, "Rhetorical Sensitivity and Social Interaction," *Speech Monographs*, 39 (1972), 75–91.

[31]A. L. Sillars, "Expression and Control in Human Interaction: Perspectives on Humanistic Psychology," *Western Speech*, 38 (1974), 269–277.

8

Understanding and Influencing Human Attitudes and Behavior through Persuasion

One of the roles of an architect is getting others to agree with his or her perception of what the edifice should look like. In his or her head, the architect knows what pleases; the task is to communicate that knowledge to others. Just as architects have a variety of ways to express their ideas, the communication theorist has a variety of approaches to the study of *persuasion.* The architect may point to aesthetic qualities of the edifice's design, its structural integrity, or its function. Along these same lines, communication theorists may look at underlying psychological constructs, such as attitudes, beliefs, and values ("aesthetic qualities"), or at the change in some behavior ("structure") or the function(s) a message performs. We are now at the stage of building our communication edifice that examines how our materials (verbal and nonverbal) are used by the communication architect to persuade. Like our structural architect, we, too, have a variety of psychological approaches that may be employed in persuading our "audiences."

A close examination of the study of communication leaves an impression that the central concern of most communication is to *influence.* Many people study communication to gain an understanding of how people use verbal and nonverbal messages. From understanding comes prediction. With prediction, control of others becomes possible. The central concern of this chapter is to examine theories of influence and persuasion.

Influence suggests that *all communication is a purposive act* because it is directed toward the achievement of some goal. Communication events are consequences of attempts to manipulate the environment around the communicator. Persuasion theorists see this purpose or goal as *social influence,* the altering of the behavior of others (and sometimes of ourselves) to achieve

155

our goals or needs. In accepting this premise—that all communication is manipulative—the persuasion theorist is at home with our rhetorical tradition. Today's increasing variety of social situations, coupled with a varied population, demands that the theorist create sophisticated and complex models to explain people's responses to attempts at modifying behavior.

The link between *attitudes* and *behavior* is important if we want change to occur that internalizes and fuels future change. Most contemporary persuasion theorists are concerned with the linkage among an established attitude, a person's behavior, and their alteration in predictable and controllable ways. Why should students of communication be concerned with the altering of attitudes and behavior? There are at least three reasons.

First, we are more comfortable when we understand our own and others' expectations. This comes from a desire for order in the world. Order, however, is desirable only to the degree that it increases predictability. As predictability increases, so do efficiency, security, and comfort. The psychological basis for studying expectations seeks to answer the questions, "Why do we act as we do?" and "Why do other people want me to do this?"

Second, to achieve the goals we desire, we must communicate with others. To exert social influence, we must understand what motivates others to act as they do. Persuasion theories provide the basic information necessary to achieve some degree of social influence.

Third, we are constantly subjected to the persuasive attempts of others. Other people have goals that require our assistance—they are going to try to manipulate us. Perhaps the most important reason for studying persuasion is for the protection it affords. By understanding the basis for changing attitudes and behavior, we may become more resistant to persuasive attempts. As we learn how and why people are motivated to change, we become better predictors of successful persuasive attempts. This success yields the potential for control. Through the study of persuasive communication, you should (1) become uncomfortable as you learn how communication is used to induce attitude and behavioral change and (2) become more comfortable as you learn how to control and resist such attempts.

SOME PROBLEMS WITH DEFINITIONS

We are not so much concerned with providing the "right" definition of persuasion as we are with helping you understand the different ones that have evolved. We can isolate three elements that set the foundation for the specific methods or theories that explain persuasion: conscious intent on the part of the persuader, attempts to change behavior, and symbol manipulation.

Conscious Intent

Most theories assume that persuasion is reserved for those situations that involve an *awareness* that we are trying to influence others. The problem comes in determining whether intent is present in a particular communication. Nevertheless, in most cases, the assessing of intent is feasible, even if on an intuitive basis. Consider, for instance, someone overhearing a message that causes an *unintended* change in the behavior of the eavesdropper. Is this persuasion? If you subscribe to the premise that all participants must be aware of the message, the answer is "no."

Attempts to Change Behavior

Most of us agree that persuasion involves the *effort* to influence others. Attitude-oriented persuasion theorists believe that attitudes *mediate* behavior, that the relationship among attitudes, behavior, and persuasion is of the order shown in Figure 8–1.

If we consider the motives underlying persuasion, it is obvious that behavior is the reason why we attempt persuasion. Attitudes, after all, are not a tangible part of our reality. They are implicit, unstated concepts existing only in our minds. In themselves, attitudes cannot affect others because there is no way of directly knowing about the attitude. If, however, a certain attitude leads us to engage in a given behavior, then we can better comprehend it. The link is still to behavior, but by focusing on the attitude, we adopt an indirect rather than a direct attempt to manipulate the behavior.

In any persuasion attempt, behavior is the only external measure of success. We infer that attitude change has occurred, but it must remain an inference based on the observation of behavior. For example, one way to explore the attitude–behavior relationship might be to examine attitudes toward a particular political candidate (will a voter vote for this person?) and the actual number of voters going to the polls.

Symbol Manipulation

Finally, most of us agree that communication is not persuasive unless change (behavioral or attitudinal) results from a verbal or nonverbal message. We acknowledge that often behavior results from physical phenomena or coercive processes. Since neither of these involve any decision on our part, neither can be said to be persuasive. It is not persuasion when a mugger knocks us on the head and takes our wallet while we lie on the ground. We do not normally surrender our wallets to strangers on the street. A change in behavior has occurred due to a conscious intent on the part of the mugger, but it resulted from physical force, *not* from the use of symbols. This form of influence is

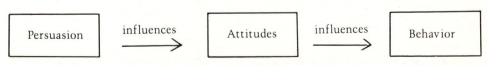

FIGURE 8–1 Persuasion, Attitudes, and Behavior.

excluded from the realm of persuasion. Communication theory is not the source to use if you desire to explain the actions of the mugger. We can explain con artists and politicians, but not violence.

THE NATURE OF ATTITUDES

Attitudes, whether directly or indirectly influencing behavior, consist of three interrelated constructs: opinions, beliefs, and values. The *opinion* is a verbal or nonverbal expression of an attitude. It may not represent the *actual* attitude, or a single attitude, but it usually indicates some aspect of an attitude. A *belief* represents an expectation about how something will occur. Beliefs tend to look toward the future and predict behavior. *Values* express an evaluation of what has happened, may happen, or will happen on some positive or negative scale. Attitudes, then, are composed of beliefs that arise from a value system. Historically, they have been defined as consisting of several "elements."[1] Attitudes comprise affective (feeling), cognitive (thoughts), and connotative (behavior) components. Attitudes emerge from the cognitive component, as influenced by their affective and behavioral counterparts.

Although we have attitudes about most things, some are more salient than others. Typically, we view our attitudes as being positive, negative, or neutral. Positive and negative attitudes reflect strongly held beliefs. Abortion, as an attitude "object," is associated with strongly held attitudes, rooted in religious or personal beliefs. Neutral attitudes usually concern either objects that do not affect us (are out of our environment) or things we know little about. For instance, fifteen years ago, most Americans had a neutral attitude regarding AIDS. Today, AIDS often is associated with stronger attitudes. The same may be true of drunken driving, the Vietnam War, the drafting of eighteen-year-olds, or energy conservation.

Attitudes typically lie dormant until a stimulus awakens them. If the stimulus is tied to a strongly held belief, or system of beliefs, we act on that attitude. Once the attitude surfaces, we evaluate it based on knowledge (cognitive elements), feelings (affective elements), and previous behaviors (connotative elements). This process provides various strategies (theories) from which to change or reinforce held attitudes. This is the strategy persuasion is made of.

As already noted, there are two major schools of persuasive theory. One revolves around behavioral tenets and is closely associated with a learning theory orientation to attitude change. The other revolves around internal psychological tenets and is associated with cognitive consistency–seeking theories of persuasion. We begin by looking at the behavioral perspectives.

BEHAVIORAL THEORIES OF PERSUASION

The behavioral orientation to persuasion seeks to demonstrate the impact of external stimuli on the formation of attitudes. As Charles Kiesler, Barry

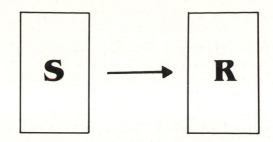

FIGURE 8–2   The Stimulus–Response Model of Human Behavior.

Collins, and Norman Miller note, persuasive behavioral theories are based on "generalizations" or analogies with learning theories.[2] The basic assumption of the behavioral orientation is that we "learn" our attitudes from our environment or from our responses to that environment.

Figure 8–2 presents the basic learning model of persuasion. The stimulus act, or communication, is linked to a response or reaction in ways that can be defined and measured. Once these links are known, the planning and preparation of persuasive messages becomes very precise. By creating an appropriate stimulus, we can elicit a desired response. In its most fundamental sense, this orientation minimizes the role of human attitudes. A simple example would be that you are hot and ask a friend to open a window, and he or she does it.

Other learning theory models of persuasion insist that attitudes have a part or role in the process. Typical of these are the works of Leonard Doob, Arthur Staats, and Clark Hull. Each took the position that attitudes serve to *mediate* the response of the organism to the environment (pp. 89–154). The most direct way to represent the concept of attitudes as mediating processes is shown in Figure 8–3. Attitudes are seen as a response (R) by the organism (O) to some overt stimulus (S). The attitude has, to some extent, been conditioned by that stimulus, but it also becomes a stimulus itself. Hence, the behaviorists argue, the attitude is a stimulus associated with an overt behavior.

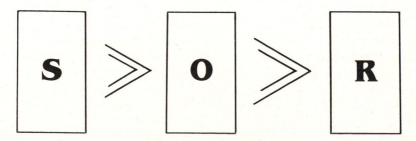

FIGURE 8–3   The S-O-R Model of Human Behavior.

Early Behavioral Considerations

The major assumptions of behavioral theory concern learning. The early theories were not concerned, however, with motivation for change or with the classical concept of reward. Instead, early theory centered on two major assumptions about the link between message and response: (1) the *association between a stimulus and a response*, and (2) the *effects of repetition of stimuli over time*. In terms of association, when two experiences occur simultaneously or in close succession, the recurrence of one tends to reinstate the other. This is quite similar to the concepts originated in Pavlov's classical conditioning experiments. For example, if an experience (public speaking) is associated with an attitude generating a certain amount of fear, then that attitude, when associated with a similar stimulus (interpersonal communication), will become associated with the new stimulus. In similar ways, the attitude becomes an *internal stimulus* bonded to some new behavior.

The behavioral orientation also places heavy emphasis on the repetition of a stimulus. Early theories placed little importance on motivation, preferring instead to rely on repeating the stimulus over and over again. The stimulus, once learned, is then used *habitually.* The more a stimulus is repeated, the more it is reinforced and the stronger the association between stimulus and response. Because of this, repetition creates an internal *drive.*[3]

The Yale Studies

In the 1950s, Carl Hovland, Irving Janis, and Harold Kelly proposed adding the concept of incentive to the behavioral orientation as the result of a series of studies which came to be known as the *Yale Program.*[4] Incentive is closely associated with motivation, but the two concepts are not the same. Hovland, Janis, and Kelly were interested in the relationships between attitude and opinion, both of which they viewed as implicit responses to a stimulus. Although attitudes and opinions are analogous to anticipations and expectations, attitude was defined in the Yale studies as being "used exclusively for those implicit responses which are oriented toward approaching or avoiding" some stimulus (p. 7).

They were interested in the effects of communication in three areas. First, *the perceived characteristics of the source* were seen to function as important stimuli. These results, of course, tended to confirm the position of classical rhetoricians such as Aristotle, with his emphasis on *ethos.* Second, *the communication "environment"* was assigned a major role in assessing the impact of a message. Third, *the actual communication itself* was viewed as a stimulus (the arguments and appeals used in message construction). The Yale researchers felt that the combined effects of source, environment, and message created a drive to attune to the message (see Fig. 8–4). The message itself served to provide a "recommended opinion" evoking an "answer response" in which we rehearse the arguments provided to the initial question. Rehearsal serves to increase the association between the new arguments (stimuli) and the desired behavior (response).

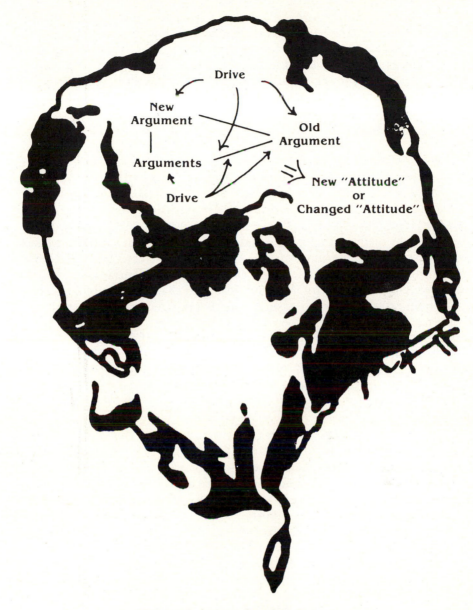

FIGURE 8–4 Stimuli and Responses.

At this stage, *incentive* becomes important. As a receiver of a message, we must be made to rehearse the message. The incentive for rehearsal is found in the appeals and arguments carried within the message. Hovland, Janis, and Kelly argued that learning new stimuli was not sufficient in and of itself to produce change. The receiver must find some "motivation for choosing that particular response to the attitude question in preference to other available responses."[5] An important feature of their work was an orientation toward *message strategies* that created incentive (e.g., fear appeals). Based on this approach, we now have several options available in selecting arguments for our messages. We might try to motivate the receiver by indicating adverse consequences if the requested action is not fulfilled (e.g., the room is hot; without air we might get a heat stroke; therefore, open the window). Or, we might appeal to reason ("It's hot. I'm tired. Please open a window").

Inoculation Theory

William McGuire developed a theory of persuasion that looked at a different application of the persuasive process.[6] Most theorists had studied the process of *changing* attitudes and behaviors. McGuire looked at the process of *not* changing. He was interested in making us resistant to a forthcoming persuasive message. Perhaps the easiest way to understand McGuire's work is to examine it by medical analogy. To make someone less susceptible to a disease, we have learned to use *inoculation*. As a result of effective inoculation programs, once dreaded diseases such as typhoid, diphtheria, and polio have been brought under control. McGuire reasoned that, just as a biological inoculation serves to ward off disease, a properly prepared communication inoculation could make us immune to *future* arguments. Inoculation theory is based on the premise that we are not in the practice of defending our beliefs. McGuire observed that, for many, a large number of our beliefs fall into a category he labeled "cultural truisms," beliefs that are so thoroughly embedded in society that they have never been attacked (e.g., brushing teeth). McGuire reasoned that such beliefs, because of their existence in a psychologically "germ free" environment, might be vulnerable to future attack.

McGuire's research suggests that providing the receiver of a forthcoming message with motivational material in the form of a *pretreatment* attack creates a defensive response. The key element is the ability of the receiver to associate new arguments (stimuli) with those already possessed and to create a new, reinforced, and therefore stronger belief. To provide this form of defense, several variables are important.

First, the *type of defense* to be created is considered. McGuire found that a defense that attacks the belief and then refutes the attack (*refutational defense*) is superior to one that merely provides additional information to support the existing belief (*supportive defense*). The refutational defense accomplishes two results that strengthen the belief being treated. By attacking the cultural truism, the receiver is alerted to a possible attack. This attack creates a threat, and the threat provides the motivation needed to build defenses.

An extension of the public health analogy should help to understand why this is vital. Forty years ago, polio was one of the most feared of the childhood killer diseases. After the development of the Salk vaccine, almost universally, parents had their children inoculated. Public health authorities estimated that the inoculation rate approached 100 percent, and the incidence of polio in the United States fell to insignificant proportions. People no longer feared the disease. As time passed, parents neglected the need for inoculation. There was not much motivation, since the disease was not prevalent. Of course, without inoculation, the disease began to reoccur. The same is true for measles, which was almost wiped out in the 1960s, but is reemerging due to a lack of inoculation. Similarly, motivation is critical if the message receiver is going to put forth the effort to develop defenses.

Second, the refutational defense provides information we can use to *build defenses against future attacks.* The persuasive impact of a new or novel attack is thereby undercut. By providing information, we give the receiver the basic materials needed to construct defenses. With both resources and a motivation to use them, the receiver is more likely to resist future attacks on his or her beliefs.

Third, the creation of defenses takes *time.* McGuire demonstrated that a communication-based inoculation, as with the biological analogy, takes a certain amount of time before it becomes effective.[7] When an attacking message comes immediately after the inoculation, a supportive defense coupled with some threat facilitates resistance; however, when sufficient time has lapsed between inoculation pretreatment and actual attack on the belief, the refutational defense is superior. In this case, stimuli are associated with *new* concepts, creating an incentive to rehearse the defense.

In extending McGuire's theory, Michael Burgoon and associates found that beliefs and attitudes other than cultural truisms are also susceptible to inoculation.[8] Burgoon's research focused on beliefs that, although they are strongly held by the individual, do not fall into the realm of truisms as defined by McGuire. He reported fairly consistent results. Therefore, we may expect that the inoculation model proves effective as a way of inducing resistance to persuasion in many situations, as long as the target attitude or belief is one that is strongly held by the receiver.

REVIEW

The discussion thus far is intended to provide an understanding of what we use to create the framework of our attitudes. Our knowledge of attitudes and how they function has limits. Within those limits, we can say that people react to their environment, but not in the same ways. Each of us serves not only as an object–target, but also as a stimulus–mediator in interpreting experience. On the basis of experience, we each construct an attitudinal "framework," which provides the basis of our approach to our symbolic world and a foundation for the methods we use when communicating to change or reinforce attitudes and beliefs. As such, behavioral persuasive theory falls into classifications of both theories of knowledge and theories of action.

CRITIQUE

The construct of attitude itself, while possessing a logical appeal, is inherently immune to direct testing. Behaviors may be measured, opinions may be recorded, but attitudes remain sealed in our minds. As a result, some theorists suggest that for all practical purposes, attitudes do not exist. The majority of communication theorists, however, are probably willing to grant the existence of attitudes, even if they quibble over their precise definition. Most of us believe that attitudes mediate human behavior, although the exact dimensions of that mediatory process remain cloudy. Learning theory as an approach has generated a vast body of research dealing with how we process information and react to our experiences. As this research continues to accumulate, our theories will become more refined and usable.

COGNITIVE CONSISTENCY THEORIES

We dealt in the previous section with the construct of human attitudes. In this section we examine in more detail theories that explain how we can modify attitudes. The architect sometimes begins the construction process with a bare plot of ground, but at other times the job is to remodel or redesign an existing structure. Likewise, one approach to the process of behavioral change is to see it as an exercise in remodeling. This is the basic focus of a group of attitude theories falling under the label of *cognitive consistency theory*.

We have been discussing situations in which a stimulus, through an association with other stimuli, causes behavior to change. However, many psychological studies have centered on the internal forces that mediate the attitude–behavior link. Where do these forces come from? What do they consist of? Cognitive consistency theories attempt to answer these questions. These theories are based on four basic assumptions about us and the way we deal with information:

1. *We are rational.* We are capable of cognitive processes and can deal logically with our environment; however, we are not always logical in the way we make decisions.

2. *We are rationalizing creatures.* Although we occasionally act irrationally or in ways incompatible with commonly held logic, we are aware of what constitutes rational behavior and value such behavior.

3. *We are consistency-seeking creatures.* We define consistency among our attitudes and behaviors as a desirable state. We are aware of behavior that is internally inconsistent and regard this awareness as painful.

4. *We adjust our behavior and/or attitudes to avoid inconsistency.* We tend to avoid pain, and since inconsistency is perceived as painful, we avoid it whenever possible. When inconsistency cannot be avoided altogether, we engage in behavior designed to minimize the resulting discomfort.

Although we dislike *inconsistency* and actively avoid situations in which inconsistency presents itself, inconsistency nevertheless is created.

McGuire suggests five ways that inconsistency is created.[9] First, inconsistency is created through our own logical shortcomings. Even when we are acting in a logical and rational manner, we do not always achieve 100 percent success. We sometimes diverge from the path of logic and reason. Emotions interfere with the pursuit of logic, as does the reliance on the symbolic value of words to express internal feelings and thoughts.

Second, inconsistency is created when we are placed in conflicting social roles. Each social role we occupy has differing expectations and demands. Sometimes these expectations are in conflict with each other and create disequilibrium (see Chapter 7), as in the role demands found in "professional" versus "parent." Interfamily relationships often create conflict between the expectations of "spouse" and those of "child."

Third, the environment in which we exist changes, sometimes leaving us with a world view or a set of attitudes that are no longer congruent with reality. A number of World War II veterans had difficulty adjusting to having Germany and Japan as allies and trading partners. It also causes significant inconsistency for them to visit the U.S.S. *Arizona* Memorial in Pearl Harbor, along with Japanese tourists. We sometimes find that our situations are different, that we have not changed as the situation changed. This source of inconsistency is sometimes identified with people who "live in the past."

Fourth, we are often pressured into behaving in ways that are inconsistent with our beliefs. The inconsistency comes from being forced to comply with a request or a persuasive message that seeks behavior that we previously found unacceptable. Young people, especially teenagers, experience inconsistency as they wrestle with the competing pressures associated with their peers as opposed to their parents. In many cases, the inconsistency is relieved by changing internal attitudes to fit new patterns of behavior.

Fifth, once we have changed an attitude, we may find that it is now inconsistent with other held attitudes. At any given moment, we have many attitudes. Most attitudes are not especially salient, and therefore we may not think about them. We may not immediately notice that a change in one attitude creates opposition to other attitudes, but when that conflict is noticed, inconsistency occurs.

Consistency theorists assume that we are consistency-seeking creatures. We seek a state of *homeostasis* or balance between behaviors and attitudes, which is obtained by ordering attitudes or beliefs in logically consistent and comfortable ways. The behavioral theorists studied in the previous section placed their emphasis on external and observable phenomena. Consistency theorists emphasize an understanding of *how and why* we seek comfort or consistency. Since we do not always act in ways that accommodate learning theory predictions (e.g., martyrdom is hard to explain from behavioral theory), cognitive consistency theory explains many outcomes of interest to the persuasion student that may not require a change in behavior to reflect attitude change. As such, they typically are categorized as theories of knowledge. In the next few pages, we briefly discuss four major cognitive consistency theories: balance theory, symmetry theory, congruity theory, and cognitive dissonance theory. As we discuss each, note how they build on each other.

Balance Theory

The earliest consistency theory was developed in 1946 by Fritz Heider.[10] Heider argued that we seek to maintain a state of consistency in our relationships, which he defined as "balance." In this balanced state, we can resist influence from outside sources. In the state of balance, we feel no pressure to change our behavior. The major source of inconsistency ("imbalance") is a tension felt through perceived interpersonal relationships vis-à-vis some attitudinal object. Heider considered interpersonal relationships as being either positive or negative; that is, we either like or dislike other people or things. Accordingly, we can determine whether we (S) find a relationship with an other (O) to be balanced or imbalanced by examining the relationships among S, O, and some idea or attitude object (X). As illustrated in Figure 8–5, there are eight possible relationships; four are balanced and four are not.

The basic nature of relationships is relatively easy to grasp. Consider, for example, the following situation. Greg (S) likes school (X) and Gretchen (O). Gretchen, however, dislikes school. This relationship, Type 6 of Figure 8–5, is unbalanced. As a result, it creates stress for Greg. To achieve balance, Greg can do any one of three things. He could (a) change his mind about

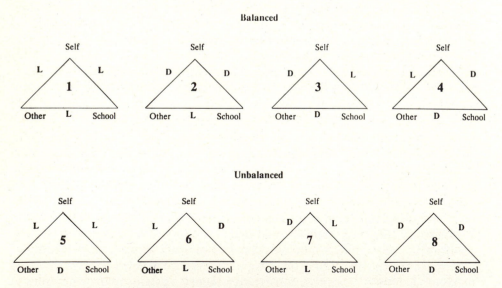

FIGURE 8–5   Heider's Balance Theory of Relationships.

Liking relationships are shown as **L**; disliking relationships are shown with a **D**. All relationships are shown from the point of view of the self and are unidirectional. Adapted from C. A. Kiesler, B. E. Collins, and N. Miller, *Attitude Change* (New York: John Wiley & Sons, 1969).

Gretchen, (b) alter his attitude about school, or (c) try to convince Gretchen to change her approach to school. If he implements Option *a*, the relationship shifts to Type 3. Option *b* would be illustrated by Type 4, and Option *c* would produce the sort of relationship shown in Type 1. In any case, the result would be the elimination of tension and stress from the relationship.

Balance theory is limited in several ways.[11] First, because Heider did not consider any differences in the *intensity* of liking–disliking, the model is not always realistic. It assumes a highly simplistic state of either liking *or* disliking. In fact, we may mildly dislike an object while strongly liking the other person. In such a case, the stress, if any, is ineffectual. Second, Heider's theory does not take into account the *reciprocal* effects of the object, the feelings of the other person in the triad, and the other's feelings about us (*S*). All of Heider's formulations are in terms of the stress felt by the *perceiver*. This produces an awkward and cumbersome tool to use in the analysis of relationships. Finally, Heider does not consider the nature of the relationship between *S* and *O*.

Relationships can also be *competitive*, rather than cooperative. Consider the case of two people who are friends and coworkers. Jane likes Sue, but both Jane and Sue want a promotion that has just become available in their agency. According to Heider, this would be a balanced situation, with Jane feeling no stress or tension. In fact, however, Jane is likely to feel stress in her relationship with Sue because of the competition between them.

Research has provided some important implications that support Heider's model. This body of research suggests that predictions of change may be made on the balance model in relation to valance, polarity, duration of the held attitude, perceptions of sources and content, and commitment. Research has supported the following predictions: (1) *Positive valances are preferred to negative valances.* We will change a negative relationship before we change a positive one. (2) *The degree of polarization in the relationship, however, mediates such change.* As we think more negatively about an object, positive change becomes less likely. (3) *The longer an attitude has been held, the harder it is to change.* Older, more long-standing attitudes are more resistant to change than those formed more recently. (4) When we feel differently about the source and the message, *attitudes toward the message change before those toward the source of the message.* finally, (5) *the more committed we are to an attitude or a relationship, the more resistant we are to change.*[12]

Balance theory is *truly* attitudinal. There is no concern for overt behavior or even messages. A change in attitude can occur without the other people even being aware of it. Because change is perceived as a simple liking construct, we may change feelings almost at will. The focus is, in terms of previous chapters, *intrapersonal.* Balance theory is useful, however, in predicting the relationship between a message source, an audience, and an attitude object. In effect, we might use it as a tool for audience analysis.

Because balance theory operates in a simple like/dislike relationship, it provides some relatively simple uses. Suppose, for instance, you and a friend (your "audience") are considering renting an apartment together. Your friend, you *think*, is unsure about potential financial problems since the lease must be signed in only one name. To predict your friend's final attitude, you need the following information: what his or her relationship to you is, how he or she feels about financial commitment, how long these beliefs have existed, and how important renting an apartment is. Assuming your relationship is positive (liking), any persuasive message about the apartment might be grounded in the three related ideas. Because balance theory does not focus on messages, however, you are left with *potential message strategies.* To look at messages, we need to move on to symmetry theory.

Symmetry Theory

Theodore Newcomb applied balance theory to communication, evolving an idea that he termed the "strain toward symmetry" theory of attitude change.[13] Newcomb adapted balance theory by suggesting that the relationships among self, other, and object are *interdependent* on each other. He saw us as constantly straining toward some type of symmetry (consistency). Important features of symmetry theory are *the intensity of the held attitude* and *the amount of attraction between people.* Symmetry theory predicts that an increase in the intensity of the held attitude or in the degree of attraction will (1) increase our strain toward symmetry, (2) increase the likelihood of symmetry, and, most importantly, (3) increase the probability that we will communicate to the other about the attitude object.

    Newcomb's theory brings communication into the realm of attitude change. Symmetry theory assumes that increasing the strain toward symmetry results in communication as we adjust our relationships so our attitudes and relationships become consistent. This adjustment of relationships over time, for instance, provides a theoretical foundation for theories of *stereotyping.* Over time, groups of people to come to think alike, share important values, and move in the direction that is under the strain toward symmetry.

    The ability to use communication as the persuasive agent suggests an interactive effect between attraction and attitude change. Change is valued as a way of retaining or achieving attitudinal similarity with friends or with people to whom we are attracted. Communication is a way of achieving change *and* a way of altering others to the change when it has taken place.

    Although symmetry theory allows us to predict the degree of liking in a relationship, it is still limited. Symmetry theory is more closely aligned with theories of *interpersonal attraction* than with studies directly examining attitude change.[14] Other than some fairly sketchy predictions, it does not specifically indicate *why* attitude change occurs. Although groups of people adjust their attitudes toward symmetry, the theory does not explain exactly which shifts will be made and who will exhibit those shifts. Furthermore, attitude change may not occur if our relationship is bound by factors significantly strong to overcome the antibonding caused by differences in attitude. Symmetry theory also suggests that we do not associate with those whose attitudes differ from our own.

Our earlier example is relevant here. Now, we can make some predictions about the persuasive outcome and message strategy. Assume that you and your potential roommate are attracted to each other. The situation requires that some message strategy be employed. Since the bond between the two of you is strong, change *should* come in favor of your position if you employ a message strategy that focuses on your friendship and financial responsibility.

Congruity Theory

Some ten years after Heider first advanced balance theory, Charles Osgood and Percy Tannenbaum presented a model of attitude change built on the principle of *congruity*.[15] Osgood and Tannenbaum were concerned with the problems associated with balance theory, especially with knowing the direction of attitude change. Congruity theory provides a mathematical formula predicting the *amount* and *expected direction* of attitude change. Both are dependent on the degree of inconsistency.

Osgood and Tannenbaum prefaced their work on the assumption that, given a change, we adjust our attitudes toward extreme or bipolar judgments. Figure 8–6 examines the difference between a simple bipolar decision and one that must discriminate among five possible decisions. It is much easier to make a bipolar decision. This movement toward "black-or-white," "all-or-nothing" is known as the principle of *maximization of simplicity*. One consequence of this principle is our inability to discriminate among ideas and sources, relying instead on stereotypical judgments. Thus, we may view a candidate as a party member, rather than as an individual political candidate.

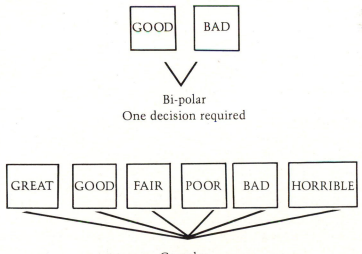

FIGURE 8–6   Making Judgments.

Association with a stereotype may be desirable at times. When a candidate seeks to avoid such stereotypes, however, we may perceive him or her at the opposite extreme, not somewhere in the middle. Consider, for example, a party you attended lately. Was it good or bad? If neither, how do you describe it? Which is *easier* to describe: the stereotyped "good" or "bad" party or the "sort of good" party?

The persuasive impact of simplified judgments is found in the link between the position of a source and our attitude. Osgood and Tannenbaum were concerned with the message a source sends in inconsistent situations. Congruity theory is specifically concerned with the incongruity existing between a source's assertions and our privately held attitudes. They predict that attitudes are linked by an assertion to the position of the source. This link yields two bonds: an *associative bond*, which is linked to an assertion by a source indicating something positive about an attitude object we perceive as "good," and a *disassociative bond*, which is linked to the source's saying something "bad" about the attitude object.

Congruity theory predicts that change is dependent on how much we like both the source and the attitude object. In other words, congruity theory examines *multiple relationships.* Any attitude change due to an inconsistent state is thought to influence perceptions of both the source *and* the attitude object. This change is reflected in our attempt to make the statements of the source conform to a reasonably consistent attitude position (to "balance" the perceptions of the source and the message). Congruity theory predicts that more polarized perceptions yield less attitude change. Attitudes toward topic and s   rce will change in inverse proportion to their intensity or polarity.

As a communication strategy, the source might "sacrifice" established credibility or goodwill for a change in our attitude. This may have been the effect of President Gerald Ford's 1974 pardon of President Richard Nixon. He may have seen the sacrifice of credibility necessary to neutralize negative attitudes toward the pardon by the nation. In the same way, if someone you dislike makes positive comments about a candidate you like, you will dislike the source less and like the message more. When a source or message is too extreme, however, neither will be believed (e.g., a janitor coming to class and dismissing it versus the known departmental secretary doing the same).

Cognitive Dissonance Theory

The latest step in the evolution of consistency theory was taken by Leon Festinger with the development of *cognitive dissonance* theory.[16] Festinger posited that people possess "cognitive elements" or attitudes that coexist in one of three relationships: (1) they may be *irrelevant* to each other (you are reading this book and someone is sleeping); (2) they may be *consonant* (you are reading this book and learning about a number of different psychological theories); or (3) they may be *dissonant* (as you read this book you find many ways that your communication may be interpreted). Festinger believed the first two relationships cause little inconsistency. The third relationship, dissonance, causes discomfort and motivates people to change at least one of the three elements to achieve consistency.

Cognitive dissonance occurs in four ways.[17] (1) As with most consistency theories, there is our own logical inconsistency. (2) Cultural mores create dissonance. (3) One specific opinion that, by definition, is included in a more general opinion, creates dissonance (e.g., mothers for abortion, veterans against war). (4) Past experiences that differ from present experiences create dissonance. According to Festinger, the existence of dissonance creates a psychological tension that motivates people to reduce it and achieve consonance between the dissonant elements. When dissonance exists, we try not only to reduce it, but to actively avoid situations and information that increase it. The first assumption is central to all consistency theories; the second is unique in that it suggests we actively avoid conflict. In general, the greater the dissonance, the greater is the pressure to reduce it.

Dissonance theory offers three general strategies to reduce inconsistency: (1) we can change the elements related to the behavior causing the dissonance, to include denying that the behavior occurred; (2) we can change the elements causing dissonance; and (3) we can add new elements, reducing the dissonance by adding information or creating new attitudes about the situation. For example, a person who smokes may (1) deny that smoking causes cancer, since almost anything seems to cause cancer; (2) seek people who smoke as friends; or (3) find new reasons for smoking (weight control, relaxation).

Dissonance often occurs when we believe we will be forced to make a decision. In most decision-making situations, at least one, if not many, alternative choices can be ignored or ruled out as not possible for any number of reasons. When we are left with two equally attractive choices, however, dissonance occurs. Typically, the importance of the decision and the advantages provided by each alternative predict the amount of dissonance generated. The more important the decision, the greater the dissonance. The fewer the distinctive advantages of any alternative relative to the other, the greater the dissonance. After the decision, *postdecisional* dissonance sets in due to the attractiveness of the nonselected option or the importance of the decision just made ("Did I do the right thing?").

If there was no solution to dissonance, dissonance theory would be an interesting but largely irrelevant theory. It is the presence of *reduction mechanisms* that allows Festinger's theory to explain communication behavior. Dissonance theory advances five strategies, discussed in the following sections, which we may use in messages designed to reduce perceived inconsistency brought about by dissonant conditions, or, conversely, to increase dissonance.

Altered Attractiveness. Frequently, after choosing between two or more options, we deal with dissonance by reducing the perceived attractiveness of the rejected option(s). We may lie to ourselves. We look for information that lowers our opinion of the rejected alternative and we magnify the good points of our selected option to the point that it seems as if no choice really ever existed. By convincing ourselves of the inevitability of the choice we made, we effectively eliminate dissonance.

Compartmentalization.   It is not unusual to exhibit behaviors inconsistent with our values, or to subscribe to values that have inconsistent premises. As children, we are taught that people have worth and value irrespective of their race or ethnic origin. We are taught to respect others and to refrain from violence in dealing with them. Yet, drafted into the armed forces, we are given another set of values. We are taught that the enemy is evil and despicable. We are taught how to kill, the ultimate violence, and rewarded when we learn how to kill effectively. In this situation, millions of people have experienced dissonance. The most common solution is to compartmentalize: to divide life into distinct cells or compartments. Military life is one compartment with one set of values; civilian life is entirely another. Compartmentalization helps us tolerate the inconsistency arising from beliefs in conflicting value systems. It is not good or bad; it is simply a device that we use to escape the pain of dissonance.

Source Derogation.   Dissonance often arises as a result of information that challenges or disagrees with information already in our heads. Usually, we are aware of a "source" for that inconsistent information. We also know that the impact of any message is influenced by our evaluation of its source. Through source derogation, which functions as an escape mechanism from cognitive dissonance, we diminish the credibility of the source of the dissonant information and reduce the dissonance created by that information.

Most of us have experienced receiving negative information about a friend or a loved one. We may hear gossip which says that somebody we like has done something of which we disapprove. This makes us feel uncomfortable, dissonant. To avoid the dissonance, we frequently dismiss the gossip as coming from an unreliable source. Parents are frequently guilty of resorting to source derogation when they receive negative information about their children.

Source derogation is not necessarily irrational. Sometimes the information source is unreliable and the message should be viewed with caution, but we need to recognize the danger of using the technique simply because we do not want to deal with a challenge to our existing beliefs. In those instances, source derogation can be used as a device to mislead ourselves.

Message Distortion.   Message distortion might be defined as hearing what we want to hear instead of what the message actually says. Like source derogation, distortion is most commonly used with messages or new pieces of information that conflict with previously accepted attitudes. The use of existing attitude systems as a filter to distort perception is widely demonstrated and should be a familiar concept. Message distortion is extremely common and is related to the degree of personal involvement we have with the attitude object under consideration.

Rationalization. The final dissonance avoidance mechanism is rationalization, sometimes known as ignoring the facts. It usually involves claiming immunity from some law of nature. For example, some friends go to a local bar for an afternoon. Later that evening, they realize that they have to return home, and that they have drunk too much. They are not drunk, but definitely are not sober. Dissonance arises from an awareness that driving and drinking are a dangerous combination. At least one usually begins to rationalize: "I can handle myself. I'll be perfectly safe, and it's only a short drive home. Nothing could possibly happen in such a distance, and besides, I'll be especially careful . . . " Most of us are guilty of rationalizing from time to time; it is a lot easier than facing facts that we do not like. The danger arises when rationalization leads us to ignore important truths simply so that we can avoid dissonance.

Dissonance theory has produced a large volume of persuasion research. In using it to persuade others, we are provided many message strategies. In situations where change is desired, the message may seek to create dissonance concerning the held position and then provide an avenue of consonance (the source's position). Also, a message may be used to make people feel responsible for a course of action and then employ dissonance theory as the strategy for implementing reducing mechanisms. In such cases, the attributions of responsibility for others' actions yields dissonance, and the only way to achieve consonance is to alter perceptions of the *original* attitude.

Table 8–1 summarizes the strengths and weaknesses of the cognitive consistency theories discussed: balance/symmetry theories, congruity theories, and cognitive dissonance theories. We now turn to two related cognitive theories. Social judgment theory takes a more practical approach to message strategy. Functional theory looks at how attitudes develop and their uses.

Social Judgment Theory

Social judgment theory attempts to answer the question, "How do we perceive an advocated (persuasive) position that is discrepant from our own?"[18] In answering this question, Carolyn Sherif, Muzafer Sherif, and Roger Nebergall proposed that the process of changing attitudes occurs in two stages. First, we judge the position taken by someone and compare it with our own position. Second, changes in attitude are then made. These changes are dependent on the *degree of ego-involvement* involving the attitude object, and the size of our *latitudes of acceptance, rejection, and noncommitment.*

According to social judgment theory, when we are exposed to a persuasive message, we can discriminate between our position and the one advocated. This discrimination produces an attitude anchored somewhere between acceptance and rejection of the statement. If the statement advocates a position

TABLE 8–1   Strengths and Weaknesses of Cognitive Consistency Theories

Theory	Strengths	Weaknesses
Balance/ Symmetry	1. Easy to understand and use 2. Emphasizes coordination 3. Somewhat testable	1. Predicts change, but not the locus of change 2. Is two-valued: attitudes are either positive or negative 3. Considers only one attitude at a time
Congruity	1. Easy to understand and use 2. Predicts degree of attitude 3. Very testable	1. Intensity of assertion is ignored 2. Considers only one attitude at a time 3. Does not consider alternative theories of inconsistency reduction
Cognitive Dissonance	1. Provides a useful explanation of decisionmaking behaviors 2. Generates considerable research	1. Difficult to predict degree of dissonance arousal 2. Difficult to predict precise modes of dissonance reduction

close to ours, it falls within our latitude of acceptance. The latitude of acceptance is the anchor position, plus a group of closely clustered positions that we find acceptable. If the message advocates a position that is neither acceptable nor unacceptable, it falls within our latitude of noncommitment. Finally, if the message advocates a position that is so far from the anchor position as to be clearly unacceptable, it falls within our latitude of rejection.

The size of these various latitudes is dependent on our personal involvement with the idea being advocated. If we are highly ego-involved (highly committed and involved), it is probable that our latitude of acceptance on the issue or topic will be small, our latitude of noncommitment very small, and our latitude of rejection much larger. On the other hand, if we are relatively noninvolved with the issue, our latitudes of acceptance and rejection are smaller than our latitude of noncommitment. Research indicates that any message falling within our latitude of acceptance tends to be *assimilated*, perceived as closer to the anchor position than it actually is. Any message landing within our latitude of rejection triggers a *contrast* effect; that is, we see it as *more* different from the anchor position than it truly is. Messages advocating positions within the latitude of noncommitment of an ego-involved person would not be likely to produce attitude change; however, that same message presented to a non–ego-involved person would produce movement and attitude change.

Where social judgment theory improves on other theories is in its implementation. Social judgment theory suggests that a *series of messages*, each within our latitude of acceptance or noncommital, will move us toward an advocated position. It also suggests that messages may "boomerang," reinforcing our original position if they advocate positions too extreme in either direction or away from the anchor (this includes being too favorable). Advocating that *all* abortions should be illegal, for instance, would cause rejection of the message by many prolifers. Abortion to save a mother's life, for example, *may* be within the prolifer's latitude of acceptance.

Functional Theory

Daniel Katz extends the study of persuasion beyond the two-phase social judgment model.[19] *Functional theory* is a persuasive approach that examines the functions of attitudes in day-to-day activity. Katz argues that we must understand why people hold an attitude and what functions it serves. His argument is based on the premise that attitude formation is a complex process relating to both behavioral (instrumental) and cognitive (consistency) considerations *and* must take into account personal idiosyncrasy. Katz suggests a four-functioned theory of attitude change based on the needs for the attitude.

Katz begins with the behavioral position that attitudes serve an associated or *utilitarian/instrumental* function; that is, attitudes serve to supply either a positive or a negative reinforcement. Our attitudes serve to create approach–avoidance tendencies (habits) which serve as motivations to behave. Katz argues that knowledge of these tendencies can be used to affect attitude change through reward–punishment contingencies and threats to needs.

Two closely related functions are those of *ego-defensiveness* and *value-expressiveness*. The ego-defensive function relates to the internal conflicts we have and the use of attitudes to maintain a stable view of self. This function is closely related to psychoanalytic theory and helps us to understand motivations in attitude formation. Katz suggests several ways to induce change associated with ego-defensive attitudes, including threatening the person, using appeals to authority, and frustrating the person. The value-expressive function, on the other hand, reflects an enhanced view of the self and is reflected in positive feelings of self-worth. Unlike the ego-defensive attitudes, which are hidden from the world, value-expressive attitudes are reflective of our public self-worth. Effecting change in attitudes formed via this function has been linked to threatening the self-concept and depriving us of the chance to express attitudes as reflective of personal positions based on some conviction.

Finally, attitudes are formed to serve a *knowledge function*. These attitudes serve to provide us with a frame of reference. Katz argued that our world is chaotic and disorganized, and that attitudes function to make order out of disorder. Attitude change through this function is influenced most by attaching ambiguous attitudes or associating attitudes with stereotypical views to the attitude object.

Functional theory tries to forge a link between why an attitude is formed or held and possible strategies for changing it. It provides for different uses of attitudes and tries to reflect the world as we view it. Finally, functional theory tries to understand the complex motivations behind the formation of attitudes.

INDIVIDUAL CHARACTERISTICS INFLUENCING ATTITUDE CHANGE

There is considerable disagreement among theorists over the existence of any general traits of persuasibility (persuasibility that is bound neither by content nor by situation). The best known researcher associated with a traits approach is Janis. The evidence is not conclusive, but Janis and others believe that five different characteristics can be used as predictors of persuasion: self-esteem, hostility, richness of fantasy, sex, and authoritarian personality.[20]

Janis and Rife report research indicating a high negative correlation between personal *self-esteem* (feelings of inadequacy, social inhibitions) and persuasibility.[21] As feelings of self-esteem decrease, attitude change increases. This finding may be explained by noting that people with low self-esteem do not place high values on themselves, instead depending more on the advice and approval of valued others. Some indicators of low self-esteem include shyness, lack of self-confidence, high concern for rejection, timidity, communication apprehension, and feelings of sadness and hopelessness.

Most research implies that *hostility* is negatively related to persuasiveness.[22] People induced to be hostile (through abusive message pretreatments) become less persuasible. A problem with hostility research, however, is the type of action the persuasive message calls for. Weiss and Find have found, for instance, that abusive pretreatments yielded more persuasion toward *punitive* appeals than *altruistic* appeals.

Significant positive correlations between individual *levels of fantasy* and persuasibility have been found in several studies.[23] People with rich fantasy responses may be able to imagine the consequences that result from a persuasive message's appeals. If the appeals were rewarding, people with rich fantasy levels would be able to "see" themselves enjoying the reward. Conversely, if the appeals were punishing, they would be able to "see" themselves suffering the adverse consequences. In either case, the persuasive result would be the same: a greater susceptibility to the message.

Some research has demonstrated that of the two sexes, females are more susceptible than males to a persuasive message in impersonal matters such as social, political, and intellectual issues.[24] Possible explanations for these results are that our cultural role model for women has placed a premium on yielding or conformity or that females lack self-confidence or self-esteem. Research by Charles Montgomery and Michael Burgoon, however, suggests that it may be the *sex role* that predicts attitude change rather than the *biological sex type*.[25] They found that females with traditionally feminine sex-role expectations (women should stay in the home, be nurturing, remain quiet, etc.) are more susceptible to persuasive messages, but that females not traditionally sex typed, as well as both "traditional" masculine (males who are strong, argumentative, loud, etc.) and nontraditional masculine sex-typed males, are less susceptible to persuasive messages.

Finally, social psychologists have given much attention to a combination of traits associated with the *authoritarian personality.* In general, the authoritarian is seen as rigid in perceptions, absolutist in values, and compulsive in behavior. A closely related personality syndrome is dogmatism, studied by Milton Rokeach.[26] In trying to influence a dogmatic personality, the persuasive message must place great stress on authorities who support a particular position and in whom the dogmatic person places a great deal of trust rather than focusing on the merits of the issue involved.

MESSAGE STRATEGIES

If we were to criticize the focus of psychological persuasion research to date, we would note that it has been on specific variables associated with the persuasive process. Given an understanding of what influences persuasion, it follows that certain message strategies may yield compliance in certain situations, especially in person-to-person influence attempts. The focus here is on the *message choices* available to persuaders.[27]

Initial thoughts in message strategy, or typologies of message strategies we choose in influence attempts, suggest that five strategies may be employed in compliance-gaining situations. Gerald Marwell and David R. Schmitt, in their initial research on message typologies, suggest that message strategies could be collapsed into socially acceptable and socially unacceptable strategies.[28] Socially acceptable strategies include rewarding messages (promises, appeals to liking) and appeals to impersonal commitments (use of positive or negative expertise). Socially unacceptable strategies include punishing messages (threats, aversive appeals) and appeals to personal commitments (positive or negative self-esteem, altercasting [i.e., a good person would do this], positive or negative self-feeling). Marwell and Schmitt suggest, then, that persuaders may choose from as many as sixteen different compliance-gaining strategies.

To explain compliance-gaining strategies, John Hunter and Franklin Boster explored the dimensionality of the typologies. They suggest that compliance-gaining strategies are a function of the emotional influence of the message on the receiver:

> Attempts to persuade others often produce emotional reactions. These reactions lead others to act in ways that have consequences for the persuader. For example, depending on the compliance-gaining message used, the listener may become angry, flattered, resentful, or experience a host of other emotions. These emotional responses lead to either immediate or delayed reactions to the persuader.

Suppose that a student attempts to persuade a roommate to spend more time studying. The roommate might conclude that the student has a good point, that the student's persuasion attempt is an expression of concern for the roommate's welfare, and begin to study more frequently. Or the roommate might become incensed, suggest that the student mind his or her own business, and eventually try to find a new roommate. Or the roommate might go along for the moment, begin to study more, and harbor resentment against the student. This resentment might then be manifested later by avoidance or anger over trivial matters. In each case there is an immediate emotional response by the listener, and a subsequent reaction by the listener that has consequences for the persuader.

Since there is a subsequent consequence for the persuader, he or she probably becomes sensitive to the emotional reactions of listeners. Moreover, the persuader's selection of a compliance-gaining message doubtless depends, in part, on the perceived (i.e., predicted by the persuader) emotional response of the listener. Simply put, it is generally functional for the persuader to avoid messages that produce negative emotional reactions in listeners.[29]

Hunter and Boster obtained support for the one-dimensional model. They suggest that, based on the emotional impact of the message on the receiver (listener), it will be used if it falls within a positive emotional "threshold"; otherwise, it will not be used.

Message strategy theory and research suggests that certain messages will be selected, depending on the people and the situation where the message will be enacted. The focus is on individual characteristic variables, situations, and new typologies of strategies. Its limitation has been on the nature of the research testing the theory. Reliance on checklists of strategies that "would be used" in a given situation only approximates the actual process of message selection; however, responses to such stimuli might, when related to other variables, yield compliance-gaining strategies.

Message strategy theory provides a cogent end to our examination of attempts to change attitudes and behavior. We have come full circle; beginning with the concept of persuasion as a purposive act, we end with an analysis of the strategies underlying that act.

_____ REVIEW _____

This chapter examined several theories of attitude and behavior change (see Table 8–2). It has stressed that attitude and behavior are related concepts, but that the link between the two is not precisely understood. The concept of an attitude, whether as an intervening variable or as the direct object of study, has become central to the study of social influence. Persuasion theory owes much to the contributions of the learning theorists, as well as the cognitive theorists. The act of changing an attitude is a complex procedure affected by both internal and external variables. Social influence strategies are aimed at either affecting change in some held attitude or inducing resistance to some future attack on a held attitude.

TABLE 8-2 Summary Table

Name of Theory	Primary Theorists	Basic Principle	Constructs	Criteria	Analytic Approach	Limitations
Human Attitudes		All communication is purposive.	• Attitude(s)			
Learning Theory	Hovland, Janis, and Kelly	Attitudes are learned through experience.	• Stimulus–Organism–Response	Predictability	Empirical Observation	Assumes a relatively simplistic explanation for what are in many cases highly complex relationships.
Inoculation Theory	McGuire	Inducing resistance to persuasion.	• Refutational defense	Motivation and information		Majority of research in support of the theory has been limited to cultural truisms.
Consistency Theories		Humans dislike and will avoid inconsistency.	• Consistency			
Balance	Heider	The search for balanced relationships.	• Balance	Analysis of interrelationships		Doesn't account for intensity of valence; doesn't consider competitive relationships.

179

TABLE 8-2 (*Continued*)

Name of Theory	Primary Theorists	Basic Principle	Constructs	Criteria	Analytic Approach	Limitations
Symmetry	Newcomb	Liking as relationship.	• Symmetry	Strain toward symmetry		Doesn't explain where adjustments will be made.
Congruity	Osgood and Tannenbaum	The maximization of simplicity.	• Congruity	Associative and dissociative bonds	—	Doesn't explain which adjustments will be made.
Cognitive Dissonance	Festinger	Avoiding dissonance.	• Dissonance	Advoidance mechanisms	—	Doesn't provide quantification needed for prediction.
Social Judgment	Sherif, Sherif, and Nebergall	Placement of messages relative to anchor.	• Anchor • Latitudes of acceptance, Rejection, Noncommitment	Placement, assimilation, contrast	—	Untestable constructs of latitudes of acceptance, rejection, etc.
Functional	Katz	Attitudes are behavioral and cognitive and individual.	• Utilitarian • Ego-defensive • Value-expressive • Knowledge functions	Complex motivation for change	—	Not adequately tested.

CRITIQUE

The problems mentioned earlier relating to the testability of the construct attitude are of course applicable here. Each of the early stages in the development of consistency theory had significant theoretical flaws, many of which were resolved by the work of Festinger. The concepts involved in cognitive dissonance are relatively clear and straightforward, although it is difficult to quantify dissonance or even to provide a qualitative estimate of how it will affect behavior in a given situation. The problem of quantification also plagues social judgment theory. The descriptive terminology offered by the theory is unambiguous, but there are no objective measures available that we can use before the fact to determine an individual's latitude of acceptance. As a result, the theory is more useful as an explanation for what *has* happened rather than as a device for predicting what *will* happen. Functional theory, for all its promise, has not been adequately tested. Little research has actually demonstrated the impact of personality on attitude change. The future of persuasion research may be found in extending message strategy to other variables and then across situations. The problem lies, however, in obtaining *actual psychological strategies as they are about to be employed*, rather than self-report measures to simulated situations.

The various attitude and behavioral theories have certainly been heuristic. There are a lot of them, however, and they tend to be low in parsimony. In the case of some, no communication is necessary for change to occur, or at least no communication between the interactants (e.g., balance theory). These psychological approaches have attempted to deal with individual attitudes and behaviors. The next section is concerned with society's effect on the communication process.

NOTES AND REFERENCES

[1] D. R. Siebold, "Communication Research and the Attitude Report–Overt Behavior Relationship: A Critique and Theoretical Reformulation," *Human Communication Research*, 2 (1975), 2–32.

[2] C. A. Kiesler, B. E. Collins, and N. Miller, *Attitude Change* (New York: John Wiley and Sons, 1969), p. 152.

[3] See C. L. Hull, *A Behavior System: An Introduction to Behavior Theory Concerning the Individual Organism* (New Haven, CT: Yale University Press, 1952); W. F. Hill, *Learning: A Survey of Psychological Interrelations* (Scranton, PA: Chandler, 1971); G. R. Miller, M. Burgoon, and J. K. Burgoon, "The Functions of Human Communication in Changing Attitudes and Gaining Compliance," in eds. C. C. Arnold and J. W. Bowers, *Handbook of Rhetorical and Communication Theory* (Boston: Allyn and Bacon, 1984), pp. 418–430. An excellent review of learning theory can be found in J. K. Burgoon, M. Burgoon, G. R. Miller, and M. Sunnafrank, "Learning Theory Approaches to Persuasion," *Human Communication Research*, 7 (1981), 161–179.

[4] C. I. Hovland, I. L. Janis, and H. H. Kelly, *Communication and Persuasion* (New Haven, CT: Yale University Press, 1953).

[5]Kiesler, Collins, and Miller, p. 105.

[6]W. J. McGuire, "Inducing Resistance to Persuasion: Some Contemporary Approaches," in ed. L. Berkowitz, *Advances in Experimental Social Psychology, Vol. 1* (New York: Academic Press, 1964); W. J. McGuire, "The Nature of Attitudes and Attitude Change," in eds. G. Lindzey and E. Aronson, *Handbook of Social Psychology, Vol. 3* (Reading: MA: Addison–Wesley, 1969).

[7]McGuire, "Resistance to Persuasion."

[8]M. Burgoon, M. M. Cohen, M. D. Miller, and C. L. Montgomery, "An Empirical Test of a Model of Resistance to Persuasion," *Human Communication Research*, 5 (1978), 27–39.

[9]W. J. McGuire, "Attitudes and Opinions," *Annual Review of Psychology*, 17 (1966), 475–514.

[10]F. Heider, "Attitudes and Cognitive Organization," *Journal of Psychology*, 21 (1946), 107–112.

[11]See Kiesler, Collins, and Miller, pp. 188–190.

[12]N. Jordan, "Behavioral Forces That Are a Function of Attitudes and of Cognitive Organization," *Human Relations*, 6 (1953), 273–287; W. J. McGuire, "The Current Status of Cognitive Consistency Theories," in ed. S. Feldman, *Cognitive Consistency: Motivational Antecedents and Behavioral Consequents* (New York: Academic Press, 1966), pp. 1–46.

[13]T. M. Newcomb, "An Approach to the Study of Communicative Acts," *Psychological Review*, 60 (1953), 393–404; C. E. Osgood and P. H. Tannenbaum, "The Principle of Congruity in the Prediction of Attitude Change," *Psychological Review*, 62 (1955), 42–55; T. M. Newcomb, "The Predictions of Interpersonal Attraction," *American Psychologist*, 11 (1956), 575–586.

[14]Kielser, Collins, and Miller, pp. 189–190.

[15]See Osgood and Tannenbaum.

[16]L. Festinger, A *Theory of Cognitive Dissonance* (Stanford, CA: Stanford University Press, 1957).

[17]Kiesler, Collins, and Miller, p. 192; Festinger, p. 13.

[18]C. W. Sherif, M. Sherif, and R. W. Nebergall, *Attitude and Attitude Change: The Social Judgment–Involvement Approach* (Philadelphia: W. B. Saunders, 1965).

[19]D. Katz, "The Functional Approach to the Study of Attitudes," *Public Opinion Quarterly*, 24 (1960), 163–204.

[20]See I. L. Janis, "Personality Correlates of Susceptibility to Persuasion," *Journal of Personality*, 22 (1954), 504–518; Hovland, Janis, and Kelly.

[21]I. L. Janis and D. Rife, "Persuasibility and Emotional Disorder," in eds. C. I. Hovland and I. L. Janis, *Personality and Persuasion* (New Haven, CT: Yale University Press, 1959).

[22]W. Weiss and B. J. Fine, "The Effect of Induced Aggressiveness on Opinion Change," *Journal of Abnormal and Social Psychology*, 52 (1956), 109–114; I. L. Janis and P. B. Field, "Sex Differences and Personality Factors Related to Persuasibility," in Hovland and Janis, *Personality and Persuasion*; Janis and Rife.

[23]See Janis; Hovland, Janis, and Kelly.

[24]Janis and Field; T. M. Scheidel, "Sex and Persuasibility," *Speech Monographs, 30* (1963), 353–358; M. Burgoon, S. B. Jones, and D. Stewart, "Toward a Message-Centered Theory of Persuasion: Three Empirical Investigations of Language Intensity," *Human Communication Research, 1* (1975), 240–256.

[25]C. L. Montgomery and M. Burgoon, "An Experimental Study of the Interactive Effects of Sex and Androgyny on Attitude Change," *Communication Monographs, 44* (1977), 130–135; C. L. Montgomery and M. Burgoon, "The Effects of Androgyny and Message Expectations on Resistance to Persuasive Communication," *Communication Monographs, 47* (1980), 56–67.

[26]M. Rokeach, *The Open and Closed Mind* (New York: Basic Books, 1960); M. Rokeach, *Beliefs, Attitudes, and Values* (San Francisco: Josey–Bass, 1968); M. Rokeach, *The Nature of Human Values* (New York: Free Press, 1973).

[27]For more on this area of persuasion research, see G. Marwell and D. R. Schmitt, "Dimensions of Compliance-Gaining Behavior: An Empirical Analysis," *Sociometry, 30* (1967), 350–364. A series of communication-based research studies have extended this initial attempt at persuasive strategies. See F. J. Boster and J. B. Stiff, "Compliance-Gaining Message Selection Behavior," *Human Communication Research, 10* (1984), 539–556; R. A. Clark, "The Impact of Self Interest and Desire for Liking on the Selection of Communicative Strategies," *Communication Monographs, 46* (1979), 257–273; J. P. Dillard and M. Burgoon, "Situational Influences on the Selection of Compliance-Gaining Messages: Two Tests of the Predictive Utility of the Cody–McLaughlin Typology," *Communication Monographs, 52* (1985), 289–304; J. E. Hunter and F. J. Boster, "A Model of Compliance-Gaining Message Selection," *Communication Monographs, 54* (1987), 63–84; S. Jackson and D. Backus, "Are Compliance-Gaining Strategies Dependent on Situational Variables?" *Central States Speech Journal, 33* (1982), 469–479; G. R. Miller and M. Burgoon, "Persuasion Research: Review and Commentary," in ed. B. D. Ruben, *Communication Yearbook II* (New Brunswick, NJ: Transaction Books, 1978), pp. 29–47.

[28]Marwell and Schmitt.

[29]Hunter and Boster, pp. 64–65.

SECTION FIVE

Building the Edifice for Society: Sociological Approaches to Communication

We began our building of communication theory from the perspective of the type of society in which we find ourselves. Ancient societies were monolithic entities; all power was in the hands of the dominant group. As we moved from ancient to contemporary perceptions of communication, however, society changed. Our more pluralistic society accepts more diversity. This change helped focus communication on the *individual* communicator and the psychology of communication.

We are influenced by our society and other people deemed "significant." We can see how social forces influence the architect. In American architecture, we see the influence not only of other societies (classical Greek, Victorian, Spanish), but of individual architects (Frank Lloyd Wright, William Le Baron Jenney [the architect of the first metal skyscraper]). In building communication theory, several social architects have influenced our view of communication: Hans-Georg Gadamer, George C. Homans, Karl Marx, Abraham Maslow, and George Herbert Mead. Each has added a social focus to the building of communication.

This section begins with an examination of Mead's concept of symbolic interactionism (Chapter 9), an approach bridging psychological and sociological theory. It examines how we communicate *within* our society. It also redefines some of the concepts originating in the humanistic school. The focus in this chapter is *self and society*, with special interest in the development of mind and intrapersonal communication.

Chapter 10 examines how we communicate from an exchange perspective. Homans's theory of communication as exchange is examined from a bargaining or negotiation perspective. The focus is on the type of relationship we expect and maintain based on expected personal payoffs.

Finally, we turn to theories that deal with how society *as a whole* reacts to communication. These "conflict theories" examine how suitable a message may be to a particular society. The theories examined include Marxist theory (Chapter 11) and critical interpretive theory (Chapter 12). The section ends with a discussion of communication as a reflection of class consciousness.

Sociological theories of communication place responsibility on our relationships. There is still a concern for individual communication, but it focuses more on how we use our communication as a reflection of society, or on how society should be. Thus, there is conflict between the individual and the society, which is reflected in our uses of language and nonverbal communication.

9

Symbolic Interactionism: George Herbert Mead's Perspective

Somewhere, the communication focus on the individual must meet and mesh with the focus of others. This meshing takes the form of both our psychological needs and the structural needs of our society. Thus, we find the norms of society reflected or rejected in the individual communicator. We also find that some people or elements in society are more important than others—they are significant in their impact on us. We can see this clearly in our architectural metaphor. Looking around, we see that certain buildings reflect the society of their times—from Victorian to Modern, plantation to condo—and the influence of individual architects.

Obviously, we are not simply clones of "significant others." We add our own psychological identity to the roles others expect of us, the roles others help us become. This is explained best by noting that we become a part of society, a society that influences the "I." While the humanist views communication as the individual as seen by the individual, the social theorist views communication as the individual as *reflected* in society, a society that influences the individual.

We begin our study of the sociological approaches to communication with George Herbert Mead, the "father" of social psychology. Mead developed a theory known as *symbolic interactionism*.[1] This theory has had a significant impact on communication theory and, because of Mead's work earlier in this century, symbolic interactionism might be considered the first study of *intra*personal communication in the field of sociology. Symbolic interactionism provides a bridge between the psychological theorists interested in the individual and the sociological theorists interested in society. From a communication perspective, we see the relationship of self to society through the language and nonverbal communication we use as reflected in social norms.

187

SOCIETY AND CULTURE

We communicate in an environment that *we* define. In our own little corner of the world, "reality" is what we see and its impact is direct and immediate. In actuality, we communicate with other people who are both like us and unlike us. The combination of all of these people forms a culture and different societies from within that culture, each with differing views of the world and ways of expressing them.

Alfred G. Smith defined *culture* as the way we communicate. To define explicitly what culture is, we should consider the composition of its elements. To do so, we must include all of the possible ideas, values, and institutions that occur in our *Weltanschauung* (world view). This world view includes social, economic, religious, political, aesthetic, and intellectual values. These values are not reality; rather they are qualities that make up our lives. Institutions for each of these values eventually develop—social: families; economic: banks; religious: churches; political: legislatures; aesthetic: museums of art; and intellectual: schools. Furthermore, each culture is part of a time and place. Thus, we are constantly reformulating, or rebuilding, our own culture.[2]

Society may be defined as a group, perceived as having a similar culture. According to Mead, we are born into a society. Significant symbols (language) help us to create and maintain society; therefore, we need communication to maintain society. Society establishes the standards or boundaries of communication for us. Abnormalities in standards provide the criteria for measuring normalcy.[3] Mead explained the importance of the social in a reference to Helen Keller:

> With a blind person, such as Helen Keller, it is a contact experience that could be given to another as it is given to herself. It is out of that sort of language that the mind of Helen Keller was built. As she recognized, it was not until she could get into communication with other persons through symbols which could arouse in herself the responses that arouse in other people that she could get what we term as mental content, or a self.[4]

TERMINOLOGY

To understand the symbolic theory of Mead and his followers, ten terms need to be defined: society, gesture, socialization, significant symbol. "I," "Me," taking the role of the other, mind, self, and definition of the situation. Each term is essential for understanding how we communicate from a social perspective.

Society

Because Mead felt that humans are different from their animal counterparts, he distinguished between insect society (infrahuman) and human society. He felt that insect society is strictly a biological and physiological entity.[5] Mead believed that human society is based on cooperation. Our gestures (words), he argued, are essentially stimuli that have become "symbolic."[6] We agree that a gesture "stands for" something else and, in a general sense, we agree on what that gesture *represents*. Since our interpretations of gestures differ, the concept of society for each of us means that we have the capacity for "being several things at once."[7]

For instance, we are simultaneously son or daughter, lover, student, and so forth. How each thing is interpreted, however, will depend on the culture's interpretation of it. Consider being born a daughter in India and one in the United States, a Viet Nam veteran today and one twenty years ago (remember, society changes over time, as do its interpretations). Two of this book's authors are Viet Nam–era veterans. How do you interpret such a label? Would your interpretation have been the same twenty years ago? Fifteen years ago? Ten years from now?

To Mead, communication is "a relationship between one part of the social act, the gesture, and the response of adjustment by a second form of that gesture."[8] It is important to note here that *society precedes the individual:* "Society inculcates a set of rules and behaviors enforced less by individual will and political sovereignty than by the individual pre-existence of society itself."[9] We discover the "rules" and abide by them by *empathizing* or *taking the role of the other.*

Role taking is a process whereby one person identifies with another's position. Through imaginative technique (an ability to step "outside" oneself), we share the response of others and respond to ourselves as others do. By taking this attitude, we put ourselves outside the self and inside the other. This book's authors, who completed undergraduate studies in the late 1960s, were students of the 1960s—of Woodstock, and the Viet Nam War. Stop a moment and reflect on the role of "student," then and now. What happens to today's male student if he drops out of school? Would you (empathize, females, a male role for a moment here) face the same trauma: either being drafted or "going underground"? Are *the* perceptions of the roles associated with "student" similar in the 1960s and the 1990s? Based on these different role expectations, try taking the role of your mother and father, your boyfriend or girlfriend, or someone from a different culture.

Society also has a set of unstated rules that constitute the "game" we call communication. In this sense, society is not significantly different from a baseball game. For each player,

> Each of his own acts is determined by his assumption of the acts [rules] of the others who are playing the game. What he does is determined, in large measure, by his "being" everyone else on his team, at least as far as their attitudes affect his responses. We get, then, an "other" which is an organization of the attitudes of those involved in the same process.[10]

What we are now and how we behave, then, is a composite of our understanding of both how we see ourselves through the eyes of others and of how we perceive others perceiving "the rules of the game." We become one with society. Our communication, both verbal and nonverbal, reflects that society and its unstated rules. We "know" to stand in line if a line is there, and to not ask questions in a mass lecture class.

Society is also an active process. According to Herbert Blumer, "Human society is to be seen as consisting of acting people, and the life of society is to be seen as consisting of their actions."[11] Society is a phenomenon that exists before any particular person. It is based on cooperation. To become part of society, we must use gestures that are symbolic. The use of gestures is governed by rules that are *dynamic* and *action-oriented*.[12]

A simple example of social impact occurs when we enter college. The particular institution existed prior to our entrance and will continue to exist long after we depart. Upon entering the college, however, we adopt the role of a "college student," which differs from that adopted in high school and may actually differ from particular college to college, or, as some would argue, from "college" to "university." Once we enter this *society*, however, we begin to take roles: freshman, pledge, premed, athlete. Each role or combination of roles has particular rules, which are learned from observing others and often from taking their roles through role playing (practice) or by imagining how others would act (empathizing).

Gesture

According to Mead, gestures allow us to learn the rules of society. Gestures are the "keys" that "unlock the doors" to society's requirements. David Miller has defined a gesture as "an act performed by an organism, but for the act to be a gesture, it must be sensed by a second organism and it must evoke a response by the second organism."[13] There are two types of gestures: nonsignificant and significant. *Nonsignificant gestures* are those used by lower animals that do not have the "same meaning for the individuals participating in the social act. Such gestures do not, therefore, evoke universal or shared meanings" (p. 70). Nonsignificant gestures include a dog barking in the middle of the night; other dogs might react, but not for the same reason. Similarly, a horse or cow swishing its tail at a fly is a nonsignificant gesture, as is a frog catching a fly with its tongue.

Significant gestures are those that "are used for the purpose of making requests, or for inciting action in another participant in a social act" (pp. 76–77). They are needed for the development of the self. Gestures may be either verbal or nonverbal, but, from the perspective of symbolic interactionism, the verbal gesture becomes the focus of attention. (Mead's "gesture," then, is different from that discussed in Chapter 3).

Upon entering college, we have a variety of significant verbal and nonverbal gestures. Being considered an "Aggie" or a "Bulldog" creates a feeling of belonging to the college. In pledging a fraternity or sorority, we learn "secret" gestures—key words and handshakes—that are used at specific (rule-generated) times. Many times, simply shouting the name of your cross-state rival can incite action among the students in your immediate society.

Socialization

When we are born into a particular society, we learn to operate within the bounds of that society. People must learn what is normal and what is abnormal. This learning process evolves through what Mead felt were three stages of the genesis (or development) of the self:[14] (1) The *preparatory stage* occurs when an infant meaninglessly imitates the perceived role of others, for example, "reading" the newspaper, "sweeping" the floor, and so forth. *Roles* are complex entities. As noted by Don Fabun, each of us has a number of roles we play.[15] We may play several of these roles simultaneously, such as father, mate, lover, and so on. At the preparatory stage, however, the infant simply learns the fundamentals of playing a role. (2) The *play stage* begins the actual role playing and includes the ability to act toward oneself; for example, the child may slap his or her own hand and say "no, no." (3) The *game stage* is the final stage in which the child learns to play a number of roles simultaneously. At this stage, Mead felt that the child had become *socialized.*

We continue to follow these three stages later in life as we learn different roles and rules associated with them. Consider, for example, a hypothetical female student. She may begin college socialization by imitating the cultural stereotype, "student." This student attends classes, prepares for those classes each night, and carries her books to class each day (and even carries extra pencils and paper). As the student socializes, she may begin to realize that this "student" role is not her—and her attendance begins to slip, she prepares less for class, and often she forgets to bring paper and pencil to class. Finally, the student may enter the game stage: She may decide that different classes require different student roles, such as those in major classes (prepared student, similar to that found in the preparatory stage) and nonmajor classes (unprepared student).

Significant Symbol

Arnold Rose has suggested five propositions relevant to the development and use of *significant symbols,* which are "cooperative gestures" employed in complex societies:

1. We live in a symbolic environment as well as a physical environment and can be stimulated to act by symbols as well as by physical stimuli [nonsignificant gestures].
2. Through symbols, we have the capacity to stimulate others in ways other than those in which we are ourselves stimulated.
3. Through the communication of symbols, we can learn large numbers of meanings and values—and hence ways of acting—from other people.
4. The symbols . . . do not occur only in isolated bits, but often in clusters, large and complex.
5. Thinking is the process by which possible symbolic solutions and other future courses of action are examined, assessed for their relative advantages

and disadvantages in terms of the values of the individual, and one of them chosen for action.[16]

Rose has stressed the importance of symbols in the communication process. According to Mead, a significant symbol is a gesture, a sign, a word *addressed to the self at the same time it is addressed to another person.*[17] The significant symbol is used to link us to two worlds: the physical and the social.

Objects in the world are both *objective* and *subjective.* They are objective in the sense that their descriptions are similar among various people. They are subjective in that their images are unique; they are memories of experience. Because our memory is unique, experiences are subjective. The point of view established by the significant symbol is the objective view of the object. The significant symbol is used to bring us together, to share, to commune, to communicate.

Significant symbols may "stand for other language signs, as where 'reptile' stands for 'snake,' but ultimately every dimension of the meanings of signs stems from the responses they elicit."[18] By using these symbols, we bring into the present shared perspectives of the past or of the future. The ultimate test of objectivity, however, is found in the *application* to the social act.[19] In this sense, information (new data) may or may not be shared, but is applied when the desired action is achieved. Thus, through the process of socialization, we learn to take on the role of the other. By taking on the role of the other, we use gestures. Some gestures become significant symbols; they take on shared meanings and persuade others to act in a certain manner.[20] These symbols are, then, developed with the role of the self.

When college alumni hear certain significant symbols, they often reenter that group (society). So, when we hear "Hook 'em Horns," "War Eagle," "Go Bulldogs," or "Go Big Blue," we reidentify with those groups. *The symbols have become a part of the self.* We find the same occurrences in occupations, in clubs, and at work. We identify with and become one with the significant symbol(s).

The "I"

According to Miller, the "'I' is the novel that calls for adjustment . . . and to become novel the old system with reference to how it is exceptional must give way to a new past."[21] The "I" has been defined in numerous ways. Mead writes, "It is because of that 'I' that we say that we are never fully aware of what we are, that we surprise ourselves by our own action."[22] Hugh Danziel Duncan claims, "The 'I' talking to its 'Me' is . . . an internalization of the 'I' talking to its 'You,' just as in turn the 'You' we address in part by the 'Me' we assume the 'You' to be."[23] Don Faules and Dennis Alexander write, "The I . . . refers to the self as actor. Your answer to the question 'Why are you doing that?' deals with your self as an actor, as a being-in-process."[24] The 'I' is the impulsive tendency of the individual. It is the initial, spontaneous, unorganized aspect of human experience. Thus, it represents the undirected tendencies of the individual."[25] The "I" "becomes accountable for everything that cannot be explained by the organized set of rules which the individual takes over in the processes of social interaction."[26]

What, then, is the "I"? Based on these definitions, the "I" cannot be evaluated empirically. The "I" is an impulsive tendency, operating in opposition to the rational roles found in the "Me." According to Miller, "Thinking is a conversation between the generalized other and the person, or more specifically, between the Me and the I."[27] Thinking is, then, "betwixt and between the old system [Me, rule and socially oriented] and the new [I, impulsive]" (p. 204). The "I" might want to skip class because of an important out-of-town game or formal dance. The "I" might want to go out "with the guys or gals" the night before a major examination. The "I" might want to act "dumb" or "cool" to get a date.

The "Me"

The "Me" is all the "I" is not. The "Me" urges conformity to the rules and roles established by society. "The 'Me' represents the incorporated other within the individual."[28] These "others" are comprised of a number of role takings. Several of these others have been developed by other symbolic interactionists since Mead developed the original theory. They include the generalized other, significant others, orientational others, primary groups, reference groups, and the "looking-glass self." These others are combined within Mead's generalized other.

Mead argues that the *generalized other* represents society. It is that aspect that is given to us by our society and causes us to have a "unity of self."[29] Thus, "The attitude of the generalized other is the attitude of the whole community" (p. 154). The generalized other differs from a *particular other*. Particular others "are specific social others we assume to be saliently related."[30] The generalized other represents society, whereas the particular other represents "people" isolated from the society and placed within our reference group. All professors, for instance, are generalized others, whereas *your* professors *at this moment in time* (school term) are particular others.

Particular others have traditionally included significant others and orientational others. In describing Harry Stack Sullivan's *significant other*, Norman Denzin suggests that this other is one whose actions and attitudes are considered valuable. Self and meaning arise through interaction with significant others.[31] Manford Kuhn's *orientational other* is one who plays an important role in our vocabulary and self-concept. The main difference between the two is that significant others are situational and change over time, whereas orientational others have historical significance. Individual professors are often significant others, whereas your advisor may become an orientational other. Your best friend from childhood may be an orientational other, whereas other friends—significant others—may come and go.

Two groups also place certain restraints on the individual: primary groups and reference groups. The family, the neighborhood, and the community may function as primary groups. These groups have influence as a result of fellowship with us.[32] Reference groups "involve some identifiable grouping to which an actor is related in some manner."[33] These groupings are of three types: "(1) Groups which serve as comparison points, (2) Groups to which men'aspire and (3) Groups whose perspective is assumed by the actor" (p. 162).

Finally, Adam Smith's *looking-glass self*[34] has been further developed by Charles Horton Cooley.[35] For Cooley, three principles of self-development were relevant: (1) we imagine how we appear to other people; (2) we imagine their judgment of our appearance; and (3) these self-feelings result in hurt or pride (p. 231). The looking-glass concept is best described through an alleged situation many years ago presented by John Kinch:

> A group of graduate students in a seminar in social psychology became interested in the notions implied by the [symbolic] interactionist approach. One evening after the seminar five of the male members of the group were discussing some of the implications of the theory and came to the realization that it might be possible to invent a situation where "others" systematically manipulated their responses to another person, thereby changing that person's self concept and in turn his behavior. They thought of an experiment to test the notions they were dealing with. They chose as their subject (victim) the girl in the seminar. The subject can be described as, at best a very plain girl who seemed to fit the stereotype (usually erroneous) that many have of graduate student females. The boys' plan was to begin in concert to respond to the girl as if she were the best-looking girl on campus. They agreed to work into it naturally so that she would not be aware of what they were up to. They drew lots to see who would be the first to date her. The loser, under the pressure of the others, asked her to go out. Although he found the situation quite unpleasant, he was a good actor and by continually saying to himself "she's beautiful, she's beautiful . . ." he got through the evening.
>
> According to the agreement it was now the second man's turn and so it went. The dates were reinforced by the similar responses in all contacts the men had with the girl. In a matter of a few short weeks the results began to show. At first it was simply a matter of more care in her appearance; her hair was combed more often and her dresses more neatly pressed, but before long she had been to the beauty parlor to have her hair styled, and was spending her hard-earned money on the latest fashions in women's campus wear. By the time the fourth man was taking his turn dating the young lady, the job that had once been undesirable was now quite a pleasant task. And when the last man in the conspiracy asked her out, he was informed that she was pretty well booked up for some time in the future. It seems there were more desirable males around than those "plain" graduate students.[36]

In the same way, how we describe others has an impact on their self-evaluations and their self-behavior. For instance, parents quickly learn that calling their children "fat," "bad," or "ugly" can have dire consequences on those children. From such situations, we see that the other is an important factor in terms of what we think of ourselves.

Others (generalized, significant, orientational) and group others (primary and reference) are important factors in developing the "Me." They are formed through the looking-glass self and through the process of socialization developed by Mead. This process results in our taking the role of the other.

Taking the Role of the Other

To understand how and why we communicate, the symbolic interactionist suggests that we take the role of the other and communicate based on how we perceive the other would think and behave. Miller notes that "in role taking, one anticipates the response to be carried out by the other."[37] The process is initially developed in our attempt to manipulate physical objects (p. 18). Later, through socialization, we use a similar process to manipulate others. This is learned through play, games, and language.[38] With these processes, we learn to learn: "Learning consists of the modification of impulses and the transference of modified behavior to various particulars 'belonging to the same class.'"[39] Through learning, the "Me" develops. Through the process of socialization, the individual learns to combine the impulsive "I" and the regulated "Me" in attempting to communicate with others.

Mind

Learning, then, consists of developing classes and using classes to make evaluations. These are not sequential phenomena, however. "The structuring of the world by classes and uses made of them arise concomitantly" (p. 10). The classes (as a function of the "Me") are used to interplay with the "I." This interaction is the process of the mind. *Mind* then, is a conversation that takes place within us; it is thinking: "Thinking is an internalization of the social process and consists in a conversation of the individual with the generalized other" (p. 35). Mind occurs when we pretest what may happen in the future. The conversation within oneself is an interactive one. In this sense, it is similar to what goes on in the brain. According to Peter Andersen, John Garrison, and Janis Andersen, "The corpus callosum relays information from one hemisphere to the other in approximately 30 to 40 milliseconds through a complex process that is not fully understood."[40] Thus, the "I" and the "Me" interact as Mind, while the right and left hemispheres interact as the brain. The thinking process is often so fast that we do not recognize it. (The mind–brain relationship is discussed further in Chapter 13.)

Self

The *self*, then, is developed through the process of socialization. Within the self, the "I" and the "Me" interact socially (and linguistically) to form mind.[41] At the same time, the right and left hemispheres function together in the brain to create the impetus and analysis for the mind to use in communication.[42] The self provides a general base of operation, but certain adaptations must be made regarding the pertinent others for a given occasion; that is, the self creates an *expectation* that will be tested by the situation and others in that situation.

Definition of the Situation

Definition of the situation refers to the period of examination and analysis before we act in a self-determined manner. We determine our immediate acts, our life-styles, and even our personalities by defining the situation. We are born into groups in which certain behavior for specific situations has already been defined. Varying from this specific behavior implies deviation. There are always conflicts between the definitions of society and the spontaneous definitions of some of its members.[43] The moral code itself is the generalized other's generally accepted definition of the situation. This code specifies the rules and behavioral norms that regulate the acquisition of one's wishes.

The smallest social unit, *the family*, serves as the primary defining agency. Speech, signs, and pressures are among several techniques used by the family in defining the situation. The parent may tell the child, "Don't play in the street," "Wash your hands before eating," and so forth. The community also serves as a defining agency for us. Gossip is one of the less formal ways of defining the situation in the community. Similar to gossip, the community also relies on words offering disgraceful characterizations: "bitch," "cheater," "coward," and so on. Finally, gestures such as smiles, waves, and sneers are expected in certain situations.

A more elaborate system of sanctions exists today in the legal system whose basis is formulated and approved in laws. Laws perform the same purpose in that they deter people from following their own desires (the "I") and conforming to the norm held by the group (the "Me"). When behavior fails to fall within that defined by society as situationally correct, we are expected to give an *account*, a statement that explains unexpected behavior.[44] An account is divided into two types: *justifications* and *excuses*. In justifications, we accept the responsibility for the behavior, but deny the definition of the act under the specific circumstances. We may admit an act of murder, but deny it was immoral because it was a situation of self-defense. An excuse is an account in which we admit that the actions in question are wrong, but deny the responsibility for the actions. We may admit that murder is an immoral act, but may claim that we were not responsible for our actions because we were possessed by a demon.

Like the mind, the definition of the situation is a social phenomenon and "is possible only when physical space and chronological time are transformed into social space and social time."[45] Generally, then, the definition of the situation consists of at least two properties: *emergence* and *relativity*. According to Peter McHugh, "Emergence concerns the temporal dimension of activity, wherein past, present, and future are analytically distinct and, at the same time, inextricable, for they are not correspondingly distinct in their influence upon concrete behavior" (p. 24). Because of rules and the general unwillingness to adapt, we develop what is called the *et cetera assumption;* that is, "People assume that future events will occur as they have in the past, a procedure that makes it possible to routinize the environment, which in turn makes an order possible" (p. 26). Thus, the factors that call for a new definition of the situation are novelty and surprise.

Relativity "begins with the idea of the interchangeability of standpoints in taking the role of the other" (p. 42). One of the most important points here is to establish *typicality:* Is our behavior representative of a group? We examine the probability of the behavior's representativeness. If it is not, we examine the possible reasons, excuses, accounts for why it is not. In this sense, we can evaluate the behavior of others as appropriate or inappropriate. All of these steps must be considered in the context of rules and games. Finally, a definition of the situation can be described as "the individual's prior conception of and attitude toward a given situation that influences his behavior when he meets that situation" (p. 61). We attempt to anticipate what is going on and why it is going on so that we can adjust our own behavior accordingly.

Thus, we change our appearance/behavior in accord with what others think about us in context. Others respond to us differently, and we consequently respond differently toward ourselves. A similar feedback process occurs when we meet a stranger. Russell Jennings developed a seven-stage model of the definition of the situation as the *cumulative impression* we make on others over time (see Fig. 9–1). This model suggests that we take account of each other (Stage 1). Based on this account, we group the other in one of several ways (generalized, primary, reference). We then begin the socialization process (Stages 3 to 5), engage in coping behaviors (Stage 4), and finally complete the role-taking process (Stage 5).[46]

COMMUNICATION AND SYMBOLIC INTERACTIONISM

The symbolic interactionist, much like the humanist, assumes that communication exists both within and between people. Our communication with others is founded in part on the interdependence of self and society; that is, how we communicate depends on how others perceive us and how we *think* they perceive us. Our communication is in large part influenced by others, who help to determine how we perceive "self" at any given moment in time. Of major import to symbolic interactionism is the symbol or gesture. Through the manipulation of significant symbols, we alter our environment and persuade others. Thus, symbolic interactionism falls in both the categories—theories of knowledge and theories of action.

Of particular interest to any interpretation of communication is the process of role taking. Through role taking, we make assumptions about how others would act and how others see our actions. Role taking becomes a major process through which we learn the rules of society. Based on our

Stage 1.   As a stranger, the speaker subvocally *takes account* of the way another views a particular situation.

Stage 2.   As a stranger, the speaker depends on characteristics, categories of need which, in his or her past experience, have a contiguous relationship to some observable aspect of the recipient. He or she then forms an initial message.

Stage 3.   The stranger then observes the response of the recipient and calculates a subsequent response based on his or her understanding of the recipient's responses and other acts in his or her past.

Stage 4.   No longer a total stranger, the speaker begins to form messages based on his or her own reconstruction of the way the recipient views the world.

Stage 5.   The speaker continually attempts to bring the audience into his or her psychological field; the speaker attempts to create a target assumptive set.

Stage 6.   The speaker engages in coping behavior, attempting to eradicate and/or replace ways of looking at the world which tend to block acceptance of the target assumptive set. These are coping themes.

Stage 7.   In analysis, the critic takes advantage of this role-taking experience of the speaker by application of the interactionist model, which, when applied, interprets the coping behavior of the speaker's interaction with the audience in such a way as to produce the resident set of assumptions of the audience.

FIGURE 9–1   Cumulative Impression.
Source: R. W. Jennings, Laboratory in Interpersonal Communication, Southern Illinois University, Carbondale, 1969, unpublished.

perceptions of role, and the ways we take those roles, our communication patterns may change.

From our roles and understanding of roles in action, the concepts of "I" and "Me" come together to form the concept of mind. Mind, in conjunction with society, creates the concept of self, and it is through self that we communicate with others. This interaction of "I" and "Me" creates a grouping through which we learn to share our world by using and manipulating symbols.

REVIEW

We are born into a society, and through the process of socialization we learn the norms, rules, and games of our particular society. Society uses gestures (significant and nonsignificant) to teach us. Many of these gestures become significant symbols within that society and are used for communication.

In the process of socialization, we form a "Me." The "Me" is composed of significant others, orientational others, reference groups, primary groups, and a generalized other. These take on significance as looking-glass selves, a self interdependent with others, society, and culture.

The "Me" interacts with the impulsive tendencies of the "I." Mind—or intrapersonal or self-communication—is a continual, social process that functions only through taking the roles of others. The combination of "I," "Me," and mind forms self. The self operates using the *et cetera assumption* unless it encounters a surprise or unique situation. When surprised, we must redefine the situation relative to time and space.

Although this theory is rather cumbersome and vague in the way it defines constructs and concepts, it does predict how society serves to model and manipulate our communication. It sets forth certain rules for the learning of roles and how those roles allow us to communicate with others. Symbolic interactionism, as a theory of human communication, approximates both the best and worst qualities of human communication. (See Table 9–1.)

CRITIQUE

If there is one indictment of symbolic interactionism, that indictment would be that the theory is not testable. It rests on an assumption that we perceive our worlds differently, depending upon who our significant others are at a particular point in time. Thus, as with humanistic theories, we are relegated to individual "case studies" which do not easily generalize to larger groups.[47] As a process orientation to human communication, the theory follows a logical base, but the concepts and constructs need further elaboration before they become clear enough to be tested. Based on research in self-conceptualization and role-taking, symbolic interactionism has received support, but that support does not generalize well to other groups of people, as Mead himself would probably have argued.

The theory, as might be guessed, is not parsimonious, but parsimony is not a critical factor in evaluating symbolic interactionism. The concepts, although vague and fuzzy, allow limited operationalization. They also allow for individual differences. The theory most certainly has been heuristic and has influenced other communication theory in a number of ways, including theories involved with shared meanings, conversational analysis, socialization, and role taking. Reliability is questionable; however, since generalizability is not a positive feature of symbolic interactionism, reliability becomes a somewhat moot point. If we assume that people change as those people

TABLE 9-1 Summary Table

Name of Theory	Primary Theorists	Basic Principle	Constructs	Criteria	Analytic Approach	Limitations
Symbolic Interactionism	Mead	To be accepted by a group or society as a whole, individual must learn to predict how the group expects him/her to respond.	• Society • I • Me • Mind • Socialization • Self • Taking the role of the other	The use of Mind should be fundamental for human interactions.	I Me Mind Self	Does not define the "I" clearly; does not explain the existence of society; does not explain deviant communicative behavior.

within their "inner group" change, then symbolic interactionism is highly reliable and serves a predictive function. From the concept that society shapes the individual, the theory certainly helps to explain how that shaping takes place and why. It fails, however, in establishing how that shaping takes place.

—————— Notes and References ——————

[1]For a more detailed intellectual biography of Mead, see D. L. Miller, *George Herbert Mead: Self, Language, and the World* (Austin: University of Texas Press, 1973).

[2]A. G. Smith, "Introduction: Communication and Culture," in *Communication and Culture: Readings in the Codes of Human Interaction*, ed. A. G. Smith (New York: Holt, Rinehart and Winston, 1966), pp. 1–10; T. Shibutani, "Reference Groups as Perspectives," in *Symbolic Interaction: A Reader in Social Psychology*, 2nd ed., eds. J. G. Manis and B. N. Meltzer (Boston: Allyn and Bacon, 1972), pp. 160–171; O. T. Ivey and M. Hickson, III, "A Basic Approach to Social Studies: An Overview for Teachers and Parents," *The Researcher*, 9 (1985), 33–40.

[3]G. H. Mead, *Mind, Self, and Society: From the Standpoint of a Social Behaviorist*, ed. C. W. Morris (Chicago: University of Chicago Press, 1962), pp. 227–336; G. H. Mead, *The Philosophy of the Act*, ed. C. W. Morris (Chicago: University of Chicago Press, 1938), pp. 473–474; G. H. Mead, *Movements of Thought in the Nineteenth Century*, ed. M. H. Moore (Chicago: University of Chicago Press, 1936), pp. 202–203.

[4]Mead, *Mind, Self, and Society*, pp. 202–203.

[5]B. N. Meltzer, "Mead's Social Psychology," in *Symbolic Interaction: A Reader in Social Psychology*, 2nd ed. eds. J. G. Manis and B. N. Meltzer (Boston: Allyn and Bacon, 1972), p. 5.

[6]Meltzer, p. 7. Mead felt that other than obvious psychological differences, "there is practically no physiological distinction between the individuals that go to make up the human community." See Mead, *Mind, Self, and Society*, p. 231.

[7]G. H. Mead, *The Philosophy of the Present*, ed. A. E. Murphy (LaSalle IL: Open Court, 1959), p. 49.

[8]Miller, p. 47.

[9]P. McHugh, *Defining the Situation: The Organization of Meaning in Social Interaction* (Indianapolis: Bobbs–Merrill, 1968), p. 7.

[10]Mead, *Mind, Self, and Society*, p. 154. See also E. Berne, *Games People Play: The Psychology of Human Relationships* (New York: Grove, 1964), pp. 48–65. E. Goffman has also viewed the human communication process as a game; see *Encounters: Two Studies in the Sociology of Interaction* (Indianapolis: Bobbs–Merrill, 1961); *Frame Analysis: An Essay on the Organization of Experience* (New York: Harper Colophon, 1971); *Behavior in Public Places: Notes on the Social Organization of Gatherings* (New York: Free Press, 1963); *Stigma: Notes on the Management of Spoiled Identity* (Englewood Cliffs, NJ: Prentice–Hall, 1963); *Strategic Interaction* (Philadelphia: University of Pennsylvania Press, 1969); *Interaction Ritual: Essays on Face-to-Face Behavior* (Garden City, NY: Anchor, 1967); *The Presentation of Self in Everyday Life* (Garden City, NY: Anchor, 1959); *Asylums: Essays on the Social Situation of Mental Patients and Other Inmates* (Garden City, NY: Anchor, 1961); *Forms*

of Talk (Philadelphia: University of Pennsylvania Press, 1981); R. S. Perinbanayagam, *Signifying Acts: Structure and Meaning in Everyday Life* (Carbondale, IL: Southern Illinois University Press, 1985), pp. 59–83.

[11]H. Blumer, *Symbolic Interactionism: Perspective and Method* (Englewood Cliffs, NJ: Prentice–Hall, 1969), p. 85; H. Blumer, "Symbolic Interaction," in *Interdisciplinary Approaches to Human Communication*, eds. R. W. Budd and B. D. Ruben (Rochelle Park: NJ: Hayden, 1979), pp. 142–144.

[12]J. P. Hewitt, *Self and Society: A Symbolic Interactionist Social Psychology* (Boston: Allyn and Bacon, 1976), p. 167. Hewitt defines society as consisting of "extended linkages of joint actions and collectivities in which diverse people and activities are connected over space and time."

[13]Miller, p. 70.

[14]Meltzer, p. 9.

[15]D. Fabun, *Communications: The Transfer of Meaning* (Beverly Hills, CA: Glencoe, 1968), p. 40.

[16]A. M. Rose, *Human Behavior and Social Processes: An Interactionist Approach* (Boston: Houghton Mifflin, 1962), pp. 5–12.

[17]G. H. Mead, "A Behavioristic Account of the Significant Symbol," *The Journal of Philosophy*, 19 (1922), 157–163.

[18]Miller, p. 139.

[19]Mead, *The Philosophy of the Present*, pp. 1–3.

[20]Mead, *The Philosophy of the Act*, pp. 151–152.

[21]Miller, p. 193.

[22]Mead, *Mind, Self, and Society*, p. 174.

[23]H. D. Duncan, *Communication and the Social Order* (London: Oxford University Press, 1962), p. 288.

[24]D. F. Faules and D. C. Alexander, *Communication and Social Behavior: A Symbolic Interactionist Perspective* (Reading, MA: Addison–Wesley, 1978), p. 44.

[25]Meltzer, p. 10.

[26]W. Kolb, "A Critical Evaluation of Mead's 'I' and 'Me' Concepts," *Social Forces*, 22 (1944), p. 292.

[27]Miller, p. 204.

[28]Meltzer, pp. 1–10.

[29]Mead, *Mind, Self, and Society*, p. 154.

[30]E. L. Quarantelli and J. Cooper, "Self-Conceptions and Others: A Further Test of Meadian Hypotheses," in *Symbolic Interaction: A Reader in Social Psychology*, 2nd ed., eds. J. G. Manis and B. N. Meltzer (Boston: Allyn and Bacon, 1972), p. 276.

[31]N. K. Denzin, "The Significant Others of a College Population," *The Sociological Quarterly*, 7 (1966), 298–310.

[32]C. H. Cooley, "Primary Groups and Human Nature," in *Symbolic Interaction: A Reader in Social Psychology*, 2nd ed., eds. J. G. Manis and B. N. Meltzer (Boston: Allyn and Bacon, 1972), pp. 158–160.

[33]Shibutani, p. 161.

[34]Miller, p. xix.

[35]C. H. Cooley, "Looking-Glass Self," in *Symbolic Interaction: A Reader in Social Psychology*, 2nd ed., eds. J. G. Manis and B. N. Meltzer (Boston: Allyn and Bacon, 1972), pp. 158–160.

[36]J. W. Kinch, "A Formalized Theory of the Self Concept," in *Symbolic Interaction: A Reader in Social Psychology*, 2nd ed., eds. J. G. Manis and B. N. Meltzer (Boston: Allyn and Bacon, 1972), p. 248.

[37]Miller, p. 18.

[38]Mead, *Mind, Self, and Society*, pp. 150–152, 160–161.

[39]Miller, p. 10.

[40]P. A. Andersen, J. P. Garrison, and J. F. Andersen, "Implications of a Neurological Approach for the Study of Nonverbal Communication," *Human Communication Research*, 6 (1979), 80. See also R. A. Filbey and M. S. Gazzaniga, "Splitting the Normal Brain with Reaction Time," *Psychonomic Science*, 17 (1969), 335.

[41]See, for example, D. W. Stacks, "Toward a Preverbal Stage of Communication," *Journal of Communication Therapy*, 2 (1983), 39–60; D. W. Stacks and D. E. Sellers, "Toward a Holistic Theory of Communication: The Effect of 'Pure' Hemispheric Reception on Message Acceptance," *Communication Quarterly*, 34 (1986), 266–285; D. W. Stacks and L. A. Dorsey, "Toward a Psychoanalytic–Neurophysiological Interpretation of Nonverbal Communication," *Journal of Communication Therapy* (in press); D. W. Stacks and D. E. Sellers, "Understanding Intrapersonal Communication: Neurological Processing Implications," in *Intrapersonal Communication Processes: Original Essays*, eds. C. Roberts and K. Watson (New Orleans, LA: SPECTRA, 1989), pp. 243–267.

[42]D. W. Stacks and P. A. Andersen, "The Modular Mind: Implications for Intrapersonal Communication," *Southern States Communication Journal*, 54 (1989), 263–293; D. E. Sellers and D. W. Stacks, "Toward a Hemispheric Processing Model of Communication Competence and Apprehension," *Journal of Social Behavior and Personality* 5 (1990), 45–59.

[43]W. I. Thomas, "The Definition of the Situation," in *Symbolic Interaction: A Reader in Social Psychology*, 2nd ed., eds. J. G. Manis and B. N. Meltzer (Boston: Allyn and Bacon, 1972), pp. 331–336; J. T. Wood, *Human Communication: A Symbolic Interactionist Perspective* (New York: Holt, Rinehart and Winston, 1982), pp. 37–60.

[44]M. B. Scott and S. M. Lyman, "Accounts," in *Symbolic Interaction: A Reader in Social Psychology*, 2nd ed., eds. J. G. Manis and B. N. Meltzer (Boston: Allyn and Bacon, 1972), pp. 404–405.

[45]P. McHugh, *Defining the Situation: The Organization of Meaning in Social Intercourse* (Indianapolis: Bobbs–Merrill, 1968), p. 3.

[46]R. W. Jennings, Laboratory in Interpersonal Communication, Southern Illinois University, Carbondale, 1969, unpublished.

[47]M. Hickson, III, J. B. Roebuck, and K. S. Murty, "Creative Triangulation: Toward a Methodology for Studying Social Types," in *Studies in Symbolic Interaction*, Vol. XI, ed. N. K. Denzin (Greenwich, CT: JAI Press, 1990), pp. 103–126.

10

Exchange Theory: George C. Homans's Perspective

Exchange theory purports that, when we enter into communication, we anticipate the outcome of that communication. Part of this expectation is rather self-centered: We look at what we will *get* from the communication. In Chapters 7 and 8, we examined the psychological forces behind communication. This chapter focuses on the give-and-take of communication between people. The architect exchanges knowledge of design and structure for the client's money. The exchange is two-way: Each has something the other desires or values. The same may be true of communication. We enter into a conversation with an expectation of getting something out of it, an *exchange*.

Like many sociological theories, exchange theory views communication as a process, involving movement. An essential part of this movement is the interaction among the participants in a communication situation. George C. Homans provided a model for studying such interaction. His view reflects a capitalist economic system: "interaction between persons is an exchange of goods, material and non-material."[1] Homans meant that we are interested in getting the most out of our resources (time, effort, or money). Most people, for example, do not go into business with the expectation of losing money.

Homans stated that we approach relationships in a similar way. We do not put time and effort into a relationship we feel we are getting little or nothing out of. The foundation of all relationships is communication, which Homans defined as "a frequency variable; it is a measure of the frequency of emission of valuable and costly verbal behavior" (p. 597). Thus, we tend to communicate less with those whom we feel are not providing us enough reinforcement, defined here as whatever reward appeals to us in a particular situation.

Examples of interaction are easy to find on any college campus, and should be familiar to you. More than one person has suggested that a male–female dating relationship is based on a bargaining situation in which one attempts to parlay at least the promise of sexual favors into an entree for a desirable social situation.[2] Even the most mature relationships recognize that we must undertake some unattractive acts for the sake of pleasing the other to maintain a relationship. As teachers, we have experienced the student who is very interested during the term, but disappears from sight once final grades have been received. The basic premise is that people communicate with one another in expectation of a profit from that interaction. When we use the term profit, we have in mind a formula such that:[3]

$$\text{Profit} = \text{Reward} - \text{Cost.}$$

Another way to view this concept is to refer to Chapter 6 and the work of Kenneth Burke. Basically, exchange theory says that there are no "friendlies" in your world, no one who will do things for you without considering what they will receive for it.

Interaction with people is not "free." All interactions have costs associated with them. At the very least, maintaining a relationship takes time, a limited resource. Time spent with one person cannot be spent with other people or in other situations. Economic theory deals with this idea under the label of "opportunity costs." Any resource (time, money, mineral wealth, etc.) is limited. When you elect to go out with your friends on the night before a major test, the cost of the evening's fun is not only what you spend at the bar. It also includes the lost opportunity to study and the grade you receive on the test.

"Cost" is not the only term in our equation that can be confusing. "Reward" is not as obvious as it might first seem. What do you get out of a relationship? It depends. Rewards are both time-bound and situation-bound (pp. 42–45). Values change with time. Some things that were important to you as a young child are of no concern now. Today, things that will be important in ten years seem almost insignificant.

One source of troubles with a relationship is our tendency to change the values that we assign, both to material possessions and to activities. Values also change as situations change. An old saying notes, "A glass of water is one thing to someone dying of thirst and quite another to one whose house is burning down." You probably have heard the old cliche, "We all have our price." The exchange theorist believes that this is true. There is *nothing* you would not do, if the "price" were right. Remember, however, that you put your *own* value on possible rewards. What is valuable to you may not be at all valuable to your roommate. What is valuable for you today may not be valuable tomorrow. It is the constantly shifting evaluation of rewards and costs that makes the prediction of human behavior so difficult.[4] But it is also what makes "profitable" relationships possible.

BARGAINING AND NEGOTIATION AS EXCHANGE

Contemporary bargaining research supports Homans's approach to communication behavior. Many people think of bargaining as a rather formal process that takes place around an impressive conference table. In fact, the bargaining process touches all aspects of our life and is applicable to a wide range of communication situations.[5] It may be formal, and labeled as bargaining, or it may be informal and not generally recognized as bargaining. The fact remains that in our interdependent society, few things are available to us without the cooperation of others. Food, shelter, love, entertainment, safety, and much, much more demand that we interact with others. We all want something from others. Bargaining occurs any time that two or more people realize that they can reach an agreement in which each will be better off (p. 52).

Altruistic philosophies notwithstanding, most people will not cooperate with us unless they gain something in the process. The profit-based formula, in other words, works both ways. Additionally, some conflict is typical, since for every gain we achieve, a cost is paid by the other party. The question to bargainers is simple: How much are you willing to give up to get the amount conceded by your adversary? James T. Tedeschi and Paul Rosenfeld suggest that four factors regulate the outcome of bargaining situations: *structure, power, concessions* and *norms.*[6]

Structure

The first factor is the *structure of the bargaining situation*, which is usually described with the aid of three terms. First, the *resistance point* is each party's "bottom line," the absolute minimum each is willing to accept from the transaction. If you are bargaining over the price of a new car, the dealer's resistance point is the absolute minimum price he or she will take for the car, whereas your resistance point is the absolute maximum you are willing to pay. Second, the distance between resistance points is referred to as the *bargaining range.* Of course, if the dealer's resistance point is $9,000 and your resistance point is $6,500, no sale is going to take place. Because the range is so great, $3,500, bargaining is not likely to take place. Third, the *level of aspiration* refers to what each party hopes to get out of the bargain. You may be willing, if necessary, to pay $8,500 for the new car. But you believe that, if you bargain successfully, the car can be bought for $6,800, which represents your level of aspiration.

Power

The second factor operating in bargaining situations is the *power of the parties involved.* Power is important in all interpersonal communication situations. In bargaining, we need to be aware of both absolute and relative powers. *Absolute power* reflects the ability of each party to create meaningful threats against the other. In formal labor–management bargaining, the ability of the union to strike is a threat. The willingness and the financial capacity of the union members to sit out a long strike determines the power that the threat represents. *Relative power* is often a function of timing and the importance that each party places on achieving its goals. Bargaining situations seldom occur between power equals.[7]

Power is a constant factor in interpersonal relationships. The ultimate threat in a relationship is termination of the relationship itself. Although each of us theoretically has the absolute power to terminate a relationship, in practice our relative power varies. Consider people with extremely low self-concepts entangled with abusive "friends." Why do they put up with it? Why don't they get rid of the jerks? Because they are *relatively* powerless. With no self-confidence, they do not believe that things could be any better ("If I end this relationship, maybe I won't be able to find another one"). An abusive friend may be better than no friend at all.

Power within a relationship varies over time. It is important to realize that power is seldom equally distributed. At any given time, one person seems to feel that he or she would suffer more if the relationship were to end. That person's costs would be higher. This feeling causes a sense of relative powerlessness.

Concessions

The *pattern of concessions* made by each party also influences the outcome of bargaining situations. Research suggests that we tend to make high *initial* demands and then offer concessions to negotiate a way toward an agreement.[8] Concessions, however, are dangerous in that they tend to reveal to the other party information about our resistance point. Moreover, a great deal of research has shown that people who are too eager to make concessions cause their adversary to "get tough."[9] Because they are viewed as admissions of less power, concessions should be offered carefully.

Norms

The final influence controlling bargaining situations comes from the *norms* that specify acceptable outcomes. We do not negotiate in a vacuum. We are aware of what others in similar situations have worked out as a solution. There seems to be a fairly widespread desire to be perceived as "fair."[10] In a bargaining situation, the best definition of fair is "staying within the norms." One norm that seems universally true is the idea of reciprocity: We should help those who have helped us.[11]

Because adherence to social norms is such a basic limit on negotiation behavior, it is important to understand that some communicators choose deliberately to violate the norms as a negotiating *strategy*. Examples of deliberately going beyond socially accepted limits are fairly easy to discover. The extraordinarily rude person is not rare, and both history and literature contain instances of the overly aggressive, promiscuous rake. In the campus riots of the 1960s, violating the "rules of the game" was exploited as a tactic by many radical groups (see Chapter 11).

The motive behind such tactics is to achieve a competitive advantage from a momentary incapacitation of the opponent. If the departure from the norm (the excessive act) is sufficiently shocking, the opponent's ability to cope is correspondingly reduced. If the shocking act is gross enough, the opponent will be completely unable to react, and victory is assured. Thus, we might view the hostage takings in Lebanon during the 1980s—and subsequent murders of some hostages—as shock tactics. A more common example is the threat to break off a relationship.

The only consistently successful response to the ploy is to end the "game" or the series of negotiations. Any negotiation process is a social act, carried out within a social context that establishes certain limits to the behavior of all players. When others go beyond the limits, continuing to negotiate simply reinforces their behavior. (Note that continued talking, or "complaining" about the violation, is a continuation of the negotiation.) When faced with negotiation behavior that goes beyond accepted limits, do not talk, do not complain. Walk out. Do not attempt to explain *why* you are walking out; simply go. Do not argue, and do not attempt to point out that the offender is violating social rules. Such people, by action, have indicated that they do not regard the rules as binding.

This is sufficiently important to deserve repeating: *negotiation is a social act*. It assumes that all parties function within the limits set by their society. If this is not the case, do not negotiate; take a walk.

Such a policy will not, as might be expected, lead to final stalemate. How many times have you seen, in the movies, that when one party walks out, the other calls him or her back? People enter into negotiations because of a desire for mutual gain through exchange. Withdrawal as a strategy penalizes those who initially violated the limits. The potential gain that attracted them to the negotiation in the first place will create pressure to reopen the exchange. Most bargainers find it easy to gain concessions when the effort to reopen negotiations takes place. Your relative power in the negotiation situation is weakened when you are forced to recontact the offended party.

PROPOSITIONS

The exchange situation produces predictable outcomes. Homans derived a number of predictions stated as lawlike propositions within the framework of exchange theory.[12] From these propositions, we can begin to understand why we communicate as we do. The following discussion centers on those propositions (quoted from Homans), with an emphasis on the *motivational* aspects of the exchange.

Proposition 1: Reward

> For all actions taken by persons, the more often a particular action of a person is rewarded, the more likely the person is to perform that action (p. 53).

If you have been rewarded for participation in class, you will probably continue to participate in class. Rewards are not always expressed in terms of money; being rewarded means only that we receive something that is of value to us. It is unnecessary that others agree that the reward received is valuable. Valuation is a personal decision and differs from person to person.

The stress placed on individual, situational determination of the reward of things is not new. Benjamin Franklin, in the 1733 edition of *Poor Richard's Almanac*, wrote, "Hunger never saw bad bread." Abraham Maslow attempted a systematic explanation of how values are assigned with his well-known "hierarchy of needs" (see Fig. 10–1).[13]

The hierarchy is a pyramid that is read from the bottom up. According to Maslow, we all have physiological needs—food, shelter, water, air, clothing, sex—that must be satisfied before we can move to the next level. The amount of any physiological item needed, or the value placed on each, varies from person to person. For example, some people eat only one meal a day; others eat constantly. After we have satisfied our physiological needs, we become concerned with satisfying security (safety) needs of ourselves and loved ones with an eye on the future. We save food, put locks on our doors, buy various forms of insurance, or open a savings account.

Once security needs have been satisfied, we tend to be oriented toward affection; that is, we have a need to belong. This need is similar to what Schutz has discussed in his inclusion type (see Chapter 7). It is also similar to the symbolic interactionists' concept of a significant other. We need to have the idea that others care about our welfare. Once affection needs have been

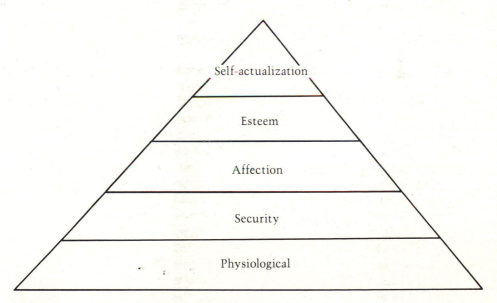

FIGURE 10–1   Maslow's Hierarchy of Needs.
Source: A. H. Maslow, *A Theory of Human Motivation* (New York: Harper and Row, 1970).

satisfied, we are concerned with self-esteem, that is, power and the need to feel important. We need to feel that what we are doing is meaningful.

Maslow suggests that less than 10 percent of people ever consistently satisfy the first four levels of needs. If we could satisfy these needs, however, we could begin working on self-actualization. These are needs that are altruistic (other-oriented). We feel like doing things for others without reward. Some theorists believe that no such people really exist.

Maslow's hierarchy suggests that communication will be increasingly valued and needed as we move *up* the hierarchy. At the physiological level, most communication is survival-oriented and nonverbal in nature.[14] Once we have an established security, we turn our attention to others. We begin to value the participation of others in our society. Through communication with others, we enhance our survival through mutual security. Ensuring security, however, requires that we communicate—negotiate—with others to establish a common sense of security. We find this, for instance, in governmental alliances such as NATO, political parties, fraternal groups, families, and so forth. The key is that security and higher hierarchical levels are valued. We communicate to achieve the rewards associated with each level.

Proposition 2: Experience

> If in the past the occurrence of a particular stimulus or set of stimuli has been the occasion on which a person's action has been rewarded, then the more similar the present stimuli are to the past ones, the more likely the person is to perform the action or some similar action, now (p. 54).

We view a person's experiences as connected. Behavior that leads to reward in one situation is likely to be used in other situations. If two classes are similar, and you are rewarded for participation in one of them, you will likely participate in the other. Since many schoolteachers prefer a quiet classroom, they tend to reward children who sit quietly at their desks and do their assignments. They often do not reward children who interrupt with questions, even creative questions. Teachers' praise and good grades go to children who do not cause "problems," who learn the material as it is taught in the textbook. This is one reason why it is difficult to get students to participate when they get to college. They have "learned" that this is not proper exchange behavior. In simple terms, we all tend to generalize from our experiences. Of course, in so doing, we often violate the principles of general semantics discussed in Chapter 4. Nevertheless, we persist in generalization as a necessary way of predicting the consequences of our actions.

Proposition 3: Value of Outcome

> The more a person values the result of an action, the more likely he is to perform that action (p. 55).

All rewards are not of equal value. We live in a complex environment that offers many different rewards. You will decide, in any situation, what you want most, and then act in the way most likely to obtain your rewards. For example, you will probably continue to participate in class as long as the reward is *worth* the cost. However, if you are sitting next to a good friend who gets embarrassed by your participation, you will begin to weigh the alternatives. What becomes more important (valuable) to you will ultimately determine whether you continue to participate in class.

Proposition 4: Diminishing Returns

The more often in the recent past a person has received a particular reward, the less valuable any further unit of that reward becomes (p. 55).

You may have learned this proposition in a basic economics class as the law of diminishing returns. Suppose that you receive a piece of candy every time you participate in class. The reward of candy is likely to be effective only for a certain number of rewards. Thirty statements in one class may be all the participation you will provide, because you are no longer hungry for the candy. Money (increased salary) is often viewed as a continual motivator for workers. There are times, however, when a "pat on the back" may be more rewarding than an increased salary. Many corporations have recognized this and have started to include nonmonetary rewards in the type of compensation offered. As a student, it may be hard to realize this, but the value of money is not always the same. If your annual income is $12,000, the prospect of a $1,000 raise is more of a thrill than it is to a person whose salary is $100,000. Just as you can have so much candy that another piece does not mean anything, some workers have so much money that another dollar means little. The same principle underlying Proposition 4 applies to *any* reward you care to imagine.

Proposition 5: Distributive Justice

When an action does not produce an expected reward or causes unexpected punishment, a person will be angry and become more aggressive. When an action produces an unexpected reward, or when it does not produce expected punishment, a person becomes more likely to perform approving behavior, and the results of such behavior become more valuable (p. 75).

Proposition 5 deals with what Homans called "distributive justice," the perception that we have a right to expect a fair exchange in our interactions. Essentially, it examines the relationship between what we expect (level of aspiration) from a relationship (situation) and what is actually experienced. Failure to get an expected reward produces frustration. On the other hand, sometimes we receive an unusual (unexpected) positive reward, such as when a worker receives an unanticipated raise, promotion, or bonus. The worker is likely to perform in accordance with a quote from one of the author's former employers: "If you pay people more than they're worth, they will probably be worth more than you're paying them."

Proposition 6: Rationality

> In any decision situation a person will choose that one action for which, as perceived by him at the time, the value . . . of the result multiplied by the probability . . . of getting the result, is the greater (p. 75).

Essentially, this proposition is an adaptation of the profit formula introduced earlier. In other words, we tend to take actions (and communicate with others and build relationships) based on the probability of a reward exceeding our costs. This final proposition seems to cause the most hardship for students of communication theory to understand and accept. Another way of phrasing it is to say that *no one ever does anything that he or she thinks is wrong*. Of course, we all do things that we know will be considered wrong by others; when we do, we often articulate such statements as, "If they only *really* knew . . . ." Most of us have also done things that we have regretted, but at the time and under the circumstances, we had worked out a formula in which the reward exceeded the costs. It was "right" then, no matter what happened later. Because communication is the foundation of relationships, we can see that the status of relationships can be determined by observing human interactions. While interactions are going well, and while both parties feel they are "profiting" from a relationship, the relationship is viable.

Take, for instance, a dating relationship. We expect that over time the relationship will increase proportionally; that is, as time increases one unit, the reward value of the relationship will also increase one unit. We know, however, that relationships also have costs: time spent with someone must come from somewhere. Norms must be negotiated, some of which may not be what we want. Also, we must balance *our* values and needs with the values and needs of the *other*. Thus, although we tend to hope that the imaginary chart of this relationship will increase steadily over time as a straight line, it actually comprises a series of peaks (rewards) and valleys (costs), with the line approximating the difference between peak and valley per time unit. As long as the rewards are greater than the costs, the relationship is rewarding and will continue. When rewards equal costs, however, the relationship begins to stagnate. When the rewards are less than the costs, the relationship begins to deteriorate. Thus, when one person begins questioning the value of the relationship, the relationship becomes tenuous. If either person decides that the costs have exceeded the rewards, action will be taken to terminate the relationship. Relationships, like societies, are stable only when all involved have a sense of reward.

REVIEW

Homans's exchange theory (see Table 10–1) is based on the notion that people will begin and maintain relationships only if each feels that he or

TABLE 10–1 Summary Table

Name of Theory	Primary Theorists	Basic Principle	Constructs	Criteria	Analytic Approach	Limitations
Exchange Theory	George Homans	Relationships and communication exchanges operate like economic exchanges.	• Profit • Reward • Cost • Resistance point • Bargaining range • Level of aspiration	Profit = Reward − Cost	Probability and reciprocity	Reciprocity is untestable in a quantitative sense. Because profit, reward, and cost are based on perception, they are difficult to evaluate.

she is getting more out of it than he or she is putting into it. The formula, *Profit = Reward – Cost*, is used as the basic principle of the theory. As we have mentioned, the concepts of reward, cost, and profit vary among individuals. In each case, however, we have a bargaining range, which indicates the level of flexibility on the part of each person involved. As such, exchange theory is classified as a theory of knowledge.

CRITIQUE

Exchange theory is a rule-based theory that is stated in a lawlike fashion. The formula is definitional in its structure (as is typically the case with formulas). An exchange theorist might argue that a person left a relationship because no profit remained. When asked why, the theorist might argue that the reward was less than the cost. Since reward and cost vary, however, it would be impossible to prove. Like many theories that are stated in a lawlike fashion, exchange theory is hard to prove or refute. Because nomic necessity is used, the theory is grounded in its language, not in empirical tests. In addition, the theory is somewhat simplistic in its formulation. For example, other relationships often affect one particular relationship as either a reward or a cost. Thus, relationships may be more like an international firm that must please the home country, which owns the company's resources and others, than they are like an owner of a clothing shop in a small, American town. When we create a new relationship, we want to maintain the ongoing profitable relationships at the same time; however, this is often difficult and sometimes impossible.

Not all agree with Homans's central assumption that we communicate for profit. Exchange theorists generally believe that people are motivated by a relationship's rewards and costs; however, we all engage in relationships that have no *apparent* payoff. While this concept runs counter to exchange theory, supporters would argue that *any* positive relationship is its own reward. We may not be conscious of the costs associated with the relationship until it infringes on some other relationship. Whichever side you take—that we are profit seekers or that we are altruistic—exchange theory offers a powerful analysis of human communication.

While Homans's theory is based on capitalistic economic notions, we find in the next chapter that Marxian theory is based on the concept that capitalism is a negative system. According to Karl Marx and others, when capitalism is used, there is always a winner and a loser. In Homans's exchange theory, both parties perceive of the relationship as profitable. Marx has argued that although both parties may perceive capitalism as profitable for all, such is not actually the case.

NOTES AND REFERENCES

[1]G. C. Homans, "Social Behavior as Exchange," *The American Journal of Sociology,* 62 (1954), p. 597.

[2]The concept of exchange in human sexual relationships is discussed in K. Davis, *Human Society* (New York: Macmillan, 1949).

[3]The formula is explained in further detail in G. C. Homans, *Social Behavior: Its Elementary Forms* (New York: Harcourt, Brace, and World, 1961).

[4]Some sociologists have pointed to what they call "imbalanced" relationships, where one party gets more than it gives. For example, see A. W. Gouldner, "The Norm of Reciprocity: A Preliminary Statement," *American Sociological Review*, 25 (April, 1960), pp. 165–167. It is more likely, however, that what Gouldner and others see as "exploitation" is in fact the result of differences in the assignment of values.

[5]M. Deutsch and R. M. Krauss, "Studies in Interpersonal Bargaining," *The Journal of Conflict Resolution*, 6 (1962), 52–76.

[6]J. T. Tedeschi and P. Rosenfeld, "Communication in Bargaining and Negotiation," in *Persuasion: New Directions in Theory and Practice*, ed. M. E. Roloff (Beverly Hills, CA: Sage, 1980), pp. 227–228.

[7]Power in interpersonal bargaining situations has been examined by a number of researchers. See A. S. Tannenbaum, *Control in Organizations* (New York: McGraw–Hill, 1968); D. G. Pruitt, "Power and Bargaining," in *Social Psychology*, ed. B. Seidenberg (New York: Free Press, 1976); J. T. Tedeschi and T. V. Bonoma, "Measures of Last Resort: Coercion and Aggression in Bargaining," in *Negotiations*, ed. D. Druckman (Beverly Hills, CA: Sage, 1977).

[8]O. J. Bartos, "Concession-Making in Experimental Negotiations," in *Sociological Theories in Action*, ed. J. Berger (Boston: Houghton Mifflin, 1966).

[9]W. C. Hamner and G. A. Yukl, "The Effectiveness of Different Offer Strategies in Bargaining," in *Negotiations*, ed. D. Druckman (Beverly Hills, CA: Sage, 1977), pp. 137–159.

[10]S. S. Komorita and J. M. Chertkoff, "A Bargaining Theory of Coalition Formation," *Psychological Review*, 80 (1973), 149–162.

[11]Gouldner, p. 171.

[12]Homans discusses three basic propositions in Chapter 4 of *Social Behavior: Its Elementary Forms*. They have been slightly adapted here. See also G. Phillips and N. Metzger, *Intimate Communication* (Boston: Allyn and Bacon, 1976).

[13]A. H. Maslow, *A Theory of Human Motivation* (New York: Harper and Row, 1970).

[14]For a discussion of Maslow and survival behavior, see D. W. Stacks and D. E. Sellers, "Understanding Intrapersonal Communication: Neurological Processing Implications," in *Intrapersonal Communication Processes: Original Essays*, eds. C. Roberts and K. Watson (New Orleans, LA: SPECTRA, 1989), pp. 243–267.

11

Conflict Theory:
Karl Marx and Saul Alinsky

ommunication is often used as a vehicle for change. Change, as explored earlier, may occur on an individual level, on a level between individuals, and sometimes within entire societies. Many times, change comes through armed revolution; often, however, change comes through communication.

In our architectural metaphor, we note that different architects look at the edifice they build from differing perspectives. Sometimes those perspectives clash. When this happens, one's perspective must change. Sometimes an architect comes along who radically changes our view of what buildings *should be*. William Le Baron Jennings is such an architect. His design of the first modern skyscraper revolutionized urban architecture. Although most of us do not recognize Jennings's contributions to architectural theory, his impact can be seen in the skylines of many large cities.

Sometimes a *social* architect comes along and turns society upside down. Karl Marx was such a theorist. Marx has influenced the human race as much as anyone. His impact on the Soviet Union and the People's Republic of China is well known, but his writings have also had impacts on many third-world nations.[1] Marx has influenced almost every area of the social sciences, including economics, political science, and sociology. He is considered a heretic among many of the theorists in all of these fields. In a sense, he may be considered a heretic among communication theorists as well.[2]

Marx's original training was in communication. As a journalist, he supported the "little person's" bringing about a revolution to create a world in which people were more equal.[3] Marx would have strenuously opposed Homans's exchange theory (see Chapter 10) as capitalistic and supportive of differentiation among people. Whereas Homas provided a means for *operating within* the system, Marx provided a means for *changing* the political and economic systems. In this chapter, we present an overview of Marx's "negative dialectics," adapted from the dialectical model originated by Georg Wilhelm Friedrich Hegel. We focus on three characteristic elements in Marx's rhetorical thinking and negative dialectics: (1) the concept of consciousness, particularly class consciousness, examining the work of Saul Alinsky as an example of the use of tactics; (2) the problem of the human referent in language meaning, and (3) the process of social alienation.[4]

NEGATIVE DIALECTICS

Aristotle wrote, "Rhetoric is the counterpart of Dialectic."[5] In the communication discipline (since Aristotle), we have studied rhetoric extensively, but for many years dialectic has taken a secondary status. Following Plato, the next significant student of dialectic was Pierre de la Ramee (Peter Ramus) in the 16th century,[6] and the next use of dialectic was encompassed in the works of Hegel.[7] In Hegel's dialectic, there were three basic concepts (thesis, antithesis, and synthesis), referred to as a triad (see Fig. 11–1).

Hegel's *dialectical* method may be defined as a method "of reasoning in which the conflict or contrast of ideas is used as a means of detecting the truth."[8] "The all inclusive triad in Hegel's philosophy, described just above, is (1) *thesis*, the Idea; (2) *antithesis*, Nature; and (3) *synthesis*, Mind or Spirit" (p. 136). Like Plato and Ramee, Hegel was an idealist, and ideas were the focal points of his philosophy. As an "antiphilosopher," Marx used a negative approach to Hegel's dialectics with a new triad of *totality, negativity,* and *alienation.*[9] In this sense, Marx turned Hegel's view of society upside down.

Marx's "society" was based on nature, consisting of land, capital, and labor (see Fig. 11–2).[10] Land comprises the natural elements of production (the land itself, fruit, trees, grass, etc.). Capital is the means of production from a simple hoe to the more sophisticated tools we have today: hay balers, tractors, bulldozers, and so on. In addition, the money used to buy these tools is considered capital. Labor is the use of *human* physical and mental energy for the purposes of production.

For Marx, labor was used in two ways. First, labor was used in natural relations (e.g., planting vegetables for our own use; picking cotton to make our own clothes). Second, as society became more complex (and pluralistic), labor became an element in social relations; that is, people were hired to do work, establishing a *social relationship* in which some people were superiors

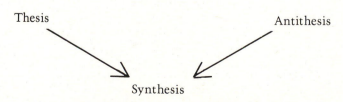

FIGURE 11–1   The Triad.

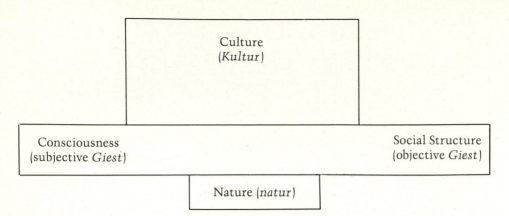

FIGURE 11–2   Marx's Model.

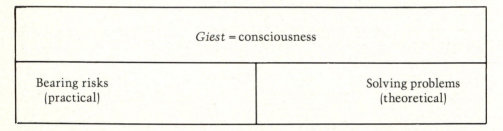

FIGURE 11–3   Types of Consciousness.

and others subordinates. Marx felt that this relationship influenced all other relationships in a given society. It also affects subjective mind (*Geist*, consciousness), which is composed of two parts (see Fig. 11–3): a *theoretical mind* (solving problems) and a *practical mind* (bearing risks).

CONSCIOUSNESS (SUBJECTIVE MIND)

Consciousness has to do with how we feel about ourselves in the areas of bearing risks and solving problems. We know that it is easier for some people to take chances than it is for others. For Marx, the concept of risk taking was directly associated with what we consider the probabilities of losing or being penalized in some way, which is tied to class consciousness. Risk taking is much different for a member of the *proletariat* (a blue-collar worker) than for a member of the *bourgeoisie* (a capitalist). The proletarian must work for a living. Today, most of us must work simply to make ends meet. Therefore, any risk that might put us "out of commission" probably would not be taken by a blue-collar worker. (A blue-collar worker may be afraid to go to a physician out of fear that the physician might recommend staying away from work for a period of time.) At the other end of the spectrum, the capitalist does not have to work. Some capitalists do not spend the interest on their income; others do not even spend the interest on the interest. For this reason, capitalists look at a risk quite differently from their blue-collar counterparts. Marx believed that we need to know and understand our place in the class system. Through this knowledge, we can better understand risks. In addition, the level of bearing risks directly affects our decision making. The more open to risks we are, the greater our options in making decisions.

Subjective mind in turn affects *objective mind* (social structure, institutions). Some institutions are changed as a result of society's consciousness, whereas others are destroyed. Together, consciousness and social structure (the class system) influence what we know as culture (*kultur*), the institutional values of a society. Whereas Hegel felt that values were the bases of society, Marx felt that *nature was basic and influenced all of the other factors in the society*, including subjective mind, objective mind, and culture.

According to Marx, if the proletariat understands its position in the world (has a class consciousness), a revolution will occur to change the situation. For such a change to occur, however, two factors are needed: (1) the proletariat must be *politically active*, and (2) the *change must come from below*, not from above. There appear to be three problems associated with bringing about this class consciousness: the problem of legitimacy, the problem of elite support, and the problem of mass support. There is a problem of *legitimacy* because people in subordinate positions often have a sense of fatalism. They do not believe *they* can change anything. Subordinates view the established order as the proper order. They accept their position of lower status as legitimate, and they believe they will be in a higher class some day. Marx indicated that lower status people must learn to take a positive view toward their own cause, and they must oppose those in power as "illegitimate." To do so, they must have the support of two groups. For *elite support*, the proletariat must recruit a small number of highly committed and politically active members. Eventually, the proletariat must draw *mass support* by convincing the masses that change is necessary and possible. To do so, the elite must use a materialist conception of history (nature is most important) to bring about *class consciousness.*[11]

Marx suggested a simplistic, deterministic method. Using the dialectic described above, he illustrated how the proletariat had evolved from the *slave class.* With knowledge about the status of one's own class, Marx anticipated worldwide changes in the socioeconomic structure. For such social change (based on social conflict), much information must be exchanged, and a great deal of rhetorical discourse must occur to bring about class consciousness. An example of tactics used to do this is found in the works of Saul Alinsky in the United States.

SAUL ALINSKY

Saul Alinsky, a radical community organizer of the 1960s, presented a persuasive strategy based more on practical ends than on Marxist ideology. The *ideal radical organizer*, according to Alinsky, had two distinct reputations. For the establishment, Alinsky's opposition, he was viewed as a "bad person speaking too well." Alinsky had a reputation for manipulating the establishment into "tripping on its own feet." For the outside group, Alinsky's "clients," the radical organizer needed to have "a knowledge of the facts, a high ethical sense, and a sense of the public good."[12] The concepts of ethics and public good were different for the ancient Roman orator (in Quintilian's terms) and the radical organizer in the United States of the 1960s. For a radical organizer such as Alinsky, legitimate tactics included actions used by powerless groups to gain power: diversion, agitation, and sometimes violence.[13] The "public good" became more ambiguous, since the radical organizer had to consider public good *for whom?* Alinsky was called a rebel, a revolutionary, and an agitator; he accepted all of this name calling with pride.[14] Whereas Machiavelli wrote *The Prince* to tell the establishment how to maintain its power, Alinsky helped the people outside of the power base in formulating ways to take power away from the establishment.[15] Alinsky broke several "rules" of traditional rhetorical theory, but he conformed to contemporary radical techniques. His approach was based upon a practical sociopolitical theory, active tactics, and an ethical system.

Alinsky's Sociopolitical Theory

Alinsky claimed to possess no political dogma, and he said he was never certain he was right. "My only fixed truth is a belief in people, a conviction that if people have the opportunity to act freely and the power to control their destinies, they'll generally make the right decisions." Only one ethic must be followed: *We cannot compromise on the principles of a free and open society where we can control our destinies. The people cannot vote out democracy.*[16]

Alinsky maintained that there are two means of power: people and money. Thus, the low-income population must use people to gain power since they lack money. Organization, then, becomes paramount. Individuals within the low-income group, however, must not become contaminated with power, because power foreshadows ruin. "Once you get fat and comfortable and reach the top, you want to stay there. You're imprisoned by your so-called freedoms. The result is a compromise of a free society open to change."[17]

In a free, open society, people are motivated by self-interests just as much as they are in a totalitarian state. An open society functions with power politics. Conflict, confrontation, and compromise perpetuate society by constantly disturbing the balance of power. Consensus without confrontation and compromise results in a totalitarian state. In a democratic state, there is a constant vying for power between the "haves" and the "have-nots."[18]

The usual outcome of such a situation is that the establishment desires the maintenance of power *because it has the power.* Even within the establishment, however, people vie for one another's power. In this way, the status quo provides impetus for the radical element. Eventually, the establishment makes mistakes, causing its own downfall. For example, Alinsky had trouble organizing a group in Chicago until the University of Chicago set itself up as the establishment and attacked Alinsky as a radical. This action by the university convinced the radical group of Alinsky's importance and brought about group cohesion. The establishment reinforced itself as "the face of the enemy," giving the opposition a cohesion it probably would not otherwise possess. As Alinsky noted,

> A Bull Connor with his police dogs and fire hoses down in Birmingham did more to advance civil rights than the civil-rights fighters themselves. The same thing goes for the march from Selma to Montgomery. Imagine what would have happened if instead of stopping the marchers that first day with clubs and tear gas, chief state trooper Lingo had courteously offered to provide protection and let them proceed. By night the TV cameras would have gone back to New York and there would have been no national crisis to bring religious leaders, liberals, and civil-rights fighters from the north into Selma.[19]

Alinsky called this turning of the establishment against itself, "mass jujitsu." Said Alinsky, "I can always depend on the Establishment to do the wrong thing at the right time."[20]

"Power is the reason for being of organizations," said Alinsky. "The powerless must organize to take power from the elite. This is citizen participation."[21] Thus, Alinsky suggested five rules for the radical to follow to understand and use power:

1. To know power and not fear it is essential to its constructive use and control.
2. Irreverence toward power figures, indeed toward all people, is essential "to the democratic faith."
3. Power is not in what the establishment has but in what you think it has.
4. You only have power as long as the opposition knows that you can and will do what you say you're going to do.
5. The radical must be adaptable so that he or she can maintain control of events in power politics.[22]

Tactics

The revolutionary organizer needs an open mind, political relativity, optimism, a good sense of humor, a strong ego, curiosity, and irreverence. The organizer must also *be himself or herself*, an integrated personality, a free person. He or she must have a well-developed imagination and be able to "realistically appraise and anticipate the probable reaction of the enemy . . . [and] to identify [with the enemy] in his imagination and foresee [the enemy's] reactions to his actions."[23] The true revolutionary should be a political schizoid, with the ability to split into two parts. On the one hand, the revolutionary sees events in the absolute: the enemy is 100 percent wrong. On the other hand, when it comes to negotiations, the revolutionary must realize that there is really only a 10 percent difference. The revolutionary should be both a firebrand and a communicator. A revolutionary's curriculum should include communication, tactics, analysis of power, organizational problems, the education and development of community leaders, and methods of introduction to new issues. With this background, the revolutionary is prepared "to agitate to the point of conflict."[24]

The *modus operandi* (mode of operation) of a revolutionary is simple. First, the revolutionary must be invited in by the people as a listener and observer. In this way, credibility is established; the people know that the leader is on their side. Through listening carefully and observing diligently, the leader shows trust and respect for the people. In the same light, the people learn to trust and respect the leader. Second, the leader must analyze the materials available, including human resources. Third, he or she must "break down . . . justifications for inertia."[25] (This is Marx's stage of establishing legitimacy.) An opening monologue illustrates this point:

> Look, you don't have to take this; there is something you can do about it. You can get jobs, you can break segregated patterns. But you have to have power to do it, and you'll get it only through organization. Because power just goes to two poles—to those who've got money, and to those who've got people. You haven't got money so your fellow men are your only source of strength.[26]

Only after we are concerned or feel threatened will we listen. Fourth, the organizer must "Bait the power structure into publicly attacking [it],"[27] for such attacks immeasurably increase the leader's *ethos* with the people. Such has been the case in the success story of *Solidaritae* in Poland.

The organizer must be circumspect in using symbols, both verbal and nonverbal. Taken to its logical conclusion, this may mean that the leader will have to get a haircut; in an Orthodox Jewish community, it means not to eat ham sandwiches. "You have to talk straight English, using a small word every time you can instead of a big one."[28] It becomes graphically clear that organizers cannot go outside the people's realm of experience. Nor should they appeal to abstract values but rather to those that are real and practical. Neither should the organizer "be trapped by tact at the expense of the truth."[29] In reality, obscenities are often the best to use, for citizen's groups grow weary of "bureaucratese." In contrast, they want the organizer "to tell it like it is." Again, the organizer must analyze the raw material. Having completed this task, he or she starts with where the world is, where the power is. Accordingly, an evaluation of personal assets and liabilities is in order, and the weak points of the opposition must be analyzed. Only then can tactics be pondered.

"Tactics mean doing what you can with what you have" (p. 126). Thus, tactics vary according to the situation. For example, they should throw the opponent off guard. Furthermore, they should be fun for the participants, imaginative, and legal, but without legal precedent. Finally, and most importantly, they should be effective.

Alinsky made a number of recommendations for determining what tactics should be used. Tactics should be within the realm of participants' experience, but outside the opposition's experience. Additionally, a target must be picked, and the target must be considered 100 percent wrong (pp. 127–130). Although the threat itself can be more effective than the tactic, the organizer should never try to "bluff" the opposition.

Alinsky has related the following as an example of a good tactic.[30] A department store in Illinois had refused to hire blacks. Alinsky took three thousand blacks to the store, where they remained inside all day keeping the sales force occupied. They moved from counter to counter, looking at merchandise, but made no purchase. At the end of the day, they made mass requests for merchandise to be sent to their homes COD. When the merchandise arrived, it was refused. Characteristically, the department store suffered economically several ways. First, many white customers would not enter the store because of the enormous number of blacks milling around. Second, when bona fide customers did enter, they had a lengthy wait, causing potential customers to leave without making a purchase. Third, the COD orders busied the accounting and delivery departments for nought. The store soon complied with the blacks' demands that they be hired.

Alinsky's Ethics

Having considered the organizer in action, the question then becomes one of whether such tactics *should* be used. Alinsky denied that these tactics were coercive, saying instead that "the judgment of the ethics of means is dependent upon the political position of those sitting in judgment."[31] Alinsky also readily discussed his ethics of ends: "Their base is the preciousness of life. [The] . . . values include freedom, equality, justice, peace, the right of dissent; the values that were the banners of hope and yearning of all revolutions" (p. 47).

Were Alinsky's tactics manipulative? According to Alinsky, "Certainly, just as a teacher manipulates, and no less, even a Socrates" (p. 92). Alinsky sought out the weaknesses in the opposition, focused in on them, predicted a response, and took action. In many cases, the opposition was "trapped" into taking a particular action. The opposition either complied with the requests of the revolutionary or took opposing action. In either case, Alinsky won. Compliance meant the establishment had lost power. If the establishment acted against the revolutionary, the revolution itself triggered cohesion. Eventually, the establishment had to comply. It appears Alinsky at least admitted his use of sophistry, whereas Socrates did not.

For Alinsky, success meant that the organization no longer needed the organizer. The organizer's ultimate purpose is his or her own elimination. For the people, there is never success, only victory. Once one problem is solved, others are created. The old is disorganized, and the new is organized: "life is a series of revolutions . . . each bringing society a little bit closer to the ultimate goal of real personal and social freedom."[32] Alinsky's approach has been compared with Herbert Simon's work on campus confrontation during the 1960s,[33] as well as with Paul Friedman and Gerald Phillips's work on the poverty class.[34] Said Alinsky, "If the end does not justify the means, what the hell does?"[35]

When a group has no power, the only "ethical" method is a pragmatic one. Alinsky's methods worked. For the powerless, that was justification enough. During a period of social change, perhaps ends do justify means. In a period of social and individual consciousness, old grounded definitions of ethics become archaic dust. Even Alinsky admitted, however, that in a period of time, "when the have-nots become the haves, they, too, must be shaken."[36]

Five principles best summarize the notion of class consciousness from the viewpoints of both Marx and Alinsky:

1. "Men make their own history . . . but they do not do it under conditions of their own choice."[37]

2. The proletariat must be "conscious of its own strength, conscious of its own interests, and unite for a determined struggle against the bourgeoisie."[38]

3. "Any given society is to be understood in terms of the specific period in which it exists."[39]

4. Rhetoric goes hand-in-hand with action; indeed, rhetoric is useful only as a stimulus for action.

5. "Success is based on a balance between praxis (practice) and theory. A lack of theory brings about anarchy, while a lack of praxis makes all statements academic at best."[40]

Thus, Alinsky provided for radicals of the 1960s an approach similar to Marx's in terms of tactics if not in terms of theory. These tactics have rarely been used in this country since the late 1960s, but they are still likely to work.

THE PROBLEM OF THE HUMAN REFERENT IN LANGUAGE MEANING

Marx was analyzing *social* relationships, which he thought underlay *economic* relationships as expressed in values, prices, and so forth. It is important to recognize, however, that Marx felt social and economic relationships were inseparable. Indeed, economics forms the foundation of society.

Economics is based on natural resources and the means of transforming those resources through capital and labor. According to Marx, economic resources and the means for transforming them have been the bases of human social relationship since the beginning of humankind. As populations increase and as societies become more pluralistic, human relationships also become more complex. The family was created, among other reasons, as an institution for dividing labor. Nations were created for self-defense and for the protection of natural resources within a particular geographic area. Extremely complex social and economic relationships have resulted from one nation's owning the raw materials, another the labor power, and a third the technology for transforming nature.

Each technological change has brought about a corresponding social change. For example, when we began digging for food using some form of a hoe, we created a change in technology. We created a *tool* for transforming nature. We created capital. Over a period of years, this change caused changes in social relationships. Some people manufactured hoes and sold them to others. This created buyers and sellers.

Relationships became more and more complex. Just as the farmer bought the hoe from the manufacturer, the seller of the hoe had to buy food from the farmer. Often a barter system developed. But society became even more complex, so that today, for example, one person places a bolt in an automobile. Hundreds of others perform similar tasks. The automobile is sent from the assembly line on a truck or a train to a dealer who sells the completed automobile to the same person who initially inserted the bolt. Between inserting the bolt and buying the completed automobile, the worker sees little relationship. In this Marxian sense, we become *alienated*.

As production increases in complexity, classes are formed. Some people take an active role in the labor of transforming nature. Others manage. Still others invest. Many of us are unaware of the relationships between the insertion of the bolt and the production of the automobile. We do know, however, that the managers and the investors are not required to use their own physical labor for maintaining a living. Instead, they are dependent on the labor of others. They own the tools needed for transforming nature. They are capitalists, members of the bourgeoisie. But their counterparts are not so fortunate. They must use their labor to live; these are the proletarians.

Interdependent relationships evolve. Just as many would be upset about General Motors losing money on the New York Stock Exchange, they would be equally upset about a lengthy labor strike. Unfortunately, according to Marx, although the laborers *should* have power, the investors actually have it. Marx felt that everyone should be a laborer. The interdependent relationship falls heavier on the laborer for the simplest of reasons: because he or she *is* the laborer. The investor has an opportunity to accumulate capital, whereas the laborer lacks this opportunity. Laborers must work, and their only apparent means of rebellion is through a strike, a work stoppage, or a work slowdown. Even more important than the physical and economic relationships is the psychology of the worker. The workers *feel* that they cannot change their predicament.

What is it that makes the worker feel this way? Several answers to this question bear consideration. In general, however, Marx's answer is that the bourgeoisie created an environment that causes the workers to feel this way. This can be observed by looking at some of the *language* of contemporary society through the eyes of the powerful. For the powerful, "welfare" is taking what is not ours. It is something for nothing. Although it is not stealing, it closely approximates the same. If we tell an untruth about our welfare status, we are lying. A $300,000 tax write-off is not welfare, but an "offering to maintain the economy." When a high government official tells an untruth, it is an "inoperative statement." These are but a few of the many possible examples indicating how the powerful do not control society simply with their money. They also control it with words. With the legal profession, a primary resource of the powerful, it is not surprising that most of the "thieves" who steal a loaf of bread from the neighborhood grocer have never heard the term *nolo contendre* (no contest).

Marx claimed that for workers to change their status, it was first necessary to have a consciousness of the situation, to understand the historical meanings and ramifications of the concept of class. Like consciousness, language arises only from the need for interaction with others. *Language and consciousness, then, form the basis for any social change derived from Marxian tenets.* "Civilization exists because material and intellectual conquests do not vanish with their conquerors. Man exists only by virtue of tradition, that is, the transmission of goods and knowledge. Language is, so to speak, the receptacle in which the acquisitions of intelligence are preserved. When we inherit a language, we are inheriting a culture created by our ancestors."[41] In essence, language is *class centered.*

With these limitations, the antiestablishment must begin from the beginning. To bring about meaningful social change, there must be a clear understanding of the place of language in a capitalistic society. It is important even for communication researchers to realize the limitations of being reared in such a society. Social change becomes possible only through a revision, if not a revolution, in the language structure. The powerless need to do two things to revise their language structure. First, the powerless need to establish a new vocabulary to be used by the "out group" as a vehicle for creating and maintaining cohesion within the group. Second, they must evaluate the establishment's semantics in an opposite (dialectical) evaluative system so that "negative" words become "positive," and vice versa. This new language must necessarily express the antagonisms between contemporary ideologies and the current economic base.

From what we have said, it would seem that communication researchers have been somewhat negligent in their evaluations and analyses of *protest rhetoric.* Marx would say that this is due to a blindness that appears as the result of living in a capitalistic society. No doubt a Marxist view is biased; so, too, is the bourgeois interpretation. Only by balancing these approaches toward language can one gain a better understanding of the natural forces operating in society.

ALIENATION

Because language is such a major power source in our society, language influences the extent to which we feel we have choices in a society. The feeling of not having much choice in a society has been explicated largely by Marx.[42] This is known as Marx's theory of alienation. This alienation takes the form of separation: from one's work, from others, and from oneself.

Hegel has written the following concerning alienation:

> Spirit is at war with itself; it has to overcome itself as it's more formidable. That development which in the sphere of Nature is a peaceful growth, is in that of Spirit a severe, a mighty conflict with itself. What Spirit really strives for is the realization of its Ideal being, but in doing so, it hides that goal from its own vision, and is proud and well satisfied in this alienation from it.[43]

Marx's alienation is a social alienation; that is, it is an alienation of groups (the proletariat). However, more recent psychological alienation researchers have indicated that people have an individual alienation as well. Melvin Seeman, for example, has characterized psychological alienation as comprised of powerlessness, meaninglessness, normlessness, isolation, and self-estrangement.[44]

Powerlessness is concerned with how "the worker is alienated to the extent that the prerogative and means of decision are expropriated by the ruling entrepreneurs" (p. 88). Seeman wrote, "This variant of alienation can be conceived as the expectancy or probability held by the individual that his own behavior cannot determine the occurrence of the outcomes, or reinforcements, he seeks" (p. 88). Powerlessness results in an inertia, and the result of the inertia is the anticommunication of the interactants in society. Rhetoric is viewed as useless, communication as impossible.

Meaninglessness is when "the individual is unclear as to what he ought to believe when the individual's minimal standards for clarity in decision-making are not met" (p. 91). We feel that we cannot adequately or accurately predict the future. This frustration results in giving up basic goal seeking in a rhetorical sense.

The third aspect of psychological alienation is Emile Durkheim's *anomie,* or what Seeman refers to as *normlessness.* Normlessness is defined as "a high expectancy that socially unapproved behaviors are required to achieve given goals" (p. 94). Thus, to gain a goal, we have to break society's rules: steal, lie, cheat.

Isolation is a characteristic of those who "assign low reward value to goals or beliefs that are typically highly valued in the given society" (p. 95). Here we find our needs in direct conflict with society's demands. The expression of disagreement with society's values causes us to be placed outside the group; thus, these attitudes are often not communicated.

Self-estrangement is defined as "the degree of dependence of the given behavior upon anticipated future rewards" (p. 98). The individual feels alienated from himself. With this constant tension between the acceptance of self and social conformity, alienation develops. Alienation then results only in hope, which is opposed by false consciousness through external controls. Hence, a number of people use alcohol, sensitivity groups, drugs, religious groups, and other forms of what Marx would call a *false consciousness.* [45]

Alienation is often associated with the language we use. As noted earlier, power is often found in language. How that language is used may indicate the degree of alienation felt by a particular group within society. Alienation should be evident in a language that is powerless and not very meaningful (e.g., women often end a statement with a tag question which reduces the power of the statement: "This sure is a nice day, isn't it?"). As alienation increases among the particular group, we might find language indicating normlessness and an isolation from the rest of society. This language would reflect a growing self-estrangement from society, a withdrawal from active participation in decision making. An example might be, "I can't beat the system unless I go around it [normlessness], but I'm not really a part of the system anyway [isolation]."

REVIEW

Social conflict theory (see Table 11–1) has been identified with the work of Marx, who felt that a constant tension in society was a positive factor. He indicated that such a conflict has occurred since the beginning of time. Marx turned Hegel's dialect upside down to show that social problems are nature based. Marx was concerned with how a capitalistic society could use conflict to create an ideal society in which people were more equal. We used Saul Alinsky's work in the United States to show how one can develop tactics for such a conflict. Three of Marx's rhetorical issues were included: class consciousness, the problem of the human referent in language meaning, and social alienation. Conflict theory, as adapted from Marx, may be classified initially as a theory of knowledge; based on Alinsky's adaptation, however, conflict theory may be seen as a theory of action.

CRITIQUE

Social conflict theory can be evaluated only by taking a Marxian perspective. It is testable by evaluating the role of material things (nature) in one's society. The theory is inherently logical, except for the fact that class is considered the only important element in society. The theory is not supportable or refutable because it is law based. One primary argument against Marx's approach is that he misunderstood human nature. Marx assumed that the masses were selfish enough *as a group* to bring about social change. It appears that individual selfishness (as noted by Homans) tends to take precedence over the group concept. The theory is extremely parsimonious, suggesting that changes in the allocation of natural resources would change

TABLE 11-1 Summary Table

Name of Theory	Primary Theorists	Basic Principle	Constructs	Criteria	Analytic Approach	Limitations
Social Conflict Theory	Karl Marx	Social concepts have their bases in nature. To change social concepts, changes must be made in nature (distribution of land, labor, and capital).	• Dialectic • Proletariat • Bourgeoisie • Nature • Social structure • Class consciousness • Culture • Alienation	Movement from a hierarchal society to a society of relative equality.	Negative dialectic.	Presumes the nature of humans to challenge their social structure (under certain conditions). However, conditions rarely exist. Presumes humans to be altruistic, sharing beings. There is never a very explicit statement how to create class consciousness where there is none.

consciousness, social structure, and culture. Marx's theory has been heuristic to some extent. Its most important heuristic use has been by those who use what they refer to as the "critical interpretive" approach, examined next in Chapter 12.

NOTES AND REFERENCES

[1] See, for example, D. Threadgold, *Twentieth Century Russia* (Chicago: Rand McNally, 1972); J. Laurence, *A History of Russia,* rev. ed. (New York: Mentor, 1965); B. Pares, *Russia* (New York: Mentor, 1962); A. Moorehead, *The Russian Revolution* (New York: Perennial Library, 1958); D. Sheeb, *Lenin: A Biography* (New York: Mentor, 1948); V. I. Lenin, *State and Revolution* (New York: International, 1943); V. I. Lenin, *On Workers' Control and the Nationalization of Industry* (Moscow: Progress, 1970); V. I. Lenin, *"Left-Wing Communism, An Infantile Disorder* (Peking: Foreign Language, 1970); L. Trotsky, *The Revolution Betrayed: What Is the Soviet Union and Where Is it Going?* (New York: Pathfinder, 1972); Mao Tse-Tung, *Quotations from Mao Tse-Tung* (Peking: Foreign Language, 1966).

[2] R. Fletcher, *The Making of Sociology: A Study of Sociological Theory, I* (New York: Charles Scribner's Sons, 1971), p. 339.

[3] M. Borden, "Some Notes on Horace Greeley, Charles Dana, and Karl Marx," *Journalism Quarterly, 34* (1957), 457–465; M. Borden, "Five Letters of Charles Dana to Karl Marx," *Journalism Quarterly, 36* (1959), 314–316; T. Carver, *Marx and Engels: Their Intellectual Relationship* (Indianapolis: Indiana University Press, 1983), p. 12.

[4] R. W. Wilkie, "Karl Marx on Rhetoric," *Philosophy and Rhetoric, 9* (1976), 232–246. See also R. W. Wilkie, "The Marxian Rhetoric of Angelica Balabanoff," *Quarterly Journal of Speech, 60* (1974), 450–458; D. Abbott, "Marxian Influences on the Rhetorical Theory of Kenneth Burke," *Philosophy and Rhetoric, 7* (1974), 217–223; R. W. Wilkie, "Rhetoric and Knowledge Among Some Contemporary Marx–Leninists," *Central States Speech Journal, 32* (1981), 153–159.

[5] L. Cooper, *The Rhetoric of Aristotle* (New York: Appleton–Century–Crofts, 1960), p. 1.

[6] P. A. Duhamel, "The Logic and Rhetoric of Peter Ramus," *Modern Philology, 46* (1949), p. 164.

[7] G. W. F. Hegel, *The Philosophy of Right and The Philosophy of History* (Chicago: Encyclopedia Britannica, 1952).

[8] J. D. Butler, *Four Philosophies and Their Practice in Education and Religion,* 3rd ed. (New York: Harper and Row, 1968), p. 44.

[9] H. Lefebvre, *The Sociology of Marx* (New York: Vintage, 1968), p. 4. Additionally Marx wrote that "Positive Philosophy [functionalism] means ignorance of everything positive," in T. B. Bottomore, *Karl Marx: Selected Writings in Sociology and Social Psychology* (New York: McGraw–Hill, 1956), p. 13 [cited in a letter from Marx to Engels, July 7, 1866]. See also J. Piaget, *Structuralism* (New York: Harper and Row, 1970), Chapter 7.

[10] N. J. Smelser, *Karl Marx on Society and Social Change* (Chicago: University of Chicago Press, 1973), pp. 3–6.

[11]G. Welty, "Communication in the Totality of Things," in *Marxian Perspectives on Human Communication*, eds. M. Hickson, III, and F. E. Jandt (Rochester, NY: PSI, 1976), pp. 1–25; R. T. Williams, "Class Consciousness: The Central Rhetorical Problem in Karl Marx," in *Marxian Perspectives on Human Communication*, ed. M. Hickson, III, and F. E. Jandt (Rochester, NY: PSI, 1976), pp. 26–35.

[12]T. Thonssen, A. C. Baird, and W. W. Braden, *Speech Criticism* (New York: Ronald Press, 1970), p. 555.

[13]S. E. Lucas, "The Rhetorical Critic and the Rhetoric of Protest," *Interchange, 1* (1971), 26–27; J. W. Bowers and D. J. Ochs, *The Rhetoric of Agitation and Control* (Reading, MA: Addison–Wesley, 1971); F. Haiman, "The Rhetoric of the Streets: Some Legal and Ethical Implications," *Quarterly Journal of Speech*, 53 (1967), 99–104.

[14]See S. D. Alinsky, *Reveille for Radicals* (New York: Vintage, 1969), p. 237; and C. E. Silberman, *Crisis in Black and White* (New York: Vintage, 1964), pp. 321–328. Alinsky was born in Chicago in 1909, the son of Russian Jews who emigrated to the United States. He attended the University of Chicago and was graduated with a bachelor's degree in archaeology. He entered graduate school, completing his field research in criminology by working with Al Capone's gang. He worked for a while as a criminologist and a professor before deciding on his life's work, community organization and action. In June 1972, Alinsky died of a heart attack. For a warm, meaningful tribute, see N. von Hoffman, "The Happy Death of Saul Alinsky, Who Was Ready, If We Were Not," *Washington Post*, June 16, 1972, p. B-1. The "Back of the Yards" refers to the area of Chicago made famous by Sinclair Lewis in *The Jungle*.

[15]H. W. Simons, "Confrontation as a Pattern of Persuasion in University Settings," *Central States Speech Journal, 20* (1969), 163–169; P. Friedman and G. M. Phillips, "Toward a Rhetoric of the Poverty Class," *Journal of Communication, 17* (1967), 234–249. These two works are used to analyze Alinsky's methods later in this section.

[16]S. D. Alinsky, *Rules for Radicals* (New York: Random House, 1971), p. 4; and S. D. Alinsky, "Playboy Interview: Saul Alinsky," *Playboy Magazine, 19* (March 1972), p. 150. Alinsky was interviewed by Eric Norden. See also T. L. Thorson, *The Logic of Democracy* (New York: Holt, Rinehart and Winston, 1962).

[17]Alinsky, "Interview," p. 72. The epitome of such a breakdown is described by George Orwell in *Animal Farm*.

[18]Alinsky, *Rules*, pp. 12–13. A third category, "have some, want-some-more" is used by Alinsky, but is omitted here since this is a transient period between the other two. For more information on the power concept, see W. D. Jacobson, *Power and Interpersonal Relations* (Belmont, CA: Wadsworth, 1972).

[19]M. Sanders, *The Professional Radical* (New York: Perennial Library, 1970), p. 42. Sanders interviewed Alinsky for this book; for all practical purposes it may be considered a primary source since all remarks were made by Alinsky.

[20]"Radical Saul Alinsky: Prophet of Power to the People," *Time, 95* (March 2, 1970), p. 56.

[21]Alinsky, *Reveille*, pp. 64–75.

[22]Alinsky, *Rules*, pp.6–7; Sanders, pp. 43, 56; Alinsky, "Interview," p. 62.

[23]Alinsky, *Rules*, p. 74.

[24]Alinsky, *Rules*, pp. 64, 78, 117.

[25]Alinsky, *Rules*, p. 99; Alinsky, "Interview," p. 76.

[26]Sanders, p. 33.

[27]Alinsky, *Rules*, p. 89; Alinsky, "Interview," p. 76.

[28]Sanders, p. 15. See also J. Rubin, *Do it! Scenarios of the Revolution* (New York: Simon and Schuster, 1970).

[29]Alinsky, *Rules*, p. 50.

[30]Alinsky, "Interview," p. 170.

[31]Alinsky, *Rules*, p. 26. See also Alinsky, *Rules*, pp. 169–183.

[32]Alinsky, "Interview," p. 76.

[33]Simons, pp. 163–164.

[34]Friedman and Phillips, pp. 234–249.

[35]Martin, p. 59.

[36]See also M. Hickson, III, "Saul Alinsky: American Marxist Strategist?" in *Marxian Perspectives on Human Communication*, eds. M. Hickson, III, and F. E. Jandt (Rochester, NY: PSI, 1976), pp. 36–43.

[37]C. W. Mills, *The Sociological Imagination* (London: Oxford University Press, 1959), p. 190.

[38]A Commission of the Central Committee of the Communist Party of the Soviet Union (Bolshevik), *History of the Communist Party of the Soviet Union: Bolshevik* (Moscow: Foreign Language, 1950), p. 10.

[39]Mills, p. 149.

[40]See M. Hickson, III, "Toward a Marxian Analysis of the Rhetorical Situation," *Canadian Speech Communication Journal*, (1976), 8–17; and M. Hickson, III, "Toward a Marxian Theory of Communication: A Humanistic Perspective," *Kentucky Journal of Speech Arts*, (1975), 12–14.

[41]R. Aron, *Main Currents in Sociological Thought, I* (Garden City, NY: Anchor, 1968), p. 109.

[42]See, for example, O. J. Hammen, "Alienation, Communism, and Revolution in the Marx–Engels Briefwechsel," *Journal of the History of Ideas*, (1972), 77–100; J. S. House and W. M. Mason, "Political Alienation in America, 1952–1968," *American Sociological Review*, 40 (1975), 123–147; K. N. Cameron, *Marxism: The Science of Society* (South Hadley, MA: Bergin and Garvey, 1985).

[43]Hegel in R. Fletcher, *The Making of Sociology, I*, p. 134.

[44]M. Seeman, "On the Meaning of Alienation," *American Sociological Review*, 24 (1959), 783–791, as reprinted in R. S. Denisoff, *Theories in Conflict*, pp. 86–99.

[45]M. Hickson, III, "Alienation and Communication: A Theoretical Perspective," *Internationale Zeitschrift fur Kommunikationsforchung*, 2/3 (1981), 123–134. See also M. Hickson, III, and S. R. Hill, Jr., "Alienation and Communication Theory in the United States," *Canadian Speech Communication Journal*, (1980), 14–25; and K. Giffin, "Social Alienation by Communication Denial," *Quarterly Journal of Speech*, 56 (1970), 347–357.

12

Critical Interpretive Theory: Lukacs, Habermas, Freud, and the Feminists

The conflict theory studied in Chapter 11 has provided contemporary communication theorists with a socially based theory that has been extended to cover a variety of situations. Whereas Marx envisioned change in absolute (class) terms, the new theorists applied his theory in different ways, focusing more on how language relates to culture and the limits that language places on our view of culture (and ourselves).

Going back to our architectural analogy, the influence of an architectural visionary results in new architects playing with the now established aesthetic and pragmatic perspectives of that vision. Certainly, Jennings and Wright brought new form and structure to architecture, but their influence did not stop there. Students of their theories took the best of their ideas and applied them to different situations. Some attempted to build in their master's manner; others *interpreted* their master's manner in novel ways. In so doing, the "new" architect infuses the old with the new. Likewise, the "old" Marxian theory has been infused with "new" ideas. In this case, conflict theory has been coopted to a new sociological approach: critical interpretive theory.

According to Stanley A. Deetz and Astrid Kersten, the critical approach is the synthesis of three main lines of thought: Marxian social theory, as provided by members of the Frankfurt School;[1] "Freudian discursive intervention,"[2] as demonstrated in the works of Wilhelm Reich and others;[3] and hermeneutics, as presented by Hans-Georg Gadamer.[4]

MARXIAN THEORY OF THE FRANKFURT SCHOOL

In Germany, the Frankfurt School (or the Institute for Social Research) has claimed writers of significance, including Jurgen Habermas, Karl Korsch, Georg Lukacs, and Walter Benjamin. In this section, we are concerned with the rhetorical works of Lukacs and Habermas, as well as some of Habermas's interpreters.

"Marxist thought is interested in what drives the direction of social construction."[5] The concern is with *domination*, where one person or group has privileged access over another group or person. The Frankfurt School viewed domination in economic, political, social, and aesthetic terms, whereas traditional Marxists (whom the Frankfurt School called "vulgar Marxists") were concerned only with economic domination.[6] The overall view was "an aversion to closed philosophical systems" (p. 41). A critical theory is, then, a "reflective theory which gives agents a kind of knowledge inherently productive of enlightenment and emancipation."[7] According to the critical theorist, it is *ideology* that prevents societies from allowing enlightenment and emancipation. Ideology includes ideas and beliefs (discursive elements), as well as rituals and gestures (nondiscursive elements).

The Critical Theorists' Dialectic

For one member of the Frankfurt School, Lukacs, the core of Marx's writing was in his method.[8] Lukacs argued,

> Let us assume for the sake of argument that recent research has disproved once and for all every one of Marx's individual theses. Even if this were to be proved, every serious "orthodox" Marxist would still be able to accept all such modern findings without reservation and hence dismiss all of Marx's theses in toto—without having to renounce his orthodoxy for a single moment. Orthodox Marxism, therefore, does not imply the "belief" in this or that thesis, nor the exegesis of a sacred book. On the contrary, orthodoxy refers exclusively to method.[9]

The method to which Lukacs has referred is Marx's historical (negative) dialectic whose concern is "the relation between subject and object in this historical process" (p. 3). The central problem for this dialectic is to change reality.

To develop any such method, we must first begin with facts. Social scientists, however, must discover their facts (data) differently from physical or biological scientists. Facts must be developed totally from history, not from the creation of variables: "Concrete reality is, therefore, the category that governs reality" (p. 10). Reality is a process, an ever-changing social process, a totality.

The underlying premise of Lukacs's dialectic states, "It is not men's consciousness that determines their existence, but on the contrary, their social existence that determines their consciousness" (p. 18). Historically, capitalism made this consciousness possible. In this process, the proletariat (workers) became "at the same time subject and object of its own knowledge" (p. 20). Because economic circumstances created the proletariat, it is only through a knowledge of the historical process that the proletariat can give direction to any action it may take.[10]

The first assumption of the dialectic, therefore, is that *history is comprised of subjects and objects; the combination of subjects and objects equals totality.* The second assumption is that *this totality can be understood only by object–subjects.* The third assumption is that *only one group in capitalistic society is capable of being object–subjects: the proletariat.* The proletariat, in turn, must be aware of the dialectical relationship in the history of philosophy: the *dialectic* of theory and praxis.[11] Finally, through the development of *reification* and the creation of class consciousness, the proletariat can determine the proper approach to the theory–praxis dialectic and grasp the "moment" for class conflict. This moment is the exact time that conflict should take place.

Reification

Reification, in its simplest form, has been demonstrated in the works of Korzybski and others.[12] The general semanticists have claimed that the word is not the thing. Contemporary researchers have warned us that assuming the word is the thing may lead to breakdowns and problems in communication. Making such invalid assumptions may even cause "mental illness" or "irresponsibility."[13]

Andrew Arato, writing on Lukacs's theory of *reification*, defines the term as the "phenomenon (and resulting phenomena) of a 'definite social relation between men [sic] appearing [emerging and seeming]' in the form of a 'relationship between things.'"[14] This definition appears consistent with both Marx's work and that of the general semanticists; that is, concepts (or constructs) begin to take on the characteristics of physical objects.

Lukacs contended that nineteenth century Marxism could not transcend reification because it treated the social world as a "second nature" (p. 25). As we can easily see, the consciousness of any "slave" is historically reduced to "thinghood," because the slave becomes an instrument or tool to be used by the master (p. 29).

Instead of becoming things as a result of their work, Lukacs suggested that a reverse process should occur. The "imparting of human forms to objects" should make those objects recognizable as human qualities. In developing this approach to reification, Lukacs was never criticized by his opponents, neither the Stalinists nor the bourgeoisie. His originality in this realm lay in his ability to bring together Marx's critique of the political economy and the development of western rationality taken from sociologist Max Weber (p. 30).

The dialectic of reification is first concerned with economics. We must distinguish between abstract and concrete categories that have dialectical relationships depending on whether one is concerned with thought or reality (see Figure 12–1). In thought, the abstract is the beginning, followed by the concrete. In reality, the concrete is the beginning point and the abstract the result.

The "second nature of appearances" is presented in a "moment of recognition" (p. 32). The next stage is the development of the "moment

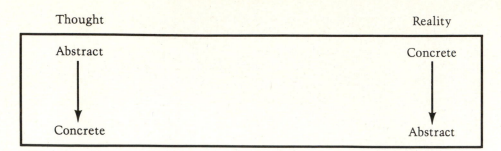

FIGURE 12–1   Dialectical Relationships: Thought versus Reality.

of overcoming."[15] Lukacs found that labor power and its result both became commodities. This *commodification* from an objective view means creating "pseudo-things." From a subjective view, we are forced to face our activities within this second nature.[16] Labor power becomes a quantitative item, a commodity. The object of production becomes separate from the labor power that created it. Lukacs suggests that this fragmentation of the workers in the work process results in having a passive and mechanical attitude toward the object of production, as well as toward our work. This produces *alienation*, a process, argues Lukacs, that is at the center of scientific study as well. Thus, in a capitalistic system, reification takes two forms: (1) our work becomes an instrument, and (2) the object of our work becomes naturalized.

The overcoming of reification may not necessarily mean the overcoming of "our technological mastery of nature" or of the "objectivity of nature."[17] We can see nature at various levels. The type of reification more easily overcome would be the relationship of human to human. The price we must pay is human activity, or *praxis* (p. 45).

There are objective aspects of the dialectic. At the first level, we assume that all of reality is contemplation; this is the objective side. Lukacs contended, however, that we cannot arrive at the subject–object interaction by way of an objective philosophy (as did Hegel). Instead, we must find a subject–object in the same location. By critiquing German philosophy, Lukacs arrived at the same conclusion as did Marx via another route. Success is found in the proletariat. The second dialectic is mediation, the objective historical process. This notion of Lukacs has been criticized by Habermas for its creation of an objective necessity as opposed to an objective possibility, making Lukacs's position deterministic or law governed.[18]

If the proletariat has a "glimpse" of the meaning of history, of what value is it? Lukacs wrote, "In the first instance nothing at all."[19] This is not to say, however, that the proletariat and the bourgeoisie would see the same meaning. Two other forces, however, would have to be exerted for any meaningful change to take place. First, there would have to be a collapse of capitalism. Second, the proletariat (as a voluntary agent) would have to intervene near the end of such a collapse (pp. 70, 79, 164). Thus, the proletariat has been moved from a position of object by the consciousness of the bourgeoisie, and only through becoming objectivized can it act as a voluntary agent, as the objective possibility.

In the final analysis, then, reification is a step first taken by the individual members of the proletariat. Realizing that this would create only minimal consciousness, Lukacs claimed that the next step would be the development of a class struggle. Many of the workers, then, had to realize their alienation and transmit that alienation to their coworkers. Even this action, however, would create only a moment of revolutionary praxis.[20]

Reification occurs in any subordinate group when that group sees itself as a "thing." For example, students are a subordinate group in the educational system or society. As a "student," you are both the result of your work and a commodity. You are your own result because as a class you are an object to your faculty (student). You are a commodity because you are seen as a product of the educational institution. Interestingly, the same analysis can be made of the faculty. They are "teachers," a class of workers or a class unto themselves to the administration (usually made up of former "teachers"). They are a commodity, as well. Their product is education, per se, something you purchase through tuition. To overcome reification, you must first realize that you—as a student or a teacher—are isolated and powerless within the educational system, or society. To change that society, however, means that you must convince others (students, teachers) that they, too, are alienated.

Lukacs's Class Consciousness

According to G. H. R. Parkinson, the "objective possibility" was at the heart of Lukacs's consciousness. In this view, class consciousness "is not the sum, or even the average, of what the individual members of a class think, feel, etc.; it is what they would do in a situation of a certain type, if they were to grasp that situation properly."[21] To assert itself in the class struggle, the proletariat must grasp its *self-knowledge*.

Lukacs wrote that class consciousness is "the appropriate and rational relations . . . 'imputed' . . . to a particular typical position in the process of production."[22] *Consciousness*, then, is not reducible to sums, averages, or psychological states of given individuals. It is a holistic, practical analysis of the historical function of class in society.[23] Sometimes, however, a false consciousness occurs.

How does *false consciousness* occur? It may be either in objectives chosen or in terms of action. Lukacs related an example. The petit bourgeoisie (middle class, merchant) is exposed to the influence of capitalism and is unaffected by the fact of class conflict between the bourgeoisie (upper class) and the proletariat. The petit bourgeoisie imagines itself "to be above all class antagonisms."[24] Thus, this middle group does not take an active part in any class struggles. Neither will the workers unless there is some type of external upheaval (war; depression).[25] The bourgeoisie cannot accept consciousness because it would spell ruin for the entire group. False consciousness arises out of self-interest, selective perception, or lack of organization. Only the proletariat can overcome these moves toward false consciousness.

Consciousness is expressed "as the irreconcilable antagonism between ideology and the economic base" (p. 64). To "cover up," the capitalists developed a coherent theory of false consciousness based on economics, politics, and society. The proletariat must uncover these contradictions to defeat false consciousness. Thus, consciousness is an awareness of the *historical role of class.*

Lukacs believed that we are subjects "in a world of objects, and everything that attests to their creative power is a step toward that complete self-determination which Marx calls freedom."[26] This achievement can occur only by combining philosophy and aesthetics into a meaningful new view of history. In the final analysis, "the whole of history has to be written; the events of the past have to be sorted, arranged, and judged from the point of view of historical materialism."[27]

COMMUNICATION THEORY AND IMPLICATIONS

The objective possibility of class consciousness remains with us today. The question is how this concept may fit into contemporary communication theory. In Western society, induction, deduction, and dialectic help us to arrive at some of the conclusions. Although each of these logical approaches has had its place, dialectic has been used only sparingly.[28] Scholars of communication theory need to develop a clearer understanding of the role of history and the role of dialectic in the current state of affairs. There are some promising signals regarding "blue-collar" studies[29] and the influence of technology on dehumanizing people,[30] as well as overall views on the subject.[31] Unfortunately, little study has been undertaken by communication scholars.

Lukacs's conceptualization of reification and class consciousness also fits with other analyses of communicative behavior. As symbolic interactionist Herbert Blumer noted, "The first premise [of symbolic interactionism] is that human beings act toward things on the basis of meanings that things have for them."[32] More important, however, is the second premise whereby "the meaning of such things is derived from and out of the social interaction that one has with one's fellows" (p. 401). When we are seen as things, false consciousness takes precedence over an overall subjective–objective view. This "new Marxism" provides a view of human communication predicated on the dialectical nature of humans and their social interactions.[33] Thus, we need to communicate with an awareness of our past as it affects our means to improve our lives. Knowing that we are individuals first and students second, and knowing how we have been treated in the past, opens the way to consciousness. Once consciousness has been achieved, communication can be used to improve our lives as students. Much of the student movement of the middle to late 1960s can be analyzed in such a light.

Jurgen Habermas

Habermas has been studied in the communication field more extensively than has Lukacs. Recently, articles by Philip Wander and Robert Francesconi have discussed Habermas's views on rhetoric and communication.[34] Wander has discussed what he refers to as an "ideological turn" in rhetorical criticism that imitates the concerns of Lukacs and especially Habermas. He claims that previous rhetorical analyses have focused on rhetoric giving blame or, for the most part, praise. In his analyses, Wander indicates that there is a "third persona" in any given communication: those being *neglected* in it. They are the nonpersons in a society who receive neither praise nor blame for they are the easily forgettable.

Francesconi's view is similar, but his concern is with Habermas's "legitimation" views. He is particularly concerned with what he refers to as "emancipatory knowledge," information the people need to be free. The view is essentially sociological in that social norms form the foundation of what is "best" for emancipation. Francesconi's view is of the traditional modes of persuasion, however. Oral and written discourse are the artifacts to be discovered and analyzed under the new criteria. It could be suggested that in fact what are needed are *new artifacts.* For example, would Habermas analyze the effects of the use of credit cards in the United States as an emancipatory device or its opposite? What about birth control pills? It may well be that the social artifacts of the society are becoming the norms instead of verbal discourse, per se.

Freudian Discursive Intervention

Several Freudian analogues are also applicable to critical interpretive theory. In Freudian discursive intervention, ideology is the nemesis and "neurosis of society."[35] In this sense, *ideology coexists with domination.* Hickson has presented a critical case study based on a Freudian–Reichian psychology of the motion picture, *Taxi Driver.*[36]

> In *Taxi Driver* we have a man in New York City who is lonely; he cannot sleep and yet he cannot find things to do 24 hours a day. All of this time, energy is building up in his body (and in his mind). Because of his perception of morality, the taxi driver does not have sex with anyone (writes Ernest Becker: "Morality is merely a prescription for choice; and 'meaning' is born as the choice is carried into action.").[37] Constantly there is a building up of energy; the only symbolic release for the taxi driver is found in what he writes into his diary every day. On occasion, he pops pills and drinks beer to try to escape the shackles that he himself and/or his society have thrust upon him.
>
> Then he meets the girl he wants. The girl is of the petit bourgeoisie class; he is proletariat. She strings him along and they go out. But the taxi driver makes a mistake, a social (class?) mistake when he takes the girl to a pornographic film. The girl is indignant that he took her to such a place, and the relationship is over as far as she is concerned. Meanwhile, the energy continues

to build up, even more so now, because the orgasmic target has been taken away. According to Wilhelm Reich, the Marxist psycho-analyst, the energy (libido) is built up in the ego, which continues to delay responses.[38] At this point, the taxi driver decides his life is miserable and that he is a worthless person (alienated), but he feels he has the capacity to change all this through some dramatic event. At first he decides to assassinate a man who is running for President of the United States (the employer of the ex-girlfriend), but as with all losers, he "blows" it. But he goes home and pops pills and drinks enough beer to subdue the social (class?) restraints on the self. He goes to a pimp and the pimp's colleagues and kills them. Society praises him as a hero; yet he has not performed any kind of social act lest one considers his own false orgasm, (consciousness) an act with bullets serving as his symbolic semen.

The release of energy (libido) from the ego to the id brings the taxi driver back to where he was in the beginning of the picture. He had a "false orgasm" in that he did not use his body to perform a bodily function. Clearly the most obvious way that he could have brought mind and body into focus was to have had an affair with the girl; a secondary mode, violence, could have been used more appropriately had he choked his victims to death with his hands (his OWN hands) instead of using a symbolic weapon created by bourgeois society. No doubt, the target of his violence was somewhat misplaced also. He should have focused on those who economically backed the pimps instead of on those who were virtually on the same socio-economic level as he.

Thus, Reich's view was that the relationship between bodily states and symbolism are not only analogic; bodily states, according to this view, but also are inevitably intertwined with symbolism. This film, of course, provided the stimulus for the real-life attempted assassination of President Ronald Reagan by John Hinckley.

Gadamer and Hermeneutics

Unlike other concepts of understanding, Gadamer did not view understanding as synonymous with empathy. He felt that, as communicators, we should be concerned with the messages that are sent, not with understanding the other person; that is, *our concern should be on a description of the message as it relates to us in day-to-day interaction.* As such, understanding is steeped in description, not prediction. To analyze these messages, Gadamer argued that "understanding is historic, linguistic, and dialectic."[39] *Hermeneutics* is the phenomenological interpretation of conscious experience.

In saying that *understanding is historic*, Gadamer was indicating that there is no pure sense of an idea's being perfect. He argued, for instance, that prejudice could open our minds for understanding. Openness, he claimed, is "not the lack of bias but the ability to distinguish productive from unproductive prejudices" (p. 18). Instead of attempting to eliminate our prejudices (which realistically we can never do), we need to understand our prejudices as well as their historical underpinnings. We need to be aware of the entire matrix of *past* messages that causes us to assign meanings to the *current* message.

Because tradition itself is linguistic, *understanding is also linguistic.* Tradition arises out of a linguistic context. "Experience and language arise together" (p. 18). Thus, experience is "always biased, interpreted, due to its linguistic character (as is the experience of the other), but since its interpretation is linguistic rather than subjective it is available to others" (p. 19). The function of language is to share experience and tradition with others. New experiences color and add to our old experiences, thus developing new interpretations of our world for ourselves and others.

The third characteristic of understanding is that *understanding is dialectical.* According to Gadamer, understanding goes beyond the people participating in the act of meaning exchange. As Deetz has described it, "the meaning of a text [communication] goes beyond its author" (p. 19). "Understanding is a 'fusing' of horizons of possibilities, opening that which is beyond yet limited by what is presently held. In that sense understanding starts from and is made possible by presumptions about what is to be meant but must be open to refinement, change, or rejection as the message unfolds further" (p. 19). With each new linguistic message placed in the text, we open a new possibility of still another new possibility. "Understanding is change with the loss and gain associated with it" (p. 19). *Genuine conversation* takes place when we allow the dialectic of possibilities to be uncovered, recovered, and discovered. We must allow the text to be opened to these possibilities. The search is to listen for strengths in the words, not the weaknesses. We should be searching for a communion, a new communion based on the new text. However, in "communion one looks forward to both the past and the future."[40] Thus, we can see that *communication is the text of what is understood* for Gadamer.[41]

Feminist Theory

Habermas and others in the Frankfurt School have been primarily interested in the concept of emancipation. Whereas Marx's emancipation was devoted exclusively to class freedom, others (including Lenin) were concerned with other issues that tend to place us within a particular class.[42] For example, some would argue that simply being black places one in a certain class in terms of how society views the person. Others have taken a similar tact regarding gender.

In the United States, for example, movement to sexual freedom has lapsed even behind that of racial freedom. Although blacks technically were emancipated over one hundred years ago, many theorists feel that women have just begun to arrive at a consciousness within the past twenty-five to fifty years.

The theoretical movement in the discipline of communication has been based on nonverbal power struggles,[43] as well as verbal ones.[44] In addition, some theorists have argued that the nature of theory itself is constructed in a "competitive male struggle for dominance."[45] Emancipation for women, then, lies in overcoming a male false consciousness and in creating a new consciousness for themselves in the process of communicating.

Carole Spitzack and Kathryn Carter suggest that the male (false) consciousness developed as an attempt to identify females with nature and with the body.[46] Nancy Henley's thesis that males attempt to dominate females nonverbally is symbolic of this process. For example, Henley contends that males touch females more often than vice versa. Although this contention is disputed in some research, the general metaphor of males "talking down" to females, treating females as children (a pat on the head), and generally acting in a paternalistic fashion is rarely disputed. Similarly, males tend to verbally subordinate women, often by changing the topic of conversation to a "men only" topic (sports, work) in an attempt to trivialize the content of female conversation.

In academia, the feminists contend that males use statistics and objectivity as a means for "closing out" the views of women. They argue that research can never be truly objective when researching human beings. Such a view has been expounded by Hickson and Julian Roebuck.[47]

Feminist views on rhetoric and communication draw highly on the cooperative and communicative aspects of the process; males view the competitive and persuasive aspects of the process.

Some audience analysis, some empathy, is needed in this research for men to understand what it is like to walk in high heel shoes or to wear panty hose. In a similar manner, a consciousness regarding verbal communication might lead us to investigate why certain words are used when talking about females, whereas others are used when talking about males. We would have to evaluate the basic assumptions. For example, suppose that this text were written in such a way that every time an architect was mentioned, we talked about "her." Only through a negative dialectic such as this could the reader see the obvious male chauvinism apparent in our language use. The same may hold true for watching a television newscast in which all of the anchors were women.[48]

The primary criticism of feminist theory and research has been that it is political in nature. Although the feminists do not deny this, they argue that all research is in fact political, that traditional research is simply supportive of the *status quo* (in Perelman's terms, "education"; see Chapter 6) whereas their research supports change ("propaganda"). Thus, both the interpretive approaches and Marxist approaches advocate social change in society.

REVIEW

In this chapter, we have viewed the critical interpretive approach as an extension of Marxist theory (see summary in Table 12–1). The works of the scholars in the Frankfurt School, as well as Reich and other Freudians, have contributed to the changes in traditional Marxist approaches. Gadamer's hermeneutics have added further change. The basic approach of each is to add to what Marx had to say. They believe that we are discriminated against in our daily communication because of the social class in which we fall. These classes, however, may go well beyond the traditional socioeconomic classes. Sex roles

TABLE 12–1 Summary Table

Name of Theory	Primary Theorists	Basic Principle	Constructs	Criteria	Analytic Approach	Limitations
Critical Interpretive Theory	Hans Georg Gadamer Frankfurt School Wilhelm Reich The Feminists	Understanding is historic, linguistic, and dialectical. . . . and gender based.	Reification			At this juncture, these are not unified as such.

and race play a part as well. In addition, we sometimes discriminate against a person without even knowing that we are doing so. The building up of a Freudian energy (libido) may force us to act negatively to another. The attribution of a limited number of behavioral motives may cause a similar negative response.

CRITIQUE

Critical interpretive theory has eliminated the singular (class) dimension of Marxist thinking. In the process, it has allowed us to view a message from a number of different perspectives. Perhaps it is much more of a rule-based, descriptive approach than is Marxist theory. Absolutes are the enemies of interpretive theory. In fact, maybe it is actually more of a new critical method than a theory itself. The intentions of the critical interpretive theorist are similar to those of the general semanticist: to help us realize the constraints that language places upon us. However, the critical approach is much more open-ended and more a receiver-based approach. Thus, it is less prescriptive and more descriptive in its overtones.

SUMMARY

In this section, we have been concerned with theories' suitability to society. To what extent are messages appropriate for the situation? In Chapter 9, on symbolic interaction, we focused on how the individual learns the norms of society and attempts to understand the rules of his or her partner in social conversation. Exchange theory (Chapter 10) suggested that reciprocity is the important element in these conversations. In fact, reciprocity seems to be the rule of rules for Homans and his followers. Marx's conflict theory is based on the need for conflict (a view opposite that of Homans, in that Homans's concern is for maintenance). Alinsky provided an example of how we can strategically use an approach with conflict as its end. The critical interpretive theorists seem to be asking us to question, to have inquiring minds about what we say to others and what they say to us. The primary message of Section Five seems to be to think before you speak, assume others will not think before they speak, and attempt to give others the benefit of the doubt in their motives. These theories of knowledge ask us to increase the bounds of our consciousness.

NOTES AND REFERENCES

[1]M. Jay *The Dialectical Imagination: A History of the Frankfurt School and the Institute for Social Research, 1923–1950* (Boston: Little, Brown, and Company, 1973); M. Hickson, III and F. E. Jandt, eds., *Marxian Perspectives on Human Communication* (Rochester, NY: PSI, 1976).

[2]S. A. Deetz and A. Kersten, "Critical Models of Interpretive Research," in *Communication and Organizations: An Interpretive Approach*, ed. L. L. Putnam and M. E. Pacanowsky (Beverly Hills, CA: Sage, 1983), p. 148.

[3]W. Reich, *The Function of the Orgasm: Sex–Economic Problems of Biological Energy* (New York: Pocket Books, 1975); W. E. Mann, *Orgone, Reich, and Eros: Wilhelm Reich's Theory of Life Energy* (New York: Simon and Schuster, 1973); M. Cattier, *The Life and Work of Wilhelm Reich* (New York: Avon, 1971).

[4]H-G. Gadamer, *Truth and Method*, trans. G. Barden and J. Cummings (New York: Seabury, 1975); S. Deetz, "Conceptualizing Human Understanding: Gadamer's Hermeneutics and American Communication Studies," *Communication Quarterly*, 26 (1978), 12–32.

[5]Deetz and Kersten, p. 150.

[6]Jay, pp. 3–40.

[7]R. Guess, *The Idea of Critical Theory: Habermas and the Frankfurt School* (Cambridge: Cambridge University Press, 1981).

[8]G. Lichtheim, *Georg Lukacs* (New York: The Viking Press, 1970), p. vii. Other biographical information on Lukacs is found in A. Feenburg, "An Introduction to the Young Lukacs," *Alternatives*, 18 (1966), 21–28; M. Harrington, "Georg Lukacs: Dialectical Career of a Dialectician," A. Kazin, "Introduction," in *Studies in European Realism*, by Georg Lukacs (New York: Grosset and Dunlap, 1964), pp. vii–viii; A. Arato, "Lukacs Theory of Marxism (1910–1923)," *Telos*, 7 (1971), 128–136; V. Zitta, *Georg Lukacs Marxism: Alienation, Dialectics, Revolution* (The Hague: Martinus Nijhoff, 1961), pp. 24–25. For a view of his aesthetics, see G. Lukacs, *Marxism and Human Liberation: Essays on History, Culture, and Revolution* (New York: Delta, 1973), pp. 107–240. Notes on Lukacs's part in the Hungarian revolution may be found in D. Kettler, "Culture and Revolution: Lukacs in the Hungarian Revolution of 1951," *Telos*, 10 (1971), 35–92. Lukacs political views are found in G. Lukacs, *History and Class Consciousness: Studies in Marxist Dialectics* (Cambridge, MA: MIT Press, 1968), p. xiii.

[9]Lukacs, *History and Class Consciousness*, p. 1.

[10]This interpretation of the dialectic differs somewhat from other views, even within the Marxian camp. See J. Stalin, *Dialectical and Historical Materialism* (New York: International, 1940), pp. 12–23.

[11]P. Breines, "Praxis and Its Theorists: The Impact of Lukacs and Korsch in the 1920s," *Telos*, 11 (1972), 67–103; and K. Korsch, *Marxism and Philosophy* (New York: Modern Reader, 1970).

[12]A. Korzybski, *Science and Sanity: An Introduction to Non-Aristotelian Systems and General Semantics* (Lancaster, PA: International Non-Aristotelian Library, 1933).

[13]W. Johnson and D. Moeller, *Living with Change: The Semantics of Coping* (New York: Harper and Row, 1972); W. Glasser, *Reality Therapy: A New Approach to Psychiatry* (New York: Harper and Row, 1965).

[14]A. Arato, "Lukacs Theory of Reification," *Telos*, 11 (1972), 25.

[15]Arato, "Reification," 33. See also G. Lukacs, "The Old Culture and the New Culture," *Telos*, 5 (1970), 29–30.

[16]Arato, 33. See also G. H. Homans, "Social Behavior as Exchange," *The American Journal of Sociology*, 62 (1954); G. H. Homans, *Social Behavior: Its Elementary Forms* (New York: Harcourt, Brace, and World, 1961). P. M. Blau, *Exchange and Power in Social Life* (New York: John Wiley and Sons, 1964).

[17]Arato, "Reification," 42.

[18]J. Habermas, *Theory and Practice*, trans. J. Viertel (Boston: Beacon, 1974).

[19]Lukacs, *History and Class Consciousness*, p. 149

[20]A. Feenburg, "Reification and the Antimonies of Socialist Thought," *Telos, 10* (1971), 93–118.

[21]G. H. Parkinson, "Introduction," in ed. G. H. R. Parkinson, *Georg Lukacs: The Man, His Work, and His Ideas* (New York: Random House, 1970), p. 11.

[22]Lukacs, *History and Class Consciousness*, p. 51. Although we have not seen this idea expressed elsewhere, it would not be unlikely that "typical" for Lukacs would be closely related to M. Weber's "ideal type." See M. Weber, *The Methodology of the Social Sciences*, trans. E. A. Shils and H. A. Finch (Glencoe, IL: Free Press, 1949); M. Weber, *The Theory of Social and Economic Organization*, trans. A. R. Henderson and T. Parsons (London: Hodge, 1947).

[23]Lukacs, *History and Class Consciousness*, pp. 51–52. Later in this section Lukacs describes the reasons why the bourgeoisie can never achieve a class consciousness.

[24]Lukacs, *History and Class Consciousness*, p. 59. Lukacs quotes from Marx's, *The Eighteenth Brumaire of Louis Bonaparte*, p. 252.

[25]Lukacs, *History and Class Consciousness*, p. 60.

[26]Lichteim, p. 76.

[27]Lukacs, *History and Class Consciousness*, p. 223.

[28]Following Plato's dialectic, the use of dialectic has since been found in the works of Hegel, Marx, and Ramus. See G. W. F. Hegel, *The Logic of Hegel*, trans. W. Wallace (London: Oxford, 1892); P. Ramus, *The Meaning of Dialectic*, trans. E. E. Wedeek and D. D. Runes (New York: Philosophical Library, 1962), pp. 640–653; P. Ramus, *Dialectical Institutions* (Stuttgart Bad Constatt: Friedrich Frommann Verlag, 1964); K. Marx, *Early Writings* (New York: Vintage, 1975); M. M. Bober, *Karl Marx's Interpretation of History* (New York: W. W. Norton, 1965); R. Tucker, ed., *The Marx-Engels Reader* (New York: W. W. Norton, 1972); D. McLellan, *The Thought of Karl Marx: An Introduction* (New York: Harper Torchbooks, 1971); L. D. Easton and K. H. Guddat, eds. and trans., *Writings of the Young Marx on Philosophy and Society* (Garden City, NY: Anchor, 1967); and H. Lefebvre, *The Sociology of Marx* (New York: Vintage, 1968).

[29]R. Sennett and J. Cobb, *The Hidden Injuries of Class* (New York: Vintage, 1972); J. B. Roebuck and M. Hickson, III, *The Southern Redneck: A Phenomenological Class Study* (New York: Praeger, 1982).

[30]W. B. Key, *Subliminal Seduction* (New York: Signet, 1973).

[31]See Becker.

[32]H. Blumer, "Symbolic Interaction: An Approach to Human Communication," in *Approaches to Human Communication*, ed. R. W. Budd and B. D. Ruben (Rochelle Park, NJ: Hayden, 1972), p. 401.

[33]M. Hickson and D. W. Stacks, "The Communication Theory of Georg Lukacs," *The Researcher, 9* (1981), 49–60.

[34]R. Francesconi, "The Implications of Habermas' Theory of Legitimation for Rhetorical Criticism," *Communication Monographs, 53* (1986), 16–35; P. Wander, "The Third

Persona: An Ideological Turn in Rhetorical Theory," *Central States Speech Journal, 35* (1984), 197–216; P. Wander, "The Ideological Turn in Modern Criticism," *Central States Speech Journal, 34* (1983), 1–18; M. C. McGee, "Another Phillipic: Notes on the Ideological Turn in Criticism," *Central States Speech Journal, 35* (1984), 43–50; L. Rosenfeld, "Ideological Miasma," *Central States Speech Journal, 34* (1983), 119–121.

[35]Deetz and Kersten, 151–152.

[36]M. Hickson, III, "The Anti-Art: Marxist Thought," *The Center Design, 1* (1977), 24–25.

[37]E. Becker, *The Birth and Death of Meaning* (New York: Free Press, 1971), p. 79.

[38]Cattier; Reich; Mann.

[39]Deetz, 18; Deetz and Kersten, 148. See also S. W. Littlejohn, *Theories of Human Communication* (Columbus, OH: Charles E. Merrill, 1978).

[40]Deetz, 20. See also S. A. Deetz, "Critical Interpretive Research in Organizational Communication," *Western Journal of Speech Communication, 46* (1982), 131–149.

[41]See H. Flick, "Gadamer and the Nature of Human Understanding," paper presented to the convention of the Southern Speech Communication Association, Hot Springs, AK, April 1982.

[42]V. I. Lenin, *The Emancipation of Women* (New York: International Press, 1934).

[43]N. M. Henley, *Body Politics: Power, Sex, and Nonverbal Communication* (Englewood Cliffs, NJ: Prentice–Hall, 1977).

[44]C. Kramarae, M. Schulz, and W. M. O'Barr, eds., *Language and Power* (Beverly Hills, CA: Sage, 1984).

[45]P. A. Treicher and E. Wartella, "Interventions: Feminist Theory and Communication Studies," *Communication, 9* (1986), 3.

[46]C. Spitzack and K. Carter, "Research in Women's Communication: The Politics of Theory and Method," in eds. K. Carter and C. Spitzack, *Doing Research on Women's Communication: Perspectives on Theory and Method* (Norwood, NJ: Ablex, 1989).

[47]M. Hickson, III, J. B. Roebuck, and K. S. Murty, "Creative Triangulation: Toward a Methodology for Studying Social Types," in ed. N. K. Denzin, *Studies in Symbolic Interaction, 11* (1989–90), pp. 103–126.

[48]See C. Spitzack and K. Carter, "Women in Communication Studies: A Typology for Revision," *Quarterly Journal of Speech, 73* (1987), 401–423; and K. A. Foss and S. K. Foss, "The Status of Research on Women and Communication," *Communication-Quarterly, 31* (1983), 195–204.

SECTION SIX

Integrating and Living with the Edifice

Communication is not a simple phenomenon. By now, you should be aware that many forces interact to motivate us to communicate. Some motivations come from our individual, psychological needs; others come from our interaction with society. Little research and theory, however, has attempted to integrate communication across both psychological and social needs. To do so, we must view human communication as a system consisting of not only psychological drives and social forces, but also biological elements. Thus, the human communication system is comprised of constructs and principles that produce behavior in lawlike and rule-governed ways.

Drawing our architectural metaphor to a close, we note that once the plans have been drawn and the client's needs accommodated, the physical building must be constructed. All elements—architect, client, materials, land, and so forth—are integrated, and the edifice is constructed. It becomes in many ways an extension of the people dwelling within it, a persona of the inhabitants. It serves to reflect how the inhabitants view the world and their relationships in that world. How well the architect has done ultimately is tested by the inhabitants' feelings of comfort with the building. Does it meet their needs? Does it do what they wanted it to do? Does it reflect how they view their relationship to their community? In communication theory, our architecture must reflect our needs for prediction, understanding, and control. How well individual theories integrate to answer *communication* questions in a variety of contexts often supports the utility of the theory. However, we must also view the process of building communication theory not from the individual elements (theories) that influence us, *but from the entire course of theories* from which we have been influenced. Such a view sometimes requires that we take from and add to our personal theory of communication. Sometimes, it requires that we take a larger, metatheoretical perspective.

The final section of this book examines the interrelationships of psychological, sociological, and biological influences on communication. In a sense, we are integrating the edifice into a *living* structure. As such, communication is viewed as holistic: an outgrowth of our biological needs (while being affected by the biological organs), reflected in our psychological needs, and contrasted with society's roles and expectations. Chapter 13 presents such an analysis in exploring the biosocial approach to communication.

Finally, in Chapter 14, the entire process of communication theory is tied together to present a metaperspective on communication theory. We seek to combine the various approaches and perspectives with a focus on the communication variables of interest to today's student. We end with nine basic principles of communication theory.

13

Integrating the Edifice:
The Biosocial Approach

In the introductory chapters to this text, we noted that we can choose from many competing designs in deciding on our edifice. Sometimes, the architect becomes complacent, falling back on designs that have worked over the years. At other times, however, the architect finds new ways of creating. Communication architects sometimes become complacent, too, relying on the foundations that were taught for years, sometimes centuries. At times, however, they seek new ways for explaining communication. In this chapter, we discuss a relatively new way of integrating the communication edifice. While not forgetting or disputing the psychological or sociological approaches, this *biosocial* approach adds the dimension of biology to the study of communication.

In particular, we examine the foundations of biosocial thought as it originated in the middle 1970s and explore some assumptions concerning behavior and communication. We begin with an examination of the impact of Edward O. Wilson and Ernest Becker on biosocial thought, as well as the ethological tradition. We then identify the major assumptions of biosocial theory. Finally, we consider theory and research about how the brain processes information and enables humans to communicate.

ORIGINS OF BIOSOCIAL THOUGHT

Although we can trace biosocial thought to Charles Darwin, current interest resurfaced with Wilson's *Sociobiology.* [1] Wilson pursues a line of thought similar to that advanced in Darwin's *The Origin of the Species.* [2] Darwin developed three major assumptions about human survivability and adaptation. First, we began as single-celled organisms and, over hundreds of thousands of years, evolved into what we now know as *Homo sapiens.* Second, we are a genetically improved animal, due to "survival of the fittest"; that is, the concept that natural selection allows the best characteristics to evolve into a superior form. Third, evolution involves variation and deviation. Once a species varies or deviates, it will not reappear in its original form.

Biological Foundations

Sociobiology examines how we survive through adaptability, adaptation, and the ability to group. Wilson's theory, however, limits what we might comfortably call "communication." Wilson's "biological communication" encompasses both verbal and nonverbal modes of communication.[3] He argues that

> All man's unique social behavior pivots on his use of language, which is itself unique. In any language words are given arbitrary definitions within each culture and ordered according to a grammar that imparts new meaning above and beyond the definitions. . . . Even communication about the system [metacommunication] is made possible. This is the essential nature of human language. The basic attributes can be broken down, and other features of the transmission process itself can be added. . . . Most of the features can be found in at least rudimentary form in some other animal species (pp. 555–556).

Wilson suggests that our nonverbal communication gives us an advantage in the ethological hierarchy. He notes, "The study of nonverbal communication has become the flourishing branch of the social sciences" (p. 556). What differentiates us from other species is our evolutionary (biological) ability to produce a verbal language *and* the accompanying nonverbal language.

Although some suggest that Wilson's sociobiology centers on the nonverbal "displays" or "sets of rigidly invariant behaviors or body structures that have been specialized through evolution,"[4] Wilson argues for more than simple (actually complex) displays. He notes that human language probably stemmed from *paralanguage* cues (phonemes and sounds), which were "richly graded vocal signals not unlike those employed by the rhesus monkey and chimpanzee. . . . Human infants can utter a wide variety of vocalizations resembling those of . . . chimpanzees. But very early in their language development they convert to the peculiar sounds of human speech."[5] This uniquely human production of phonemes or sounds, he argues, is due to evolutionary changes in the tongue position and the lengthening of the pharyngeal track.

Wilson's perception of communication is found in Table 13–1. Note that verbal communication is defined as the "utterance of words and sentences." How these words and sentences are combined (i.e., grammar) may be explained through Noam Chomsky's innate deep-structure model of grammar which posits a universal grammar (see Chapter 4) and our innate ability to relate grammar to "words" (surface structure).[6] Nonverbal communication, however, is perceived as two-fold: (1) *prosody,* or vocal quality, differentiates us from

TABLE 13–1   Sociological Modes of Human Communication

 I. Verbal Communication (Language): The utterance of words and sentences.

II. Nonverbal Communication

   A. *Prosody:* tone, tempo, rhythm, loudness, pacing, and other qualities of voice that modify the meaning of verbal utterance.

   B. *Paralanguage:* signals separate from words used to supplement or to modify language.

     1. *Vocal* paralanguage: grunts, giggles, laughs, sobs, cries, and other nonverbal sounds.

     2. *Nonverbal* paralanguage: body posture, motion and touch (kinesic communication); possibly also chemical communication.

Source: E. O. Wilson, *Sociobiology* (Cambridge, MA: Harvard University Press, 1975), p. 556.

lower species in that the meaning of a verbal (and abstract) statement can be altered through the way the statement is verbalized, and (2) *paralanguage* comprises "signals" that are not words, but function to modify or substitute for the word or statement. This area is further divided into *vocal paralanguage* and *nonverbal paralanguage,* or all other aspects of nonverbal communication (kinesics and olfaction). Wilson's orientation to survivability and communication precludes what we examined in Chapter 3 as nonverbal communication *subcodes.* His approach to communication deals with the behaviors associated with expression (voice and gesture) and with the potential to *smell* trouble or fear, as found in lower animals.

Wilson's sociobiology has not met with popular acceptance among those who study communication.[7] Along with the limitations suggested by the evolutionary line taken, sociobiology seems to offer a too simple, unidimensional approach to the study of human communication. It does not address human *complexity.* Sociobiology places less stress on *communication* than on survival strategies. It does, however, offer an understanding of the *biological* side to our communication, that which may indicate certain pressures that are mediated in the human via symbolic (social) logic. Examples of this include territorial aggression, sexual reproduction, and sexual differences found in both the human and other species, but "created" differently by society. For instance, we increase the probability of territorial defense with language that includes such abstractions as "motherland" or "fatherland" or "home," symbolic attachments to the land. We suppress urges aimed at sexual reproduction (although we may chemically or behaviorally "signal" the other) through symbols and "rules" of conduct. Also, we have created gender (social) differences (masculinity and femininity) from sex (biological) differences (male and female).

To understand our communication, we must go beyond the biological or the sociobiological. By taking the best of the sociobiological and adding it to the social–psychological, we create the *biosocial approach.*

Sociological Foundations

One clear distinction between us and lower animals is our ability to create order. This creativity is found in the way we *perceive* our world and label (symbolize) the parts of our environments. Symbolization allows us to create societies and roles within those societies according to some rules. We use rules in an attempt to control our *destiny*, the time between life and death. One sociologist distinguishes between us and other animals based in part on the notions of survival and adaptability. Two of these distinctions are as follows:

> (1) Men have hands, by virtue of which, through the manipulation of physical objects, a distinction can be made between the manipulatory phase of an act and the consummatory phase. (2) Since physical objects lend themselves to being manipulated in many alternative ways, thereby making it possible for one individual to take the role of another in a social act, language gestures (significant symbols) emerge and are means for controlling and directing social behavior.[8]

Language is a socially learned phenomenon for a way of constructing reality. As biological entities, we each create a *multidimensional* social "person," which reflects how we relate to our society through a variety of roles, each with its own expected role behaviors and expectations. These social factors interact with the biological to produce rules for that time between life and death.

Becker, an anthropologist, suggests that the end of life produces a fear that our reality will end. Although this ending is a certainty accepted by other animals in daily life, we tend to put off thinking of death and, at the same time, fashion our reality in such a way as to deny death. As Becker notes, "the idea of death, the fear of it, haunts the human animal like nothing else; it is the mainspring of human activity—activity designed largely to avoid the final destiny for man."[9] We have no control over our beginnings or over our deaths (except for suicide). Between birth and death, however, many of our functions are both biological and social.

The idea that between birth and death we create a "self" helps to promote socialization. That we take responsibility for our own actions and behaviors suggests that we are driven by some need to establish ourselves in our environments. This drive resembles Abraham Maslow's claim that our most basic needs are for physical needs and security.[10] Lower animals seek food, shelter, and reproduction. Our needs, however, also include *self-esteem*, which is secured through the manipulation of symbols within a society. Self-esteem becomes a reflection of self to other selves in particular settings.[11] According to Becker, regard for oneself first comes from others, second from bodily needs, and finally from the symbols and dramatizations that are part of our culture.[12]

Thus, we have a socially oriented perception of self influenced by others through their perceptions of us. This peer group perception is not much different from the concept of *pecking order* in lower animals. Lower animals continually reflect on their own species in the biological order of survival in domination, physical size, and, to a lesser degree, cunning. We have been made socially conscious of our own bodies. This consciousness, much like that of lower animals, yields perceptions of power and status; however, we symbolize certain aspects of the body for socially appropriate and inappropriate roles, roles that function *naturally* in other species. Thus, we are guilty or envious when our body parts are either superior or inferior to those of others.

Finally, we come to the crux of the matter. We are what our symbols and our actions (based on those symbols) indicate. We become a product of our society, but we remain a product of our own bodies, which results in our "paradoxical nature, the fact that [humans] are half animal and half symbolic" (p. 26). Hickson has argued that "Humans' symbols constantly bring them out of their animal nature, and their bodies constantly put them back into their animal states. Humans obviously have trouble dealing with these contradictory terms. The general tendency is to deny the body."[13] We prefer to associate with the freedom of symbolism and abstraction as found in the *mind* and to disassociate the deterministic and bounded body.[14]

As we socialize, we find that biological drives materialize at certain points in time. For instance, maturity yields a natural progression of growth in both the male and female; however, we socialize that growth as good or bad. Thus, males approaching puberty must survive the social stereotypes of immaturity as the pitch breaks associated with their voices develop through maturation. Females must survive the social pressures associated with breast enlargement and the onset of menstruation. The female often grows faster, becoming physically larger than her male counterpart, providing a chance for control. Because we place many social stigmas on such natural change, however, we make the natural something to be envied or embarrassed about.

Biosocial Thought

The dualism of mind and body creates a tension commonly understood as the *mind–body problem*. We exist within a unidimensional construct known as the body, an exoskeletal device that has through evolution come to house the brain. The brain, through its control of the mind, the body, and the interaction of mind and body, has become the central concern in the biosocial study of human behavior.

Based on the discussion of sociobiology and ethology, and of the symbolic nature of human society, several assumptions regarding biosocial thought can be stated:

1. We have no control over our births or our deaths (except through suicide).
   - Between birth and death, many human functions are both biological and social.

- We are biologically similar to other animals.
- We are socially superior to other animals in that we have developed a capacity to think and speak (use abstractions in a socially shared way).

2. The body is unidimensional. It operates on an input-to-output basis.
3. The brain is multidimensional. It operates in such a way as to create social reality out of biological time clocks. The brain controls the human clock.
4. The brain and the body interact to produce communication patterns. The interaction of brain and body creates the concept of "mind," which, in turn, yields "reality."

THE BRAIN

For many years, researchers in psychology, linguistics, biology, physics, anthropology, sociology, and even theology, have been concerned with how the brain functions. Only recently, however, have communication researchers begun to address the complex issues related to the brain–mind communication potential. Models of how the brain processes information leading to communication not only have been challenged, but have quickly replaced much of what we thought we knew about the human information-processing system. Biologically, psychologically, and socially, the brain has become a central concern in understanding how and why we process, interpret, and communicate about stimuli in both the physical and abstract environments in which we live.

Biological Evidence

Harold Jerrison has argued that verbal and nonverbal communication complemented each other as a form of evolutionary variation that allowed us to gain mastery over our environment and to survive.[15] He argues that space and time considerations played an initial role in our survival, but, as we began to interact as social predators, nonverbal messages became more refined and abstracted into concepts related to time and place. As these images were further refined, they became linked to language through a symbolic process associated with socialization. This shift from predominantly nonverbal modes of communication to symbolic modes also created a brain that was different in both size and function.

The brain, as we know it today, consists of two hemispheres, each with specialized functioning. At one time, it was suggested that we had a dominant (left) hemisphere and a minor (right) hemisphere. The left side controlled both language and abstract thought, the uniquely human behaviors; the right side was relegated the evolutionary duties associated with nonverbal behaviors.[16] This model existed up to the middle to late 1970s. Several events occurred during the late 1970s to question this parsimonious explanation of how the brain controlled communication.

Evolutionary Evidence.   Evidence suggests that we possess not one "brain," but three evolutionary brains, each with a particular function or specialized operation.[17] This evolutionary perspective was first advanced by Paul MacLean in 1972. Based on physiological evidence, he argued that we have brains approximately equal to two major classes of lower species. Our most primitive brain, the *R-Complex*, is closely associated with reptiles and has as its major duties such basic functioning as instinctive behaviors, territoriality, aggressive–defensive behaviors, and reproductive behaviors. This brain is found just around the brain stem. The next evolutionary level is represented by the "old brain" (*Paleomammalian* brain), which comprises the limbic system in man and is equated with the brains of most dogs, cats, and chimpanzees. Located around the R-Complex brain, it functions to recognize and evaluate emotions. The most recent brain, the *Neomammalian* brain, represents the neocortex, or those convoluted brain masses we normally associate with the "brain." This brain is responsible for symbolism, language, and the creation of rules; additionally, it is representational, allowing for abstraction.

TABLE 13–2   Functions, Focus, and Structures of the Human Brain

Function/Focus		Motivational Level*
Neomammalian Brain		
Relationships between internal and external world, words/information, experience, images, novelty		Esteem
Right Hemisphere	*Left Hemisphere*	
Space	Logic	
Patterns	Words	
Holism	Intellect	
Association	Transformation	
Imaging	Time	
Connotation	Denotation	
"Forest"	"Trees"	
Paleomammalian Brain		
Sound, taste, smell, touch, emotion, love, hate, morality, family, passion, values, play		Belonging
R-Complex Brain		
Survival, safety, ritual, repetition, food gathering, territoriality, reproduction, regularity, defense		Safety

*After Maslow (1975).

The role of each "brain" is to process information about the environment. Normally, the Neomammalian brain controls the two earlier brains. As it controls each brain, it also interprets information it receives from them and, based on its analysis, acts. At times, the stimuli may become so intense that this brain may relinquish control to the Paleomammalian brain, which would then react in emotional response to the stimuli. If the stimulus was so intense as to cross-circuit this brain, then instinctive R-Complex behaviors (e.g., flight or fight) may predominate. Under normal circumstances, however, the Neomammalian brain retains control, and we communicate "normally" according to the rules laid down by society.

Evolution, however, produces more than a simple three-tiered brain. Jason Brown has suggested that what actually differentiates us from lower animals is the formation of a "symbolic consciousness."[18] This formation is found in the asymmetrical nature of our brain—the left and right hemispheres working in concert to process information—and allows for the manipulation of visual and verbal symbols (see Table 13–2). Our evolutionary brain, as we know it today, may be thought of as three brains, each with left and right hemispheres.

Dominance. The concept of brain dominance posits that we have a "left brain" (for language and abstraction) and a "right brain" (for nonverbal imaging and emotion). Based on this rationale, certain functions and processing differences of communication could be expected. Albert King, examining the type of decisions made by the brain in advertising, suggests that the direction of an individual's gaze can suggest either the type of appeal or thought processes going on (see Fig. 13–1).[19]

The major problem with the dominance explanation lies in the concept that function (e.g., language, abstraction, nonverbal imaging) is localized. The dominance perspective, although sufficient to explain some behavior, does not adequately answer how we integrate complex verbal and nonverbal messages into a message "corpus."[20] John Campbell suggests that

> the right brain is not a linguistic idiot. It has its own codes, its own rules, and these are worth examining. It does have some comprehension of spoken language, and it is good at detecting pitch, intonation, stress, cadence, loudness, and softness. It knows whether a sentence is asking a question, giving an order, expressing a condition, or making a statement . . . It can recognize the ridiculous and inappropriate, and be aware that words and sentences are embedded in a wide matrix of relationships.[21]

Hemispheric Style. Like Campbell, Stacks and Daniel Sellers argue that the concept of hemispheric style more adequately explains how the brain operates. Stacks and Sellers have argued that, based on evidence from *neuro-maturational* studies (studies of how the brain matures and processes language), the brain may be less rigid in processing information than suspected.[22] As the child ages from five to thirteen years, a strong evolutionary

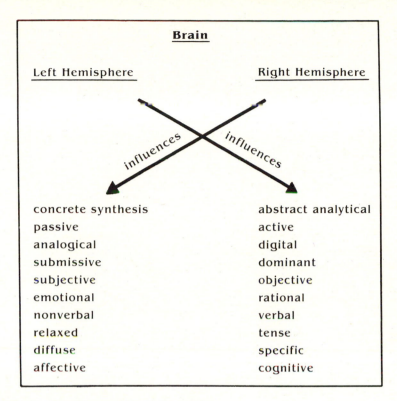

FIGURE 13–1   Cognition and Brain Processing.
Adapted from: A. King, "The Eye in Advertising," *Journal of Applied Communications Research*, 2 (1974), p. 8.

left hemisphere advantage for language *begins to disappear*. Stacks and Sellers suggest that "The fact that the left hemisphere has shown this predisposition to language has led some researchers to consider the left hemisphere dominant for language."[23] They note that while the *processing* of language is found in *both* hemispheres, qualification and modification are more akin to the right hemisphere's style, while the left hemisphere remains more logical and analytical.[24]

What type of language might each hemisphere process? J. E. Bogan suggests that the left hemisphere's language is more "propositional" (analytical, syntactical, and deliberate), and the right hemisphere's language is more "apropositional" (rational, instinctive, and perhaps unconscious).[25] Along this line, Ross Buck has suggested that right hemispheric language is more spontaneous, more "nonpropositional."[26] By this, Buck means that right hemispheric language may be verbalized, but is an unconscious phenomenon. Much like a Freudian slip, this right hemispheric language may be a simple statement tied to a particular emotional or physical referent.[27]

In normal activity, the left hemisphere controls. It is responsible for "normal" information processing. What is normal? We know, for instance, that normal verbal and nonverbal information reflects a low to moderate intensity. We also know that the mind has the capacity to make the "abnormal" normal. When we process information that is not normal, the right hemisphere adds its interpretation (usually emotive) *before* the left finishes its interpretation. For instance, when we confront someone we dislike, we establish a safe distance from the other person. As the confrontation heats up, our verbal messages go from nonthreatening to threatening, logical to emotional. As our language (both specific symbols and more general phrases) intensifies, our nonverbal (right hemisphere) behavior intensifies also.

At some point, the left hemisphere may lose control of the interaction. The right hemisphere's emotive interpretation may take charge of the communication. This might include unconscious obscenities and aggressive behavior. We might clench a fist, wave it in the other's face, and *close* distance. As the situation reduces in intensity, left hemisphere control is reestablished. Our communication in times of rage is often unconscious to us, reflecting right hemisphere control of the communication.

Message Transmission.   Perhaps the most controversial interpretation of the brain's processing of information is the concept of *interhemispheric communication*, which suggests that the brain hemispheres communicate with each other. Julian Jaynes, in an analysis of how the brain operated before the introduction of "self" (a self-volition suggesting responsibility for our actions and thoughts), said that the brain communicated with itself through "commissars" or connections located deep within the brain.[28] Most research now suggests that such communication occurs, but as an *alerting mechanism* for an oncoming message within, not between, hemispheres.[29]

The *corpus callosum* is a biological bridge where messages and analyses are transmitted between the two hemispheres. Little research has been conducted on its *message* potential. Severing this thick band of nerve tissue has shown to control epilepsy (a brain problem where massive electrical charges are transmitted between hemispheres, resulting in a total disruption of normal information processing).[30] Jerre Levy argues that such a transmission across the corpus callosum is due to hemispheric stylistic differences and the brain's ability to incorporate interpretations of complex messages.[31]

When a hemisphere is activated, alpha brain (task-related) activity is reduced or suppressed. Walter R. Moore found, for instance, that recall tasks (cognitive and analytical) yielded left hemisphere alpha suppression, whereas recognition tasks (cognitive and visually oriented language) yielded right hemispheric alpha suppression.[32] Since the brain processes its analyses in a symmetrical, left–right nature, transmission across the corpus callosum seems the most parsimonious and adequate explanation for complex message processing.

Toward a Biosocial Model of Communication

A biosocial model of communication takes into consideration the natural processing of information and the creation of symbolic or normative expectations based on how society expects us to act. To this point, we have examined how the brain receives information, how it begins to process it, what processing "styles" it uses, and what effects result.

The biosocial model of communication begins with the concept that information is received and processed by the brain in a "natural" way; that is, information received by both hemispheres is no different, but is interpretated differently. (In normal communication, *both* hemispheres of the brain receive the same information almost simultaneously, or at least within microseconds of each other.) This model suggests that the right hemisphere possesses a rudimentary form of language, one steeped in unconscious and qualitatively based processes, and that the human brain consists of six (three evolutionary brains, each with a right and a left hemisphere) rather than two (left and right hemisphere) brains.

As such, each hemisphere and level of the brain becomes a processing *module*. According to Stacks and Peter Andersen, modules act as processing and filtering entities within the brain. Furthermore, we might view the two hemispheres as superprocessing modules.[33] They posit that each module (and there are modules within modules) possesses the capacity to *think*, and that each influences and is in turn influenced by other modules as they communicate with each other. Michael Gazzaniga suggests that such modules act as a loose federation of governments, each cooperating and fighting with each other:

> A cognitive system composed of mental modules, each one of which could act independently from the other but all together forming a mental federation [self, self-concept], would be most likely to assign to one cognitive system the chore of establishing and maintaining a theory about the federation's actions. Part and parcel of the process would be the necessary concept that the organism was acting freely, that in fact the organism was governable. . . . Because our brains are organized in terms of independent modules each capable of action . . . One implication is that one value of the brain being organized the way I propose is that it allows for constant testing and retesting of our beliefs. The responding exploring human being will have a higher probability of constantly reevaluating his or her beliefs . . . If the brain were a monolithic system with all modules in complete internal communication, then the value we place on our beliefs would never change . . . [We] would be doomed to repeat the cant of . . . preceding generations in a reflexlike manner.[34]

Stacks and Sellers further argue that this modular communication be used to explicate why people differ in their communication competence and why some people avoid communication altogether by suggesting that dissonance produced by modular communication may yield inappropriate evaluation of either the situation (e.g., public speaking) or the person (individualized fears or apprehensions).[35]

An important function of modular processing is the control of chaos involved in information processing. Modular processing requires the stimulation that information provides the brain, but not so much stimulation as to overcome (information overload) its processing abilities.[36] Modularity suggests how the "normal" mind operates. Simply put, the greater the number of active modules, the more the order. As the brain, through its various modules, processes information, the *more ordered it becomes.* On the other hand, a few *key* modules can produce extreme disorder or chaos and abnormal communicative behavior. Some modules important to a *communicative situation* may weigh more heavily on the interpretation of that situation, producing, for example, communication apprehension.

Most of us realize that we need some delay to produce competent messages; however, there are times when each of us is apprehensive about communicating. This apprehension can be caused by internal or external stimuli. In most cases, we can reason through the dissonance caused by the situation ("I am giving a speech to a group of strangers and I'm scared." "I talk to other people each day about this; there is little difference." Etc.) and produce normal competent communications; however, self-concept may be low, a bad experience in the last presentation may be remembered, or someone in the audience who is important may produce abnormal behavior. Attempting to add variables to the equation (arguments as to why we should not be apprehensive) should increase modular dissonance and produce less apprehension. On the other hand, by focusing on one or two important reasons (modules), apprehension will increase as dissonance decreases. As the modules process the various reasons for apprehension, no one reason should outweigh the others. When one or two modules is given more weight, the dissonance-reduction modular communication is short circuited and abnormal communication results.

Based on this brain–mind model, five theoretical principles may be derived, which suggest a biosocial orientation toward communication:

1. *The two hemispheres of the brain act as superprocessing modules, processing information according to both semantic (verbal and nonverbal) and syntactic style.* Perception comes from the processing of information received through our senses and interpreted by the brain's hemispheres. Our perceptions, then, are a product of the information processing associated with our brain.

2. *Complex messages are analyzed by modules in* BOTH *the left and the right hemispheres; interpretation, however, depends upon the intensity and structure of the message.* As this information from our inner and outer environments is received and processed, it is interpreted by each brain hemisphere and module. These interpretations yield complex interpretations of both cognitive and affective information; that is, both brain hemispheres and their modules have the capacity not only to process complex messages, but also to create those messages.

3. *Modular transmission occurs both between hemispheres and between brain levels.* In *normal* communication, brain modules transmit messages between and among themselves. When

combined, these messages create an interpretation of the communication stimulus.

4. *The corpus callosum transmits modular messages between the left and right hemispheres (and their associated modules) for proper interpretation and analysis.* To communicate effectively, the brain hemispheres must interact. This occurs across the corpus callosum, which serves as a bridge for message transmission. At times, this bridge becomes overloaded, and abnormal processing, interpretation, and communication occur.

5. *The MIND is the result of the brain's processing of messages between modules in both hemispheres and their associated brain levels, each adding a little more to the total "picture" for final analysis, normally controlled by the left hemisphere's Neomammalian module.* Finally, the mind is created. The mind is the total of *all* modular processing. The mind, however, also is the product of the society in which we reside. The brain and its modules provide the processing mechanisms for the mind's creation. The mind organizes brain modules and creates a conscious awareness of the communication event.

Other Potential Biological Influences on the Mind

It would be simpler if our model of the brain and its influence on communication had only to deal with the symbolic or normative nature of life; however, three other areas influence how the brain operates: biological sex differences, culture and language, and internal and external mind-altering devices (hormones and drugs).

Sex. Biological sex seems to influence how our brain processes messages.[37] In Western society, males typically process nonverbal communication in the right hemisphere and language in the left. For females, however, this strict duality of thought is not followed as rigidly. Females process some nonverbal communication in the left hemisphere along with language. Although this accounts for greater communicative sensitivity, females have more difficulty when faced with abstractions requiring time and space analysis (e.g., those boxes in aptitude tests that ask what *should* this look like). Some evidence indicates, however, that being raised masculine or feminine may alter this difference.

Robert Ornstein suggests that our senses also follow this left–right asymmetry. He asks that you answer ten questions to see which side of the brain you associate with (note which are more feminine):

1. Which side of you is more feminine?
2. Which is more masculine?
3. Which do you consider the "dark" side of yourself?
4. Which side is "lighter"?

   5. Which is more active?

   6. Which is more passive?

   7. Which side is more logical?

   8. Which side is more "intuitive"?

   9. Which side of you is more mysterious?

   10. Which side is more artistic?[38]

Culture and Language.   The culture in which we grow up and the language we speak alters how we process messages. Jaynes suggested that the spoken language of the early Greeks influenced their behaviors through the processing of a primarily vowel-oriented language.[39] Along this line of thought, Tsunoda believes that culture and the type of language (the way in which it is spoken) helps to determine how the brain processes verbal and nonverbal stimuli.[40] He found that children growing up *and* learning language in Japan and some Polynesian cultures processed verbal and nonverbal communication less asymmetrically; they processed some time–space relational material in the left hemisphere. Children growing up in Western culture, however, exhibited our usual left–right asymmetry. Interestingly, it is not race, but culture, that makes this difference. Japanese children raised in the United States exhibit left–right asymmetry, whereas American children raised in Japan exhibit the Japanese asymmetry. Tsunoda attributes these differences to the difference between a consonant-heavy language (English) and a more tonal language (Japanese and most Polynesian languages).

Mind-Altering Devices.   Finally, how the brain operates is affected by mind-altering devices, including drugs and hormones. Interestingly, the brain creates its own drugs. To reduce the effect of pain, for instance, the brain creates its own morphine. A number of researchers are now examining the effects of drugs, from those that are prescriptive to those commonly available (e.g., alcohol, caffeine, chocolate), to see how each influences the brain and perceptions of others.[41] This body of research centers on the *normal* drugs we take without thinking (e.g., caffeine and chocolate) and those we use socially (e.g., alcohol). What effects these drugs have on brain processing and communication are only now being understood.

   Hormonal changes also alter how the brain operates and how we perceive others.[42] Hickson and colleagues have suggested that the interaction between hormone level and perception of gender (a socialization process) may produce changes in the behavior of males and females.[43] Such changes involve the production of hormones and the suppression of the brain's normal interpretations through symbolization.

   Whether the altering devices are hormone- or drug-related, changes in the chemistry of the brain (a complex of electrical activity and chemical interchange) clearly alter perceptive abilities. These changes yield differences in communicative behaviors. Changes in biological brain functioning

TABLE 13–3 Summary Table

Name of Theory	Primary Theorists	Basic Principle	Constructs	Criteria	Analytic Approach	Limitations
Biosocial Approach	Edward Wilson Charles Darwin Ernest Becker	Biological (physical and neurological factors) interact with social phenomena to create communication situations.	• Brain hemispheric dominance • Sex differences	To understand one person's motives, biological considerations must be made.		Little is known about these biological functions and their influence on the communication process.

produce changes in how we socialize. Interestingly, however, changes in socialization may also produce changes in the brain. *The process is interactive.* Future research, from a variety of disciplines, will help to answer the questions posed by the brain–mind duality on communication, especially those related to variables such as sex, culture, language, and mind-altering drugs and hormones.

REVIEW

Beginning with the nineteenth century research of Darwin, some researchers have observed similarities between humans and other animals. Wilson suggested that what we consider social and what we consider biological interact with one another. Interpreting the work of Darwin and others, Becker indicated that we are *unidimensional* in our bodily functions and *multidimensional* in our social functions. From these researchers, we have developed what we refer to as the biosocial approach (see Table 13–3). We have indicated how the brain's functioning, sex, culture, language, and mind-altering devices influence the communication process.

CRITIQUE

Because this theoretical approach is new, it is impossible to evaluate it critically at this time; however, we can say the theory is *potentially* heuristic. Although still incomplete at this time, it certainly provides for a number of constructs that can be measured.

We end this chapter with several questions. Where are we in terms of a communication edifice? Should we be concerned about developing one approach to human communication, or should we view communication according to context and framing? Are there any general principles that can be derived from all that we have discussed to this point? In Chapter 14, we attempt to answer these questions. In so doing, we create other questions, urging you to consider what your own views of communication are.

NOTES AND REFERENCES

[1] E. O. Wilson, *Sociobiology: The New Synthesis* (Cambridge, MA: Harvard University Press, 1975).

[2] C. Darwin, *The Origin of the Species* (New York: Mentor, 1958).

[3] Wilson, *Sociobiology,* p. 176.

[4] G. Zivin, "What Use Sociobiology?" *Journal of Communication* (1978), 194–200.

[5] Wilson, *Sociobiology,* p. 556.

[6] N. Chomsky, *Syntactic Structures* (Hague: Mouton, 1957).

[7] Zivin, "What Use Sociobiology?"

[8] D. L. Miller, *George Herbert Mead: Self, Language, and the World* (Austin: University of Texas Press, 1973), p. 238.

[9]E. Becker, *The Denial of Death* (New York: Free Press, 1973), p. ix; see also E. Kubler-Ross, *On Death and Dying* (New York: Macmillan, 1969), pp. 1–10; E. Becker, *The Structure of Evil: An Essay on the Unification of the Science of Man* (New York: Free Press, 1968); E. Becker, *Escape from Evil* (New York: Free Press, 1975); E. Becker, *The Birth and Death of Meaning: An Interdisciplinary Perspective on the Problem of Man*, 2nd ed. (New York: Free Press, 1971).

[10]A. H. Maslow, *Toward a Psychology of Being*, 2nd ed. (New York: Van Nostrand, 1968).

[11]See G. H. Mead, *Mind, Self, and Society: From the Viewpoint of a Social Behaviorist*, ed. C. W. Morris (Chicago: University of Chicago Press, 1962).

[12]Becker, *The Denial of Death*, pp. 229–230.

[13]M. L. Hickson, "Toward a Bio-Social Theory of Human Communication," master's thesis, Mississippi State University, 1981.

[14]Becker, *The Denial of Death*, pp. 41–42.

[15]H. J. Jerrison, "Evolution of the Brain," in *The Human Brain*, ed. M. C. Wittrock (Englewood Cliffs, NJ: Prentice–Hall, 1977), pp. 39–62.

[16]The brain operates through reception of stimuli from the various senses. Basically, the brain receives information either *contralaterally* or *ipsilaterally*. Contralaterality indicates that the *left* hemisphere controls the *right* side of the body and the *right* hemisphere controls the *left* side of the body. Input of sensory information is also ipsilaterally and contralaterally related. As you might expect, ipsilateral information (going from right nostril, for instance, to right hemisphere) would be much faster than that having to cross over from one side of the brain to the other. Ipsilateral processing occurs with the olfactory (smell) sense. The other senses are more contralateral. What you hear in your right ear is processed in the left hemisphere; what you hear in the left ear is processed in the right hemisphere. With the eyes, however, we have "backup" systems. That is, you have two "hemifields" in each eye, what you see in the left hemifield of the eye is processed in the right hemisphere; what you see in the right hemifield is processed in the left hemisphere. Obviously, interpretations of stimuli would differ according to which (major or minor) hemisphere received the message.

[17]P. MacLean, "The Brain's Generation Gap: Some Human Implications," *Zygon/Journal of Religion and Science, 193* (1972), 137–149.

[18]J. Brown, *Mind, Brain, and Consciousness* (New York: Academic Press, 1977); see also R. M. Restak, *The Brain* (New York: Bantam, 1984).

[19]A. King, "The Eye in Advertising," *Journal of Applied Communications Research, 1* (1974), 1–12.

[20]D. W. Stacks, "Toward the Establishment of a Preverbal Stage of Communication," *Journal of Communication Therapy, 2* (1983), 39–60; D. W. Stacks, "Understanding Communication Processing As a Function of Brain Hemispheric Style," paper presented at the Conference on "Meeting the Methodological Challenges of a Process Notion of Communication," Tampa, FL, April 4–5, 1983; D. W. Stacks and D. E. Sellers, "The Effect of 'Pure' Hemispheric Reception on Message Acceptance," *Communication Quarterly, 34* (1986), 266–285; D. W. Stacks and D. E. Sellers, "Hemispheric Style and the Process of Discourse: An Integration and Extension of Recent Theory and Research," paper presented at the Southern Speech Communication Convention,

April 1984, Baton Rouge, LA; D. W. Stacks and L. A. Dorsey, "Toward a Psychoanalytic–Neurophysiological Interpretation of Nonverbal Communication," *Journal of Communication Therapy,* (in press).

[21]J. Campbell, *Grammatical Man* (New York: Simon and Schuster, 1982).

[22]Stacks and Sellers, "The Effect of 'Pure' Hemispheric Reception"; R. W. Keith, ed., *Central Auditory and Language Disorders in Children* (Houston: College–Hill, 1981); and J. Williford, "Sentence Test of Central Auditory Dysfunction," in J. Katz, ed., *Handbook of Clinical Audiology,* 2nd ed. (Baltimore: William and Wilkins, 1978).

[23]D. W. Stacks and D. E. Sellers, "Hemispheric Processing and Human Communication Style: Toward an Integrative Theory of the Processing of Verbal and Nonverbal Messages," paper presented at the Southern Speech Communication Association Convention, Winston-Salem, NC, April 1985; L. J. Shedletsky, "Cerebral Asymmetry for Aspects of Sentence Processing," *Communication Quarterly, 29* (1981), 3–11; L. J. Shedletsky, "Cerebral Asymmetry for Aspects of Sentence Processing: A Replication and Extension," *Communication Quarterly, 31* (1983), 78–84.

[24]Stacks and Sellers, "Hemispheric Processing and Human Communication Style."

[25]J. E. Bogan, "Some Educational Aspects of Hemispheric Specialization," *UCLA Educator, 17* (1975), 24–32.

[26]R. Buck, "Spontaneous and Symbolic Nonverbal Behavior and the Ontogeny of Communication," in ed. R. S. Feldman, *Development of Nonverbal Behavior in Children* (New York: Springer–Verlag, 1982), 29–62.

[27]Stacks and Dorsey, "Toward a Psychoanalytic–Neurophysiological Interpretation of Nonverbal Communication."

[28]J. Jaynes, *The Breakdown of Consciousness in the Bicameral Mind* (Boston: Houghton Mifflin, 1976).

[29]Stacks and Sellers, "Hemispheric Processing and Human Communication Style."

[30]D. R. Sisk, "Use of Auditory Masking to Estimate Carryover of Correct Phoneme Production," master's thesis, University of South Alabama, 1985.

[31]Stacks and Sellers, "The Effect of 'Pure' Hemispheric Reception"; J. Levy, "Right Brain–Left Brain: Fact and Fiction," *Psychology Today* (1985), 38–44.

[32]W. R. Moore, Jr., "Alpha Hemispheric Asymmetry of Males and Females on Verbal and Non-Verbal Tasks," *Cortex, 15* (1979), 321–327.

[33]D. W. Stacks and P. A. Andersen, "The Modular Mind: Implications for Intrapersonal Communication," *Southern Communication Journal, 54* (1989), 273–293.

[34]M. S. Gazzaniga, *The Social Brain: Discovering the Networks of the Mind* (New York: Basic Books, 1985), p. 146.

[35]D. W. Stacks and D. Sellers, "Toward a Hemispheric Processing Model of Communication Competence and Apprehension," *Journal of Social Behavior and Personality, 5* (1990), 45–49.

[36]See D. W. Stacks, "The Modular Mind and Intrapersonal Communication Processes," paper presented at the Speech Communication Association, San Francisco, CA, November 1989.

[37]R. Restak, *The Brain: The Last Frontier* (New York: Doubleday, 1979).

[38]R. E. Ornstein, *The Psychology of Consciousness*, 2nd ed. (New York: Harcourt Brace Jovanovich, 1977).

[39]Jaynes, *The Breakdown of Consciousness in the Bicameral Mind.*

[40]T. Tsunoda, *The Japanese Brain: Brain Function and East–West Culture,* 1978. Cited in A. Sibatani, "It May Turn Out that the Language We Learn Alters the Physical Operation of Our Brains," *Science* (1980), 24–26.

[41]Restak, *The Brain: The Last Frontier;* see, for example, J. Timson, "Is Coffee Safe to Drink?" *Human Nature* (1978), 56–58.

[42]Restak, *The Brain: The Last Frontier.*

[43]M. Hickson, D. W. Stacks, S. Cullinane, and M. L. Sandoz, "New Directions in Nonverbal Research: Gender-Role Socialization," paper presented at the Speech Communication Association Convention, Chicago, November 1984.

14

Living with the Edifice

To this point, we have learned that communication theories are derived from various perspectives. They have come from different eras of time, and from persons with different academic training and differing basic assumptions about the nature of symbols, norms, human beings, and societies. We traced these theories from the doctrines of subjectivity and opposites developed by Protagorus over two thousand years ago to the contemporary idea that biological and social phenomena influence one another and the communication process.

We have learned that the development of communication theory is similar to architectural theory. As time passes, the building materials (nonverbal and verbal symbols) become easier to use because we know more about them. Framing improves because we learn that people have different needs. Although traditional rhetorical theory may not appear as important to us today as it was two thousand years ago, it remains a primary means of developing rhetorical strategies in interpersonal communication and political communication.

When we have the materials available and the framing in mind, we then build an edifice that suits us and our community, including all the perspectives previously discussed. In this chapter, we use our theoretical edifices in several *communication contexts*. As Lee Thayer has indicated, we use communication in seven different levels (see Fig. 14–1).[1]

UNDERSTANDING THEORY AS METAPERSPECTIVE

What we believe to be theory, as should be evident by now, may be approached in a number of ways, some of which are indicated in Figure 14–1. Perhaps a more appropriate way of looking at *communication* theory is to view communication as *the* integrating principle that ties psychological and sociological (and rhetorical) perspectives into one "grand" theory. In this way, we are forced to take a *metaperspective*: a perspective on a perspective.

270

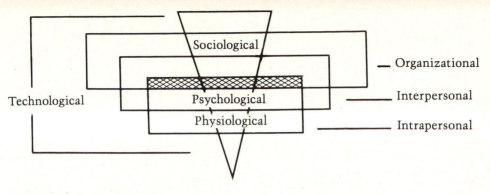

FIGURE 14–1   Levels of Communication.

Adapted from: L. Thayer, "Communication and Organization Theory," in *Human Communication Theory: Original Essays*, ed. F. E. X. Dance (New York: Holt, Rinehart and Winston, 1967), p. 87.

This approach to communication theory differs significantly from previous approaches. Historically, we might argue that the field of communication borrowed heavily from other fields in creating its theory, if it actually had theory. In the middle 1970s, however, concern over theory as a way of understanding, predicting, and controlling the behavior of others, came to the forefront. Emphasis during this period was on *understanding* and creating "theories" based on one of three general approaches to human communication: laws, rules, or systems. Why we identified with a particular approach may have been more a function of our training than an actual outlook on the phenomena under study.

This influence created an impression that the communication student had to follow a particular approach, now labeled "theory." Thus, the approach to communication suggesting regularities in behavior and thought (covering law) became a theoretical perspective. Researchers and theorists adopting this approach/theory advocated a behavioral perspective in which communication is viewed as *lawlike*; that is, people are seen as habitual and predictive within degrees of error. Many did not agree with this approach.

Reacting to the covering-law approach, which reduced the "humanness" of communication, some researchers suggested that people are *rule-governed* and responsible for their communication. The obvious advantage of this perspective is that we can incorporate the rhetorical principles inherent in the field with the symbols and norms that constitute communication. The rules approach to studying communication became a theoretical framework.

The third perspective, *systems*, argues for a holistic approach to communication. The systems approach provides a way to examine "metacommunication" events where all possible variables or behaviors are examined for their impact on communication. Although systems approaches are found from intrapersonal through technological communication contexts, they seem better adapted to larger, more complex communication situations, such as organizations. Within the systems approaches, both lawlike and rule-governed explanations can operate. The major problem with the systems approach, however, is its general inability to make precise predictions about different systems over time.

In the late 1970s and early 1980s, concern with communication shifted toward a *contextual* analysis, that is, that the type of communication (intrapersonal, interpersonal, small group, organizational, technological) influenced how we approached and defined communication. However, theorists continued to take the perspective of laws, rules, or systems. Thus, communication theory became more fractionalized. As a discipline, our "theory" tended to become reductionist. Even critical theory examined the phenomenon of communication in deeper but not wider holes. We pigeonholed communication.

A more appropriate view of communication theory might be to strip away the structure of our current model and rethink where we are going. In the following pages, we suggest a slightly different way of viewing "theory" in communication. This view presupposes that communication theorists *actively* borrow from other disciplines, taking what is important or what helps us understand how and why we communicate. This metaperspective suggests that *any* approach to communication theory uses something from other approaches. The way we approach the study of communication determines which theoretical perspective we take. Thus, lawlike, rules, and systems theories are viewed not as mutually exclusive entities, but as interdependent aspects of understanding human communication.

For instance, some communication *is* lawlike. When we walk down a sidewalk and a stranger passes, several communicative behaviors occur that are lawlike. First, we glance at the other until he or she is about twelve feet from us. We avoid eye contact but continue to watch to avoid collision. If the other person makes contact, says "hello" for instance, our reaction is usually to respond back with "hello." If, while in a crowd, you see someone wave at you from across the street, you may wave back, even though you may not be the targeted person. Some communication, then, is lawlike in that we exhibit it with regularity and within some tolerable degree of error.

Some communication is rule bound. Perhaps a better word for rule is "convention." We agree (explicitly or tacitly) to behave in a certain way, and our adherence to these rules is perceived as both intentional and goal directed. We have not actually established a "rule," but have agreed to some type of convention that allows for both regularity (lawlike and probably rule oriented) and idiosyncrasy. We can, however, predict that rule adherence will be within a degree of some accepted tolerance.

All communication, either lawlike or convention oriented, is bound by context. When two people interact, they interact as two selves, two intrapersonal systems. When more than two people get together, we have groups that differ in terms of number of people and tasks. Even in complex organizations such groups actually comprise smaller groups, which in turn comprise interacting selves. Communication may be viewed from a meta-perspective suggesting that *both* context and theoretical approach are equally important.

Finally, this metaperspective requires that our reliance on context be lessened. The *individual* should become the focus of communication theory and research. Whether we are concerned with interpersonal, small group, organizational, cultural, technological, or mediated forms of communication, we must take the individual communicator into account. *We begin with the individual and end with the individual.* In this regard, all forms (contexts) of communication become interdependent. The following pages outline an interpretation based on this perspective.

CONTEXTS OF COMMUNICATION THEORY

Theory and Intrapersonal Communication

Intrapersonal communication theory has been influenced by George Herbert Mead and the humanistic psychologists. At the most fundamental level, these researchers have been concerned with the creation, maintenance, survival, and enhancement of the construct, *self.* The primary use of theory in communication is in directed courses in interpersonal communication, although many communication departments across the country now teach courses in intrapersonal communication. Additionally, an emphasis on self in therapeutic and mental health communication is on the upswing.

The basic intrapersonal approach has been to define what constitutes a "good" self. How do we know when we have a good self? The practice of interpersonal communication would tell us that "it depends on our perspective." But what exactly does it depend on? A good self-concept means having a fair evaluation of who you are. This evaluation may be based on physical appearance, intelligence, number and quality of friends, one's relative success in school or business, and so forth. A good self-evaluation, however, means that what others think of you and what you think of yourself are similar and reflect the basic values of your society and culture.

If we use Mead's notion of self, we know that the self results from an interaction between the "I" and the "Me." Although we may have an impulsive tendency to take actions, generally we are constrained by the social conventions. Because the "Me" is other oriented, an evaluation of who we are requires knowledge of what others think of us. Intrapersonal communication is the first step in communicating because this is the stage at which we decide whether to attempt communication at all.

Intrapersonal communication, however, cannot be "seen" or even "felt." Testing the constructs of self, "I," and "Me," let alone their interactive effects, is both difficult and open to serious methodological concern. Humanistic theory, which sees the individual as the unit of analysis, rests on an in-depth knowledge and prediction at a *micro*level of analysis. Although prediction *across* individuals is minimal, knowledge and understanding of particular people leads to better "interpersonal" prediction.

Theory and Interpersonal Communication

Interpersonal communication is based on symbolic interactionism, humanistic psychology, behavioral psychology, and exchange theory. Perhaps humanistic psychology has been most valuable in the development of courses and research in interpersonal communication. Recently, interpersonal communication has been viewed as a long-term process. Words make up sentences, which make up conversations, episodes, and ultimately relationships. Relationships begin when two strangers meet. They test one another (typically using a version of Homans's exchange theory) to predict the potential of the relationship. These relationships undergo growth stages, go through stagnation periods, and terminate (one party moves away, breaks up with the other, or dies). The rules about how to form, strengthen, weaken, and terminate relationships create an important area of study. Students of interpersonal communication need to learn that there are rules, and they need to learn that breaking the rules carries sanctions.

Certain elements of interpersonal communication have been influenced by research from the covering-law and systems approaches. These elements concern the personality variables that influence our predispositions toward interpersonal relationships. Dogmatism, self-concept, communication apprehension or avoidance, and extroversion are but a few. The construct *self-disclosure* (from both rules and systems perspectives) is an important feedback mechanism in healthy interpersonal relationships.

Integrating Intrapersonal and Interpersonal Relationships

Interpersonal communication cannot occur without intrapersonal communication. We might consider interpersonal communication as the probing by two selves in an attempt by both to understand themselves better through each other. Effective interpersonal communication might be perceived from the perspective of trying to understand both one's self and the other person from one unique view of the world. This is accomplished through the use and misuse of symbols and norms, goaded perhaps by some desire to dominate or be dominated and to relate to or with the other person. Interpersonal communication also allows us to create and reflect societal rules, which in some cases become lawlike and in others become conventions for future behavior. Interpersonal communication also allows for the creation of *idiosyncratic conventions.* For instance, a couple that attends a party may make eye contact every few minutes as a way of signaling togetherness. Through this "convention," both people can enlarge their circle of acquaintances, yet feel together without threatening to interfere on the other's relationships.

Our outlook for interpersonal communication is influenced by our self's ability to integrate behaviors found in the context. Such an approach suggests that our perspective-taking ability is dependent on our *intra*personal communication. Thus, an ability to adapt to different interpersonal contexts may be a function of our psyche, or our brain's modular processing, or our perception of correct from incorrect. In short, the intrapersonal communication process includes making a decision whether to begin interpersonal communication and whether at a later time to reenter the relationship.

Theory and Group Communication

Group communication theory has been based on many of the sociological aspects of our field. Systems theory and rules theory have added considerably to our understanding of how communication works in groups such as the family and organizations such as IBM or General Motors and how this context differs from interpersonal communication. When systems theory is used, we can learn what communication strategies are needed to maintain or move the group; how to increase morale, satisfaction, or other variables; where inputs are too low or high; whether task demands are too high or low; what leadership strategies are used; whether interaction with the environment is needed; and so on.

Rules theory also has been useful in group communication, especially that of the complex organization. The use of vertical and horizontal communication (and knowing how they differ) is helpful to the new employee. Learning to ask questions and not to ask questions, how to "cover up" for a fellow employee, and how to assess relationships with fellow employees can be handled using a rules approach.

Exchange theory can be used to determine whether other members, groups, or organizations are reciprocating and perhaps why they are not reciprocating. Understanding the levels of acceptance and rejection can help one to decide whether to move to a position with another employer.

Marxist theory and critical interpretative theory can help those in an organization to understand how some may be discriminated against and how to bring about organizational change. Recently, research has emphasized the importance of the critical interpretative approach to bringing about greater equality and, thus, increased productivity through such constructs as organizational and group "climate" and "satisfaction."

Integrating Interpersonal Communication and Group Communication

Regardless of the level of group communication, from the small to the large group, from the organization to the society, groups are composed of individuals. Even the critical interpretive perspective must establish the individual as its base. For communication to occur within the group, it must occur between at least one self and another. Whether the level of analysis is symbolic or behavioral, how that communication occurs and what form it takes is influenced by the intrapersonal perception of the *event*. The interaction of two or two million people is dependent on the perceptions and needs of people *in their own minds*. Thus, communication context (intrapersonal, interpersonal, group) and theoretical perspective operate together and through four levels of communication: physiological, psychological, sociological, and technical.

LEVELS OF COMMUNICATION THEORY

The Physiological Level

To this point, the only theory that emphasizes the physiological level has been the biosocial approach. What are the effects of a worker's being tired on the company's productivity? How do hormones affect our attitude on the job? Biorhythms, drugs, general physical fitness, brain hemisphere dominance, and so forth, all influence how we work on the job.

At the physiological level, communication theory attempts to integrate biological *and* sociological–psychological thought. Systems theory, to include cybernetics and the concept of holism, has contributed much to what we know about the brain and its processes. We know that certain parts of our communicative behavior are lawlike—action–reaction, antecedent–subsequent—but that "mind" reacts on a more rule-based approach. Integration of all these approaches may signal yet newer approaches to the study of human communication.

The Psychological Level

At times, it is important to use a behavioral approach when trying to motivate another person. At other times, it is important to listen carefully to find out where the other person "is" so that messages can be constructed to meet that person's needs. At the psychological level, we treat communication for its truly unique factors. The contributions of various humanistic theorists provide insight into the individual psyche.

The major contributions at the psychological level come from systems theory, until we treat behavior as the outcome of some response to a stimulus, when the covering-law approach provides useful insight into automatic, "phatic" forms of communication.

The Sociological Level

Although many of us have not been trained to think about communication at the sociological level, this area has become more important in the study of communication. The critical interpretative theorists, for instance, use sociological approaches to establish criteria for improving the lot of those who suffer from class, race, and sexual discrimination. The study of both social rules and symbolic interactionism have assisted in developing a communication theory concerned with the needs of society.

The Technological Level

Marxist theory has demonstrated the relevance of social change to technological change. However, increased mediation of communication may cause alienation, and the long-term repercussions of alienation are detrimental not only to the individual, but also to the person's contacts and the society at large. Here, the influence of the media comes into play. We have intentionally left the media unexplored in this text for two reasons. First, our focus has been on *human* communication and how the human communicates. We tend to view the media as a technological tool that can be used to advance communication, not a theoretical concern in and of itself. Second, media "theory" is not very well developed. It borrows heavily from political models, such as "agenda setting." Not that the same critique can be advanced within intrapersonal, interpersonal, and group theories, but the focus in such research and theory is the individual and the individual's communication. We perceive media theory as sociological in nature. Media theory, along the lines of critical interpretative and conflict theory, might provide important future insight into human communication.

PRINCIPLES OF HUMAN COMMUNICATION THEORY

By now, it should be apparent that theory is an important aspect of human communication. At this point, it is useful to summarize some basic theoretical principles derived from the communication perspectives discussed in earlier sections. In the following pages, we summarize a number of communication principles and briefly discuss their ramifications.

1. *The use of communication in a society is dependent on the nature of that society.*

   A. *In a monolithic social structure, the need for communication is only as a simple maintenance device.*

Perelman's notion that communication is needed only as a maintenance device appears consistent with everything we know about communication theory. As a maintenance device, communication functions as simple feedback, as indicated in cybernetic systems models. Because people in such societies have similar needs and values, there is little need to attempt persuasion. Not needing a rhetorical strategy to persuade means that people lack the necessity for such framing either in psychological or environmental terms. Monolithic societies lack inequities strong enough to require a need to overthrow the existing system. In such societies, the rules are so readily apparent as to appear to be laws. It is important to realize, however, that ours is *not* such a society. Ours is a *pluralistic* society in which values differ and people, either as individuals or groups, have a need or drive to change the attitudes, beliefs, opinions, and behaviors of others.

B. *In a pluralistic social structure, communication is the primary means for maintaining or changing social values.*

In a society such as the United States in the 1990s, individual and group values are different. We find a rich diversity of both value and role systems, people who range from being politically conservative to liberal, sexually liberal to conservative, and so on. Each individual and group needs to have access to the information necessary to maintain the social system. People also need to *attempt* to influence others. Maintenance perspectives (symbolic interactionism, Perelman, etc.) serve to illustrate the need to find some generalized notion of what society expects. However, when such diverse and strongly held beliefs as indicated by prochoice and prolife groups are at work, for example, such simplistic generalizations become more difficult to find.

As Perelman noted, pluralistic societies attempt to seek common values and use the institutions of those societies to reinforce them. The symbolic interactionist indicates that we can determine common values through the "Me" and through generalized others in particular. Having a knowledge of our generalized other is beneficial in determining how to act while maintaining the values of our society. At the same time, systems theory provides insight into ways of maintaining balance within the system, as well as balance between the system and its environment. Homeostatic (balancing) theories may be used for changing individual attitudes and behavior without changing the superstructure of society.

The development of cognitive dissonance, balance, and congruity theories provides a strong base to change others in the context of a single behavior, attitude, or opinion. Typically, these theories do not advocate change in the entire system or even clusters of values. They have been useful, however, in creating states of imbalance within such structures or about certain variables to cause change.

Many studies in human communication have used a *variable analytic* approach (the study of a variable, usually under laboratory conditions, to learn how it is affected or affects other variables) to define constructs and variables. Researchers have used this approach to develop theory involving a particular variable (i.e., credibility, fear arousal, communication apprehension or avoidance). Many of these studies have been valuable in specifying certain directions for theory through the found importance or lack of importance for a particular variable.

In the application of communication theory, homeostatic approaches have been beneficial in political communication and advertising campaigns. In political communication, the use of dissonant information about the opposition may help in electing a candidate. In some cases, indicating what the opposition is going to say in the future may add credibility to a candidate's position and bolster the audience's held attitudes or beliefs. In advertising campaigns, balance and congruity theories are used to show how some product or product line is associated with other positive features of our lives. Automobiles and personal products are associated with beauty and prestige.

It is important to note, however, that these approaches are most effective when dealing with only one idea and not a cluster of ideas.

The conflict theory of Karl Marx and the critical theorists is useful in bringing about major changes in society as a whole. To some extent, Saul Alinsky also used these approaches in bringing about changes in communities. These approaches are useful for creating dynamic changes in society. To use them for minor changes would probably prove ineffective. They require elite support (a small number of extremely dedicated individuals who believe the changes they want are important), mass support (over the long run), and legitimation (acceptance by society at large as a nonradical entity).

The changes obtained from conflict and critical theories, which may range from eliminating class differences to eliminating chauvinism, require not only rhetorical strategies, but *systems of strategies.* They typically take more time than changes brought about by homeostatic theories, but their repercussions last longer. A rhetorical exigency (a need for something to be said at this time and place) is critical for these approaches to work. Currently, conflict approaches are most useful for bringing about fundamental changes within complex organizations that operate as social systems in and of themselves. Thus, in a pluralistic society, maintenance, homeostatic, and conflict theories are all useful as points of departure in the study of differing values and serve as bases for understanding and predicting communicative outcomes.

2. *Human action and the accompanying motives for that action are established through nonverbal and verbal codes.*

One of the few statements about communication that can be made without much controversy is that nonverbal and verbal codes form the materials used in constructing the communication edifice. Most research in nonverbal communication indicates that, without its accompanying verbal messages, nonverbal communication lacks meaning. Although some researchers have placed great importance on the nonverbal component in the total communication process (estimating as high as 93 percent of total meaning is communicated nonverbally), they have also indicated that the nonverbal portion of the message is emotive and provides little cognitive information. At the same time, numerous studies have been concerned with the verbal message alone, such as conversational analysis and networking. Very little, if any, communication research has actually examined the contributions of *both* code systems simultaneously. Although contemporary study of nonverbal and verbal communication is still in its infancy, positions now advocating more holistic approaches to communicative meaning should show a high propensity for success.

General semantics, as a tool for studying communication, has recently met with strong opposition. The theory is still used, however, as a device for establishing *what we said* as opposed to *what we thought we said.* Motives also may be assessed through this approach to communication.

3. *Nonverbal and verbal codes are used to prepare rhetorical strategies.*

Although traditional rhetorical theory emphasized five canons of rhetoric, *memoria*, or memory, was later dismissed as a "lost canon." The remaining four canons could not exist without nonverbal and verbal coding. Because *inventio*, or invention, involves the content of the communicative act, it is based on verbal coding. The gathering of evidence and the creation of arguments are based upon thinking, listening, and reading, which inherently involve verbal coding behavior. *Dispositio*, or organization, also involves the use of the verbal code. Ordering arguments or deciding to omit an argument are "word games" that we use in developing the speech. *Elocutio*, or style, is the language of the speech. *Pronuntiatio*, or delivery, is almost exclusively nonverbal coding. Eye contact, facial expression, and paralanguage are important for getting messages across. Although many communication studies analyze the use of verbal communication, few public speech analyses involve nonverbal coding.

4. *Intrapersonal communication (symbolic interactionism, humanistic psychology, homeostatic theories) involves setting a goal and establishing lines by which that goal may be achieved.*

In this way, we can see that rhetorical strategies are themselves first intrapersonal in nature. As message constructors, we first analyze our situation in our minds. In this sense, we learn that language is a tool for thinking, as well as a tool for interacting with others.

A. *"I"-oriented (symbolic interaction) or animalistic tendencies (biosocial) or simple stimulus–response mechanisms (behavioral psychology) are generally useful only for shortterm, immediate goal setting.*

B. *"Me"-oriented (symbolic interaction), symbolic tendencies (bi social, general semantics), and humanistic psychology are useful for longer term, interpersonal goal setting.*

C. *Conflict theory and critical interpretative theory are useful for social system rhetorical strategies directed toward change.*

5. *Rhetorical strategies are audience- and situation-based. Depending on the audience and the situation, a particular strategy should be chosen.*

6. *Individual goals (humanistic psychology and behavioral psychology) assist us in establishing a rhetorical strategy that is meaningful to us, as well as the audience, in a situation.*

7. *Group goals (exchange theory, social conflict theory, critical interpretive theory, and phenomenology) assist us in gauging the overall impact of our messages.*

8. *In a pluralistic society such as ours, we must assess the available materials, the strategies, the individual, and the society (the available means of persuasion) in our study of the architecture of communication theory.*

9. *We begin our assessment with the idea that "perspectives vary," and we attempt to analyze with an array of available perspectives.*

The question we may ask at this point is, "Does this means of studying the nature of communication actually work?" Its effectiveness is based on the outcomes of those who try to study communication using these perspectives.

SUMMARY

Future Concerns of Communication Theory

We have addressed the concerns and expectations of a discipline that is seeking not only to understand itself, but also to explain the how's and why's of communication. Our trip through the various approaches has centered on numerous researchers and theorists from a variety of disciplines. The connecting thread on our map has been a concept: "Communication." Where we are now, as noted in earlier chapters, may only be at the level of asking better questions. But what are the questions we need to consider? This chapter has asked and attempted to answer several. Now we believe that more questions can be asked. The future of the field of communication is in those questions.

REFERENCE

[1] L. Thayer, "Communication and Organization Theory," in *Human Communication Theory: Original Essays*, ed., F. E. X. Dance (New York: Holt, Rinehart and Winston, 1967) p. 87.

APPENDIX A

Building a Theory

When preparing to design a building, the architect weighs many factors before putting that design to paper. This pre-design period includes creating and testing different ideas and concepts according to many criteria. Regardless of how the architect finishes a design, he or she understands what is needed, *given what he or she has to work with* (materials, aesthetic features, etc.). At a more basic level, the architect understands the theoretical concepts underlying all buildings.

Communication architects are no different. Like the building architect, the communication architect is educated about *general* designs. Here, we provide the basic foundations for communication edifices by discussing *theory*. As noted in Chapter 1, we all perceive things differently. In relation to theory, however, we do so on a formal level, which is open to evaluation. Here, we provide an understanding of different approaches to theory *in general*, as well as the tools with which to evaluate theories.

Today, many courses are taught in the field of communication, including public speaking, interpersonal communication, radio broadcasting, television broadcasting, cablecasting, filmmaking, theatre, aesthetic appreciation, print journalism, and public relations. In addition, the realm of data processing using computers may be referred to as information processing (or communication). *Communication has become the single most important element in our lives.* The underlying assumptions of what communication is are found in communication theory. The purpose of this book has been to introduce you to some of the people and ideas that have transformed communication from what it was twenty-five hundred years ago to what it is today. In this appendix, we define theory, discuss types of theories, delineate the components of a theory, illustrate how theory is related to research, show how theory is important in a learning context, and provide a simple means for evaluating theories.

DEFINING A THEORY

The word theory conjures up different ideas for different people. For example, Abraham Kaplan writes that a theory is "a way of making sense of a disturbing situation to allow us to bring to bear our habits and to modify habits or discard them altogether, replacing them by new ones."[1] Nicolas S. Timasheff notes that a theory is "couched in terms of exactly defined concepts; consistent with one another; such that existing generalizations could be deductively derived; and fruitful [increases our scope of knowledge]."[2] C. David Mortensen provides a specific definition of *communication theory* as "an umbrella term for a host of general principles and orienting statements designed to specify causes and key relationships among given facets of communicative behavior."[3] Given all this, we use "theory" in the general sense of trying to answer questions about what communication is, how it works, and how it does not work.

TYPES OF THEORIES

In working with theories, we should remember that they can be categorized in many different ways. As noted in Chapter 2, one of the more common ways of categorizing is by *level of generality*. There are at least three common levels of theory generality: (1) grand (universal), (2) middle-range (general), and (3) hypothesis testing. Grand theories generalize to a global society and are presumed to hold over a long period of time (Marxian theory). Middle-range theories may concern only a particular group in society or may be particular in content and universal in the groups they generalize to (cognitive dissonance). Hypothesis testing is limited in scope of content, as well as in the group of people under investigation. Although attempts are made by some to generalize the results of hypothesis testing, such generalizations are valid only after testing has occurred across many groups of people.

Thus, the level of theory generality primarily considers how many people are involved and the specificity of content. A theory that concerns only certain people in certain situations—for example, the communication rules pertinent to standing in an elevator—uses hypothesis testing. At the other extreme, a theory that concerns how communication is used to maintain the existence of an entire society is a grand theory. The level of generality indicates boundaries of a theory.

A second way of categorizing a theory is by its *substantive base* (or metaphor). Many theories use metaphors to explain what communication is like and how the process works. At least eight such communication theories have been produced: (1) *dramatistic* (communication is like a play), (2) *journalistic* (communication is like the questions a reporter asks), (3) *rhetorical* (communication is persuasion), (4) *psychophysical* (communication is similar to the human body), (5) *value* (communication is based on the relative needs of the sender and the receiver), (6) *information* (communication is intended to provide new data and the channels for those data), (7) *systems* (communication is like an ever-changing process), and (8) *servo-mechanistic* (communication is like a thermostat used to help maintain the best temperature).

Two examples of categorizing the types of theory by substance are found in the works of B. Aubrey Fisher and Leonard Hawes. Fisher saw communication theory as falling into four general categories: *mechanistic, psychological, interactional,* and *pragmatic.*[4] The mechanistic perspective is concerned with messages being transmitted and received through a channel, as well as the effects of such messages. The psychological perspective adds the dimension of having the receiver actively process the information; the focus is on this active receiver. The interactional perspective views the two participants as changing throughout their transferring of messages. The pragmatic view deemphasizes the internal perceptions of the interactants and is concerned with the social situation previously established.

Hawes divided communication theories into four types: *literary, academic, eristic,* and *symbolic* (see Table A–1).[5] Kenneth Burke exemplifies a theorist with a literary approach, using a great many words (see Chapter 4). Hugh Danziel Duncan used the academic type by incorporating some of the work of Burke and George Herbert Mead, eliminating some of the wordiness, and classifying many propositions from their works (see Chapter 6). Ego-involvement theory, developed by Sherif, Sherif, and Nebergall, is Hawes's example of an eristic theory, which is much less wordy (substantive) and more controllable (form oriented). Eristic theory provides a means whereby other researchers can test it (see Chapter 8). Information theory, developed by Shannon and Weaver, is Hawes's example of a symbolic type. This type of theory is mathematically oriented, although it may not contain numbers.

A third way of categorizing theories is by *specific purpose.* Among the purposes are (1) *description* (explanation), which provides an answer to WHAT? (2) *prediction,* which provides an answer to WHY? (3) *heuristic,* which provides an answer to HOW? and (4) *control,* which would provide ultimate prediction.

The final means of categorizing communication theories is by focus, or what we call *orientation.* One can take several different views. The orientation may be holistic, considering the entire overview of sender, message,

TABLE A–1 Communication Theories

Content-Oriented			Form-Oriented		
Literary	Academic	Eristic	Symbolic	Postulational	Formal
WORDS/STATISTICS . . . . MATHEMATICS/LOGIC					

This scale was devised by Mark Hickson, III, Mississippi State University, 1977, after the work of L. Hawes in *The Pragmatics of Analoguing: Theory and Model Construction in Communication* (Reading, MA: Addison-Wesley, 1975), and A Kaplan, *The Conduct of Inquiry: Methodology for the Behavioral Sciences* (San Francisco: Chandler, 1964), p. 295.

medium (or channel), and receiver. Another orientation may look only at the sender of the message. The message itself may be the focus of the theory. The medium (or channel) may be used to identify the most important element in the theory. Finally, the theory may be receiver oriented. In general, however, all these categories will be used to verify potential answers to a communication question (justification) and to discover new communication questions and answer them (heurism).[6]

COMPONENTS OF A THEORY

Throughout this book, numerous words are used to explain perspectives on human communication, including *construct, relationship, principle,* and *theory.* A term (a word or a phrase) in a theory may be called a construct. A construct may have a particular definition in a theory that may differ from the ordinary or dictionary definition of that word. Just as an architect must consider the building materials when planning a building, so must the theorist consider the constructs of his or her theory.

Constructs may fall into various categories. Interpersonal attraction, for example, may be characterized through the nonverbal communication "materials" of smiles, touch, physical attraction, or tone of voice. Credibility, as a construct, may fall in the realm of a rhetorical strategy (a framework for the communication). Exchange, as a construct, may be an aspect of a social edifice for the community. These terms are similar to the architect's concrete, brick, and so on, or in language terms we may consider the constructs as *nouns.*[7]

Architects do more than simply devise lists of items needed to construct a building. They must also consider how the various aspects of the building will be combined. Just as mortar and bricks naturally work together, certain constructs in communication theory work well together. Thus, we must consider the *relationships* between the constructs (or *verbs* in the language metaphor). Constructs can be combined in several ways.

Hans L. Zetterberg, for example, has illustrated five ways in which constructs can be blended to form relationships. Relationships may be (1) reversible or irreversible, (2) deterministic or stochastic, (3) sequential or coextensive, (4) sufficient or contingent, and (5) necessary or substitutable. Reversible means "if X, then Y" and "if Y, then X." Irreversible means "if X, then Y," but there is no conclusion about "if Y." Deterministic means "if X, then *always* Y." Stochastic means "if X, then *probably* Y." Sequential means "if X, then *later* Y." Coextensive means "if X, then also Y." Sufficient means "if X, then Y regardless of anything else." Contingent means "if X, then Y, but only if Z." Necessary means "if X, and *only* X, then Y." Substitutable means "if X, then Y; but if Z, then also Y." These relationships are easier to understand if you substitute words for X, Y, and Z.[8] Thus, a particular relationship may be irreversible, stochastic, sequential, contingent, and substitutable; however, a relationship between constructs cannot at the same time be reversible *and* irreversible, or deterministic *and* stochastic.

Constructs and relationships form the basic structure of theories. A statement about how constructs and relationships work together is called a principle. Some examples of communication principles are "The word is not the thing" or "ALL communication is persuasion" or "You cannot not communicate." Such principles are like "The hammer must force the nail into the wood." In a sense, then, a principle is a combination of constructs and relationships (or a *sentence* in the language metaphor of theory).

A number of principles form what is known as a theory, which is analogous with the plan for the entire building. Theories sometimes carry the name of the theorist or sometimes have their own name based on some construct, relationship, principle, or metaphor based on the theory. A theory may be considered a paragraph or a story in the language metaphor of theory.

THEORY AND RESEARCH

At this point, we begin developing a theory using constructs. From these constructs, we develop principles (or *propositions*). We must remember, however, that we are still using theoretical notions that should be testable. Some theories (called form oriented) are much more *testable* than others (called substantive theories).[9]

In any case, some form of logical or empirical testing is usually needed. To test a theory, we must go into the domain of *research*. We must make a "transformation." Just as the architect must take the plans and begin the actual building, the theorist must use the theoretical plan as a base to test the theory through research. *Constructs* must be transformed into *variables*. A variable uses an "operational definition"; that is, a term has a particular meaning under certain circumstances. For instance, intelligence is a construct. The intelligence variable is a score on a particular intelligence test, of which there are many, each slightly different and yielding possibly different results. The variable, then, makes the construct more concrete and allows the user to test it under different circumstances.

At the same time, the principles must be transformed to enter the research domain. Principles become *hypotheses* (or sometimes *research questions*). An hypothesis is a way of phrasing a principle to test it. Take the principle that "taller women will speak more in initial interactions with men than will shorter women." To form this principle into an hypothesis, we must be more specific. We must operationalize the constructs into variables that may be tested. The hypothesis might read, "Women taller than five feet nine inches will speak more words than women five feet nine inches or shorter in the first four minutes of interaction with a male stranger." Note that the constructs "taller/shorter," "time," and "talk" have been operationalized and are now amenable to testing.

(Untested) Theory   Research (Tested Theory)

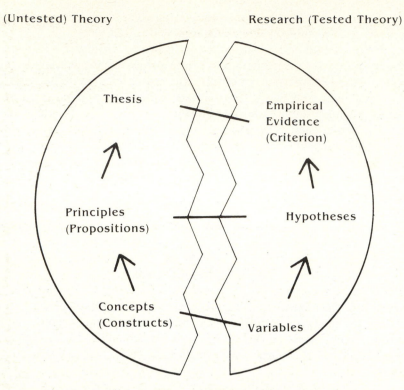

FIGURE A–1 **Theory and Research Domains.**

The outcome of hypothesis testing is *empirical evidence.* Gary Cronkhite and Jo Liska have called this the *criterion.* The criterion is a "test, principle, rule, canon, or standard by which anything is judged or is estimated."[10] Once testing has been completed, the results are used to support, modify, or refute the theory (see Fig. A–1).

The relationship between theory and research (or method) is analogous to what Gregory Bateson and others have referred to as imagination and rigor. The research forms the rigorous aspects of the discipline: the detail, the minor complexity, the harsh scrutiny. Theory (or imagination) is the quest for answers, disregarding *for the moment* the rigor that will be needed to later test the theory. Thus, in this text, we have been primarily concerned with that "imagination,"[11] or what W. Barnett Pearce and Vernon Cronen call the "wonder,"[12] or what John Grinder and Richard Bandler call "the magic,"[13] that leads us to explore communication.

Gerald R. Miller and Harry E. Nicholson see theory in less idealistic terms. They view theory as a method of asking questions.[14] Theorizing (asking appropriate and significant questions) over a longer period of time (as in a career) develops new ways of thinking. Perhaps the best statement in this regard is an anonymous, yet erudite quotation:

We have not succeeded in answering all your questions. Indeed, we sometimes feel we have not completely answered any of them. The answers we have given only serve to raise a whole new set of questions. In some ways we feel that you are as confused as ever, but we believe you are confused on a much higher level and about more important things.

Thus, we believe that learning involves the act of asking good questions, which may be the most important element in the learning process.

THEORY IN A LEARNING CONTEXT

We use research to modify theories. Indeed, sometimes research gives us the impetus for an entirely new theory (in this sense, the research based on the

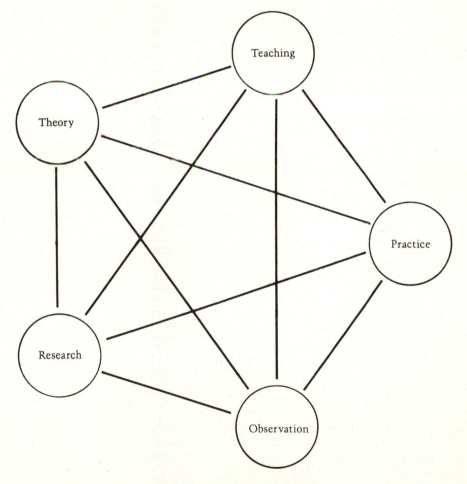

FIGURE A–2   **The Learning Web.**

old theory serves a heuristic function—it generates new theory and research). Theories are useful in teaching classes in communication. If the students learn properly, they practice what they have learned in their daily communication (see Fig. A–2). Over a period of time, changes in practice are observed and researched: We begin to observe what "works" and what does not and explore why. New theories are then formulated, they are taught, and students begin practicing in accordance with the new theory. Although this cycle is important, the order in which the elements occur may not always be the same. *Theory, teaching, practice, observation, and research form the web of the learning context.* They all work together. Any one element can change any other. Our mission here has been to determine how changes in theory affect the other dimensions of the learning context.[15]

EVALUATING THEORIES

Not all theory is "good." It is important to learn how to evaluate a theory since *a theory is only as good as the tests that judge it.* Although various evaluation methods can be used to evaluate a theory (metatheoretical criteria), we have used the following method for such evaluations. These steps should help you in your quest to understand and use different approaches to the study of communication. Remember, you may not agree with what the theory says, which may make it difficult for you to "see" where the theory is going. Try to take a disinterested look at the theory. First, look to see what the theory purports to do. What are the things it will allow you to do that other theories do not? How efficient is it in *explaining* communication phenomena? What *predictions* does the theory make? Look for the *central assumption(s)* on which the theory is based and what special definitions are used in describing this theory/approach. (Note that some terms, such as, "mind" "body," and "self," remain undefined; these are called "primitives" and help to define the entire theory.)

Observe the *constructs* of the theory (as well as variables, if the theory has been tested). How well are they defined? How valid are they? Observe the *propositions* (principles, hypotheses, research questions) of the theory. What relations do they develop? Are they new? Do they make sense, given what we know both logically and empirically? Next, look at the *order* of the propositions. The pattern should be logical within its limitations. Usually, the pattern will be chronological, inductive, deductive, or dialectical. *Chronological* means placing the first principles (in time) first, such as Darwin's theory of evolution. *Inductive* means moving from the specific cases to the general case. *Deductive* means moving from a general case to specific instances. *Dialectical* is concerned with taking a construct and comparing and contrasting it with its opposite (antithesis) to determine the result (synthesis) (see Chapter 6). The overall *thesis* should be summarized into one or two logical, coherent statements which explain the essence of the combined propositions.

In summary, the theory should be *testable, logical, supportable* (or refutable), *parsimonious* (with redundant and unnecessary items omitted), *reliable* (hold up to testing over a period of time), and *heuristic* (interesting enough to provoke others to challenge it).[16]

REVIEW

We have defined construct, relationship, principle, theory, variable, and hypothesis. We have illustrated the relationship between theory and research, and we have shown how they are important in the learning context. We have provided a learning tool for comparing and contrasting theories. Finally, we have provided an outline for evaluating theories.

What have we learned about *building* our communication theory? Just as architects must understand intuitively how their building will look, how functional it will be, and how much aesthetic appreciation it will receive, communication architects must impose certain restrictions on themselves prior to developing a blueprint. The communication architect must understand how to approach communication in general, what parts are important, and how results can be trusted. Using this approach we (1) perceive a situation or person, (2) test that perception via some result, and (3) learn from anticipated results how the theory functions. This day-to-day theorizing someday will yield a formal theory of how to communicate, with what effect, and with what limitations. Fortunately, there are many theories already stated and tested that allow us to understand, predict, and ultimately control our communication. Based on our knowledge of general theory building, like the architect, we have the basic knowledge needed to evaluate and choose a blueprint format (a metatheory).

NOTES AND REFERENCES

[1]A. Kaplan, *The Conduct of Inquiry: Methodology for the Behavioral Sciences* (San Francisco: Chandler, 1964), p. 295.

[2]N. S. Timasheff, *Sociological Theory: Its Nature and Growth* (Garden City, NY: Doubleday, 1955), pp. 9–10.

[3]C. D. Mortensen, *Basic Readings in Communication Theory* (New York: Harper and Row, 1979), pp. 1–2.

[4]B. A. Fisher, "Evidence Varies with Theoretical Perspective," *Western Journal of Speech Communication,* 41 (1977), 9–19.

[5]L. C. Hawes, *Pragmatics of Analoguing: Theory and Model Construction in Communication* (Reading, MA: Addison–Wesley, 1975).

[6]Kaplan.

[7]J. Hage, *Techniques and Problems of Theory Construction in Sociology* (New York: Wiley, 1972), pp. 9–33.

[8]To view some of the specific kinds of relationships, see H. L. Zetterberg, "On Propositions in Sociology," in *Research Methods: Issues and Insights,* eds. B. J. Franklin and H. W. Osborne (Belmont, CA: Wadsworth, 1971), pp. 101–111.

[9]Hawes.

[10]G. Cronkhite and J. Liska, "Introduction," *Western Journal of Speech Communication*, 41 (1977), 6.

[11]C. Wilder-Mott and J. C. Weakland, eds., *Rigor and Imagination: Essays From the Legacy of Gregory Bateson* (New York: Praeger, 1981).

[12]W. B. Pearce and V. E. Cronen, *Communication, Action, and Meaning: The Creation of Social Realities* (New York: Praeger, 1980).

[13]J. Grinder and R. Bandler, *The Structure of Magic, II* (Palo Alto, CA: Science and Behavior Books, 1976).

[14]G. R. Miller and H. E. Nicholson, *Communication Inquiry: A Perspective on a Process* (Reading, MA: Addison–Wesley, 1976).

[15]For more information about the development of theories, see C. A. Lave and J. G. March, *An Introduction to Models in the Social Sciences* (New York: Harper and Row, 1975); F. Suppe, ed., *The Structure of Scientific Theories* (Urbana, IL: University of Illinois Press, 1974). For more information about communication research, see P. Emmert and W. D. Brooks, eds., *Methods of Research in Communication* (New York: Houghton Mifflin, 1970). See also D. Cushman and W. B. Pearce, "Generality and Necessity in Three Types of Theory About Human Communication," *Human Communication Research*, 3 (1977), 344–353.

[16]See also S. W. Littlejohn, *Theories of Human Communication*, 2nd ed. (Belmont, CA: Wadsworth, 1983), pp. 23–24; C. C. Arnold and J. W. Bowers, eds., *Handbook of Rhetorical and Communication Theory* (Boston: Allyn and Bacon, 1984).

APPENDIX B

Glossary

Abdicrat Personality From Schutz's general need for control; a person who is submissive, refuses to take responsibility, and exhibits hostility.

Absorbed Actions One of Morris's kinesic actions; they are unconsciously acquired from friends.

Account From the symbolic interactionist perspective, a statement that explains inappropriate behavior.

Acquired Response A response that is acquired through association with a neutral stimulus over experience; general semantics.

Act An element in Burke's pentad; the communicative message itself.

Action Rules Choice-governed responses governed by practical necessity.

Adaptors An element in the meaning-centered approach to nonverbal communication; behaviors used to adjust the body, satisfy some bodily need, or satisfy some emotional need; see also *self adaptors* and *object adaptors*.

Adult Role From Harris's transactional analysis approach; a role found in the meshing of the parent and child through exploration and testing.

Affect Blend An affect display (meaning-centered approach to nonverbal communication); a blending of one or more of the six basic affect displays.

Affect Displays An element in the meaning-centered approach to nonverbal communication; displays of emotion that may or may not accompany a verbal message. Affect displays include anger, disgust, fear, happiness, sadness, and surprise. See also *neutral expression* and *affect blend*.

Agency An element in Burke's pentad; the means or instruments used in the communicative act.

Agent An element in Burke's pentad; the source of the communicative message; the one who acts.

Agreement/Disagreement A mode of analysis based on a focus on points where we differ from others (disagreement) or when our future responses tend toward consistency with previous decisions.

Alienation From conflict theory; a social alienation based on use of language that takes the form of separation from work, others, and self; Marx. Also from psychological theory as related to conflict theory; powerlessness, meaninglessness, normlessness, isolation, and self-estrangement; Melvin Seeman.

293

Alinsky, Saul   Conflict theorist and radical organizer; developed persuasive strategy based on Marxist ideology.

Allokine   An element in the linguistic analogy approach to nonverbal communication; the smallest, cultural variation of movement.

Allport, Gordon   Developmental personality theorist; suggests that the self develops through seven stages (bodily self through "the knower"); psychological approach.

Anthropological Approach   Nonverbal approach; incorporates the impact of culture and society on nonverbal communication.

Antithesis   Stylistic device associated with Gorgias; the use of opposites of terminology or meaning in contrasting clauses. See also *Marx*.

Argyle, Michael   Nonverbal theorist; best known for intimacy–equilibrium approach; psychological approach.

Aristotle   Rhetorical theorist in early Greece; tried to find a middle ground in the debate between the Sophists and Plato.

Ars Dictamen   The art of letter writing in the Middle Ages; teachers were highly prized members of the universities.

Associative Bond   A linkage to an assertion by a source indicating something positive about an attitude object the receiver perceives as "good"; congruity theory.

Attitude   A construct said to be composed of affective (feeling), cognitive (thoughts), and connotative (behavioral) components; internal feelings about some object; composed of opinions, beliefs, and values.

Autocrat Personality   From Schutz's general need for control; a person who possesses a need to dominate others and distrusts the motives and creative potential of others.

Backstage   An element of performance; an area where the person prepares for the performance; dramaturgical analysis.

Balance Theory   A cognitive consistency theory of attitude change developed by Fritz Heider; argues that people placed in a state of imbalance will attempt to restore balance by changing their attitudes toward either message or object.

Bargaining   From exchange theory; a way to limit costs and enhance rewards; see *Structure of Bargaining Situation, Power, Concessions,* and *Norms.*

Batons   A class of illustrators (meaning-centered approach to nonverbal communication) which emphasize what is being said.

Becker, Ernest   Anthropologist who suggests that the end of life produces a fear that our reality will end; biosocial.

Behavioral Theories of Attitude Change   Theories of persuasion that seek to demonstrate the impact of external stimuli on the formulation of attitudes.

Belief   An expectation about the way some event or sequence of events will occur.

Biological Communication   From Wilson's sociobiology; communication that encompasses both verbal and nonverbal modes of communication; see *Prosody* and *Paralanguage; Biosocial Approach.*

Biosocial Approach   An approach to communication that tries to take into account the biological foundations of human communication and the more social–psychological foundations of human interaction with others.

Birdwhistell, Ray L.   Nonverbal theorist; linguistic analogy approach to nonverbal communication; anthropological approach.

Boundary   Areas within the system that may be physical, spatial, temporal, or symbolic; a buffer area that separates the system from its environment, a system from its suprasystem, or a subsystem from other subsystems.

Brain   From the biosocial; an organ that creates social reality out of biological time clocks; see also *Left Hemisphere, Right Hemisphere, Contralateral, Ipsilateral, R-Complex Brain, Paleomammalian Brain, Neomammalian Brain.*

Buck, Ross   Nonverbal theorist; approach advocates ethological view in which nonverbal communication is used to adapt to situations and maintain a sense of homeostasis.

Burgoon, Judee K.   Nonverbal theorist; best known for work in proxemics, functional approach.

Burke, Kenneth   Modern rhetorician; perceived rhetoric as the use and study of persuasive resources.

Canons of Rhetoric   Attributed to Cicero; parts of oration. See *Inventio, Dispositio, Elocutio, Memoria,* and *Pronuntiatio.*

Casting   An element of the coordinated management of meaning theory; casting is used to train others for some part in an episode.

Central Assumption   That upon which the theory is based; the underlying metaphor or sense of reality upon which all else is built.

Child Role   From Harris's transactional analysis approach; a role in which feelings are developed, feelings that reflect inward and often with hurt; a role full of negatives about self and others.

Chomsky, Noam   Theorist concerned with language acquisition; language as a biological function.

Chronological   A pattern of propositions in which the propositions are placed in some time order.

Cicero (or Tully)   Rome's greatest orator; attributed to the five canons of rhetoric; systematized the work of the early Greeks.

Clark, Ruth Anne   Developed an approach to communication known as constructivism.

Class Consciousness   From conflict theory; the bringing about of change in the masses through the conception of history; Marx.

Closed Systems   Systems that are contained or isolated from their environments.

Code   Putting ideas into some form so that others can understand them. See *Verbal Communication* and *Nonverbal Communication.*

Cognitive Consistency Theories of Attitude Change   A number of theories of persuasion that suggest that people actively avoid situations or messages that cause inconsistency and prefer to remain in a state of homeostasis or balance.

Cognitive Dissonance   A cognitive consistency theory of attitude change developed by Leon Festinger; posits that the greater the dissonance (inconsistency), the greater the pressure to reduce it by changing the reasons for the dissonance, changing the perception of the environment or situation, or adding new information that reduces the dissonance or creates new attitudes.

Communication System   A system in which the states are connections or nonconnections between objects (structural).

Concessions   From exchange theory; the pattern of communication revealing information about each party in the bargaining situation.

Conclusio   A part of speech organization (*dispositio*); peroration or conclusion; the end of the speech which summarizes and makes emotional appeals to win the sympathy of the audience; Cicero.

Confirmatio   A part of speech organization (*dispositio*); confirmation; that part of the speech which lends credit, authority, and support to the case; Cicero.

Conflict Theory   A sociological theory of communication based on the works of Karl Marx.

Confutatio   A part of speech organization (*dispositio*); refutation; the part of speech that anticipates the objections or arguments of the opposition and disposes of them in advance; Cicero.

Congruity Theory   A cognitive consistency theory of attitude change developed by Charles Osgood and Percy Tannenbaum; posits that people's attitude changes are tied closely to incongruity (inconsistency) between a source's assertions and the held attitudes of the people; see also *Associative Bond* and *Disassociative Bond*.

Construct   A component of a theory; a term within the theory with a particular definition that may differ from other definitions in other theories or may differ from a dictionary or ordinary language definition.

Constructivism   An approach to communication dealing with the way people construct the messages they send; Jesse G. Delia and Ruth Anne Clark.

Consubstantiality   A concept in Burke's rhetorical theory; the sharing of a common meaning with the audience.

Content Dimension   Communication acts which provide information about the information itself; pragmatic perspective component.

Contralateral   From the biosocial; each hemisphere of the brain (right and left) controls and receives information from the opposite side of the body. Information conveyed by most of the senses is contralaterally transmitted.

Coordinated Management of Meaning   Rules theory; W. Barnett Pearce.

Corax of Sicily   Rhetorical theorist (circa 467 B.C.) of the prescriptive school.

Corpus Callosum   From the biosocial, a thin band of brain fiber that connects the right and left hemispheres.

Creative Behavior   An element of the rules approach which is determined by the following of rules "in a novel way or acting independently of the rules."

Criterion   A "test, principle, rule, canon, or standard by which anything is judged or estimated" (Cronkhite and Liska); empirical evidence.

Critical Interpretive Theory   Sociological approach to communication; a synthesis of three main lines of thought: Marxian social theory, hermeneutics, and Freudian theory.

Critical Method   Burke's dramatistic approach to the study of rhetoric; the pentad.

Cultural Relativity   Proposition that the language of a culture is directly associated with how one thinks in that culture; Edward Sapir and Benjamin Whorf.

Culture   From Alfred G. Smith, the way we communicate; sociological.

Cumulative Structure Approach   See *Meaning-Centered Approach*; Paul Ekman and Wallace Friesen.

Cushman, Donald P.   Rules advocate.

Cybernetic System   A system that focuses on feedback mechanisms and self-regulation.

Darwin, Charles   Greatly influenced the study of nonverbal communication.

Dating   An extensional device that involves using a notational system to indicate that things change through time; general semantics.

Dean, Janet   Nonverbal theorist; best known for intimacy–equilibrium approach; psychological approach.

Deductive   A pattern of propositions in which the propositions are placed from a general case and move to specific cases.

Defensive Climate A concept from Gibb's concept of defensive communication; defensive climates are formed through interaction characterized by evolution, control, strategy, neutrality, superiority, and certainty.

Defensive Communication A concept originated by Gibb; behavior which occurs when a person perceives or anticipates threat in interaction.

Definition of the Situation From the symbolic interactionist perspective; the period of examination and analysis before an individual acts in a self-determined manner.

Deictic Movements A class of illustrators (meaning-centered approach to nonverbal communication) that indicate location in space of objects.

Delia, Jesse G. Developed an approach to communication known as constructivism.

Democrat Personality From Schutz's general need for control; a person who can give or receive orders, follow or lead, and is capable of relinquishing control.

de Sola Pool, Ithiel Structural systems proponent.

Dialectic According to Perelman, a subject that is concerned not with facts or truths or reality, but with opinions (which are theses adhered to with varying degrees of intensity).

Dialectical A pattern of propositions in which the constructs are compared and contrasted with their opposites (antithesis) to determine some result (synthesis).

Dialectical Method From conflict theory; a method of reasoning in which truth is detected through conflict or contrasting of ideas.

Disassociative Bond A linkage to an assertion by a source indicating something negative about an attitude object the receiver perceives as "good"; congruity theory.

Discovered Actions One of Desmond Morris's kinesic actions; they are found at the conscious level, but are limited to the genetic structure of the body.

Dispositio One of the five canons of rhetoric attributed to Cicero; disposition or organization; composed of six parts: *exordium, narratio, divisio, confirmatio, confutatio, conclusio*.

Divisio A part of speech organization (*dispositio*); partition; a methodological statement of the topics to be discussed; Cicero.

Division A concept in Burke's rhetorical theory; the opposite of consubstantiality and identification; provides the motive for rhetoric and communication.

Doctrine of Opposites One of two major rhetorical doctrines generally attributed to Protagorus; held that one can always find at least two contradictory positions that can be rationally defended.

Doctrine of Subjectivity One of two major rhetorical doctrines generally attributed to Protagorus; taught that truth exists in a relativistic sense only.

Domain Generality Identified by the number of conditions that must be met for the principle(s) of the theory to hold true.

Dramaturgical Analysis A general approach to the study of social interactions concerned with how people stage and act out a social role in differing contexts; rules approach; Erving Goffman.

Drive A concept arising from behavioral theories of attitude change which suggests that internal states can be created through repetition of a stimulus that becomes habitual over time.

Ekman, Paul Nonverbal theorist; meaning-centered approach.

Elite Support From conflict theory; a small group of highly active and highly committed members; Marx.

Elocutio One of the five canons of rhetoric attributed to Cicero; style; deals primarily with word choice, composition, and stylistic devices or figures of speech.

Elocutionary System Nonverbal analysis which modeled natural gestures into "appropriate" gestures for dramatic presentations; Gilbert Austin.

Emblem An element in the meaning-centered approach to nonverbal communication; a gesture (facial or gestural) that has a direct verbal equivalent.

Emblematic Illustrators A class of illustrators (meaning-centered approach to nonverbal communication); substitute for some word or phrase during interaction but have no particular meaning after the interaction.

Empirical Evidence The outcome of testing an hypothesis or research question.

Engram A stimulus we receive that leaves an imprint on us, that can be later retrieved.

Enthymeme Rhetorical concept of Aristotle; a tool adapted to achieving persuasion via the use of an approximate syllogism (a syllogism with one of its premises omitted).

Entropy A state in which the system is moving toward deterioration.

Environment An aspect of systems theory; all systems exist in physical, spatial, and temporal conditions, which become the system's environment (see also *boundary*).

Episode An element of the coordinated management of meaning theory; determined by the actors in the particular situation; answers the question, "What do you think he is doing?"

Eristic Sophists Rhetoricians of the sophistic period (550–500 B.C.) primarily interested in formal logic.

Et cetera assumption From the symbolic interactionist perspective, where people routinize the environment by assuming that the future will occur much as has the past.

"Etc." Rule An extensional device that reminds the user of language that we cannot say everything about a given phenomenon at any point in time; general semantics.

Ethological Approach Nonverbal approach; offshoot of zoological approach; study of similarities between the behavior of lower species animals and the behavior of humans.

Ethos Aristotelian concept associated with persuasion; the personal character of the speaker.

Exchange Theory Sociological theory developed by George C. Homans; views communication as a process, involving movement, as an exchange of goods.

Excuse One of two types of accounts; the individual admits that the actions in question are wrong, but denies responsibility for the action; symbolic interactionism.

Exordium A part of speech organization (*dispositio*); the introduction; Cicero.

Extensional Devices Linguistic devices designed for handling problems we have with language and meaning; general semantics. See *Dating, Indexing, "Etc." Rule, Quotation Marks*.

Extensional Orientations A concept from general semantics based on observation, empirical evidence, and a recognition of uniqueness.

False Consciousness From conflict theory; the use of other "forms" that help to create alienation through external controls (e.g., drugs, religion, etc.); Marx. Also from critical interpretive theory; arises out of self-interest, selective perception, or a lack of organization; Lukacs.

Feedback   A characteristic of open systems; a control feature within the system. See also *Homeostasis, Positive Feedback, Negative Feedback.*

Fisher, B. Aubrey   Pragmatic perspective advocate; systems advocate.

Fixed Feature Space   Environmental or artifactual areas composed of relatively fixed or hard to move features; Edward T. Hall.

Frame   An element of performance; an attitude used to view performances; dramaturgical analysis.

Frankfurt School   Critical interpretive theory as proposed by Jurgen Habermas, Karl Korsch, Georg Lukacs, and Walter Benjamin; contemporary Marxian social theory.

Freudian Discursive Intervention   An approach to critical interpretive theory; posits that ideology is the nemesis and "neurosis of society"; ideology coexists with domination.

Friesen, Wallace   Nonverbal theorist; meaning-centered approach.

Front   An element of a performance; the area in which the performance is played, includes the necessary props and objects; dramaturgical analysis.

Functional Approach   An approach to nonverbal communication which places behaviors into functional groupings: power, status, and liking; Albert Mehrabian.

Functional Theory   A theory of attitude change that examines how and why people have attitudes. See also *Daniel Katz.*

Gadamer, Hans-Georg   A critical interpretive theorist who argued that we should be more concerned with the messages being sent than with an understanding of the audience or other person; analysis should be placed in history, linguistics, and dialectic.

Game Stage   From the symbolic interactionist perspective, the final stage in socialization whereby the person is socialized; the stage whereby we can play a number of roles simultaneously; Mead.

Geist   From conflict theory; consciousness; Marx.

General Semantics   A theory of language dealing primarily with the meanings of words; Alfred Korzybski.

General Systems Theory   A view of systems that examines the system as more than the simple interconnectedness between objects; presupposes an active and reactive system and a system fed on information.

Generality   The degree to which a theory may be representative of "reality"; the number of conditions that the theory meets or specifies when reflecting "reality." See also *Syntactical Generality* and *Domain Generality.*

Generalized Other   From the symbolic interactionist perspective; that aspect which is given by the organized community or social group to the individual and causes the individual to act toward societal others; Mead.

Genuine Conversation   From the hermeneutic; takes place when the dialectic of possibilities (based on messages) is allowed to be uncovered, recovered, and discovered; Gadamer; critical interpretive theory.

Gesture   From the symbolic interactionist perspective, an act performed by one person and perceived by another; may be significant or nonsignificant; the verbal gesture becomes the focus of attention; Mead.

Gibb, Jack R.   Developed the concepts of defensive communication, defensive climate, and supportive climate; psychological approach.

Goffman, Erving   Rules approach advocate; dramaturgical analysis.

Gorgias   A literary–cultural Sophist whose style was flowery; taught that words and things are different (forerunner to general semantics). See also *Antithesis, Isocolon, Parison, Homeoteleuton.*

Grammaticus   A teacher of rhetoric in the Roman period.

Habermas, Jurgen   A theorist from the Frankfurt School; critical interpretive theory; see *Third Persona*.

Hall, Edward T.   Nonverbal theorist; best known for work in the areas of time and space; anthropological approach.

Harris, Thomas   Developed the transactional approach to communication; psychological approach.

Hemispheric Style   From the biosocial; a concept suggesting that each hemisphere of the brain is primarily responsible for a type of interpretation, rather than a dominance for interpretation.

Hermeneutics   Phenomenological interpretation of conscious experience; Gadamer.

Heurism   The ability of a theory to discover new questions and/or answers to questions.

Hierarchy   The natural order of systems; the identification of a system in relation to other systems and subsystems within a given suprasystem.

Holism   Characteristic of systems whereby the system is greater than the sum of the system's parts.

Homans, George C.   Developed exchange theory; sociological perspective.

Homeostasis   A characteristic of systems whereby feedback seeks to maintain the system at the current level.

Homeoteleuton   Stylistic device associated with Gorgias; the use of a series of two or more clauses ending with the same or rhyming words in speech.

Humanistic Approach   An approach to communication concerned with the interaction of the individual's personality with his or her orientation to the world; psychological approach.

Hypothesis   The phrasing of a principle or proposition to test it.

I   From James's concept of self; the self represented in a form of consciousness in which the person becomes his or her own self-knower.

"I"   From the symbolic interactionist perspective, an impulsive tendency operating in opposition to the rational roles found in the "Me."

Identification   A concept in Burke's rhetorical theory; the sharing of substance or psychological unity with the audience.

Identity   A concept from general semantics concerned with a belief that there is an absolute sameness or an extreme similarity between "things" in the world.

Ideographs   A class of illustrators (meaning-centered approach to nonverbal communication) which represent thought processes and are used when speakers cannot get their thoughts out.

Illustrators   Elements in the meaning-centered approach to nonverbal communication which support and complement the verbal message. See also *Batons, Ideographs, Pictographs, Kinetographs, Emblematic Illustrators, Deictic Movements, Rhythmic Movements*, and *Spatial Movements*.

Impressions   From constructivism, a social cognition regarding perceptions of another person; an impression is used to establish message strategies that may be rationalized.

Inborn Actions   One of Morris's kinesic actions; they are instinctive and occur at birth.

Inborn Response   A response to a situation through some form of conditioning.

Indexing   An extensional device that involves the use of a subscript to show that not each individual or group is the same; general semantics.

Inductive   A pattern of propositions in which the propositions are placed from specific cases to a more general case.

Influenced Behavior   An element of the rules approach which is determined by the actor's "meanings and volitions."

Informal Space   The space immediately surrounding the person (personal space); Edward T. Hall.

Infracommunicational System   A principle of the linguistic approach to nonverbal communication which states that there is a high degree of interdependence among the five body senses, which, along with verbal communication, creates a communication system.

Inoculation Theory   A psychological theory of persuasion developed by William McGuire based on a biological analogy suggesting that weakened doses of a message may make the receiver less susceptible to a message.

Intensional Orientations   A concept from general semantics based on internal feelings, definitions, or associations.

Intention Display   An element of dramaturgical analysis; a person indicates to others where he intends to go and what he intends to do.

Interpreting   A view of reality based on thinking, synthesizing, and analyzing the data that have been sensed.

Intimacy–Equilibrium Approach   An approach to nonverbal communication that proposes all interactions are bound in conflicts between approach and avoidance forces; Michael Argyle and Janet Dean; psychological approach.

Intrapersonal Communication   A humanistic approach to communication; communication based on knowledge of self and how that self relates to others.

Inventio   One of the five canons of rhetoric attributed to Cicero; invention; the discovering of all available materials for use in an oration.

Ipsilateral   From the biosocial; information is transmitted from one side of the body to the same side of the brain (right nostril to right hemisphere); seems to occur mainly with olfactory sense.

Isocolon   Stylistic device associated with Gorgias; the repetitive use of two or more clauses with the same number of syllables in speech.

Isolation   From conflict and psychological theory; the needs of the individual and society are at odds with each other; Seeman.

James, William   Psychologist who first formulated the self as a three-part concept of self-experience; humanistic approach.

Justification   The verification of potential answers to a communication question via theory. Also, one of two types of accounts; where an individual accepts responsibility for an act but denies the definition of the act under specific circumstances; symbolic interactionism.

Kairos   A rhetorical principle of Gorgias; a standard used to decide such matters as organization, the means of proof, and the style to be employed; the idea that appropriateness rather than correctness should be the standard for behavior.

Katz, Daniel   Attitude theorist; functional theory.

Key   An element of performance; the central concept in the analysis of a frame; dramaturgical analysis.

Kine   An element in the linguistic analogy approach to nonverbal communication; the smallest basic movement and may be differentiated from other kines by the allokine (equivalent to the phoneme or phone).

Kineme   An element in the linguistic analogy approach to nonverbal communication; a grouping of kines or allokines which establishes the first meaningful level of analysis (equivalent to a word).

Kinemorpheme   An element in the linguistic analogy approach to nonverbal communication; a grouping of kinemes which establish social meaning (equivalent to a sentence).

Kinesics   Nonverbal subcode; the study of body movement, gestures, facial expression, eye movement; Ray L. Birdwhistell; Desmond Morris.

Kinetographs   A class of illustrators (meaning-centered approach to nonverbal communication) which represent some form of bodily action.

Knowledge   A perception retained in the perceptual memory bank.

Korzybski, Alfred   Founder of general semantics theory; basic proposition was that we live in two different environments, one physical and one symbolic.

Kultur   From conflict theory, the combination of subjective and objective mind (consciousness and social structure) creating culture; Marx.

Lateral Thinking   A model of thinking that expands upon the assumptions we make about reality and questions those same assumptions.

Laws Perspective   A view of communication with a set of universal propositions and their stipulated initial conditions (nomic necessity).

Left Hemisphere   From the biosocial; the side of the brain responsible for logical, analytical interpretation of stimuli and for complex language and societal rules.

Legitimacy   From conflict theory; a problem associated with the masses due to subordinate positioning and a sense of fatalism; Marx.

Level of Generality   A way to categorize a theory as grand (universal), middle-range (general), or hypothesis testing (specific).

Life Cycles   A human system characteristic defined as the "sequences of a person's inner experiences and production."

Linguistic Analogy   An approach to nonverbal communication that compares nonverbal communication to the linguistic structure of language; suggests that nonverbal communication is learned; Ray Birdwhistell.

Literary–Cultural Sophists   Rhetoricians of the sophistic period (550–500 B.C.) primarily interested in the study of language and grammar.

Logical/Affective   A mode of analysis based on rational or emotive responses to "reality."

Logical Necessity   Concerns the idea that necessity is based on definitional force and is determined by whether a logical calculus can be derived from the propositions.

Logos   Aristotelian concept associated with persuasion; proof or apparent proof provided by the words used in the speech.

Lukacs, Georg   A theorist of the Frankfurt School; Marxian perspective; critical interpretive theory.

Manner   An element of a performance; indicates to the audience what kind of performance is about to take place; dramaturgical analysis.

Marx, Karl   Developed "negative dialectics"; sociological perspective taking a rhetorical approach to communication.

Mass Support   From conflict theory, the support of the proletariat; Marx.

Material Self   From James's concept of self; the physical self (body and physical extensions).

Maximization of Simplicity   A principle in Osgood and Tannenbaum's congruity theory, which refers to the "all-or-nothing," bipolar form of judgment; a reliance on stereotypical judgments.

Me   From James's concept of self, the self that can be evaluated; the empirical self.

"Me"   From the symbolic interactionist perspective, that part of the self which urges conformity to rules and roles established by society; includes the incorporated other; Mead. See *Generalized Other, Significant Other, Orientational Other.*

Mead, George Herbert   Developed the theory of symbolic interactionism.

Meaning   An element of the coordinated management of meaning theory; suggests that meaning is organized over various conversations among actors and organized into units.

Meaning-Centered Approach   Nonverbal approach; study of nonverbal communication based on the meanings associated with kinesic behavior; Paul Ekman and Wallace Friesen.

Meaninglessness   From conflict and psychological theory; an inability of the individual to predict the future resulting in a frustration whereby the individual gives up basic goal seeking in a rhetorical sense; Seeman.

Mehrabian, Albert   Nonverbal theorist; best known for work in the functional approach to nonverbal communication; psychological approach.

Memoria   One of the five canons of rhetoric attributed to Cicero; memory; called the "lost canon"; the study of the materials that the orator has prepared so that they may be presented in a fluent fashion.

Metabolism   Characteristic of open systems; the sharing of inputs (energy, information) between system, subsystem, and environment.

Metafunctional Approach   Approach to nonverbal communication taking a truly communication approach; Judee K. Burgoon and Thomas J. Saine; groups nonverbal communication theories to the assumptions each makes.

Mind   From the symbolic interactionist perspective, a conversation that takes place within the individual (thinking); occurs when we pretest the future; the interaction of the "I" and the "Me."

Mind–Body   From the biosocial; a dualism of the body (which is unidimensional) and the mind (which is multidimensional), which creates tension in the person.

Mirroring   An element of the coordinated management of meaning theory; the taking on of a role when that role is needed in the particular episode.

Mixed Actions   One of Morris's kinesic actions; they are acquired in numerous ways.

Modes of Analysis   Different ways of interpreting the data used to construct reality.

Modification   A structure existing in language theory which argues that man is born with a natural ability to formulate certain combinations of words, which, even in their least sophisticated versions, make sense; Noam Chomsky.

Monge, Peter   Structural–functional advocate; systems advocate.

Morphogenesis   See *Positive Feedback.*

Morphostasis   See *Negative Feedback.*

Morris, Desmond   Nonverbal theorist; theory of nonverbal communication as kinesic actions. See *Inborn Actions, Discovered Actions, Absorbed Actions, Trained Actions, Mixed Actions; Ethological Approach.*

Movement Rules   Stimulus response behaviors governed by nomic necessity.

Multidimensional Person   From Wilson's sociobiology, the problem associated with a "person" who must follow both biological factors and social factors which interact to create rules for living; biosocial.

Multiordinality   A concept from general semantics suggesting that words have different levels of abstraction.

Narratio   A part of speech organization (*dispositio*); narrative; the exposition of events; Cicero.

Nature–Nurture Controversy   A theoretical concern over whether nonverbal communication is learned (nurture) or genetically transferred (nature); Charles Darwin.

Necessity   That which must hold true in order for the theory to be held true. See also *Nomic Necessity, Logical Necessity,* and *Practical Necessity.*

Need for Affection   One of Schutz's general categories; includes people whose need for affection is deficient (underpersonal) through excessive (overpersonal); the ideal type is the personal, a person who is comfortable in his or her relations with others.

Need for Control   One of Schutz's general categories; includes people whose need for control is excessive (autocrat) through deficient (abdicrat); the ideal type is the democrat, a person who can take and receive orders.

Need for Inclusion   One of Schutz's general categories; includes people whose need for inclusion is deficient (undersocial) through excessive (oversocial); the ideal type is the social, the person who has a healthy self-concept, is creative, and motivated by a concern for others.

Negative Feedback   A characteristic of systems in which the feedback looks for deviations or errors in the system and returns the system to its original state.

Negentropy   Actions or forces that reduce the system's movement toward entropy; an aspect of open systems.

Negotiation   An element of the coordinated management of meaning theory; negotiation is compromising about an episode.

Neomammalian Brain   From the biosocial; "new brain," the brain that comprises the neocortex; associated with symbolization, language, and creation of rules; is representational, allowing for abstraction.

Neuromaturation   From the biosocial; a concept that suggests that the brain matures to a point where the styles of each hemisphere become more-or-less locked into place.

Neutral Expression   An affect display (meaning-centered approach to nonverbal communication); lack of emotion.

Noemas   From phenomenology; a movement within a communication approach that deals with the consciousness of an object.

Noesis   From phenomenology; a movement within a communication approach that deals with the consciousness of an impending psychological act.

Nomic Necessity   Concerns the idea that the principle(s) *must* hold true.

Nonadditivity   From general semantics; no two things are the same, and reacting to "sameness" (adding two similar things) yields a difference.

Nonallness   From general semantics; people cannot say everything about anything.

Nonverbal Communication   One of two major communication code systems; sometimes defined as all that language is not; communicated via channels other than words.

Nonverbal Paralanguage   From Wilson's sociobiology; body posture, motion, touch (kinesic communication), and chemical communication. See *Olfaction, Biosocial.*

Normlessness   From conflict and psychological theory; a feeling that the individual must be deviant in order to accomplish some goal; Seeman.

Norms   From exchange theory; an awareness of past bargaining behavior creating an expectation of what is appropriate in the given situation; what is "fair."

Object Adaptors   A class of adaptors (meaning-centered approach to nonverbal communication); behaviors associated with object touching and usually associated with nervousness or negative behaviors.

Objective Mind From conflict theory; social structure and institutions; risk taking; Marx.

Olfaction From Wilson's sociobiology, a chemical form of communication based in the sense of smell; biosocial.

Open Systems Systems that are composed of prescribed, semipermeable boundaries and are interdependent on other systems or subsystems.

Opinion The verbal or nonverbal expression of an attitude.

Order of Propositions A way to test a theory based on the logical pattern of the propositions contained within the theory. See *Chronological, Inductive, Deductive,* and *Dialectical.*

Orientation A way of categorizing a theory based on what aspect of communication the theory focuses on; the view the theory takes of "reality."

Orientational Others From the symbolic interactionist perspective, one who plays an important role in the development of self and who has historical significance to the person; Kuhn.

Overpersonal Personality From Schutz's general need for affection; a person who is extremely intimate, personal, and confiding.

Oversocial Personality From Schutz's general need for inclusion; a person who fears being ignored and constantly seeks the comfort of others.

Paleomammalian Brain From the biosocial; "old brain," the brain that comprises the limbic system and is equated with the evolutionary level of cats, dogs, and chimpanzees; function is emotion, may possess rudimentary language.

Parakinesic Phenomena A construct found in the linguistic analogy approach to nonverbal communication; a combination of movements associated with verbal language. See also *Allokine, Kine, Kineme,* and *Kinemorpheme.*

Paralanguage From Wilson's sociobiology, signals separate from words used to supplement or to modify language; biosocial. See *Vocal Paralanguage* and *Nonverbal Paralanguage.*

Parent Role From Harris's transactional analysis approach; a role in which we learn through the imposed, unquestioned, externalized recordings of the events around us.

Parsimony A feature of a theory; a parsimonious theory is one that omits redundant and unnecessary terms.

Parson Stylistic device associated with Gorgias; the use of parallel structures in speech.

Pathos Aristotelian concept associated with persuasion; the emotive aspects of the speech and audience.

Patterson, Miles L. Nonverbal theorist; best known for work in the functional approach to nonverbal communication; posits five functions to nonverbal communication: providing information, expressing intimacy, regulating interaction, exercising social control, and facilitating service or task goals; psychological approach.

Pearce, W. Barnett Rules advocate; coordinated management of meaning.

Pentad Burke's organizational pattern or structure through which he studied rhetorical motivations. See *Act, Agency, Scene, Agent,* and *Purpose.*

Perelman, Chaim Modern rhetorician; interested in the process of argument and the ways in which argument functions in communication.

Performance An element of dramaturgical analysis; "the total range of behaviors displayed by an individual in the presence of a specific group of observers and upon whom the behaviors are designed to achieve some impact."

Personal Personality   From Schutz's general need for affection; a person who is comfortable in interactions and who can provide and receive genuine affection.

Phenomenology   An approach to communication that emphasizes the descriptive account of daily events.

Pictographs   A class of illustrators (meaning-centered approach to nonverbal communication) which are used to create the shape of what is being talked about.

Plato   Philosopher in ancient Greece who opposed the teaching of the Sophists; taught that truth was absolute, knowable, and capable of being communicated.

Play Stage   From the symbolic interactionist perspective, a stage in socialization whereby we begin actual role playing and includes the ability to act toward oneself; Mead.

Positive Feedback   A characteristic of systems in which the feedback amplifies deviations within the system and moves the system to another state.

Power   From exchange theory; the ability to create meaningful threats (absolute), and the importance of the bargaining situation (relative) to the parties involved.

Powerlessness   From conflict and psychological theory; rhetoric is viewed as useless, communication is impossible; Seeman.

Practical Necessity   Concerns the extent to which a person feels obligated to perform in a certain way.

Pragmatic Perspective   B. Aubrey Fisher's perspective of systems which is concerned with the interrelatedness of people in a social unit.

Preparatory Stage   From the symbolic interactionist perspective, a stage in socialization whereby we meaninglessly imitate the perceived role of others; Mead.

Prerequisites for Argument   From Perelman's rhetorical theory; three prerequisites to argument: (1) an effective community of minds, (2) consideration of the collection of people who constitute the audience (and the varying nature of the situation), and (3) the willingness to listen to the argument.

Prescriptive Rhetorical Theories   Rhetorical theories attributed to Corax of Sicily (circa 467 B.C.) and his students, which provides the practitioner a set of very specific rules to be followed in oratory.

Primitive   A term that remains undefined within a theory and helps to define the entire theory.

Principle   A component of a theory; a term that states how constructs and relationships work together in combination.

Profit   From exchange theory; the difference between reward and cost (Profit = Reward – Cost).

Pronuntiatio   One of the five canons of rhetoric attributed to Cicero; delivery; the manner in which the speech is delivered.

Proposition   A principle developed to a state whereby it can be tested through some type or form of research.

Proprium   Another term for the self.

Prosody   Nonverbal element; the study of the voice as an instrument of communication; Joshua Steele. Also, from Wilson's sociobiology: tone tempo, rhythm, loudness, pacing, and other voice qualities that modify the meaning of verbal utterances; biosocial.

Protagorus   A Sophist whose teaching methods were based on imitation of model speeches; his style ("Attic") exemplified a very plain, direct style of speech.

Proxemics   Nonverbal subcode; the study of physical space and territory; Edward T. Hall; Judee K. Burgoon.

Psychological Approach Nonverbal approach; examines the impact of nonverbal behavior as an attitudinal or behavioral modifier; incorporates not only cultural but also individual communicator differences in communication.

Purpose A way of categorizing a theory based on what it describes, predicts, controls, and asks new questions. Also, an element in Burke's pentad; the aim or goal of the message act.

Quintilian Roman teacher of rhetoric.

Quotation Marks An extensional device that indicates that the any two people may use a word differently, but that there is enough similarity between them to use the word; general semantics.

R-Complex Brain From the biosocial; an evolutionary brain located just above the brain stem; responsible for instinctive behaviors, territoriality, aggressive–defensive behaviors, and reproductive behaviors.

Reaction/Response The ability of words to condition people to respond; general semantics.

Referent In general semantics, any object, event, phenomenon, etc., that is found in the physical environment.

Regulators An element in the meaning-centered approach to nonverbal communication; gestures and facial expressions that regulate the flow of communication in an interaction.

Reification From critical interpretive theory (and general semantics); when concepts and constructs begin to take on the characteristics of physical objects; Lukacs.

Relationship Dimension Communication acts which provide information about the meaning of the content; pragmatic perspective component.

Relationships A component of a theory; a term that implies how different constructs within a theory are combined.

Research Question The phrasing of a principle or proposition to test it.

Rhetoric The counterpart of dialectic; the use of all available means of persuasion; Aristotle.

Rhetorical Exigency A need for something to be said at this time and place.

Rhetorical Sophists Rhetoricians of the sophistic period (550–500 B.C.) primarily interested in the teaching of rhetoric and oratory.

Rhythmic Movements A class of illustrators (meaning-centered approach to nonverbal communication) that indicates the timing of an event or occurrence.

Right Hemisphere From the biosocial; the side of the brain responsible for emotive, spatial–temporal interpretation of stimuli, and for impulse and simple language structure.

Rogers, Carl Established a phenomenologically based, person-centered psychology.

Role See *Social Self.*

Role Taking From the symbolic interactionist perspective, a process whereby the individual identifies himself or herself in the other person's position.

Rules Approach The transfer of symbolic information regulated by communication through code and network rules; a "class of human activity where significance is largely dependent on the existence of consensually-shared rules" (Donald P. Cushman).

Sapir, Edward Theorist concerned with semantic properties of language; cultural relativity. See also *Benjamin Whorf.*

Scene An element in Burke's pentad; the background against which the act is performed.

Schutz, William   Developed a view of the self based on personality types found in three general categories of needs: inclusion, control, and affection.

Self   A central concern of humanistic approaches to communication; "the individual as known to the individual" (Murphy). Also, from the symbolic interactionist perspective, developed through the process of socialization.

Self Adaptors   A class of adaptors (meaning-centered approach to nonverbal communication); behaviors associated with self touching and usually associated with nervousness or negative behaviors.

Self-Esteem   From James's concept of self; the ratio between successes a person has had and the pretensions that person has. Also, from the biosocial; secured through symbol manipulation within society.

Self-Estrangement   From conflict and psychological theory; the individual feels estranged from self; Seeman.

Self-Presentations   An element of dramaturgical analysis; a person's acting out of social roles.

Semifixed Feature Space   Space that is mobile and consists of furnishings and objects found within fixed-feature space; Edward T. Hall.

Sensing   A view of reality based on the five senses.

Significant Other   From the symbolic interactionist perspective, one whose actions and attitudes are considered valuable and who may change over time; Sullivan.

Significant Symbol   According to Arnold Rose, "cooperative gestures" in complex society; symbolic interactionism.

Silent Assumptions   Assumptions made concerning the meaning of a situation that go beyond the words available to the communicator; general semantics.

Social Cognition   The process of thinking that occurs prior to message transmission; constructivism.

Social Game   An element of performance; performances that take place with groups of people who may be taking on other roles or serving as an audience; dramaturgical analysis.

Social Judgment Theory   A persuasion theory developed by Muzafer Sherif, Carolyn Sherif, and Roger Nebergall; posits a two-stage process in changing attitudes: (1) people judge their position against that of others, and (2) changes are made depending on the degree of ego-involvement in the issue and the status of the attitude object in the person's latitudes of acceptance or rejection.

Social Personality   From Schutz's general need for inclusion; a person who feels comfortable in interaction, is creative, motivated by a concern for others, and has a healthy self-concept.

Social Relationship   From conflict theory; the relationship between people in society where some are in a superior role and the others in a subordinate role; Marx.

Social Self   From James's concept of self; the self that is reflected through the perceptions of how others see the person; closely associated with "role."

Socialization   From the symbolic interactionist perspective, learning to operate within the bounds of the particular society in which the person finds himself; a process in which we learn what is normal and what is deviant. See also *Preparatory Stage, Play Stage, Game Stage.*

Society   From the symbolic interactionist perspective, a group, perceived by an individual as having a similar culture; human society is based more on cooperation and symbols; Mead.

Sophists   A group of early Greek rhetoricians (550–500 B.C.) known primarily as teachers.

Space-Binding   A concept from general semantics which suggests that meanings for things differ depending upon proximity and relative position.

Spatial   A mode of analysis that emphasizes different perspectives toward "reality" based on the language we use to describe that reality through differences (i.e., "between," over," "around").

Spatial Movements   A class of illustrators (meaning-centered approach to nonverbal communication) that represent spatial relationships and differences.

Specific Knowledge   A mode of analysis based on the specificity of language through vocabulary.

Spiritual Self   From James's concept of self; comprised of inner, subjective states of consciousness; a "self of selves."

St. Augustine   Rhetorician of the Middle Ages; dealt with how rhetoric could be used to inspire and move audiences.

Stability/Change   A mode of analysis based on the importance placed by people on either keeping "reality" as it is (stability) or in a state of flux (change).

Stage   An element of a performance; the particular place or location of the performance; dramaturgical analysis.

Stereotype   A mode of analysis that looks at another person or event as similar to others in the same class.

Stochastic Probability   The sequential nature of human behavior as predicted in B. Aubrey Fisher's pragmatic perspective.

Strange Loop   A mode of analysis that leads us to a conclusion that would otherwise seem contradictory or impossible.

Structure of Bargaining Situation   The overall perception of the situation in terms of resistance point (bottom line), bargaining range (distance between resistance points), and levels of aspiration (what each person hopes to get out of the interaction).

Structural System   A view of systems in which the emphasis is on what the system does with the information flow through some set of networks.

Structural–Functional Perspective   A systems model encompassing open, closed, and cybernetic systems; advocated by Peter Monge.

Subject–Predicate Relation   A structure existing in language whereby no matter what the subject is, the predicate indicates what kind of action the subject takes; Noam Chomsky.

Subjective Mind   From conflict theory; consciousness; decision making; Marx.

Substantive Base   A way of categorizing a theory based on a metaphor that explains what communication is like and how the process works.

Subsystem   Elements that make up a system.

Sullivan, Harry Stack   Developmental personality theorist; suggested that the self develops through seven stages (infancy through adulthood); psychological approach.

Supportive Climate   A concept from Gibb's concept of defensive communication; supportive climates are formed through interaction characterized by description, problem orientation, spontaneity, empathy, equality, and understanding.

Suprasystem   An element of systems theory that presupposes that a number of systems are interrelated to form a larger entity, the "suprasystem."

Syllogism   Rhetorical concept associated with proof; a series of statements that could be proven objectively; Aristotle.

Symbolic Interactionism   Sociological approach to the study of communication developed by George Herbert Mead.

Symbols   In general semantics, representations of ideas.

Symmetry Theory   A cognitive consistency theory of attitude change developed by Theodore Newcomb; posits that people strain toward symmetry (balance) based on the intensity of held attitudes and the attraction between people or objects.

Syntactical Generality   Identified by the extent to which the words "all" or "none" are used in the principles of the theory.

System   Any continuing entity capable of two or more states; something that seeks to describe the interrelation(s) between some state(s).

Theory   "A way of making sense of a disturbing situation to allow us to bring to bear our habits and to modify habits or discard them altogether, replacing them by new ones" (Kaplan); "couched in terms of exactly defined concepts; consistent with one another; such that existing generalizations could be deductively derived; and fruitful" (Timasheff); "an umbrella term for a host of general principles and orienting statements designed to specify causes and key relationships among given facets of communicative behavior" (Mortensen); trying to answer questions about what communication is, how it works, and how it does not work; the relationship of a number of principles taken together.

Thesis   A coherent statement of a theory in one or two logical statements reflecting the essence of the combined propositions.

Third Persona   From critical interpretive theory; in any given speech, those being neglected in the speech; Habermas.

Time   A mode of analysis that places the person/event in the past, present, or future.

Time-Binding   A concept from general semantics that suggests that as time changes, so do meanings.

Trained Actions   One of Morris's kinesic actions; they are learned through practice or conscious observation.

Transactional Analysis   An approach to communication based on Thomas Harris's view of role expectations. See also *Parent, Child, Adult Role*.

Triad   From Hegel, thesis (idea), antithesis (nature), and synthesis (mind or spirit). From Marx, totality, negativity, alienation. Conflict theory.

Underpersonal Personality   From Schutz's general need for affection; a person who fails to be involved with others or whose interactions are superficial and maintained at an emotional distance from others.

Undersocial Personality   From Schutz's general need for inclusion; a person who is introverted or withdrawn.

Understanding   From the hermeneutic; understanding is historic in that there is no pure sense of an idea's being perfect, understanding is linguistic in that language and experience coexist, and understanding is dialectical in that with each message we open the possibility of a new message; Gadamer; critical interpretive theory.

Value   An evaluation of what has, may, or will happen on some positive or negative scale.

Variable   A construct that has been "operationalized" through a definition which takes into account the specific need for the construct under specific circumstances.

Variable Analytic Approach   The study of a variable, usually under laboratory conditions, to learn how it is affected or affects other variables.

Verb–Object Relation   A structure existing in language theory which expresses "the logical relationship between cause and effect"; Noam Chomsky.

Verbal Communication One of two major communication code systems; associated with our spoken and written language; typically labeled as "language."

Vertical Thinking Thinking based on the ordinary assumptions we make about "reality."

Vocal Paralanguage From Wilson's sociobiology; grunts, giggles, laughs, sobs, cries, and other nonverbal sounds; biosocial.

Voice A mode of analysis that emphasizes the structuring of the message as either passive or active.

von Bertalanaffy, Ludwig General systems theorist.

Weltanschauung World view.

Whorf, Benjamin Theorist concerned with semantic properties of language; cultural relativity. See also *Edward Sapir.*

Wilson, Edward O. Theorist whose interest in sociobiology influenced biosocial thought.

Yale Program A series of studies carried out at Yale University under Carl Hovland, Irving Janis, and Harold Kelly which added the concept of incentive (or motivation) to the behavioral approach to persuasion.

Zoological Approach Nonverbal approach; suggests a direct correlation between lower species and humans in both origin and use of nonverbal communication.

CREDITS

Figure 2–2   B.D. Ruben, "General Systems Theory," in *Interdisciplinary Approaches to Human Communication*, eds., R.W. Budd & B.D. Ruben (Rochelle Park, NJ: Hayden, 1979), p. 102.

Figure 2–3   Peter R. Monge, *Human Communication Research*, Spring 1982, Vol. No. 3, 245–261, copyright © 1982 by the International Communication Association, reprinted by permission of Sage Publications, Inc.

Figure 2–4   M. Hickson and D.W. Stacks, *NVC: Nonverbal Communication Studies and Applications*, *2nd ed.* (Dubuque, IA: Wm. C. Brown, 1989), p. 65.

Table 2–1   P.R. Monge, "The Systems Perspective as a Theoretical Basis for the Study of Human Communication," *Communication Quarterly*, 25 (1977), 22.

Figure 3–1   Burgoon, Judee K., and Thomas J. Saine, *The Unspoken Dialogue: An Introduction To Nonverbal Communication.* Copyright © 1978 by Houghton Mifflin Company. Used with permission.

Figure 3–3   J. Steele, *An Essay Towards Understanding the Melody and Measure of Speech to Be Expressed and Perpetuated by Peculiar Symbols.* (London: Bulwer and Company, 1775).

Figure 3–4   G. Austin, *Chrinomia, or a Treatise on Rhetorical Delivery.* (London: Bulwer and Company, 1806).

Figure 3–5   M. Hickson and D.W. Stacks, *NVC: Nonverbal Communication Studies and Applications*, *2nd ed.* (Dubuque, IA: Wm. C. Brown, 1989), p. 13.

Figure 3–6   R.L. Birdwhistell, *Kinesics and Context: Essays on Body Motion Communication.* (Philadelphia: University of Pennsylvania Press, 1970), p. 283.

Figure 3–7   Per Wadsworth copyright held by Oelgeschlager, Gunn and Hain, Inc. Mail sent to address provided has been returned "attempted not known." Company is not listed in LMP. We do have permission attempts in file. Source: A. Meharbian, *Silent Messages: Implicit Communication of Emotions and Attitudes*, *2nd ed.* (Cambridge, MA: Oelgeschlager, Gunn and Hain, Inc., 1981).

Figure 4–1   Figure from *The Meaning of Meaning: A Study of the Influence of Language Upon Thought and of the Science of Symbolism* by C.K. Ogden, I.A. Richards, reprinted by permission of Harcourt Brace Jovanovich, Inc.

Figure 4–2   *Meta-Talk: A Guide To Hidden Meanings In Conversation*, copyright © 1973 by Gerald Nierenberg and Henry Calero. Reprinted by permission of Simon & Schuster, Inc.

Table 4–3   Adapted excerpts and figure from *Language in Thought and Action, Fourth Edition*, by S.I. Hayakawa, copyright © 1978 by Harcourt Brace Jovanovich, Inc., reprinted by permission of the publisher.

Figure 7–3   Figure from *I'm OK—You're OK*, by T.A. Harris, copyright © 1967, 1968, 1969 by Thomas A. Harris. Reprinted by permission of Harper & Row, Publishers, Inc.

Figure 8–5   Adapted from *Attitude Change*, by C.A. Kielser, B.E. Collins and N. Miller, copyright © 1969, by John Wiley & Sons, Inc.

Figure 10–2   From *Motivation and Personality, Third Edition*, by Abraham H. Maslow, revised by Robert Frager et al. Copyright 1954, 1987 by Harper & Row, Publishers, Inc. Copyright 1970 by Abraham H. Maslow. Reprinted by permission of HarperCollins Publishers.

Figure 13–1   Adapted from: A. King, "The Eye in Advertising," *Journal of Applied Communication Research*, 2 (1974), p. 8.

Table 13–1   Reprinted by permission of the publishers from *Sociobiology: The Newsynthesis*, by E.O. Wilson, Cambridge, MA: The Belknap Press of Harvard University Press, copyright © 1975 by the President and Fellows of Harvard College.

Figure 14–1   L. Thayer, "Communication and Organization Theory," in *Human Communication Theory: Original Essays*, ed. F.E.X. Dance (New York: Holt, Rinehart and Winston, 1967), p. 87.

Index